DISCOVER
THE JOYS OF YIDDISH

A *nudnik* is a pest, a nag, a monumental bore; a *phudnik* is a nudnik with a Ph.D.

A *chassen* is a bridegroom: "Long before Freud, the Jews had this saying, 'When a son gets married, he divorces his mother.' "

***

"For delicious noshing, *The Joys of Yiddish* is hard to beat."

—*National Jewish Monthly*

"I chuckled, I roared, I wept. This is more than just a book, it is an experience."

—*Ann Landers*

"Thus the joys of Yiddish become the joys of the human spirit to be shared by all men. . . . This reviewer . . . wishes that the book and author live 120 years."

—*Book Week*

"A joy to read . . . a loving lexicon of Yiddish words, phrases and expressions that have either already won the tongues of English speakers, or are sure to do so soon. . . ."

—*The Christian Science Monitor*

"Witty, intelligent, scholarly . . . an abundance of stories and anecdotes . . . a joy."

—*Chaim Potok, The Saturday Review*

***

An *alter kocker* is a crotchety, fussy, ineffectual old man, i.e., "old fart."

Feh! is the Yiddish replacement for "phew! pee-oo! ugh! phooey!"—a crisp and exact delineation of distaste.

P9-DEF-738

Books by Leo Rosten

The Joys of Yiddish
People I Have Loved, Known or Admired

Published by POCKET BOOKS/WASHINGTON SQUARE PRESS

For orders other than by individual consumers, Pocket Books grants a discount on the purchase of **10 or more** copies of single titles for special markets or premium use. For further details, please write to the Vice-President of Special Markets, Pocket Books, 1633 Broadway, New York, NY 10019-6785, 8th Floor.

For information on how individual consumers can place orders, please write to Mail Order Department, Simon & Schuster Inc., 200 Old Tappan Road, Old Tappan, NJ 07675.

Leo Rosten

The
JOYS
of
Yiddish

POCKET BOOKS
New York   London   Toronto   Sydney   Tokyo   Singapore

The author expresses his gratitude for permission to reprint the following copyrighted material:

Excerpts from pages 379, 380–1, 385 of Volume I and pages 1196, 1725 of Volume II, *The Jews: Their History, Culture and Religion*, 3rd edition edited by Louis Finkelstein. Copyright © 1960. Reprinted by permission of Harper & Row, Publishers, New York.

Excerpt from *Akiba* by Louis Finkelstein. Copyright © 1962. Reprinted by permission of The Jewish Publication Society, Philadelphia, Penn.

Excerpt from *American Judaism* by Nathan Glazer. Copyright © 1965. Reprinted by permission of The University of Chicago Press, Chicago, Ill.

Excerpt from the notes by Harry Golden in *The Spirit of the Ghetto* by Hutchins Hapgood. Copyright © 1966. Reprinted by permission of Funk & Wagnalls Company, New York.

Excerpts from *The Earth Is The Lord's* by Abraham Joshua Heschel. Copyright © 1964. Reprinted by permission of Abelard-Schuman, Limited, New York.

Excerpt from *The Promised City* by Moses Rischin. Copyright © 1962. Reprinted by permission of Harvard University Press, Cambridge, Mass.

Excerpts from *The World of Sholom Aleichem* by Maurice Samuel. Copyright 1943. Reprinted by permission of Alfred A. Knopf, Inc., New York.

Excerpts from *Historical Essays* by H. R. Trevor-Roper. Copyright © 1962. Reprinted by permission of Macmillan & Co., Ltd., London. Also by permission of Harper & Row, Publishers, New York. From *Men and Events*. Copyright © 1958.

POCKET BOOKS, a division of Simon & Schuster Inc.
1230 Avenue of the Americas, New York, NY 10020

For my mother
who taught me the *mama-loshen*
and
for my children
and their children
and theirs

Contents

Contents

vi

Preface

I wrote this book because there was no other way in which I could have it. For many years I had craved and sought and failed to find a lexicon of just this type.

What This Book Is Not

This is not a book about Yiddish. It is not a dictionary of Yiddish. It is not a guide to Yiddish. It is not written for experts in, or students of, Yiddish.

What This Book Is

This is a book about language—more particularly, the English language. It shows how our marvelously resilient tongue has been influenced by another parlance: Yiddish. It illustrates how beautifully a language reflects the variety and vitality of life itself; and how the special culture of the Jews, their distinctive style of thought, their subtleties of feeling, are reflected in Yiddish; and how this in turn has enhanced and enriched the English we use today.

So, this book explores a fascinating aspect of English: those words and phrases from Yiddish (some I call "Yinglish," some "Ameridish") that we today encounter in English books, magazines, newspapers; or hear on television or radio, in movies or nightclubs; or may overhear on the street or in a bus in many a large city in the United States.

By "Yinglish" I mean Yiddish words that are used in colloquial English in both the United States and the United Kingdom: *kibitzer, mish-mash, bagel,* etc.

By "Ameridish" I mean words coined by, and indigenous to, Jews in the United States: *kochalayn, utz, shmegegge,* etc.

"Yiddish," "Hebrew," and "Jewish"

For the benefit of innocents, I hasten to add that Yiddish and Hebrew are entirely different languages. A knowledge of one will not give you even a rudimentary understanding of the other. True, Yiddish uses the letters of the Hebrew alphabet, employs a great many Hebrew words, and is written, like Hebrew, from right to left, thusly:

UOY EVOL I ACIREMA

—which should delight any reader under fourteen. But Yiddish and Hebrew are as different from each other as are English and French, which also use a common alphabet, share many words, and together proceed from left to right.

Nor is "Yiddish" a synonym for "Jewish." "Yiddish" is the name of a language. Technically speaking, there is no language called "Jewish." Strictly speaking, Jews do not speak "Jewish" any more than Canadians speak Canadian, or Baptists read Baptist. But it would be foolish to deny that in popular English usage, "Jewish" *is* used as a synonym for "Yiddish." After all, "Yiddish" comes from the German *Jüdisch,* meaning "Jewish," and in the Yiddish language itself *Yiddish* means "Jewish." We may as well accept reality.*

The Scope of This Wordbook

This book, accordingly, is a lexicon of certain foreign-born words that:

(1) are already part of everyday English (*shmaltz, gonif, shlemiel*);

(2) are rapidly becoming part of English (*chutzpa, megillah, shlep, yenta*);

---

* The distinction between "Jewish" and "Yiddish" is, I may say, ignored by many Jews: those who do not know there is a difference, and those (especially third-generation, or of German descent) who dislike and deliberately avoid the word "Yiddish."

(3) should be part of our noble language, in my opinion, because no English words so exactly, subtly, pungently, or picturesquely convey their meaning (*shmoos, kvetch, shlimazl, tchotchke,* etc.)

Were I writing all this in the style and with the impudent imagery so characteristic of Jewish humor, I would say: "This book is a collection of three kinds of simply *delicious* words: those which are naturalized citizens; those which have taken out their first papers; and those which should be drafted into our army just as soon as possible."

The Influence of Yiddish on English

It is a remarkable fact that never in its history has Yiddish been so influential—among Gentiles. (Among Jews, alas, the tongue is running dry.) We are clearly witnessing a revolution in values when a Pentagon officer, describing the air-bombardment pattern used around Haiphong, informs the press: "You might call it the bagel strategy."[1]* Or when a Christmas (1966) issue of *Better Homes and Gardens* features: "The Season's Delightful Jewish Traditions and Foods." Or when the London *Economist* captions a fuss over mortgage rates: HOME LOAN HOO-HA.[2] Or when the *Wall Street Journal* headlines a feature on student movements: "REVOLUTION, SHMEVOLUTION."[3] Or when a wall in New York bears this eloquent legend, chalked there, I suppose, by some derisive English major:

MARCEL PROUST
IS A
YENTA

Or when England's illustrious *Times Literary Supplement,* discussing the modern novel, interjects this startling sentence: "Should, schmould, shouldn't, schmouldn't."[4] Or when a musical play about the Jews in the Polish *shtetl* of fifty years ago, *Fiddler on the Roof,* scores so phenomenal a success.[5]

---

* References, with dates and sources, will be found at the end of this Preface.

Yiddish phrasing and overtones are found in, say, the way an Irish whiskey advertises itself:

"Scotch is a fine beverage and deserves its popularity. But enough is enough already."

Or in an advertisement for a satirical English movie, *Agent 8¾*:

"By Papa he's a spy,
By Mama he's a spy,
But from spies he's no spy!"*

I can cite dozens of similar uses of Yinglish idiom.⁶

Yiddish Words and Phrases in English

Every so often I run across the statement that *Webster's Unabridged Dictionary* contains 500 Yiddish words. I do not know if this is true, and I certainly doubt that anyone actually counted them. For my part, I am surprised by the number of Yiddish words, thriving beautifully in everyday English, that are *not* in *Webster's*, nor in other dictionaries of the English language—including the incomparable thirteen-volume *Oxford English Dictionary*. You will find many of these lamentably unrecognized words in the volume you now hold in your hands.

Many a scholar has commented on the growing number of Yiddish words and idioms that "invade" English. But English, far from being a supine language, has zestfully borrowed a marvelous gallimaufry of foreign locutions, including many from Yiddish; and who will deny that such brigandage has vastly enriched our cherished tongue?**

---

* This ploy of deflation originally involved the playwright Samson Raphaelson and his mother. Mr. Raphaelson, having scored a considerable success on Broadway and in Hollywood, bought himself a yacht —and a nautical cap, on which "Captain" was embroidered. Old Mrs. Raphaelson studied the cap on her proud son's head and won immortality by saying, "By you you're a captain, and by me you're a captain; but tell me, Sammy, by a *captain* are you a captain?"

** I have elsewhere pointed out that a sentence like "The pistol in our bungalow is stuffed with taffy" contains words from six languages (Slovak, Czech, Hindustani, Tagalog, Old French, English—

Take the popular usage of the suffix, *-nik*, to convert a word into a label for an ardent practitioner or devotee of something: How could we manage without such priceless coinages as *beatnik* and *peacenik? The New York Times* recently dubbed Johann Sebastian's acolytes "Bachniks"; some homosexuals dismiss nonhomosexuals as *straightniks;* the comic strip *Mary Worth* has employed *no-goodnik;* and a newspaper advertisement even employed Yiddish-in-tandem to get "NOSHNIKS OF THE WORLD, UNITE!"[8]

Many a student of contemporary mores has discovered the degree to which novelists, playwrights, joke writers, comedians, have poured Jewish wit and humor into the great, flowing river of English.[9] This is also an indication of the extraordinary role of Jewish intellectuals, and their remarkable increase during the past forty years, in the United States and England.

Who has not heard or used phrases such as the following, which, whatever their origin, probably owe their presence in English to Jewish influence?

> Get lost.
> You should live so long.
> My son, the physicist.
> I need it like a hole in the head.
> Who *needs* it?
> So why do you?
> Al*right* already.
> It shouldn't happen to a dog.
> O.K. by me.
> He knows from nothing.
> From that he makes a *living*?
> How come only five?
> Do him something.
> *This* I need yet?
> A person could bust.
> He's a regular genius.
> Go hit your head against the wall.
> You want it should sing, too?

---

via Old Frisian), and that an utterance such as "Oh, bosh! Some nitwit has put alcohol in the ketchup!" entails the uncopyrighted use of Turkish, Dutch, Arabic, French, Malay, Chinese, and pidgin Japanese.[7]

Plain talk: He's crazy.
Excuse the expression.
With sense, he's loaded.
Go fight City Hall.
I should have such luck.
It's a nothing of a dress.
You should live to a hundred and twenty.
On him it looks good.
It's time, it's time.
Wear it in good health.
Listen, *bubele* . . . ?

What other language is fraught with such exuberant fraughtage?

Colloquial Uses in English of Yiddish Linguistic Devices

But words and phrases are not the chief "invasionary" forces Yiddish has sent into the hallowed terrain of English. Much more significant, I think, is the adoption by English of linguistic *devices*, Yiddish in origin, to convey nuances of affection, compassion, displeasure, emphasis, disbelief, skepticism, ridicule, sarcasm, scorn. Examples abound:

1. Blithe dismissal via repetition with an *sh* play-on-the-first-sound: "Fat-shmat, as long as she's happy."[10]

2. Mordant syntax: "Smart, he isn't."

3. Sarcasm via innocuous diction: "He only tried to shoot himself."

4. Scorn through reversed word order: "Already you're discouraged?"

5. Contempt via affirmation: "My *son*-in-law he wants to be."

6. Fearful curses sanctioned by nominal cancellation: "A fire should burn in his heart, God forbid!"

7. Politeness expedited by truncated verbs and eliminated prepositions: "You want a cup coffee?"

8. Derisive dismissal disguised as innocent interrogation: "I should pay him for such devoted service?"

9. The use of a question to answer a question to which the answer is so self-evident that the use of the first question (by you) constitutes an affront (to me) best erased either by (a)

repeating the original question or (b) retorting with a question of comparably asinine self-answeringness. Thus:

[A]

Q. "Did you write your mother?"
A. "Did I write my mother!" (Scornful, for "Of course I did!")

[B]

Q. "Have you visited your father in the hospital?"
A. "Have I visited my father in the *hospital?*" (Indignant, for "What kind of a monster do you think I am?")

[C]

Q. "Would you like some chicken soup?"
A. "Would I like some *chicken* soup?" (Emphatically concurring, for "What a stupid thing to ask.")

[D]

Q. "Will a hundred dollars be enough?"
A. "Will a hundred dollars be enough?" (Incredulously offended, for "Do you think I'm crazy to accept so ridiculous a sum?")

[E]

Q. "Will a thousand dollars be enough?"
A. "Will a *thousand* dollars be enough?" (Incredulously delighted, for "Man, will it!")

[F]

Q. "Will you marry me?"
A. "Will I *marry* you?" (On a note of overdue triumph, for "Yes, yes, right away!")

Or consider the growing effect on English of those exquisite shadings of meaning, and those priceless nuances of contempt, that are achieved in Yiddish simply by shifting the stress in a sentence from one word to another. "Him you *trust?*" is entirely different, and worlds removed, from *"Him* you trust?" The first merely questions your judgment; the second vilipends the character of the scoundrel anyone must be an idiot to repose faith in.

Or consider the Ashkenazic panoply in which insult and

innuendo may be arrayed. Problem: Whether to attend a concert to be given by a neighbor, niece, or friend of your wife. The same sentence may be put through maneuvers of matchless versatility:

(1) *"Two* tickets for her concert I should buy?" (Meaning: "I'm having enough trouble deciding if it's worth one.")

(2) "Two *tickets* for her concert I should buy?" ("You mean to say she isn't distributing free passes? The hall will be empty!")

(3) "Two tickets for *her* concert I should buy?" ("Did she buy tickets to *my* daughter's recital?")

(4) "Two tickets for her *concert* I should buy?" ("You mean to say they call what she does a 'concert'?!")

(5) "Two tickets for her concert *I* should buy?" ("After what she did to me?")

(6) "Two tickets for her concert I *should* buy?" ("Are you giving me lessons in ethics?")

(7) "Two tickets for her concert I should *buy?"* ("I wouldn't go even if she gave me a complimentary!")

Each of the above formulations suggests a different prior history, offers the speaker a different catharsis, and lets fly different arrows of contumely. And if all emphasis is removed from the sentence, which is then uttered with mock neutrality, the very unstressedness becomes sardonic, and—if accompanied by a sigh, snort, cluck, or frown—lethal.

On the Yiddish Language

A word about Yiddish itself. It is older than the English we speak, although it did not fully come into its own, building a literature of its own, until the mid-nineteenth century—since which recent time it has produced an impressive body of stories, poems, novels, essays, and social criticism.

Yiddish is the Robin Hood of languages. It steals from the linguistically rich to give to the fledgling poor. It shows not the slightest hesitation in taking in house guests—to whom it gives free room and board regardless of genealogy, faith, or exoticism. A memorable remark by a journalist, Charles Rappaport, runs: "I speak ten languages—all of them in Yiddish."

I think Yiddish a language of exceptional charm. Like any street gamin who has survived unnamable adversities, it is bright, audacious, mischievous. It has displayed immense resourcefulness, immenser resilience, and immensest determination-not-to-die—properties whose absence has proved fatal to more genteel and languid languages. I think it a tongue that never takes its tongue out of its cheek.

Yiddish lends itself to an extraordinary range of observational nuances and psychological subtleties. Steeped in sentiment, it is sluiced with sarcasm. It loves the ruminative, because it rests on a rueful past; favors paradox, because it knows that only paradox can do justice to the injustices of life; adores irony, because the only way the Jews could retain their sanity was to view a dreadful world with sardonic, astringent eyes. In its innermost heart, Yiddish swings between *shmaltz* and derision.

I have always marveled at how fertile this *lingua franca* is in what may be called the vocabulary of insight. The Jews were forced to become self-conscious from the day Moses warned them to invest every act with piety in preparation for a strict heavenly accounting. Knowledge, among Jews, came to compensate for worldly rewards. Insight, I think, became a substitute for weapons: one way to block the bully's wrath is to know him better than he knows himself.

Jews *had* to become psychologists, and their preoccupation with human, no less than divine, behavior made Yiddish remarkably rich in names for the delineation of character types. Little miracles of discriminatory precision are contained in the distinctions between such simpletons as a *nebech*, a *shlemiel*, a *shmendrick*, a *shnook;* or between such dolts as a *klutz*, a *yold*, a *Kuni Lemmel*, a *shlep*, a *Chaim Yankel*. All of them inhabit the kingdom of the ineffectual, but each is assigned a separate place in the roll call. The sense of differentiation is so acute in Yiddish that a word like, say, *paskudnyak* has no peer in any language I know for the vocal delineation of a nasty character. And Yiddish coins new names with ease for new personality types: A *nudnik* is a pest; a *phudnik* is a *nudnik* with a Ph.D.

Were I asked to characterize Yiddish—its style, its life story, its ambience—in one word, I would not hesitate: irrepressible.

Isaac Bashevis Singer reminds us that Yiddish may be the

only language on earth that has never been spoken by men in power.[11]* Few instruments of human speech have led so parlous a life, amidst such inhospitable neighbors, against such fierce opposition. And I know of no tongue so beset by schisms and fevers and ambivalences from within the community that had given it birth: Jews themselves.

Purists derided Yiddish for its "bastard" origins, its "vulgar" idioms, its "hybrid" vocabulary. Hebraicists called it "uncivilized cant." Germans called it a "barbarous argot," a "piggish jargon."[12] But English, French, Italian, German, all began as "vulgar" tongues, as jargon, as the vernacular of uneducated masses: The priests and intellectuals and noblemen (if educated) used Latin and Greek. And not too long ago, in Russia, Poland, Scandinavia, the Balkans, the nabobs learned French, a "refined" language, but remained ignorant of the national, "the servants'," language.

English Words in Yiddish

Many English words are part of today's Yiddish. In the American households of Jewish immigrants from eastern Europe, the parents spoke Yiddish to each other—and to the children. But the passionately eager-to-be-American children customarily replied in English. (Hence the witticism, as true for other immigrants as for Jews, "In America, it is the children who raise the parents.")

The vigorous Yiddish press, striving to make life in the boom and bewilderment of the New World easier for its readers, taught them many useful English words.[13] Since these words were spelled in Yiddish, their pronunciation was necessarily determined by the pronunciational aspects of Yiddish—and by the habituated reflexes of the Jewish tongue and larynx. And so proud new patriots swiftly enlarged their vocabularies with such useful, everyday words as:

vindaw	(window)
stritt cah	(street car)
sobvay	(subway)

---

* In Israel, where Hebrew is the official parlance, they say that Premier Levi Eshkol often injected Yiddish into cabinet meetings—and was resented for it.

tex	(tax)
sax	(sex)

Let me point out that one reason for these aural transformations lay in the way many Jews pronounced *any* language—German, French, or Yiddish itself.[14]

If I may quote from an earlier work of mine:

> Some say "ship" when they mean the source of wool, or "sheep" when they mean a vessel. Others throw "bet" around with abandon to mean either "bat," "bet," "bad," or "bed."
>
> Mr. Kaplan may say "fond mine fife fit don," which suggests a devoted shaft of flutes fit for an Oxford tutor. But [the phrase means] that Mr. Kaplan, having lost something, found it five feet down.
>
> Or take Mrs. Moskowitz [who says] "I hate the brat." That is not at all what she means. . . . If I had her say, instead, "I ate the brat," which is closer to her message, Mrs. Moskowitz would be tainted with cannibalism, which is absurd. (There are certain *animals* Mrs. Moskowitz would not dream of digesting.) I would have to violate truth, in the service of truth, and write Mrs. Moskowitz's perfectly innocent thought as "I ate the bread."
>
> [Or] take Mr. Kaplan's name. Anyone in the class can spell it correctly. But notice: Mr. Kaplan refers to himself as "Keplen," Mr. Blattberg calls him "Kaplen," Mr. Plonsky always bellows "Keplan," Mr. Matsoukas mutters "Koplen," and Olga Tarnova, who could wring lurid overtones from a telephone number, moans "Koplan."[15]

Any reader who feels superior to such quaint, broken English might ponder the words written in *Harper's* back in 1915 by William Dean Howells:

> "With us [Americans] the popular taste is so bad, so ignorant, so vulgar, that it suggests the painful doubt whether literacy is a true test of intelligence and a rightful proof of citizenship. . . . The literary taste of

the Russian Jews on the East Side is superior to that of the average native American. . . ."[16*]

And we might remember that when the overwhelming majority of mankind was illiterate, it was hard to find a Jewish lad over six who could not read and write (Hebrew). Most adult male Jews could handle at least *three* languages: They used Hebrew in the synagogues and houses of study (see *Bes Midrash*), Yiddish in the home, and—to Gentiles— the language of the land in which they lived. My father, a workingman denied the equivalent of a high-school education in Poland, handled Yiddish, English, Hebrew, Polish. Jews were linguists of necessity.

Brief Note: The History of Yiddish

For the picaresque history of this spirited and gallant tongue see the entry *Yiddish* and the Appendix. Here I need only say briefly: Around the tenth century, Jews from what is now northern France, who spoke Old French and, of course, Hebrew, migrated to towns along the Rhine, where they began to use the local German dialect. Hebrew remained untouched as the "sacred," the liturgical, language—for reading *Torah* and *Talmud*, for use in prayer and in scholarly or theological discourse.

In the Rhineland, Jews wrote German phonetically, *using the letters of the Hebrew alphabet*, just as Jewish sages in Spain wrote Spanish (and Arabic) with Hebrew letters.

Yiddish really took root and flowered, as a vernacular, in the ghettos—which began in walled *juderías* in Spain in the thirteenth century. (The Lateran Councils of 1179 and 1215 forbade Jews to live close to Christians, and in 1555 Paul IV ordered segregated quarters for Jews in the Papal States.)

---

* Mr. Harvey Swados reminds us that of all the public libraries in New York City, the largest circulation of the classics was found in the Seward Park branch; and the Metropolitan Museum of Art finally opened its doors on Sundays because of a persistent campaign born in, and championed by, residents of the Lower East Side.[17] To me, one of the noblest images of human history is that of the newly arrived immigrant mother, unable to speak a word of English, who hastened to her branch library and held up one, two, three fingers—the number signaling the number of children for whom she wanted library cards.[18]

This new parlance was a mélange of Middle High German, some Old German, remnants of Old French and Old Italian, Hebrew names and phrases, and local dialects.*

But Yiddish did not really settle down and raise its own young until after the fifteenth century, when the Jews went to eastern Europe—Poland, Galicia, Hungary, Rumania, Russia. There the buoyant tongue picked up new locutions, adapting itself to the street and the marketplace. Yiddish became the Jews' tongue via the Jewish mother, who, not being male, was denied a Hebrew education.

Professor Max Weinreich has given us an exhilarating epigram: "A language is a dialect that has an army and a navy." Yiddish, unlike Hebrew, the official language of Israel, has neither army, navy, police, nor governmental mandate. It has only ardent practitioners and sentimental protectors. In Israel, Yiddish was accorded short shrift by officials and populace alike, until quite recently. The official disfavor and unofficial scorn account for the joke I heard in Jerusalem:

On a bus in Tel Aviv, a mother was talking animatedly, in Yiddish, to her little boy—who kept answering her in Hebrew. And each time the mother said, "No, no, talk Yiddish!"

An impatient Israeli, overhearing this, exclaimed, "Lady, why do you insist the boy talk Yiddish instead of Hebrew?"

Replied the mother, "I don't want him to forget he's a Jew."

That mother knew what Israel Zangwill meant when he said: "Yiddish incorporates the essence of a life which is distinctive and unlike any other."[19]

Perhaps the most eloquent statement of the case for Yiddish as the special language of Jews was penned by the writer I. L. Peretz:

Yiddish, the language which will ever bear witness to the violence and murder inflicted on us, bears the marks of our expulsions from land to land, the language which absorbed the wails of the fathers, the

---

* Interestingly enough, some ancient German words, no longer used in German, survive in Yiddish: *atsinder*, "now," comes from the obsolete German *etzust*; *lylach* is Yiddish, German uses *laken* for "sheet" or "tablecloth."

laments of the generations, the poison and bitterness of history, the language whose precious jewels are undried, uncongealed Jewish tears.[20]

Do All Jews Understand Yiddish?

No. Rabbi Morris N. Kertzer makes the point vividly:

> If an international conference were called today, bringing together Jews of a dozen different countries, no single language would be understood at all. This fact is a source of wonder to many Jews and non-Jews alike. . . . In Italy, France and North Africa, I frequently saw a look of amazement on the faces of American Jewish soldiers who addressed the elders of a synagogue in Yiddish and found no response. In Dijon, most Jews were at home only with their native French; in Algiers, Arabic and French were the languages in most Jewish homes; and in Naples, only a rare soul had ever heard a word of Yiddish.
>
> Hebrew, the language of prayer and the Bible, is spoken only by Israelis and a handful of scholars. . . . Yiddish . . . is today unintelligible to Jews of Italy, Turkey, Spain, North Africa, a goodly number of Americans, and many native-born Israelis. . . . Jews throughout the world today have as their first, and most often their only, language the tongue of the land in which they live.[21]

The Use of Stories, Humor, and Anecdotes

I have used a story, joke, or anecdote in the main body of this lexicon to illustrate the meaning of a word, wherever possible. Since this is highly unorthodox in lexicography, a brief for the defense may be in order.

I consider the story, the anecdote, the joke, a teaching instrument of unique efficacy. A joke is a structured, compact narrative that makes a point with power, generally by surprise. A good story is exceedingly hard for anyone to forget. It is therefore an excellent pedagogic peg on which to hang a point. Those who do not use stories when they try to explain or communicate are either inept at telling them or blindly forfeit a tool of great utility.

The Jewish anecdote possesses a bouquet all its own. Since almost every Jew is raised to reverence learning, and encouraged to be a bit of a teacher, the Jewish story (*myseh*) is at its best when it points a moral or moralizes a problem.

A very large part of Jewish humor is cerebral. It is, like Sholom Aleichem's, reason made mischievous, or, like Groucho Marx's, reason gone mad. Jewish jokes drape their laughter on logic—in despair.

In nothing is Jewish psychology so vividly revealed as in Jewish jokes. The style and stance of its humor reflect a culture, I think, no less than its patterns of shame, guilt, hostility, and approval.

The first riddle I ever heard, one familiar to almost every Jewish child, was propounded to me by my father:

"What is it that hangs on the wall, is green, wet—and whistles?"

I knit my brow and thought and thought, and in final perplexity gave up.

"A herring," said my father.

"A *herring?!*" I echoed. "A herring doesn't hang on a wall!"

"So hang it there."

"But a herring isn't green!" I protested.

"Paint it."

"But a herring isn't *wet.*"

"If it's just painted, it's still wet."

"But—" I sputtered, summoning all my outrage, "—*a herring doesn't whistle!*"

"Right," smiled my father. "I just put that in to make it hard."

We need not be surprised to find countless Jewish jokes mocking the Jews themselves. Self-awareness, pushed into self-analysis, turns into self-criticism.

I once defined humor as "the affectionate communication of insight."[22] Humor also serves the afflicted as compensation for suffering, a token victory of brain over fear. A Jewish aphorism goes: "When you're hungry, sing; when you're hurt, laugh." The barbed joke about the strong, the rich, the heartless powers-that-be is the final citadel in which human pride can live. "All sorrows can be borne," said the Danish writer Isak Dinesen, "if you put them into a story."

But *writing* jokes proved far, far more difficult than I ever anticipated. (Think how much you are aided, in telling a joke, by tonal variations and strategic gestures; by artful pauses and inflections; by the deliberate camouflage of chuckles, dismay, smiles, murmurs.) And certain stories, gorgeous in the telling, just cannot be put into print without suffering more than a sea change. As good an example as I know is this classic:

During a gigantic celebration in Red Square, after Trotsky had been sent into exile, Stalin, on Lenin's great tomb, suddenly and excitedly raised his hand to still the acclamations: "Comrades, comrades! A most historic event! A cablegram— of congratulations—from Trotsky!"

The hordes cheered and chortled and cheered again, and Stalin read the historic cable aloud:

JOSEPH STALIN
KREMLIN
MOSCOW
YOU WERE RIGHT AND I WAS WRONG. YOU ARE THE
TRUE HEIR OF LENIN. I SHOULD APOLOGIZE.

TROTSKY

You can imagine what a roar, what an explosion of astonishment and triumph erupted in Red Square now!

But in the front row, below the podium, a little tailor called, "Pst! Pst! Comrade Stalin."

Stalin leaned down.

The tailor said, "Such a message, Comrade Stalin. For the ages! But you read it without the right *feeling!*"

Whereupon Stalin raised his hand and stilled the throng once more. "Comrades! Here is a simple worker, a loyal Communist, who says I haven't read the message from Trotsky with enough feeling! Come, Comrade Worker! Up here! *You* read this historic communication!"

So the little tailor went up to the reviewing stand and took the cablegram from Stalin and read:

JOSEPH STALIN
KREMLIN
MOSCOW

Then he cleared his throat, and sang out:

YOU WERE RIGHT AND I WAS WRONG? YOU ARE THE
TRUE HEIR OF LENIN? I SHOULD APOLOGIZE??!! . .
TROTSKY!

Finale

I am happy to acknowledge below the many kind people
who helped me during the years it took to finish this opus.

As for the errors and lapses and shameless omissions that
will be brought to my attention by irate grammarians, dissent-
ing rabbis, philologists, historians, fervent Yiddishists, inflex-
ible Hebraicists, or readers simply devoted, as am I, to their
beloved *mama-loshen,* I shall try to console myself with the
words of Samuel Johnson, who sent his great dictionary out
into the world with this marvelous admonition:

> . . . a few wild blunders and risible absurdities, from
> which no work of such multiplicity was ever free, may
> for a time furnish folly with laughter. No dictionary of
> a living tongue can ever be perfect . . . a whole life
> cannot be spent upon syntax and etymology . . . What
> is obvious is not always known, and what is known
> is not always present. In this work, when it shall be
> found that much is omitted, let it not be forgotten
> that much likewise is performed.[23]

LEO ROSTEN
New York

FOOTNOTES TO PREFACE

1. *Newsweek,* September 25, 1967, p. 63.
2. London *Economist,* November 19, 1966.
3. *Wall Street Journal,* January 12, 1968.

4. *Times Literary Supplement* (England), February 3, 1966, p. 82.

5. For a tart criticism of the ways in which the musical play did injustice to the Sholom Aleichem stories and characters, see Joseph C. Landis, "Fiddling with Sholom Aleichem," *Arts and Sciences*, Spring, 1965.

6. *Plotzed* was used in *Time*, October 14, 1966, cinema section; *Oy gevald!* is the sole comment on a movie reviewed in the New York *World-Journal Tribune* TV supplement for January 8–14, 1967, p. 29; the *Wall Street Journal* used *mishmash* in an editorial on November 8, 1966, as did Barbra Streisand to a diplomatic audience in London, as reported in *The New York Times*, June 13, 1966; *The Saturday Evening Post* for September 24, 1966, used *schticklach* in a caption; *Time* used *klutz* in the November 4, 1966 issue, p. 15; the *New Yorker* alluded to *shticks* without italics, July 8, 1967, p. 22; *maven* was used in ads for Vita herring, *The New York Sunday Times Magazine*, December 5, 1965, p. 75, being only one example; *Time* coined *filmniks*, March 4, 1966, p. 47; Sophia Loren sprinkled an interview in New York with words like *shmegegge*, *The New York Times*, May 26, 1966, and, as reported by Earl Wilson in the New York *Post* on the same day, *megilla* and *meshpuchah*; the London *Times Literary Supplement* used *schmaltz* June 17, 1965, p. 489, and on June 3, 1965, p. 457, uses "beigles" without italics for *bagels*; the *Village Voice* (N.Y.) casually mentions *meshpucheh*, October 22, 1964; *schmaltz* is used but spelled *schmalz* by Harold Schonberg in *The New York Times*, September 30, 1966, and *"schmalzy"* is used in *Time*, September 23, 1966, p. 97; a film review of "The Return of Mr. Moto" in the late New York *Herald Tribune* was headed "Nudniks, Nonsense, Clichés"; a lapel button in New York reads LIFE IS A SHTICK; *Zayda* appears in the New York *Daily News*, January 5, 1966, p. 54; *The New York Times'* Sidney Zion used *schmoozle* on August 26, 1966; "ultra-schmultra" appeared in the San Francisco *Chronicle*, in Herb Caen's column, on November 11, 1966; in a long analysis of Sir Laurence Olivier in the London *Observer*, Mr. Kenneth Tynan cited *chutzpah*, "the untranslatable Jewish word that means cool nerve and outrageous effrontery combined," as one of the cardinal ingredients of Sir Laurence's acting genius; Frank Kermode uses *kvell* in London's *The Listener*, December 28, 1967, p. 849.

7. Leo Rosten, "Tiptoe Thru Lingo," *Look*, December 26, 1967.

8. *The New York Times*, December 18, 1966.

9. See, for instance, Wallace Markfield's "The Yiddishization of American Humor," *Esquire*, October 1966, for an amusing foray.

10. This is somewhat similar to the English "teeny-weeny," "razzle-dazzle," etc. This device is called, technically, "second-order reduplication." See Stuart Berg Flexner, in H. Wentworth and S. B. Flexner, *Dictionary of American Slang*, Crowell, 1967 ed., p. 605.

11. I. B. Singer, "A Phantom of Delight," *Book Week* supplement, July 4, 1965, p. 2.

12. See, for instance, Stephen Birmingham, *Our Crowd: The Great Jewish Families of New York*, Harper and Row, 1967, pp. 290–293. Also Joseph L. Baron, *A Treasury of Jewish Quotations*, Crown, 1956, p. 558.

13. A study by Dr. J. H. Neumann of three New York Yiddish daily newspapers in 1938 showed that 20 per cent of the words on the

advertisement pages of the newspapers were English loanwords; in the smaller and more personal ads, the percentage ran 28 per cent. See Lilian Mermin Feinsilver, "Yiddish and American English," *Chicago Jewish Forum*, Winter, 1955–56, Vol. 14, No. 2, p. 76.

14. Such pronunciational shifts affect a whole range of vowels; the teaching of English to Jewish immigrants was an undertaking pregnant with surprises. For instance:

(1) The short *a* becomes a short *e*: "cat" is pronounced *ket*, and "pat" becomes *pet*.

(2) The short *e*, in turn, emerges as a short *a*: "pet" is rendered as *pat*. I hate to think what must have occurred with "a bad bed."

(3) The short *i* becomes a long *e*—and vice versa. This means that "pill" is pronounced *peel* and "peel" comes out *pill*. An Ashkenazic dentist (his patients called him "dentnist") might well fall into this euphoric promise: "Rilex! I'll feel your cavity so you won't even fill it!"

(4) The long *o* becomes *aw* or *u*, and the *aw* sound, in turn, becomes a long *o*: thus, "phone" becomes *fawn* or *fun*; "saw" becomes *so*.

(5) The long English *oo* undergoes a transformation to a short *u*; a "pool" becomes a *pull*—and vice versa. To say that a dumbbell is drunk, a virtuoso might declaim, "That full is fool *shnaps!*"

(6) The rounded *ow* becomes *ah*: "how" is rendered *hah*, "powder" as *podder*, and "louse" sounds exactly like the Spanish article *las*.

(7) The *w* regularly becomes a *v*: "We went to Willie's wedding" is vivified into "Ve vent to Villie's vaddink."

(8) The final *g* becomes a *k*; thus "walking the Muggs' pug dog" becomes "valkink the Muck's puck duck"—a most unholy metamorphosis.

(9) The *ng* and *ngg* sounds are often confused; thus "singer" rhymes with "linger" and in Brooklynese "Long Island" sounds like "Long Guyland."

(10) Voiced final consonants tend to become unvoiced: in such a vagarious world, one eats corn on the *cop*, spreads butter on *brat*, and consumes potato chips·by the *back*.

It should be noticed that some of these vowel shifts are consistent and others are not, and that pronunciational variations appear in the speech of people who *can* conform to accepted sounds. In Yiddish itself, for instance, the word for "bread" is pronounced not *Broht*, as in German, but as *broyt* or *brayt*. What accounts for the transposition of *a*'s for *e*'s, the interchangeability of the short *i* and the short *e*, or the use of *v*'s for *w*'s when—obviously—each can be enunciated with ease, is a mystery I cannot resolve.

For technical questions about Yiddish, its grammar, vocabulary, and syntax, see Uriel Weinreich, *College Yiddish*, YIVO Institute for Jewish Research, 1965 edition. This is the first English textbook on Yiddish grammar. The late Professor Weinreich also produced the first dictionary of Yiddish-English, English-Yiddish, since Alexander Harkavy's outworn classic of 1891. Weinreich's dictionary was published by McGraw-Hill in 1968.

15. Leo Rosten, *The Return of H*Y*M*A*N K*A*P*L*A*N*, Harper, 1961, pp. 15–16.
16. Quoted by Harvey Swados, "A Sentimental Journey to the Lower East Side," *The New York Times Magazine*, September 18, 1966.
17. *Ibid.*
18. Harry Golden, in Hutchins Hapgood, *The Spirit of the Ghetto*, Funk & Wagnalls, new ed, 1965, p. 32.
19. I. Zangwill in 1906, quoted in Joseph L. Baron, *op. cit.*, p. 558.
20. J. L. Baron, *op. cit.*, p. 558.
21. Morris N. Kertzer, *What Is a Jew?*, World, 1953, pp. 116–118.
22. *The Return of H*Y*M*A*N K*A*P*L*A*N*, *op. cit.*, pp. 15–16.
23. *A Johnson Reader*, ed. by E. L. McAdam, Jr., and George Milne, Pantheon, 1964, pp. 141–142.

Acknowledgments

It is a pleasure for me to thank the following persons for their expert advice, their sharp criticism, their helpful comments, and their consummate patience with an obsessive and impatient author: None of them should in any way be blamed for my final text.

Maurice Samuel, distinguished author and *mavin par excellence* on Sholom (or Sholem) Aleichem and Jewish life, greatly encouraged me throughout, and generously read and analyzed the entire manuscript. Dr. Shlomo Noble, Secretary, the Commission on Research, YIVO Institute for Jewish Research, helped me on many troublesome points of etymology. Dr. Bernard Mandelbaum, Dean, Jewish Theological Seminary, served as a persistent critic-theologian—and a treasure-house of Talmudic stories. Chancellor Louis Finkelstein and Rabbi Seymour Siegel, of the Jewish Theological Seminary, resolved many perplexing problems in the final stages. Dr. Gershon Winer, Dean, Jewish Teachers Seminary and People's University, helped provide definitions and derivations during the very first stages of this undertaking. Rabbi Isaiah Rackowsky of Bridgeport, Connecticut, saved me from several important errors, as did Rabbi Solomon Goldfarb of Long Beach, New York. Mrs. Priscilla Fishman assisted me in research for a month.

I am especially grateful to my learned friend, Felix Kaufmann, who conducted a most difficult and painstaking critique of the entire final manuscript, to which he brought his singular acquaintanceship with ancient history, Latin, Greek, German, Italian, Hebrew, Aramaic, and Sanskrit. My rigorously analytic friend and counsel, Bruno Schachner, contributed several illuminating suggestions.

I would like to thank Alfred Hart, whose original germ of an idea grew into this opus—which I never would have undertaken had I realized how prolific and tormenting this little germ would turn out to be.

My wife was unbelievably helpful—in letting me alone during those unconscionably long stretches of time, in New York and Westhampton Beach, when I absented myself mentally from her incomparable company and conversation.

For cooperation, skill, equanimity, and patience far beyond the call of salary or duty, I cite with gratitude my assisting angels, Edna Collins Reed, Susan Klein, and Maureen Lally.

L.R.

Guide to This Lexicon

HOW TO PRONOUNCE YIDDISH

Only two sounds in Yiddish or Yinglish present any problem to the laryngeally ungifted: the *r*, and the famous *kh* (which I spell *ch*, for reasons explained below). Both sounds can be rendered without pain if the reader will heed the following hints:

I. How to Pronounce the "R"

There are two *r* sounds in Yiddish: the trilled *r*, and the deep-throated or guttural *r*. So:

(A) Place the tip of your tongue against the front edge of your upper gums and vibrate—(your tongue, not your gums). This is the lingual or trilled *r*.

(B) Gargle, which means vibrate your uvula.* This is the uvular or guttural *r*.

NOTE: The hard English *er* ending to a word is unknown to Yiddish; pronounce any Yiddish word that ends in *er* with the soft *air* sound: "father" is rendered as *fathair*, "dancer" as *dan-sair*, and so on.

---

* The uvula is the small, fleshy appendage that hangs down, above the back of your tongue, from the middle of the soft palate. The palate or roof of the mouth is hard and bony in front, soft and fleshy in back. The phrase "He has a good palate," anatomical nonsense, comes from the days when the sense of taste was incorrectly believed to reside in the palate.

II. How to Pronounce "KH" or "CH"

If you can pronounce the Scottish *loch* or the German *ach!* you can pronounce the Yiddish *ch* (or *kh*).*

Here are five different, easy ways of producing the *ch:*

(1) Prepare to say "Yes." Now, instead of pronouncing the *y*, simply expel air, in a little spurt, blowing it through the passage between the roof of your mouth and your tongue.

OR

(2) Set your tongue as if you are going to pronounce a *k;* but let the air out to pronounce an *h.* That's the *kh* sound.

OR

(3) Pretend you have a fish bone stuck in the roof of your mouth. Now *cccchh* it out. That's the sound.

OR

(4) Pretend you have a bread crumb stuck in your throat. Expel it by rattling wind and saliva around sonorously.

OR

(5) Pronounce the *YECCH!* made famous by *Mad* Magazine. Even a Cabot can do this.

If you use any of these five pronunciatory gambits, you may now delight yourself, and Semitic cynics, by pronouncing

> *cheder*
> *chutzpa*
> *ylchus*
> *chasidim*

with careless aplomb. You should even be able to pronounce *chachem*, thus becoming one.

RULES FOLLOWED FOR LISTING AND CROSS-REFERENCING WORDS

(1) All words are listed in alphabetical (English alphabet, that is) order.

(2) I have tried to list every form I have encountered for

---

* By the *ch* sound in Yiddish I mean that sound designated in phonetics as *kh.* In technical language, the phonetic *kh* is "the unvoiced velar" or "the unvoiced uvular fricative."

the spelling of a word; but I *define* the word under the spelling I consider best (see below).

(3) Each entry that is not defined is cross-referenced to the place where it is.

(4) Where three or four spellings are listed together, in columnar order, the first entry is the one I prefer and use. Thus:

> CHANUKAH
> CHANNUKAH
> HANUKA
> HANUKKAH

(5) I have listed some spellings I consider outlandish, because I did find them in English transliteration: for example, *schatchen* for *shadchen*, *schlemiehl* for *shlemiel*, etc. Such entries are cross-referenced to the spelling under which they are defined.

(6) I list no form of spelling that is not based on one that I have, in fact, seen in an English book or periodical.

(7) Hebrew words are *listed* in both their Hebrew and Yiddish spelling, where such spellings differ; they are also cross-referenced; they are *defined* under their Yiddish spelling:

> SHOLEM *(Yiddish)*
> SHALOM *(Hebrew)*
> *or*
> BES MIDRASH
> BET MIDRASH
> BETH HAMIDRASH

THE PRONUNCIATIONS USED IN THIS LEXICON

Two dialects, broadly speaking, characterized and dominated the way Yiddish was spoken in Eastern Europe: the Northern or "Litvak," which centered in Lithuania, and the Southern or "Poilish," followed by Jews from Poland to Rumania and the Ukraine. Claims and counterclaims for each fly about like swallows in the spring.

In the United States, the Southern dialect was preferred in

the Yiddish theater. The Northern pronunciation, preferred in literary discussions and on the lecture platform, was considered "standard" Yiddish.* This did not in the slightest affect those who had spoken Southern Yiddish as their first language, their *mama-loshen*, their "mother tongue." (I have heard the simple word for "where" rendered as *voo, voe, vee*.)

I trust I will be forgiven for favoring the Southern pronunciation, on which I was raised, in the case of many words. It is not simply bias on my part: An enormous number of Jews followed the Polish pronunciation and saw no reason to alter it, especially since it was used in the great Yiddish theater.

In general, I have tried to accommodate both the Northern and Southern camps as well as I could. I have followed these guiding rules for pronunciation:

(1) The pronunciation of *vowels*, as in "standard" Yiddish, follows that used by Russian and Lithuanian Jews.

(2) The pronunciation of a few *consonants* follows that used by Polish Jews. (This may seem confusing, but only because it is explained; you can be just as discombobulated by the technical preface of an English dictionary.)

(3) Hebrew words are pronounced differently in Yiddish than they are in Hebrew. (The Hebrew *th* is pronounced *s*, for instance; and whereas Hebrew words are accented on the last syllable, Yiddish words are not.) I use the Yiddish or Yinglish pronunciation throughout.

(4) Whenever a Hebrew word, or a word derived from Hebrew, appears in Yiddish, I use the Ashkenazic (Eastern Europe) pronunciation--not the Sephardic (Mediterranean) version. Yiddish is, after all, the language of the Ashkenazim. (The distinctions between the two are explained in the respective entries in the lexicon.)

RULES USED FOR THE SPELLING
OF YIDDISH WORDS

Is there a "standard" or official way of spelling Yiddish words in English? Not really. In 1937, the YIVO Institute of

---

* See "Yiddish," *The Standard Jewish Encyclopedia*, revised 3rd edition, ed. by Sir Cecil Roth, Doubleday, 1966, pp. 1945–46.

Jewish Research established governing rules for orthography, but they are widely ignored by editors and writers who use Yiddish words in English. (See Appendix.)

In this lexicon I have followed a few simple rules—choosing those forms of spelling that seem to me to offer the greatest help to readers who have not pronounced Yiddish words before.

(1) I spell words phonetically, wherever possible. (In Yiddish itself, words are spelled quite simply, according to the way they are pronounced, and without the maddening malformations of English, say, that make it possible to write the *ee* sound in sixteen different ways.*)

(2) I use *ch* instead of *kh* wherever possible, greatly preferring *chutzpa* to *khutzpa* (which no one ever spelled that way), or *cheder* to *kheder* (which some do spell in that odd way).

I am perfectly well aware that phonetic purists want the "uvular fricative" written *kh*, not *ch*. But since the reader of English will encounter the *ch* form far more often than the *kh* form, I think it best (and least misleading) to follow the most common practice.

(3) I try to use *sh*, not *sch*, to begin a word that is pronounced *sh*, not *sk*.

The *sch* is misleading to the Anglo-Saxon eye and tongue; it may misdirect the innocent into such barbarities as pronouncing *shlemiel*, if spelled *schlemiel*, as *sklemiel*.

But where a *sch* usage is so widely used and familiar as to have become "standardized," I bow to the weight of usage and conform.

(4) Certain choices on my part are admittedly arbitrary:

(a) I prefer *meshugge* to *meshuge*, or *shmegegge* to *shmegege*, because the double *g* tells the English reader to use a hard *g*, and avoids making the preceding vowel long, as in English.

(b) I select the Yiddish as against the German spelling of certain words: *gefilte* for *gefülte*.

(c) I use the opening *tch* instead of *ch*, in some cases, because I have tried to reserve the use of *ch* for the

---

* *me, feet, clean, believe, deceive, demesne, machine, obscene, people, key, Caesar, oenologist, happy, Ian, quay.* See my "Tiptoe thru Lingo," *Look*, December 17, 1967.

> phonetic *kh* sound. (This is not always possible, because of the way some spellings have caught on.)

(5) Where authorities differ over the spelling of certain words, as indeed they do, I have chosen the spelling that provides the quickest, clearest visual guidance to the reader.

In general, I spell the Yiddish words phonetically and use vowels according to their familiar English values:

LETTER	SOUND	AS IN	EXAMPLE
a	*ah*	are	*batlan*
	a	hat	(rarely occurs)
	ay	shame	*bagel*
	uh	llama	*mitzva*
e	*eh*	ten	*gelt*
	ee	eve	*tchotchke*
	ea	mere	*Yeshiva*
	ur	over	*k-nocker*
	uh	were	*levaya*
	ay	fey	*cheder*
i	*i*	hit	*shtik*
	ī	bite	*fifer*
o	*ah*	pot	*geshmott*
	oh	tone	*kosher*
	aw	horn	*loksh*
	uh	come	*bubbe* (1 variation)
u	*uh*	run	*bluffer*
	u	put	*lump*
	oo	prune	*kuni*
	u	pull	*utz*
y	*ee*	tiny	*bialy*
	i	lymph	*Dybbuk*
	ī	by	*myseh*
	y	young	*yenta*

DOUBLE VOWELS

LETTER	SOUND	AS IN	EXAMPLE
aa	*ah*	kraal	*baal*
ai	*ay*	maid	*aidem*
au	*aw*	haul	*graub*
ay	*ay*	say	*behayma*
ei	*i*	site	*Yiddishkeit*
ee	*ee*	feet	*bubbee*
ey	*ee*	donkey	*patchkey* [var. of *patchkeh*]
ie	*ee*	siege	*miess*
oo	*oo*	fool	*boo-boo*

FOREIGN SOUNDS

LETTER	SOUND	AS IN	EXAMPLE
ch	(Ger.)	ach!	*chutzpa*
kh	(Heb.)	parekh	*shekhinah*
dzh	(Slav.)	dzhlub	*dzhlub*
zh	(Slav.)	zhlob	*zhlub*

But the best-intentioned phoneticists run into the obdurate walls of demotic usage and custom: I found that I had to depart from consistency if I wanted to avoid outlandish visual departures from the familiar—e.g., *Rosh Hashanah*. So I have retained the long-established spelling of Hebrew words, even though the Hebrew pronunciation has been widely replaced by the Yiddish pronunciation. (*Shalom* is pronounced *shah-LOAM* in Hebrew, *SHAW-l'm* or *SHO-lem* in Yiddish.)

1. Where a word has been so widely used in English with a spelling I do not especially like *(shnook)* I have retained that spelling. (I would have preferred *shnuk.*)

2. Where a strict adherence to the table above would mislead the reader (for instance, many would pronounce the Yiddish *patch*—"slap"—to rhyme with "match," so I spell it *potch*, which is clearly meant to rhyme with "notch"), I have used that arrangement of letters that offers the simplest, clearest guide to the eye and ear.

3. I have added *h* to many words that end in *e*—wherever the pronunciation calls for the *eh* sound. This signals the

reader not to make the preceding vowel long, as in English (where "fat" becomes "fate," and "ton" becomes "tone" once an *e* is added). For example: *faygele* ("little bird") might well be pronounced *FAY-GEEL;* the addition of an *h,* to make it *faygeleh,* leads the reader to pronounce the word *FAY-geh-leh.* But a word like *broche,* which would be better spelled *brocheh,* is so consistently encountered in English as *broche,* that I have retained (with brief regret) the conventional orthography. Ditto for *chassene,* which is pronounced *KHA-seh-neh,* not *kha-SEEN.*

PRONUNCIATION AIDS

I have tried to help the reader manage unavoidable uncertainties, inconsistencies and confusions by offering a pronunciation aid, or phonetic indicator, for every word; thus: *"Sephardic . . . pronounced seh-FAR-dick."*

I have tried to provide a "rhymes with" device (*Shtetl . . .* rhymes with "kettle") for every word. This proved impossible for some words—and in other instances I was driven to extremes, as gruesome to me as they may seem to you. For this I can only beg your indulgence. The lot of phoneticists, like that of policemen, is not a happy one.

By and large, then, I have done my very best to give the swiftest, clearest, simplest assistances to the unpracticed or unwary tongue. Where my efforts have not proved successful, my intentions remain as pure as they were innocent.

L.R.

The Jews are just like everyone else—only more so.

—Anon.

What is lofty can be said in any language, and what is mean should be said in none.

—Maimonides

When a Jewish farmer eats a chicken, one of them is sick.

—Folk saying

When a father helps a son, both smile; but when a son must help his father, both cry.

—Folk saying

If I am not for myself, who will be for me? And if I am only for myself, what am I . . . And if not now—when?

—Hillel

Jewish dropout: A boy who didn't get his Ph.D.

—Anon.

Lexicon of Yiddish-in-English

Adonai

Pronounced *ah-doe-*NOY, to rhyme with "follow Roy." Hebrew: "My Lords." (The singular form is *Adoni*, but the plural is customarily used, perhaps to magnify God's majesty and to distinguish the deity from earthly sovereigns.)

The sacred title of God, never pronounced by pious Jews except during solemn prayer, and with head covered. When God is mentioned in ordinary discourse, devout Jews say *"Adoshem."*

Four Hebrew letters, *YHVH*, form the Hebrew name for God. *Adonai* is a substitute for these "sacred" letters.

We simply do not know how *YHVH* was pronounced by the ancients. There are no vowel letters in Hebrew; vowel *sounds* are indicated by diacritical marks (dots, dashes). But the Torah scrolls are not so marked or "vocalized."

Only in the ancient Temple in Jerusalem was the utterance of *YHVH* permitted. And when the awesome appellation *was* pronounced by the high priest, the musical part of the service swelled up loud so that worshipers would not hear The Name.

3

In English, *YHVH* is rendered vocally as "Yahweh" or "Yahveh." "Jehovah," which first appeared in Christian texts in 1516, is simply incorrect; it is based on a German papal scribe's reading of *YHVH* with the diacritical marks of *Adonai,* which had been added as a pronunciation aid.

The King James Version of the Bible usually translates *YHVH* as "Lord."

NOTE: When a religious Jew refers to God, in speaking, he changes even the substitute names: Instead of saying *"Adonai"* he says *"Adoshem";* when saying *"Elohim"* he alters one sound to make it *"Elokhim."*

See also ADOSHEM and Appendix: God's Names.

For an illuminating discussion of "God" (as an English word, as a concept with antecedents in prehistory, as one of the deity's names in the Old Testament), see James Hastings, editor, *Dictionary of the Bible,* revised edition by F. C. Grant and H. H. Rowley. Scribner's, 1963, pp. 333–338.

"If God lived on earth," goes a sardonic Yiddish saying, "people would knock out all His windows."

A remarkable directness and intimacy characterize the attitude of even the most God-fearing Jew to the Almighty. He may offer his personal orisons to God in a free-wheeling recitative that is richly garnished with complaints, irony, and critical questionings. Consider this lovely old story:

On the eve of Yom Kippur, that most solemn and sacred day, an old Jew looked up to heaven and sighed: "Dear God, listen: I, Hershel the tailor, put it to You! The butcher in our village, Shepsel, is a good man, an honorable man, who never cheats anyone, and always gives full weight, and never turns away the needy; yet Shepsel himself is so poor that he and his wife sometimes go without meat! . . . Or take Fishel, our shoemaker, a model of piety and kindness—yet his beloved mother is dying in terrible pain. . . . And Reb Label, our *melamed* (teacher), who loves all the lads he teaches and is loved by all who know him—lives hand to mouth, hasn't a decent suit to his name, and just developed an eye disease that may leave him blind! . . . So, on this most holy night, I ask You directly, God: Is this *fair?* I repeat: *Is this fair? . . .*

So, tomorrow, O Lord, on our sacred Yom Kippur—if You forgive us, we will forgive You!"

"God, I know, will provide," sighed one disconsolate Jew. "I only wish He would provide *until* He provides."

Another story tells us of a legendary *zayde* (grandfather) in "Shpolle," who was called "the Saint of Shpolle." He was said to have become so heartsick over the sufferings of the Jews and the injustices of the world that he decided to put God on trial. So he appointed nine friends as judges, himself being the tenth needed for a *minyan*, and summoned the Almighty to appear on the witness stand. (Since God is everywhere, the *zayde* simply closed his door.)

For three days and nights this remarkable juridical body tried the Lord: They presented charges, devised defenses, pondered, prayed, fasted, consulted the *Torah* and the *Talmud*. Finally, in solemn consensus, they issued their verdict: God was guilty. In fact, they found Him guilty on two counts: (1) He had created the spirit of Evil, which He then let loose among innocent and pliable people; (2) He clearly failed to provide poor widows and orphans with decent food and shelter.

Adoshem

Pronounced *ah-doe-*SHEM, to rhyme with "follow them." From Hebrew: *Ha Shem*, "the Name."

A cryptonym for *Adonai*, the title of God. *Adoshem* is used when the name of God is uttered outside of formal religious service.

Much mystification and magic, down the centuries, attended the utterance of God's Name, and many substitutes for It abound in Hebrew. Here are a few: *Elohim*—(when the attribute of God's justice is cited); *Ha Shem*—(when God's mercy is cited); *El Elyon*—God the Most High; *Hakodesh Baruch Hu*—The Holy One, blessed be He; *Ribon Olam*— Ruler of the World; and *Yah* (which is never pronounced)— a word formed from two Hebrew letters, *yud* and *hei*, which are the first and last letters of *YHVH*, God's unutterable Holy Name.

See also ADONAI and Appendix: God's Names.

aha!

> Pronounced with a note of sudden comprehension, pleasure or triumph.

> The versatile expletive, widely used by old-fashioned Jews, to signify:
> 1. COMPREHENSION. "You don't subtract, but multiply? *AhA!*"
> 2. ILLUMINATION. *"AhA! That's* why they called off the party!"
> 3. SURPRISE. "The *doctor* was wrong? *AHA!*"
> 4. SENTENTIOUS HINTING. "Just ask her—and watch her expression. *Aha!*"
> 5. DELIGHT. *"Ah-A!* Then *I* win the bet!"
> 6. TRIUMPH. *"AhA!"* (meaning, "So now do you admit you're wrong?")

Aha! is not to be confused with *hoo-ha!,* its blood cousin. Perhaps the best way to illustrate the difference is with the following story.

For twenty years Mr. Sokoloff had been eating at the same restaurant on Second Avenue. On this night, as on every other, Mr. Sokoloff ordered chicken soup. The waiter set it down and started off. Mr. Sokoloff called, "Waiter!"

"Yeah?"

"Please taste this soup."

The waiter said, *"Hanh?* Twenty years you've been eating the chicken soup here, no? Have you ever had a bad plate—"

"Waiter," said Sokoloff firmly, "taste the soup."

"Sokoloff, what's the *matter* with you?"

"Taste the *soup!*"

"All right, all right," grimaced the waiter. "I'll taste—where's the spoon?"

"Aha!" cried Sokoloff.

ai-ai-ai
ai-yi-yi

Pronounced *ay-ay-*YI, or AY-*yay-yi,* to rhyme with "my my my."

This exquisite exclamation should not be confused with the classic *oy-oy-oy.* A folk saying goes "To have money may not always be so *ai-yi-yi,* but not to have it, you may be sure, is *oy-oy-oy!*"

Ai-ai-ai is cried, crooned, or sung out in a juicy repertoire of shadings; it is sent forth *forte* or *pianissimo;* it can run up or down the tonal scale; it is counterpointed by a fruity variety of facial expressions—according to the vocalizer's intention and histrionic talent.

The three syllables should not be clipped, as Spaniards do in mouthing their stern Iberian *ay-ay;* nor should the syllables be barked out, as the Japanese do in grunting their hoarse, harsh "Hai!" (which means "yes" but sounds as though it came out of a robot greatly in need of oil); nor should the syllables be murmured genteelly, as in the fine old British nauticism, "Aye, aye, sir."

The Yiddish *ai-ai-ai* is of another and altogether different genre: it ties the consonantal "y" right into the compliant "ai" in a liquid linkage that enhances both euphony and meaning thusly:

1. SUNG OUT HAPPILY, up-scale (*ai-yi-*YI!) with a beam or laugh, it expresses admiration, envy, surprise, all-other-words-fail-me enthusiasm;

2. UTTERED SADLY, with a dolorous expression, sheep-eyes, a shake of the head, or in hollow *diminuendo* (AI-*yi-yi*), it emits monosyllabic pellets of dismay, pity, lamentation, regret, quite akin to *oy-oy-oy;*

3. UTTERED SARCASTICALLY, or garnished with a glare, a snicker, a sneer, *ai-ai-ai* is a scathing little package of scorn: "So he's on the committee for the annual picnic. *Ai-ai-ai.*"

These feeble ground rules are not to be interpreted rigidly. (My father, for instance, a virtuoso of the *ai-ai-ai,* could make it jump through hoops beyond the three delineated above.)

Many an accomplished complainer can trill an *ai-ai-ai* up-scale as if it were a dirge, which is no small feat, and some can produce a down-scale *ai-yi-yi* with so joyous and percussive a first syllable that the rest sounds not like depression but exhaustion from too much delight.

When Mr. Olinsky returned from Europe, his partner in Marlborough Men's Coats hung on his every reminiscence.

"And I even was in a group who went to the Vatican," beamed Olinsky, "where we had an audience with the Pope!"

"*Ai-ai-ai!* The Pope! . . . What does he look like?"

"A fine man, thin, spiritual, I figure a size 38, short."

alav ha-sholom (masculine)
aleha ha-shalom (feminine)

Pronounced *aw*-LUV *ha sha*-LOAM or AH-*luv ha* SHO-*lem* (the first pronunciation is Hebrew, and elegant; the second is Yiddish, and brisk). The two Hebrew words are often pronounced as if one: *alevasholem*. The feminine form is *aleha ha-shalom*, pronounced *ah-leh-ha ha*-SHO-*lem* or SHA-*loam*.

Literally: "On him (or her) peace."

The phrase is used, automatically, when referring to someone who is dead—as, in English, one says "of blessed memory," or "May he rest in peace."

When a man says "My uncle Harry, *alevasholem*, once said . . ." you can be sure that Uncle Harry is dead.

As a boy, I was fascinated by the obligatory "*alevasholem*," but puzzled to hear: "That man? A liar, a no-good, *alevasholem*." Thus realism, wrestling with ritual, resolves ambivalence. In fact, the primary purpose of ritual is to provide a routine for the management of emotion. Routine reduces anxiety by removing choices.

It also used to please me, as a boy, to hear a patriarch utter a fearsome oath thusly: "May beets grow in his belly! God forbid." It pleased me, I say, because "God forbid" took the edge off a malediction uttered in anger—*after* the anger had been healthily expressed.

Jews are at home with strong emotions. They express feelings with ease, to say nothing of eloquence, then politely dilute them—to be on the safe side of things.

It was at the great Café Royale, on Second Avenue in New York City, *alevasholem*, that I first heard this classic joke:

SCENE: *Restaurant.*

Waiter: "Tea or coffee, gentlemen?"

1st customer: "I'll have tea."

2nd customer: "Me, too—and be sure the glass is clean!"

(Waiter exits, returns)

Waiter: "Two teas. Which one asked for the clean glass?"

aleichem sholem

See SHOLEM ALEICHEM.

The famous Yiddish writer Sholom (Solomon) Rabinowitz, who took these words as his pen name, would have loved the following story.

Said Mrs. Nathan to her daughter Deborah, who was plain, thirty-one, and unmarried: "Listen, darling. Don't get excited, and don't get mad. I am your mother, who loves you and wants to see you married and happy. There's no sense just sitting around, night after night, *hoping* some nice man is going to telephone. Like that, I'm afraid, it won't be any more. I think you should put an ad in the paper!"

Cried Deborah, "Mamma, you must be joking!"

"You don't have to give your *name*. Just put down a box number. Like this." She handed her daughter a piece of paper, on which she had printed:

> CHARMING JEWISH GIRL, WELL-EDUCATED, FINE COOK,
> WOULD LIKE TO MEET KIND, INTELLIGENT, EDUCATED,
> JEWISH GENTLEMAN. OBJECT: MATRIMONY.
>
> BOX 146

Deborah turned red and blushed and stammered and muttered protestations, but her mother persuaded her that nothing was to be lost—and very, very much just might be gained.

So the advertisement appeared in the newspaper, and each morning Deborah hastened down to meet the postman. And in a few days she came running up in excitement.

"Mamma! Look! An answer to the ad, forwarded from the newspaper!" With flushed cheeks she ripped open the envelope, read the contents—and burst into tears.

"Darling," cried Mrs. Nathan, "what is it? Tell me!"

In an agonized voice, Deborah gasped: "It's from papa."

aleph-baiz
aleph-bayz
aleph-bez
aleph-baz

Pronounced OL-lif BAZE, in my Yiddish circles, to rhyme with "Ma riff haze." Hebrew: The names of the Hebrew letters a, b.

The alphabet—i.e., "abc's." "He is learning his aleph-baiz."

Aleph is the name of the first letter in the Hebrew alphabet; beth is the name of the second. The similarity of aleph-beth to "alphabet" is obvious.

The Hebrew alphabet, incidentally, came from the inhabitants of Canaan, which was that part of Palestine the Greeks called Phoenicia. Hebrew was most probably the language spoken by the Phoenicians/Canaanites (Isaiah spoke of the "language of Canaan"), who almost surely created those letters which formed a Semitic alphabet, and from which all the alphabets in Europe descended. Hebrew was one of a cluster of related languages (Aramaic, Ugaritic, Akkadian, Arabic, etc.) known as "Semitic."

See Appendix: Alphabet.

One of the most endearing customs I know involved a Jewish boy's first day in Hebrew school, or cheder. The teacher would show the boy the alphabet, on a large chart, and before (or after) he repeated the teacher's "aleph" a drop of honey was placed on his tongue. "How does that taste?" the boy would be asked.

"Sweet."

"The study of the holy Law," was the answer, "is sweeter."

Sometimes the boy's mother would give him honeycakes, shaped in the letters of the alphabet, before he went off to the *cheder* on his first day, or when he returned, to make him know and remember that "learning is sweet."

And after the boy completed his first lesson, some parents would surreptitiously drop a coin before him. "Ah, an angel dropped that from heaven to show you how pleased God is that you learned your first lesson."

alevai

See HALEVAL.

"*Alevai* you should live 120 years, plus three months!"

"Thank you. But why 'plus three months'?"

"I wouldn't want you to die suddenly."

As a child, and probably according to one of the principles of Piaget concerning the development of reason in the young, I went into stitches over this one:

"Let's go to a movie Sunday—if, *alevai*, we're alive; and if not, we'll go Tuesday."

almona
almoona

Pronounced "*oll*-MAW-*neh*," to rhyme with "Ah'll pawn a," or *oll*-MOO-*na*, to rhyme with "Altoona." Hebrew: "widow."

Widow.

Though no more than descriptive, *almona* is pronounced with a hint of sadness, for widows, orphans, and even the grown motherless or fatherless are accorded conspicuous sympathy in Jewish circles. And the reverent son or daughter of a departed virago, or a deceased wastrel, will refer to "my saintly mother" or "my sainted father." Such generous, not to say effusive, sentiments are sometimes applied to mothers-in-law, too.

When old Isadore Litvak, dealer in ribbons and buttons, died of a heart attack, he left, to everyone's surprise, insurance policies that totaled $10,000.

Did this, in some small measure, help console the widow? No. For what the *almona* wailed was: "My poor Isadore—all his life he worked, day and night, and we lived poor as mice, and just when God decides to drop a fortune in our lap, Izzy drops dead!"

alrightnik (masculine)
alrightnikeh (feminine)
alrightnitseh (feminine)

From the English "all right," with the incomparable "-nik" added. Pure Yinglish.

1. One who has succeeded, i.e., done "all right," and shows it by boasting, ostentation, crude manners.
2. *Nouveau riche,* with trimmings.

As is true of many Yiddishisms, the pungent suffix "-nik" is enlisted in the service of scorn.

Alrightniks are materialists; they parade their money; they lack modest, sensitive, *edel* qualities. They talk loudly, dress garishly, show off.

Alrightniks may be envied, but are not admired; for they have succeeded whether or not they have taste, breeding, or spiritual values. Above all, they are not learned, nor devoted to learning—hence cannot be really respected.

An *alrightnik*, drowning, was pulled out of the water, and an excited crowd gathered, crying, "Stand back!" "Call a doctor!" "Give him artificial respiration!"

"Never!" cried the *alrightnik*'s wife. "Real respiration or nothing!"

The rabbi came to a rich Jew and asked for a contribution to the poor.

The *alrightnik* refused. "They are nothing but lazy loafers! Their poverty is their own fault!"

The rabbi said, "Come to the window. Look out. What do you see?"

"I see—people," said the *alrightnik*.

"Now look into that mirror," said the rabbi. "What do you see?"

"Why, myself."

"Isn't it astonishing," sighed the rabbi, "that when you cover a clear glass with a little silver, you see only yourself?"

An attractive *alrightnikeh* was depressed by the suburb into which she and her husband had recently moved. One day she hastened to her neighbor's house and, embarrassed, said, "Shirley, you're the only one I can ask. Would you give me some—confidential advice?"

"Gladly."

The *alrightnikeh* blushed. "How—do you go about having an affair?!"

"I," beamed Shirley, "always start with 'The Star-Spangled Banner.' "

An *alrightnikeh* (or *alrightnitseh*) called a decorator to her new apartment. "I want you should fix up this place from top to bottom. Money is no object."

The decorator asked, "Would you like it to be modern?"

"Modrin? N-no."

"French?"

"French?" echoed the *alrightnikeh*. "How do *I* come to French?"

"Perhaps Italian provincial?"

"God forbid!"

The decorator sighed, "Madame, what period *do* you want?"

"What 'period'? I want my friends to walk in, take one look, and drop dead! Period."

alter kocker
A.K.

> Pronounced OLL-*ter* KOCK-*er*, to rhyme with "Sol the mocker." From the German: *alter*, "old"; *Der Alter*, "the old man." What *kocker* means I had rather not tell you in street argot, but *kock* means "defecate."

> (Vulgarism) A crotchety, fussy, ineffectual old man.

A.K. is a testimonial to the ineradicable earthiness and vigor of Yiddish. (My mother *never* let me use such a phrase, or employ such vulgarity.)

A.K. is as often used in mild, fond condescension as it is in derision: "Let him alone: He's just an *A.K.*" "He lies in bed all day, like an *alter kocker.*"

I make no special plea for *alter kocker*, but I certainly prefer *A.K.* to its English equivalent, "old fart."

Two *A.K.*'s had sat in silence on their favorite park bench for hours, lost in thought. Finally, one gave a long and languid *"Oy!"* The other replied, "You're telling *me?"*

And perhaps it was the same two *A.K.*'s on the same park bench, observing the same prolonged, silent communion. At last one said, "How are things?"

"Eh!" shrugged the other. "How about you?"

"Mn-yeh."

They rose. "Well, good-bye. It's always nice to have a heart-to-heart talk."

amen
amain

> Pronounced, according to regional variation, *aw*-MAIN to rhyme with "raw lane"; *aw*-MINE, to rhyme with "jaw line"; or even *oo*-MINE, to rhyme with "do fine." Hebrew: "So be it."

Amen.

(1) The word used during and at the end of prayer to signify affirmation. It is one of the most widely known words in all the world: Jews, Christians, and Muslims share its usage.

When services were held in the Temple in Jerusalem, a longer formula was used as the response of affirmation made by the people during the liturgy recited by the priests and Levites. After the Temple was destroyed, *amen* was retained in Jewish liturgy.

The *Talmud* ruled that *amen* was to be recited "with the full power" of the voice. (A forceful enunciation of *amen* was believed by the credulous to help open the doors of paradise.) The loud, emphatic utterance of *amen* was connected with the expression of repentance, which is very strong in Judaism.

The Great Synagogue of Alexandria was said to be so huge that worshipers in the rear, who could not hear the cantor, could not know when he had finished the prayer. To enable these unfortunates to participate in a mighty responsive *amen* at the right moment, an attendant signaled with a flag when it was time for all the faithful to thunder out in chorus: *"Amen!"*

(2) An interjection used as a response to a good wish.

"I hope you get well quickly."
"Amen."

(3) An expletive uttered in malediction, to co-wish misfortune upon someone disliked, or disaster upon someone hated. Thus:

"May a *kazarnya* [an armory] collapse on him!"
"Amen!"

"May all his teeth fall out!"
"Amen."

"Killed he should be before nightfall!"
"Amen!"

"Like a beet should he grow—with his head in the earth!"

"Ah, *amen!*"

am ha-aretz

Pronounced *am*-HOR-*etz* in Yiddish, to rhyme with "Tom Boretz." From the Hebrew: *Am ha-aretz,* "people of the soil," or, less literally, "an uneducated man."

1. An ignoramus.
2. A vulgar, boorish, ill-mannered man or woman.
3. A country bumpkin.

In the Jewish communities of Europe, learned but poor Jews were much, *much* more highly respected than rich but unlearned ones.

Am ha-aretz meant uneducated or uncultured (just as "villain," in English, originally designated a serf, and "boor," a peasant); after the Babylonian Exile, "none remained save the poorest sort of *the people of the land*" (II Kings, 24 : 14). These unlearned farmers drifted away from Judaic practices, and married into the surrounding populations. The rabbinical leaders stigmatized such backsliders as vulgarians and transgressors of the law.

The *Talmud* describes an *am ha-aretz* as one who does not respect the Law and the rabbis. Maimonides defined him as "a boor in whom is neither learning nor moral virtue." Rabbi Nathan ben Joseph called an *am ha-aretz* "one who has children and does not educate them. . . ."

An *am ha-aretz* may be shrewd, though ignorant. But not these two ignoramuses who were arguing: "Does a slice of bread fall with the buttered side up or down?"

Jacob said, "With the buttered side down!"

Max said, "With the buttered side *up!*"

So they made a bet.

Jacob buttered a slice of bread, raised it, and let it drop. It fell—buttered side up.

"I win!" cried Max.

"Only because I made a mistake," protested Jacob.

"What mistake?"
"I buttered the wrong side."

"How just is the Lord," said an *am ha-aretz* from Chelm, the mythical town inhabited by fools. "He gives the food to the rich—and the appetite to the poor!"

"The luck of an *am ha-aretz* is this: He doesn't know that he doesn't know."

—FOLK SAYING

apikoros

Pronounced *ah-peh-*KAY-*riss*, to rhyme with "Papa Bayliss," or *eh-peh-*KOY-*riss*, to rhyme with "Effie coy miss." From the Greek philosopher Epicurus, via rabbinical literature.

1. An unbeliever, a skeptic, an agnostic, an atheist. (*Apikorsus*, pronounced *ah-peh-*CORE-*suss*, means "skepticism" or "heresy.")
2. A Jew who does not observe religious practices. The *Mishnah* states: "All Israelites have a share in the future world [except] he who says there is no resurrection, he who says the Law has not been given by God, and an *apikoros*."

I have always loved the charming story about the brilliant young student who came to the old, learned rabbi and defiantly exclaimed, "I must tell you the truth! I have become an *apikoros*. I no longer believe in God!"

"And how long," asked the elder, "have you been studying *Talmud*?"

"Five years," said the student.

"Only five years," sighed the rabbi, "and you have the nerve to call yourself an *apikoros*?! . . ."

aroysgevorfen

Pronounced *ah-*ROYCE-*ge-vor-fen*, the *royce* rhyming with "choice," the *vorfen* with "orphan." From German. Thrown out.

This simple adjective carries a cargo of regret, for it means "wasted," and Jews are not second to New Englanders in their disapproval of wastefulness; *aroysgevorfen* is applied not only to material things.

My mother would often end a lecture to me with the dour lament that her words were probably in vain: *"Aroysgevorfeneh verter* (thrown out words)!" Was ever a phrase more heartfelt?

Aroysgevorfeneh yoren (years), enunciated with a sigh deep from the diaphragm, or with bitterness, refers to the wasted years that can never be relived. Jewish women are, by tradition, prone to lament their lot with this phrase.

Aroysgevorfeneh gelt (money) describes a useless purchase, an investment that did not prove fruitful, or (as in the story below) a gesture that went awry.

Benny and Moe wanted to give their mother a new and different birthday present. They went from shop to shop until, to their wonder and delight, they found—a parrot that spoke Yiddish! This astonishing bird cost $500, but the devoted sons decided it was worth it. Think of the hours and hours of pleasure their old-fashioned mother would derive from conversing with the extraordinary parrot; and think of the admiration the bird would elicit among Mamma's friends in the sisterhood!

So the sons bought a beautiful gilded cage, and placed the parrot inside, and had the singular birthday gift delivered to Mamma.

Then, in great excitement, they telephoned: "Mamma, Mamma, how did you like your present?"

"De*licious!*" said Mamma.

Ashkenazi
Ashkenazim (plural)
Ashkenazic (adjective)

Pronounced *osh-keh-*NOZ*-zee*, to rhyme with "Gosh Ben Ossie." Hebrew: *Ashkenaz*, "Germany." [Originally, *Ash-*

kenaz referred to a kingdom of sorts in ancient eastern Armenia.]

The name applied, since the sixteenth century, to the Jews of central and eastern Europe—ancestors of the vast majority of Jews in the United States.

Ashkenazim and *Sephardim* are the two main branches of Jewry. The Sephardic Jews live in, or come from, Portugal, Spain and southern France. The Ashkenazim moved from northern France to Germanic cities along the Rhine, then to central and eastern Europe, where they found settlements of Jews who had emigrated, long before, from Babylon and Palestine.

Medieval rabbis dubbed Germany *Ashkenaz* after a passage in Jeremiah (51 : 27), and decided that after the Flood, one of Noah's great-grandsons, named Ashkenaz, had settled in Germany. I have no idea what inspired the rabbis.

Ashkenazic Jews are distinguished from Sephardic Jews in many ways: the Yiddish they speak, their style of thought, their pronunciation of Hebrew, aspects of their liturgy, many customs, food habits, ceremonials. This is not surprising, given the considerable differences in history and experience across a span of a thousand years.

Yiddish is an Ashkenazic invention—and universe: the vernacular of Sephardic Jews is LADINO.

The culture of Ashkenazim is markedly different from that of Sephardim (see SHTETL). At the core of Sephardic thought, says Abraham Menes, lay the question: "What must a Jew *know?*" At the heart of Ashkenazic life, stirred the challenge: "What must a Jew *do?*"

The Sephardim were sophisticates, enlightened, cosmopolitan: merchants, physicians, philosophers, advisers to bishops and kings; the Ashkenazim were peddlers, peasants, proletarians, fundamentalist in faith, steeped in poverty, bound to orthodox tradition and superstition and fervent Messianic dreams. They resisted the secular world and scorned secular knowledge. Their intellectual world was bounded by the *Torah* at one end and the *Talmud* at the other. They held to dogged piety and boundless compassion. They were resigned to the humiliations and brutality of the world around them. They considered themselves (please note) God's hostages for the redemption of mankind!

And the Ashkenazim created a unique mode of thinking and living, an entirely distinctive civilization—in a Yiddish literature that Sephardic Jews could not understand, about a kind of person the Sephardim had never seen, celebrating passions and visions Sephardim could comprehend only by an effort.

It was in the Ashkenazic world that *Yiddishkeit* ("Jewishness") reached its golden age, and it may never return.

From 1880 to 1910, about one-third of the Jews in Eastern Europe migrated—over 90 percent of them to the United States.

See SHTETL, SEPHARDI, YIDDISH.

averah

Pronounced *ah-VAY-reh,* to rhyme with "Ah, say the." Hebrew: "sin."

1. *(Literally)* A transgression against God's will.
2. *(More loosely)* An unethical or undesirable act.
3. *(Colloquially)* "Too bad," "what a pity." "It's an *averah* to discard that dress; I've only worn it twice."

An *averah* is the direct opposite of a *mitzva,* as we shall see. The words are often contrasted, as in the saying: "One *mitzva* leads to another; an *averah* leads to an *averah.*"

Mr. Popper was challenged to fight a duel with Weishaupt, a well-known anti-Semite. The time was set for 6 A.M., in a field beyond the city.

Promptly at 6, Weishaupt appeared with his seconds.

They waited.

At 6:20, a messenger came running toward them, with a telegram:

UNAVOIDABLY DETAINED. IT WOULD BE AN AVERAH TO DISAPPOINT YOU. SO DON'T WAIT FOR ME—SHOOT.

POPPER

Centuries before Sigmund Freud published his *Interpretation of Dreams* (1900), the Jews had a saying: "In sleep, it is not the man who sins—but his dream."

"No man sins for someone else." —BABA METZIAH

aydem

Pronounced AID'*m*, to rhyme with "raid 'em." From German (archaic): *eidam*.

Son-in-law.

The Jews' extraordinary emphasis on education was expressed not only in the most extreme effort to educate one's sons, but in the longing and search for a son-in-law who would be a student, a scholar, a *talmid chachem*. It was quite common for a family, as part of a girl's dowry, to pledge support of the young couple for a number of years. The son-in-law would move into his in-laws' home, there to receive free room and board, and devote himself solely to Talmudic studies.

Aydem auf kest: "A son-in-law who boards."

Mr. Baum was showing his friend Kipnis through his new apartment, and Kipnis, greatly impressed, was clucking and marveling in the most *de rigueur* fashion.

"But you've seen nothing yet!" said Baum. "You should see how my *aydem* lives! Come!"

He hurried Kipnis up the stairs, to an apartment on the floor above, and flung the door open.

"*Ai-ai-ai!*" exclaimed Kipnis. "It's beautiful! It's magnificent! A palace—and for such a young man. . . . Tell me, what does your *aydem* do?"

"Four A's and a B-plus!" said proud Baum.

Janowitz was complaining to a friend that a disaster had befallen him. "My *aydem*—I tell you, I am cursed, cursed!"

"What's wrong with him?"

"What's *wrong* with him?" moaned Janowitz. "That boy

doesn't know how to drink and he doesn't know how to play cards!"

"*That* you call a curse? That's a blessing. Why are you complaining?"

"Because he does drink and he does play cards!"

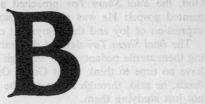

Baal Shem

> Pronounced *bol*-SHEM, to rhyme with "doll hem." Hebrew: "the master of the [good] Name."

> The name given to saintly men who were believed to be endowed with mystical and healing powers, which they attained (it was claimed) through manipulations of God's Name.

Baal Shems practiced folk medicine, employed amulets to ward off the Evil Eye, and dispelled spirits. They also dispensed psychiatric advice. They were believed, or claimed, to be chosen by the deity, as spiritually superior souls, for the performance of divine intentions.

The *Baal Shem,* or *Baal Shem Tov* ("good"), was the most famous of these holy men. Born Israel ben Eliezer (c. 1700–1760), the *Baal Shem* was an itinerant evangelist, a mystic, an ecstatic, a poet. He preached in simple language: "My teaching rests on three kinds of love: love of God, love of the *Torah,* love of man." He told his followers to laugh, to sing, to dance in adoration of the Holy One—which scandalized the traditionalists. What distinguished him from other *Baal Shems* was that whereas they dabbled in spiritualism and were steeped in mysticism, numerology, the abracadabra of endless, abstruse rearrangements of one or another of the Names of God, the *Baal Shem Tov* preached a down-to-earth, untormented gospel: He was a gentle visionary who extolled the expression of joy and the enjoyment of life.

The *Baal Shem Tov* derided the learned Talmudists, branding them sterile pedants who "through sheer study of the Law have no time to think about God." One serves God through deeds, he said, through living out the precepts of the *Torah*, not just studying them.

The rabbis of Galicia and Poland branded Israel ben Eliezer a heretic, but thousands of simple people venerated him as a true saint and miracle-worker.

He became known to his followers as the *Besht* (an acronym formed from the first letters of *Baal Shem Tov*) and his influence spread rapidly. He brought the excitement of hope into the lives of Polish Jewry, who had been decimated during a decade of savage Cossack pogroms.

The *Besht* said to the poor and the ignorant: God is in everything, including man. Every man, therefore, is good, and even a sinner can approach God with devotion. It does not matter that a simple Jew is unlearned—honest prayer is as important as erudition. Unity with God is achieved not through suffering, weeping, and asceticism, but through emotion, through rapture in spontaneous song and dance, in rejoicing and ecstasy. Man must enjoy human passions, not repress or run from them.

This extraordinary gospel (in some ways like Martin Luther's) became the basis of the Chasidic movement. Although the illustrious and revered Gaon of Vilna excommunicated the *Besht* and banned his teachings, the Chasidic movement swept with singular speed and fervor through Poland, Galicia, Bohemia, and Hungary. An entire culture within the culture of the *shtetl* grew up around the liberating visions of the *Baal Shem Tov*—and ended, as movements begun by simple men often do, in a cult.

The *Baal Shem* "rejuvenated" Jewry, says Professor A. J. Heschel, for Jews "fell in love with the Lord and felt such yearning for God that it was unbearable. . . . In the days of

Moses, Israel had a revelation of God, in the days of the Baal Shem, God had a revelation of Israel."*

"Some scholars are like donkeys: they merely carry a lot of books."

—FOLK SAYING

badchen
badchanim (plural)

Pronounced BOD-*khen*, and *bod*-KHAH-*nim*, with the uvular Scottish/German *kh*. Hebrew.

A professional funmaker, jester, entertainer.

Merrymakers, masquers, clowns, improvisers of doggerel, traveling players and musicians—all these were common figures in Europe during the Middle Ages. And the Jewish populace loved their own professional *badchanim*, who attended weddings, anniversaries, *Bar Mitzvas*, to enliven the festivities.

The *badchen* would offer a serious poem to bride and groom, would orate on the glory and sanctity of marriage, would extol the ancestors, the parents, the guests—and then would lampoon everything, teasing the nuptial couple, spoofing the ceremony itself, extemporizing poems, perhaps donning a mask, ad-libbing jokes, dancing, leading songs.

The rabbis urged Jews to "make merry" at weddings—even proclaiming it one's duty to be sportive; perhaps the singularly perceptive sages sensed how important it was for Jews, condemned to so much suffering and fear, to enjoy periodic catharsis.

The *badchen*, incidentally, often composed his own verses and music—much of it extempore; and the *badchanim* left a legacy of folk songs that have come down the centuries and form a cherished part of Jewish life and lore.

One of the most renowned of *badchanim* was Eliakim Zunser, a poet of considerable talent.

The *badchen* has all but disappeared from Jewish life (in the United States, at least) but surely left his mark and

---

* A. J. Heschel, *The Earth Is the Lord's*. Abelard-Schuman, 1964, pp. 76, 98.

example: The *badchen* is the direct lineal progenitor of the TUMMLER, which entry you ought to read.

See also KLEZMER.

bagel

Pronounced BAY-*g'l*, to rhyme with "Nagel." From German, *Beugel*, "a round loaf of bread."

A hard doughnut-shaped roll, simmered in hot water for two minutes before baking, then glazed with egg white.

If you have never tasted a *bagel*, I feel sorry for you.

Bagels are known as doughnuts with a college education—and the college is probably Yeshiva.

Because *bagels* were made of white flour, they were considered great delicacies in eastern Europe, where the poor Jews (and most Jews were very poor, indeed) ate black bread except on the Sabbath, when the queen of breads, *challa*, was eaten.

A *bagel* was supposed to be lucky, because it is round. Don't laugh at the Jews: The wise Greeks thought a circle "the perfect" form, because it had neither beginning nor end; therefore, God, being perfect, chose the circle as the basic form in constructing the universe. The orbits of the stars and planets were assumed to be circular. Even Aristotle thought so, and so did Ptolemy, and so did Copernicus, who nearly drove himself crazy trying to rearrange Ptolemy's elaborate observations into a new set of circles with epicenters. (The mystical assumption about circles plagued and stymied astronomers until Kepler.)

Bagels and hard-boiled eggs were traditionally served in Jewish homes after a funeral, for they were thought to symbolize the unending "round" processes of life and the world. The custom may have developed from interpretations of the passage in Ecclesiastes: "One generation passeth away, and another generation cometh; but the earth abideth for ever." The first printed mention of *bagels*, by the way, is to be found in the Community Regulations of Cracow, Poland, for the year 1610—which stated that *bagels* would be given as a gift to any woman in childbirth.

I suppose that you, like most people, think that a *bagel* and lox (smoked salmon) is the traditional Sunday morning breakfast for Jews. It is certainly widespread, but not traditional: It is a triumph of cuisine invented by American Jews.

Slices of tender lox, topping a layer of sweet butter on which cream cheese has been lathered, the whole enclosed by a toasted *bagel,* is so delicious that, to stop the watering in my mouth, I am going out to lunch.

INTERMISSION

A Yiddish expression: *"Er ligt in drerd und bakt bagel,"* is readily translated as "He lies in the ground and bakes *bagels.*" But what does that mean? "He's not doing so well, poor chap."

A man from Mars landed on Second Avenue and looked into a store window, fascinated. Finally, he entered the shop and asked the owner: "What are those little wheels in the window?"

"Wheels? What wheels?"

The Martian pointed.

"Those aren't wheels," smiled the *baleboss.* "They're called *bagels.* We eat them. . . . Here, try one."

The Martian bit into a *bagel* and smacked his lips. "Man! This would go great with cream cheese and lox."

On St. Patrick's Day, 1968, Macy's ran an advertisement in the New York papers such as I had never thought I'd see:

BAGELS,
BEGORRAH!
(green ones, yet)

The ad ended: "Cream cheese and lox . . . eighth floor."

Of such is the history of human culture compounded. Begorrah.

balbatim
balebatim

Pronounced *bol*-BOT-*im,* to rhyme with "Moll got him." Hebrew: "masters of the house."

Persons of high standing, impeccable repute and responsibility; community leaders.

The board members of a synagogue or temple are *balbatim*.

The crude, the vulgar, the superficial, however successful, are not *balbatim* or *balbatish* (adjective).

See BALEBOSS.

Young Rabbi Shulman finally summoned up enough courage to say to Mr. Benenson, one of the *balbatim* of the community, "I trust you won't mind my mentioning it, but I can't help noticing that—you always fall asleep when I'm preaching."

"Why not?" replied Benenson. "Would I sleep if I didn't trust you?"

balbatish
balabatish

Pronounced *bol*-BOT-*ish*, to rhyme with "doll tot-ish." Technically, the word should be *balabatish*, but the second "*a*" is slurred in pronunciation. (This is the adjective of *baleboss*.) *Balbatisher* is masculine; *balbatisheh* is feminine.

1. Quiet, respectable, well-mannered.
2. Responsible; of some consequence.

What nicer adjective is there? To call someone *balbatish* is to endow him or her with quiet, admirable traditional virtues. "What a *balbatish* child." "He is a *balbatisher* merchant." "She is a *balbatisheh* woman."

"My little *balbatishkeit*" means "my few possessions."

A Texan, driving down the great flat desert near Beersheba, in Israel, spied a tiny but *balbatish* house in the distance, and he drove up and stopped and knocked on the door.

An old Jew came to the door. "Good morning."

"My throat is so dry it's on fire," said the Texan. "I wonder if you would be good enough to give me a glass of water."

"Certainly; come in, make yourself at home."

The Texan entered and drank the water and thanked his host, then said, "Do you own this little house?"

"Yes."

"What do you do way out here?"

"I raise chickens."

"How large is your property?"

"Well," said the Jew. "In front, it's a good sixty feet—and in back, it must be a hundred, a hundred and ten, feet at *least*."

The Texan smiled. "Back home, on my ranch, I get up and get in my car around 9 A.M. and I start to drive, and I drive and drive and drive—and I don't reach the end of my property until six o'clock that night!"

"*Tchk!*" sighed the Jew. "I once owned a car like that."

baleboss (masculine)
baleboosteh (feminine)

The masculine form is pronounced either *bol-eh-*BAWSS to rhyme with "Walla hoss," or *bol-eh-*BOOSS, to rhyme with "Walla puss."

The feminine form is pronounced either *bol-eh-*BAWSS-*teh*, to rhyme with "Walla costa," or *bol-eh-*BOOSS-*teh*, to rhyme with "Walla puss ta." From the Hebrew, *baal ha-bayet*, "master of the house"; but the female, *baleboosteh*, is entirely and delightfully Yiddish.

A *baleboss* is:

1. The head of the household, the man of the house.
2. The owner of a store, shop, establishment.
3. The manager or superintendent.
4. One who assumes authority.

A *baleboosteh* is the wife of (1), (2), or (3), or

5. An excellent and praiseworthy homemaker.
6. A female owner.
7. A female manager.
8. A bossy woman.

Number 5 is the most common usage today, given the notable decline in the number of Jewish woman who (a) work behind the counter in the shop owned or managed by their husbands, or (b) are themselves owners and/or operators of businesses.

When one Jewish housekeeper calls another a *baleboosteh* it is usually with an appreciative "Pssh!", raised eyebrows, pursed lips, or with admiring *"Tchk!"*'s and clucks.

To call a woman "a real *baleboosteh*" is to bestow high praise indeed: It means the honoree is a splendid cook, baker, laundress, and, above all, keeps so immaculate a home that "you can eat off the floor." No one I knew ever did, in fact, eat off anyone else's floor, but I cannot count the number of times I heard the phrase—or the number of times that that symbolic riband of the *Légion d'Honneur* was pinned upon my mother's apron.

I was greatly impressed, as a child, by the obsession with cleanliness in our household, and the scorn with which untidiness was castigated. Cleanliness was not second to godliness; it was second to nothing.

In Hebrew, *baal* means master and *bayis* means house, and *baaleboss* originally meant a man who owned a business, a house, or a piece of land. It was extended to mean "master of the house," lord of his domain. Jewish men did dominate the home, and were respectfully obeyed by wife and children in all those domains considered man's high and exclusive responsibility.

There is a charming Yiddish expression for a Jewish girl's fond hope: *"A tisheleh, a benkele, a baleboosteh bei sich zu sein!"* "A little table, a little bench—oh, to be a *baleboosteh* of one's own!"

A newly arrived Jewish immigrant entered a kosher restaurant on Delancey Street. The waiter who poured his water was—*Gottenyu!*—Chinese! And the Chinese servitor proceeded to rattle off the menu in fluent Yiddish, even unto the idiomatic grunts, sighs and *nus*.

When the Jew was paying his bill, he asked the cashier, "Are you the *baleboss* [owner]?"

"Who else?"

"Well, I certainly enjoyed my dinner—and even more, the fact that your waiter speaks such excellent Yiddish!"

"Sha!" hissed the proprietor. "He thinks we're teaching him English!"

balmalocha
balmalucha

Pronounced *bahl-m'LUH-kheh*, or *bahl-m'LAW-kha;* make the *kh* Scottish and uvular, as in *loch;* rhymes with "Moll m'cooka." From Hebrew: "craftsman."

1. An expert. "Where pants are concerned, he is a real *balmalocha.*"
2. (In a derisive sense) Maladroit, inexpert, *"some craftsman,"* that is: no-craftsman-at-all. "His son-in-law? Oh, there's a *balmalocha!"*

In a small *shtetl* notices appeared that, at 5 o'clock on the first day of June, "The Great Isadore Bloomgarten, World-Famous Trapeze Artist," would walk across the river on a tightrope. Admission: 25 kopecks.

The whole town turned out.

They saw a rope tied to a tree, stretched tight across the river, anchored to a tree on the other side. Out came The Great Bloomgarten—but in an old suit and frayed shoes. He climbed up the tree, set one foot warily on the rope, and turned to address the audience: "Ladies and gentlemen, good Jews—I have a confession to make. I am not a trapeze artist. I'm just a poor man trying to earn a living. If I try anything as crazy as starting across the river on this rope, I'll fall, break my neck, and drown right before your eyes. Now if it's all right with you that for a miserable twenty-five kopecks a poor Jew should have that happen to him, I'll proceed. . . . So let's vote. How many want me to go on?"

As a tightrope walker, Bloomgarten was no *balmalocha,* but as a salesman———!

Bar Mitzva
Bar Mitzvah

Pronounced *bar*-MITZ-*vah*, to rhyme with "Car hits ya." From the Hebrew: "son of the commandment"; more broadly, "man of duty."

The ceremony, held in a synagogue or temple, in which the thirteen-year-old Jewish boy reaches the status, and assumes the duties, of a "man." It is held on the Saturday closest to the boy's thirteenth birthday.

The *Bar Mitzva* ceremony is not an ancient institution; it did not even exist until the fourteenth century. It is not a sacrament, nor a sacramental ritual. It simply signalizes the arrival of a Jewish boy at the age when, presumably, adult reason and responsibility commence. (The thirteenth year, in many cultures, is considered the beginning of puberty, and is celebrated with initiation rites.)

Ancient rabbinical sources contain the alarming notification that after his thirteenth birthday a Jewish boy is responsible for observing 613 (!) holy commandments. I must record my very grave doubt that a careful accounting of this is kept, even in heaven.

Please note that in traditional Jewish life the *Bar Mitzva* is a ceremony, a celebration, not a confirmation. In Reform Judaism there has arisen in addition to the *Bar Mitzva* a ceremony of confirmation; that is, the boy confirms his faith and his responsibility. But Orthodox Jews regard Jewishness as something that does not require confirmation: A Jew is a Jew; Jewish life is one long unbroken continuity; one only celebrates the arrival at the age of thirteen.

The *Bar Mitzva* signifies that a young male, now a "man of duty," is committed to lifelong religious and ethical obligations. In earlier days, "the *Bar Mitzva* boy" was obliged to deliver a scholarly address on some aspect of Talmudic law. He did not deliver a speech. In America, the custom arose of delivering a *Bar Mitzva* speech which began, "Today, I am a man." (When a rosy-cheeked thirteen-year-old announced this in a piping tenor, broad smiles, of both pride and polite dubiety, danced through the congregation.)

Today, the boy usually delivers a prayer, in Hebrew or English, pledging himself to live up to the ideals of Judaism, dedicating himself to the *Torah*, and thanking his father and mother for all they have done for him. (At this point, parental and grandparental eyes well up.) The boy is called to the altar to read the week's section from the *Torah* and the attached section (the *Haftarah*) from later parts of the Bible.

After the *Bar Mitzva*, the boy is, technically, required to wear phylacteries (TEFILLIN) during morning prayer. He can now be counted as an adult in the MINYAN of the ten males required before public prayers can begin, and can be called to the pulpit to recite a passage from the *Torah*.

To Jewish parents, the *Bar Mitzva* is a proud landmark of high symbolic meaning: i.e., their son's dedication to the lofty precepts of an ancient people and tradition. Papa, Mamma, sisters, brothers, grandparents, in-laws, friends, friends of friends, Papa's business associates, Mamma's neighbors—all are present at a *Bar Mitzva*. The parents and grandparents beam and KVELL to the bursting point.

It is customary to give gifts to the young man—who, at one time, was sure to receive at least six fountain pens, with chagrin. The father gives the boy a TALLIS (prayer shawl) of his own. A *Bar Mitzva* feast follows the service.

In the nineteenth century, some Reform temples introduced group confirmations, instead of individual *Bar Mitzvas*. Group confirmation services are held for boys and girls who are fifteen or sixteen. (It is, after all, somewhat sanguine to consider a modern thirteen-year-old a "man.") Confirmation services *en masse* are held during the feast of *Shevuoth*. Other Reform and Conservative synagogues retain the *Bar Mitzva* ceremony *and* hold group confirmations for mid-teenagers.

If you want to know more about *Bar Mitzvas*, go to one. They're charming, innocent, and always put a lump in my throat.

(For the equivalent ceremony for girls see BAS MITZVA.)

At the last *Bar Mitzva* I attended, I heard this story:

Two Martians who had landed in America happened to run into each other.

"What's your name?" asked the first.

"4286. And yours?"

"3359."

"That's funny; you don't look Jewish."

Bas Mitzva
Bas Mitzvah

Pronounced *bahs*-MITZ-*vah*, to rhyme with "Joss pits ya." Hebrew: "daughter of the commandment."

The ceremony for girls, akin to the *Bar Mitzva* for boys.

In recent years, some Reform, Conservative, and even Orthodox congregations have introduced a *Bas Mitzva* ceremony, which is a *Bar Mitzva* open to girls when they reach the age of twelve. (The ancients realized that girls mature earlier than boys.)

Many an Orthodox Jew still shudders at the idea of a *Bas Mitzva*, and others give a girl a *Bas Mitzva* at home, but not in the synagogue.

Bas Mitzva services are sometimes held *en masse*, for girls from twelve to eighteen years of age.

batlan
batlanim (plural)

Pronounced BOT-*l'n*, to rhyme with "totlin"; *bot*-LON-*im*. Hebrew: "A man who does nothing."

1. Someone without a trade or regular means of livelihood.
2. An unemployed or lazy man.
3. A misfit, such as a *Talmud* student of no promise.
4. Someone with intellectual pretensions and half-baked ideas.

Men who lived on the fringes, as it were, often spent most of their time inside the *Bes Midrash*, the House of Study, there seeking a way of picking up a few pennies—for making up the tenth (plus ninth or eighth, too, sometimes) man for a *minyan*. For this service, some congregations paid, out of a special fund.

A *batlan* might be given a small fee to join a group studying the *Talmud* in honor and memory of a deceased relative. When a bereaved family had no males, a *batlan* might be retained, in an emergency, to recite the prayer for the dead, the *Kaddish*, twice daily.

The *Talmud* says that every Jewish community must contain ten *batlanim*—that is, ten men who, since they do no work, can devote all their time to prayer and study.

The phone rang at the nurse's desk in Ward Four.

"Nurse, can you tell me how Hershel Resnick is getting along?"

The nurse consulted her charts. "Just fine. The doctor says he can go home on Thursday. . . . Who shall I say called him?"

"No one. I'm Resnick. That doctor treats me like a *batlan* and won't tell me a thing!"

behayma
behama
behayme

Pronounced *b'HAY-muh*, to rhyme with "the Dana." From Hebrew: *behama*, "animal (domesticated)."

1. (Literally) Animal—especially used for a cow.
2. A stupid man or woman; a dumbbell; an ignoramus. "Don't ask that *behayma* for an opinion." "She looks like an angel but thinks like a *behayma*."
3. A drudge; a stolid, hardworking, uncomplaining unimaginative sort. "That *behayma* works ten hours a day." "A worker is a man, not a *behayma*."

An old man was walking down a country road carrying an enormous load of wood on his shoulders. He struggled up a long hill, muttering and cursing, "I'm no more than a *behayma!*" when the bundle slipped off his shoulders and he cried out, "I can't go on! Let the Angel of Death come and take me!"

At once the Angel of Death appeared: "You called?"

Said the old man quickly, "To help me get that load back on my shoulders!"

MORAL: Men prefer misery to death.

ben

> There is no way to mispronounce this, unless you *try*.
> Hebrew: "Son."

> Son.

Before family names were common, a Jew was known by his given name plus the name of his father: e.g., Yochanan *ben* (son of) Zakkai.

Sometimes the form used was *bar*, which is Aramaic; thus: Shimon bar Kochba.

For a girl one said *bas*: Rivka *bas* Bethuel.

The old form—e.g., Yitzchok *ben* Shmuel—is still used on many wedding certificates, and in the synagogue when a man is called up to read a passage from the *Torah*.

Both *ben* and *bar* are widely used in Hebrew to form compound nouns: *ben Torah* (an educated person); *bar mitzva* (one who has reached the age of responsibility); *bar mazel* (a lucky person).

A Jew is considered a *ben brith*, or "son of the covenant." See BRITH.

bentsh

> Pronounced BENCH. From the Romanic *benedicere:* "bless."

1. To bless. "May God *bentsh* you."
2. To recite a blessing.
3. To recite the Grace after Meals.
4. To recite a particular blessing; thus, *bentsh licht:* to recite the blessing over Sabbath or holiday candles; *bentsh gomel:* to recite the blessing after having recovered from a serious illness, escaped an accident, etc.

The Grace after Meals appears to have been instituted during the period of the Second Temple. It begins with four benedictions: thanking God, who provides food; blessing the land that produces it; expressing hope for the rebuilding of Zion; attesting to God's love and kindness. These are followed by a series of petitions varied to suit the occasion (for one's guests, relatives, visitors), plus verses from Psalms, and—always— ending with a prayer for peace.

---

gebentsht (verb)

Blessed.

"He is *gebentsht* with patience."

gebentshter (adjective masculine)

gebentshteh (adjective feminine)

Talented, blessed—i.e., blessed with exceptional gifts.

"He has a *gebentshteh* mouth," means "He is an eloquent speaker, a superlative orator." Of a surgeon, one might say, "He has *gebentshteh* hands." And in irony, "With brains, he wasn't exactly *gebentsht*."

"An angry man is unfit to pray."

—NAHMAN BRATZLAV

---

berrieh

Pronounced BERR-*yeh*, to rhyme with "dare ya'." From Hebrew: *briah*, "creature."

> A woman of remarkable energy, talent, competence; a female live wire; one who gets a lot done, does it swiftly, does it well; a real *baleboosteh*.

This term of approbation is nearly always exclamatory: "My, is she a *berrieh!*" "To do a thing like that, you have to be a regular *berrieh!*"

The cardinal importance of the woman in the home has always been stressed within Jewish culture. (Jews never held with the "I'm just a housewife" nonsense.) The Jews knew that the wife and mother was *the* homemaker, and found many ways of complimenting her. (See SHABBES.)

The doctor examined the eighty-three-year-old woman and said, "Some things not even modern medicine can cure. . . . I can't make you any younger, you know."

"Who asked you to make me younger?" retorted the *berrieh*. "I want you to make me older."

Bes din
Beth din
Bet din

> Pronounced, in Yiddish, *"base din"* to rhyme with "case tin." Hebrew: "House of Judgment." Plural: *Batte din.*

> A rabbinical court.

Jewish communities in Europe usually had their own civil courts, presided over by a chief rabbi or a *dayan*. These courts dealt with religious and local (Jewish community) problems, and with those domestic and commercial disputes (marriage, divorce, inheritance, debts, etc.) in which the disputants sought advice or arbitration.

When a dispute involved litigation, at least three rabbi-judges sat.

In the Middle Ages, there were special "guild" *Batte din*, for different trades and occupations.

In the United States, many observing Jews preferred to

bring their troubles to their rabbi, or to a *Bes din* of three rabbis, instead of going into the public courts. (*"Es passt nit,"* a commonly heard phrase, means "It's not nice" or, as the English would say, "It isn't done.")

These *Batte din* had no legal authority: the Jews who came to them came voluntarily. The more orthodox the "defendant" the more compliant to the *Bes din*. Such courts are still found in religious communities.

In Israel, the *Batte din* are official, operate in the office of the central Rabbinate, and have exclusive jurisdiction over certain areas of status, marriage, inheritance, etc.

See SANHEDRIN, DAYAN.

Bes Midrash
Bet Midrash
Beth Hamidrash

Pronounced *bess*-MED-*rish*, to rhyme with "less red fish." Hebrew: "House of study."

Sometimes used as another name for synagogue. (See SHUL.)

The synagogue, from its inception, was a place for both prayer and study, and in Jewish life the distinction between the two is exceedingly difficult to draw. The *Bes Midrash* was, originally, the place where male Jews met to study. And since prayers were frequent there, the name came to be used for synagogue, too.

Study and prayer, or (better) study-prayer, was the most potent mortar in Jewish life and history. It was the linchpin in a Jew's self-esteem. It lent meaning and purpose to the most difficult and desperate of existences. It illuminated life. It ennobled, inspired, redeemed. It admitted even the humblest Jew to the company of sages, prophets, scholars, saints.

Virtually *all* of male Jewry participated in a perpetual seminar on the *Torah* and the *Talmud*. Even the cobblers. Even the tailors. The drovers and diggers, farmhands and carpenters. The peddlers and beggars and shopkeepers. Most

Jews past the age of six (except for mental deficients) could read and write! They were all arguers, dialecticians, amateur theologians—albeit their poverty was great, their living precarious, their security at the mercy of local fanatics. When studying *Talmud*, every Jew felt elevated, a participant in an eternal dialogue on divinity, truth, the purpose and obligations of life.

W. E. H. Lecky, the Irish historian, summarized the Jewish ethos during the Middle Ages in this singular passage:

> While those around them were grovelling in the darkness of besotted ignorance; . . . while the intellect of Christendom, enthralled by countless superstitions, had sunk into a deadly torpor in which all love of enquiry and all search for truth were abandoned, the Jews were still pursuing the path of knowledge, amassing learning, and stimulating progress with the same unflinching constancy that they manifested in their faith. They were the most skilful physicians, the ablest financiers, and among the most profound philosophers.*

Jewish communities all over Europe automatically established formal study groups, communally supported. Abraham Menes points out that in 1887, in the small town of Kroz, no fewer than nine separate study societies thrived. Kroz had only two hundred Jewish families, but supported twelve teachers (two women, to teach girls) and two bookbinders!**

"In almost every Jewish home in Eastern Europe," writes Professor Abraham Joshua Heschel, in his lyrical *The Earth Is the Lord's*,*** "even in the humblest and poorest, stood a bookcase full of volumes. . . . Almost every Jew gave of his time to learning, either in private learning or by joining one of the societies [for] studying the *Talmud*. . . . At nightfall,

---

* W. E. H. Lecky, *The Rise and Influence of Rationalism in Europe*, Vol. II, third edition. Appleton, 1906, p. 271.
** See articles by S. Greenberg and J. B. Maller in *The Jews: Their History, Culture and Religion*, Vol. II, third edition, Louis Finkelstein, editor. Harper, 1960, pp. 1234–1288.
*** A. J. Heschel, *The Earth Is the Lord's*. Abelard-Schuman, 1964, pp. 42, 43–44.

almost everyone would leave the tumult and bustle of everyday life to study in the *beth ha-Midrash*."

And in the house of study every Jew sat "like [an] intellectual magnate. . . . When a problem came up, there was immediately a host of people pouring out opinions, arguments, quotations. . . . The stomachs were empty, the homes barren, but the minds were crammed with the riches of the *Torah*."

"Once I noticed," writes a Christian scholar, who visited the city of Warsaw during the First World War, "a great many coaches on a parking place but with no drivers in sight. In my own country I would have known where to look for them. A young Jewish boy showed me the way: in a courtyard, on the second floor, was the *shtibl* of the Jewish drivers. It consisted of two rooms: one filled with *Talmud*-volumes, the other a room for prayer. All the drivers were engaged in fervent study and religious discussion . . . It was then that I found out . . . that all professions, the bakers, the butchers, the shoemakers, etc., have their own *shtibl* [room] in the Jewish district; and every free moment which can be taken off from their work is given to the study of the *Torah*. And when they get together in intimate groups, one urges the other: '*Sog mir a shtickl Torah*—Tell me a little *Torah*.' "*

Many, many Yiddish words are related to study and scholarship: see MELAMED, YESHIVA, TALMID CHACHEM.

An eleventh-century poet sang:

> He who has toiled and bought for himself books,
> But his heart is empty of what they contain—
> Is like a lame man, who engraved on a wall
> The figure of a foot, and tried to stand in vain.
> —SAMUEL HA-NAGID, 993–1055, *Granada*

Someone once asked a scholar, "Why is it that you study so slowly—but pray so very fast?"

"Because," sighed the sage, "when I pray, I am talking to God; but when I study, God is talking to me."

* A. J. Heschel, *The Earth Is the Lord's*. Abelard-Schuman, 1964, p. 46.

bialy

Pronounced *bee-OLL-lee*, to rhyme with "fee dolly." Colloquial abbreviation of "Bialystoker."

A flat breakfast roll, shaped like a round wading pool, sometimes sprinkled with onion.

I choose the wading pool as a model because, like it, the *bialy* has a bottom—i.e., is not empty in the center, like a tire or a bagel.

The *bialy* roll, a growing packaged favorite in food stores across the country, is second only to the bagel as a base for cream cheese and lox.

The name is taken from the bakers from Bialystok, a city in Poland, where this exquisite product was presumably perfected.

"Forty cents a dozen for *bialies*?" protested Mrs. Becker. "The baker across the street is asking only twenty!"

"So buy them across the street."

"Today, he happens to be sold out."

"When I'm out of *bialies*, I charge only twenty cents a dozen, too."

blintz
blintzeh
blintzes (plural)

Rhymes with *chintz* and *chintzes*. From Ukrainian: "pancake." *Blintz* is actually Yinglish; in Yiddish, the singular is *blintzeh*.

A pancake, rolled around a filling, most often of cottage cheese.

I list *blintz* and *blintzes* together, because I never heard of anybody eating only one. *Blintzes* are traditional delicacies for the festival of *Shevuoth*.

Blintzes today may contain jam: strawberry, cherry, blackberry; potatoes; fish concoctions; apples; peaches; etc. Hence the need to say "cheese blintzes," which once would have sounded as redundant as "wet water."

Blintzes, as eaten by Jews, are ordinarily smothered under thick sour cream. Jet-set Jews, aspiring to *crêpes suzettes,* have taken to smothering blintzes with honey or jam instead of sour cream. There is no accounting for tastes.

Blintzes have become as much a part of Jewish summer cuisine as *borsht* or *shtchav* (sorrel soup).

bluffer (masculine)
blufferkeh (feminine)

Pronounced BLUFF-*er* and BLUFF-*er-keh,* to rhyme with "Duffer" and "Duffer-keh." Yinglish.

One who bluffs, deceives, exaggerates vaingloriously, mixes hyperbole with hot air.

A *bluffer* may bluff because he is boastful, foolish, vain, or because, as in poker, he is trying to mislead or deceive you. "He is nothing but *bluff*" means "He's full of hot air." "Watch out, he's a *bluffer,*" was not an injunction to call a bluff, but urged caution in the acceptance of representations.

Among certain Jewish groups, *bluffer* is often associated with the adjective "Americaner," just as various characteristics were attributed to other groups: "Polisher *yachne,*" "Rumanian *gonif,*" "German *yekke* (pedant)."

A farmer asked his neighbor if he could borrow his horse for a few minutes. The neighbor said, "I would, gladly, but my helper took the horse to the vet, and they'll be gone all day."

At this point, the neigh of the horse was heard in the stable.

"So whom do you believe?" cried the *bluffer.* "Me or a horse—and a horse who's a notorious liar, to boot?!"

Bnai Brith

> Pronounced *b'*-NAY BRITH, to rhyme with "René Smith."
> Hebrew: "sons of the covenant." [The *th* ending never
> appeared in classical Hebrew. See BRITH.]

A national Jewish society, organized in 1843, that devotes
itself to philanthropic and community activities. It supports
the Hillel Foundations on 240 college campuses, engages in
youth and vocational services, adult education, etc. The organization founded the superb nonsectarian National Jewish
Hospital in Denver. Perhaps its best-known division is the
Anti-Defamation League, which has long studied and fought
discrimination and anti-Semitism.

Bnai Brith has branches in forty-five countries.

boarderkeh
bordekeh

> Pronounced BORD-*er-keh*, to rhyme with "for Decca."
> Ameridish.

> A female boarder (obviously) who pays for room and
> board.

Purists, of both English and Yiddish, greatly disdain and
openly deplore such "loanwords" as *boarderkeh*. I find them
delightful.

The blithe adoption of English words, to which Hebrew or
Yiddish endings were tacked on, rapidly enlarged an immigrant's vocabulary and served as a *lingua franca,* equally com-
prehensible to American and Jew. Who, for instance, could
fail to understand the meaning of *opstairsikeh? donstairsikeh?
nexdoorikeh?*

As for *boarderkeh:* when the immigration waves brought
so many newcomers to America, rare was the flat in a poor
neighborhood that did not rent out at least one room. The
foreign enclaves in every large American city were crammed
with ROOM AND BOARD signs in German, Italian, Polish, Nor-
wegian, Russian, Hungarian—and Yiddish.

Poor people had to help finance their rent by taking in a roomer or a boarder, who usually ate with the family. Greenhorns, for their part, could not afford a flat of their own. Except for immigrants from the British Isles, the language problem was staggering—hence the wisdom of living for a while amidst *landsleit* (people from your old country) whom you could understand, who understood you, and whose longer residence in the golden land made it possible for you to pick up the basic words, phrases, practices, and mores of the bustling new world.

The kind of English that immigrants of, say, six months' standing confidently passed on to newer greenhorns created a rich argot all its own: It can be dubbed Yinglish or Ameridish. It is an extremely descriptive, functional, picturesque, and vigorous vernacular.

For a brilliant eyewitness description of the Lower East Side, see Hutchins Hapgood's classic, *The Spirit of the Ghetto*. (For the 1965 Funk and Wagnalls edition, Mr. Harry Golden has written a running commentary of reminiscences of his own childhood.)

SCENE: *Classroom, Lower East Side, 1926*
TEACHER: "Who can tell us where the Rumanian border is?"
STUDENT: "In the park with my aunt, and my mother doesn't trust him!"

The galloping difficulties of a foreign tongue are suggested in this anecdote:

A Mr. Goldberg, from Pinsk, coming to America, shared a table in the ship's dining room with a Frenchman. Mr. Goldberg could speak neither French nor English; the Frenchman could speak neither Russian nor Yiddish.

The first day out, the Frenchman approached the table, bowed and said, *"Bon appétit!"*

Goldberg, puzzled for a moment, bowed back and replied, "Goldberg."

Every day, at every meal, the same routine occurred.

On the fifth day, another passenger took Goldberg aside "Listen, the Frenchman isn't telling you his name. He's say ing, 'Good appetite.' That's what *'Bon appétit!'* means."

At the next meal, Mr. Goldberg, beaming, bowed to the Frenchman and said, *"Bon appétit!"*

And the Frenchman, beaming, replied: "Goldberg!"

———

At his wife's graveside, Mr. Berman wept copiously.

The Bermans' boarder, Mr. Kipnis, wept even more—and, indeed, carried on so hysterically that Mr. Berman said, "Kipnis, don't take it so hard! I'll get married again."

(I have heard this story as typically French, too.)

bobbe-myseh
boobe-myseh

> Pronounced BOB-*eh* by Lithuanian Jews, and BAW-*beh* or BUB-*beh* (using the *u* as in "put") by Polish Jews; MY-*seh* rhymes with "Rye, suh." *Bobbe* (or *boobeh* or *baba*) is the affectionate name for grandmother; *myseh* means tale, story, from the Hebrew *ma'aseh*.
>
> Old wives' tale; nonsense; something patently silly and untrue. "Did he try to sell me a *bobbe-myseh!*" "She believes every *bobbe-myseh.*"

Bobbe-myseh is a most effective compound noun for the sarcastic dismissal of something. I know an erudite professor at Cambridge (England) who often vents his ire on pretentious social-sciencing with this epithet. It puzzles Cantabrigians.

Now that you know all this, it is my duty to inform you that *bobbe-myseh* may derive from a Yiddish adaptation of the *Story of Buvo* or *Buovo*, a romantic fifteenth-century tale which was, in turn, an Italian reincarnation of the Bevis of Hampton cycle of romances. The stories, originally written in English, were translated into Italian, and from Italian were turned into Yiddish! In this vernacular they became popular among Jewish women.

———

If you are interested, Bevis of Hampton is a fictional figure who appeared in a fourteenth-century Anglo-Norman metrical romance, then in a French *chanson de geste*, *Beuve d'Han-*

stone. Italian-poem versions called the protagonist Bovo *d'Antona;* Germanic versions called him *Boeve de Haumtone.*

Elijah Bochur (1468?–1549) wrote two novels in Italian *ottava rima* stanzas: The *Bova Bukh* and *Paris un Viene;* both are Yiddish adaptations of Italian romances.*

bonditt
banditt

Pronounced *bon-*DITT, to rhyme with "Ron, sit!" From German: *Bandit:* "rogue," "bandit."

1. A clever, resourceful, beguiling fellow.
2. Someone with a delightful sense of mischief.

"Oh, what a *bonditt!*" is uttered with a grin, or an appreciative cluck, the way westerners say, "That son of a gun!"

To ring a change on the immortal precedent of *The Virginian:* "When you call me *bonditt*—smile."

Parents may say of a boisterous, bright child, "Oh, what a *bonditt!*" ("Oh, what a little devil.")

I used to think that *bonditt* was an adaptation from the English "bandit" by way of the villains in early westerns, who were called "bandits" more often than "robbers." But *bonditt* was widely used by Jews in Russia, Poland, Rumania, long before they saw a movie.

See also GONIF, MOMZER, MAZIK.

Two lawyers met in the lobby of the Empire State Building.

"Abe Epstein!" cried the first. "What a surprise! I haven't seen you since we both lived on Eldridge Street, on the Lower East Side. How are things?"

"You want to see something?" Epstein led his friend proudly to the large directory in the lobby, and pointed. " 'Eldridge, C. R.' That's me."

---

* Yudel Mark, "Yiddish Literature," in *The Jews: Their History, Culture and Religion,* Vol. II, third edition, Louis Finkelstein, editor. Harper, 1960, pp. 1191–1231.

"Eldridge? You *bonditt!"*

Epstein said, "Don't think I'm ashamed of my origins! The initials stand for 'Corner Rivington.'"

boo-boo

See BULBA.

bopkes

See BUBKES.

borsht

> Pronounced BOARscht; from the Slavonic, where it is pronounced *bor-sh-tch.* (I see no reason to suggest an *sk* sound by spelling it *borscht* instead of *borsht.*)

> Beet soup, served hot or cold (delicious!), often with a dab of sour cream (superb!), sometimes with tiny new potatoes bobbing in it, or cucumber slices floating on it (a *mechaieh!*).

Borsht was a great staple among Jews, because beets were so cheap. "You don't need teeth to eat *borsht.*" Another saying goes, *"Billig vie borsht,"* "Cheap as *borsht.*"

In recent years, a group of language-manglers have gone around altering restaurant menus and removing the *t* from the end of *borsht.* I do not approve of this. The Russian/Polish/Ukrainian word is spelled without a *t,* to be sure, so I suppose restaurants of those persuasions have a right to protect the linguistic purity of their menus. But I see no reason for Jewish restaurants to drop the *t.* In Yiddish, it is spelled and pronounced *borsht.*

The *"Borsht Belt"* refers to that sizable suzerainty, in the Catskill Mountains, of summer (and now winter) resorts that cater to, and were once almost exclusively patronized by, Jews.

SEE TUMMLER, KOCHALAYN.

SCENE: *A restaurant.*
FIRST CUSTOMER: "Give me the *borsht*."
WAITER: "Take my advice: Have the chicken soup."
SECOND CUSTOMER: "I'll have pea soup."
WAITER: "Don't take the pea soup—take the barley."
The soup is brought, the customers served.
FIRST CUSTOMER: "This chicken soup is marvelous! The best I ever tasted!"
SECOND CUSTOMER: "Waiter! Why didn't you recommend me the chicken soup?"
WAITER: "You didn't ask for the *borsht!*"

SCENE: *A dance hall in the Borsht Belt.*
YOUNG MAN: "Are you dancing?"
YOUNG LADY: "Are you asking?"
YOUNG MAN: "I'm asking."
YOUNG LADY: "I'm dancing."

boychik
boychikel (diminutive)
boychiklech (plural)

Pronounced BOY-*chick*, rhymes with "Roy chick." Plural: BOY-*chik-lekh* (the final *"kh"* is guttural): An affectionate, more diminutive neologism is *boychikel*. Yinglish, pure and simple, though it uses the common Slavic suffix *tchik*.

1. Diminutive of "boy."

Boychik or *boychikel* is used with affection, even admiration, the way some people say, "That's my boy," or the way an earlier generation said, "Oh, you kid!"

"Hello, *boychik*," or "How are you, *boychikel?*" may be uttered to males long past their boyhood; generally, when used to or about an aging man, *boychik* carries a tinge of sarcasm —but it can be used fondly:

Affectionate: "That Sam (sigh) . . . he has the spirit of a *boychik*."

Sarcastic: "At his age to go after young girls . . . ! Some *boychik!*"

2. (Critically) A sharp operator; one who cuts corners. "He's some *boychik*" can mean anything from "He's a tricky fellow" to "Watch your pocket."

bren

Pronounced BREN, to rhyme with "wren." German: *brennen,* "to burn."

Someone of great energy, vivacity, competence and optimism; a "fireball."

"She is a real *bren*." "Don't worry about him; he was born a *bren*."

On his first day as a bus driver, Maxey Eckstein handed in receipts of $65. The next day his take was $67. The third day's income was $62. But on the fourth day, Eckstein, a *bren*, emptied no less than $283 on the desk before the cashier.

"Eckstein!" exclaimed the cashier. "This is fantastic. That route never brought in money like this! What happened?"

"Well, after three days on that *cockamamy* route, I figured business would never improve, so I drove over to Fourteenth Street and worked there. I tell you, that street is a gold mine!"

brith
bris

Pronounced BRISS by most Jews in America; pronounced BRIT by Israeli Jews. NOTE: The *th* ending was unknown in Hebrew; Gentile scholars (of Hebrew and the Bible) decided upon it a few hundred years ago. Yemenite Jews differentiate between the *t* and *th* sound.

Brith means "covenant," but usually refers to the circumcision ceremony: in Hebrew: *Brith Milah.*

The *Brith Milah* is observed on a boy's eighth day of life, even if that day falls on *Yom Kippur*.

The circumcision is usually performed by a *mohel* (pronounced MOY-*el*), who is not a rabbi but an expert in this sharply circumscribed (no pun) surgical area. Tradition-observing Jews insist on a *mohel;* others ask an M.D. to do the cutting.

If you think that circumcision is or was a peculiarly Jewish custom, see Appendix: Circumcision.

At a *brith*, the proud father raised his glass of wine for a toast, sipped, and beamed, "Lovely wine. Good year: 5721."

broche

> Pronounced *BRAW-kheh*, making that *kh* a throat-clearing sound as in *Mad* Magazine's "Yecch!" Hebrew: "benediction." Plural: *broches*.

> 1. Blessing; a prayer of thanksgiving and praise.
> 2. To "make a *broche*" is to offer a blessing.
> 3. A Jewish girl's name.

The ceremonial demands on very religious Jews are very heavy, however much the faithful rejoice in the repetition.

Broches are recited during prayers (three times daily, plus special *broches* on *Shabbes* and in festival services). The silent prayer that precedes and follows communal praying contains nineteen *broches*. In the morning prayer, there are three *broches* associated with the *Shema;* in the evening prayer, four *broches* are associated.

The formula for a benediction must include *"Shem U'Malchus,"* the name of God affirmed as King.

To a tradition-observing Jew, the occasions that call for a *broche* include:

the first act upon arising
the last act before retiring
before and after every meal
upon eating and/or drinking at any time
    (even between meals; there are separate *broches* for different foods and drinks)

upon washing one's hands—which is strictly enjoined (this
must be done as soon as one gets out of bed in the morning, before praying, before eating)

upon returning from a hazardous journey

upon recovering from a grave illness

upon performing any religious ritual

upon the arrival of a new season

upon seeing the new moon

upon donning a new garment

upon smelling a fragrant odor

upon seeing such natural phenomena as lightning, majestic
mountains, a magnificent sunset, etc.

upon seeing a beautiful person or animal

upon seeing a strangely shaped person or animal

upon receiving bad news

upon seeing a scholar or sage

upon seeing a king

Et cetera.

The *Talmud* gives the exact form to be followed in "making
a *broche*." Tradition holds that the texts were formulated during the time of Ezra (2,000 years ago) by the sages of the
time, called the Men of the Great Synagogue. In the second
century, Rabbi Meir declared it to be the duty of everyone to
say no fewer than 100 *broches* daily!

About a hundred *broches* are reserved for the Sabbath.

One of the best known *broches* is *Shehecheyanu*, which
thanks God for having enabled one to live and reach whatever
auspicious occasion; it is used when eating "the first fruit of
the year"—or any food after long abstention or hardship.

For a delightful insight into the range and psychological
function of *broches*, see Chapter 11 of Maurice Samuel's classic *The World of Sholom Aleichem*.

See also DAVEN.

When S. Y. Agnon was named Nobel Prize Laureate for Literature, in 1966, he was told he would have to go all the way
to Sweden, where he would receive the award from the king.

"Good," said Mr. Agnon, who observes orthodox religious
rites, "I have never had the opportunity to say the *broche* one
makes upon seeing a king."

Mrs. Gidwitz told her benevolent old Orthodox rabbi, "My grandchildren are driving me crazy this year: they want to have a Christmas tree. Rabbi, could you maybe make some dispensation, a special *broche* over such a tree . . . ?"

"Never!" said the rabbi. "Impossible."

So Mrs. Gidwitz consulted a more lenient rabbi, a Conservative. "No," he said. "I'm sorry."

So poor Mrs. Gidwitz went to the young new Reform rabbi. "I'll be glad to," he said. "Only tell me: What's a *'broche?'* "

bubbe

See BUBELEH.

bubee

Pronounced *BU-bee*, to rhyme with "goody." Cf. BUBE-LEH.

Affectionate term of endearment, the diminutive of *bubeleh*, used between a husband and wife, a parent and child, between siblings—and amongst members of the theatrical profession surprisingly soon after they begin to work together.

See BUBELEH.

bubeleh
bobeleh

Pronounced *BUB-eh-leh*, using the *u* of "put," not of "tub"; rhymes with "hood a la." From Russian/Hebrew. In Hebrew, *buba* means "little doll." But the Yiddish *bube* and *bubeleh* seem independent of the Hebrew, say the experts.

Grandmother; the affectionate diminutive, really: "little grandma." (*Baba*, which means midwife or grandmother in Russian and other Slavic tongues, was often used in addressing any old woman, whether one's grandmother or not.)

Bubeleh, a term of endearment, is widely used for "darling," "dear child," "honey," "sweetheart."

A husband and wife may call each other *bubeleh.*

Jewish mothers call both female and male babies *bubeleh.* This carries the expectation that the child in the crib will one day be a grandparent. It also honors the memory of the mother's mother: in calling a baby "little grandmother," a mother is addressing the child in the way the child will in time address *its* grandmother—and its child.

Bubeleh has come into vast popularity in recent years—via television. On all the night "talk" shows, the garrulous comedians, actors, actresses try to display warm, outgoing, loving natures, in fact all the obligatory coziness of show business, by greeting each other with kisses, embraces, cheek pattings— and generous doses of *"bubeleh."* Thus: "How *are* you, *bubeleh?"* or "I just loved your last picture, *bubeleh!"* or even, *"Bubeleh,* baby, where have you *been?"*

What struck me during the birth and vehement barrage of *bubelehs* among emphatically Anglo-Saxon, Italian, Greek, and Negro entertainers, was the fact that no one seemed to think it necessary to explain what *bubeleh* meant. I often wonder what residents of Idaho or Mississippi think those crazy people in New York or Hollywood are talking about.

A Jewish mother sent her son off to his first day in school with the customary pride and precautionary advice: "So, *bubeleh,* you'll be a good boy and obey the teacher? And you won't make noise, *bubeleh,* and you'll be very polite and play nice with the other children. And when it's time to come home, you'll button up warm, so you won't catch cold, *bubeleh.* And you'll be careful crossing the street and come right home . . ." etc. etc.

Off went the little boy.

When he returned that afternoon, his mother hugged him and kissed him and exclaimed, "So did you like school, *bubeleh?* You made new friends? You *learned* something?"

"Yeah," said the boy. "I learned that my name is Irving."

bubkes
bopkes

Pronounced BOP-*kess*, to rhyme with "mop kiss," or BUB-*kiss*, to rhyme with "put this," or BAWP-*kess*, to rhyme with "stalk mess," or BUB-*kess*, to rhyme with "pub mess."

Russian: "beans." But Jews say *"Bubkes!"* not to designate beans (*bebloch* does that) but to describe, with considerable scorn:

1. Something trivial, worthless, insultingly disproportionate to expectations. "I worked on it three hours—and what did he give me? *Bubkes!*" (I think *"Bubkes!"* more eloquent, because more harsh, than "Peanuts!")

2. Something absurd, foolish, nonsensical. "I'll sum up his idea in one word: *bubkes!*"

Bubkes must be uttered with either scorn, sarcasm, indignation, or contempt. The expletive takes over where "Nonsense!" "Baloney!" or "Bushwa!" stop for a rest.

I know of no English word that carries quite that deflating, even bitter, aroma.

The man who exclaims *"Bubkes!"* is a man who understands the place of pride in the protocol of humiliation.

Only the proud say *"Bubkes!"*

SCENE: *A pushcart on the Lower East Side.*

A woman customer picks up a broken fork. "How much?"

"One cent," says the proprietor.

"One cent? That's too much!"

"So make me an offer."

P.S. This bit of sociology may not illustrate *bubkes* (although that was what the argument was about), but it establishes the penurious universe in which so much Jewish life was lived, and in which so much compensatory humor was born.

bulba

Pronounced BULL'*y-beh*, with a liquid *l* (as in "million"); or BULL-*ba*, to rhyme with "full, ma." From Polish: "potato."

1. (Literally) A potato.
2. An error, a boner, a *faux pas*.

The second usage is the most frequent—and amusing. "Oh, did she make a *bulba!*" "He is famous for his outlandish *bulbas.*"

This is not literary Yiddish, mind you, nor pure, nor even high-toned, but *bulba* is used most expressively in colloquial Yiddish.

It has been suggested to me that *boo-boo*, that recently coined synonym for a *gaffe*, descended from *bulba;* but it seems more likely that *boo-boo* is pure onomatopoeia to describe the sort of *faux pas* that is made by a child and is followed by tears.

So far as I can discover, *boo-boo* came out of show business—probably Hollywood. I first heard it in a skit by Dean Martin and Jerry Lewis.

For more colorful denotations of *bulba*, see BULBENIK.

bulbenik

Pronounced BULL-*beh-nik*, to rhyme with "pull the pick." Strictly Ameridish.

1. One who is inept, clumsy, all-thumbs, who fouls things up.
2. An actor "who talks as though he has a potato in his mouth"—that is, an actor who "blows" his lines, mixes them up, commits embarrassing Spoonerisms; a Malaprop.

I once wrote an article about New York's Café Royale (alas, now defunct), the favorite congregating place for the stars and devotees of the Second Avenue (i.e., Yiddish) theater.

The Café Royale was the Sardi's, Lindy's, and 21 of the Lower East Side, all in one. The air in the Café Royale was as thick with theatrical lore, with stories, jokes, sagas, memories, as the blintzes were thick with sour cream. And there I heard heartrending tales of a famous *bulbenik*.

In one play, this earnest thespian strode front center, held forth his hands in tragic appeal, and (all through rehearsal, at least) faultlessly delivered this line:

"Oh, God, I have five children—dear, sweet children—" etc. (The Yiddish for children is *kinder*, pronounced KINN-der.) But on opening night, the *bulbenik* strode front center, extended his hands, and said, "Oh, God, I have five *finger* (fingers) . . ." Understandably, he brought the house down.

In another play (*The Dybbuk*), a white-garbed maiden is possessed by a demon or *dybbuk;* she writhes, cries out in terror, falls, loses consciousness. The maiden lies there, alone on the stage. Then villagers, each holding a candle, enter; they see the maiden's lifeless form, draw back in horror. Their leader, stepping closer, exclaims, "A *dybbuk!* A *dybbuk* has entered the maiden!" Cries, screams, swoons, etc.

All went well through rehearsals. Came opening night. The maiden, possessed by the awful spirit, writhed and cried and fell stricken. The column of villagers appeared, drew back. Their leader stepped forward, raised his candle, and cried, "A candle! A candle has entered the maiden!"

He was a *bulbenik*.*

bulvon
bulvan

Pronounced *bull*-VON, to rhyme with "full on." Slavic: "Dolt," "blockhead."

A gross, thick-headed, thick-skinned oaf.

No English word carries quite the sneer of *bulvon*, or quite

* For a nostalgic view of the place where Jewish actors, intellectuals and *bulbeniks* hung out see "Café Royale," in my collection *The Strangest Places.* Harcourt, Brace & Co., 1939.

the implicit devaluation of brute strength. "Any *bulvon* could do that." A *bulvon* has no sensitivity, no insight, no spiritual graces.

A *bulvon*, about to go on a date with a girl he had never taken out before, begged a friend to advise him: "Girls just don't like me," said the *bulvon*. "But you—you have your pick. How do you do it? What's the real way to talk to a dame?"

"I'll tell you the secret," said the Lothario. "Jewish girls love three topics of conversation: food, family, philosophy. That's all you need to remember. To inquire about a girl's likes in food is to make her feel important. To inquire about her family shows that your intentions are honorable. And to discuss philosophy with her shows you respect her intelligence."

The *bulvon* was delighted. "Food, family, philosophy!"

He met the girl and blurted, "Hello. Do you like noodles?"

"N-no," said the startled girl.

"Do you have a brother?"

"No."

The *bulvon* hesitated but a moment: "Well, *if* you had a brother, would he like noodles?" That was philosophy.

bummerkeh

Pronounced BUM-*er-keh*. Ameridish.

A female bum; one who "bums aron' "—lives loosely; a disreputable lady.

Old Mr. Trabish, sitting near the pool of a Catskill resort, could not help noticing the white-haired man at the next table: There he sat, with two beautiful *bummerkehs*, as he had every day during the week, drinking and laughing and eating. Every day he went off the high diving board and swam seven lusty laps without stopping. And every night he was in the night club, dancing with different *tsatskes* until the wee hours.

After two weeks of observing this strenuous schedule, Mr.

Trabish leaned over and said, "Mister, it's amazing the condition you're in, the way you live!"

"Thank you," said the white-haired man.

"Excuse me for asking, but how *old* are you?"

The roué shrugged. "Twenty-seven."

burtche

Pronounced BOOR-*tchen*, to rhyme with "poor gin." Slavic: "mumble."

1. To grumble, to growl, as (a) a stomach, (b) a person.
2. To complain.

"What's he *burtching* about?" is a reasonable facsimile of "What's he griping about?"—in spades.

See also KVETCH, KRECHTZ.

C

cabala
cabbalah
kabbalah

Pronounced *ca*-BAH-*la*, to rhyme with "a dolla(r)." Hebrew: "Tradition," from the verb meaning "to receive."

The Jewish mystical movement; the complex and esoteric body of Jewish mystical tradition, literature, and thought.

Cabalism was a movement of profound mystical faith fused to, and steeped in, the superstitions and occult preoccupations of pre-Middle Ages. It was a minor but meaningful stream of thought and experience, a pious attempt to fathom the awesome, fearful mysteries of God and creation. Originally, cabalism meant the Oral Tradition; in the twelfth century, Jewish mystics adopted the term, claiming an unbroken link between their ideas and those of ancient days.

Cabalists claimed that their revelation was part and parcel of Scripture. But cabalism's divinations and abracadabra, its intricate numerology (see GEMATRIA), remained in a shadowland until the eighth century A.D., when *The Book of Formation* appeared in Italy.

Not until *The Book of Splendor* (the *Zohar*) appeared in Spain in the thirteenth century did a formidable metaphysical text on cabalism appear. Two hundred years later the great Renaissance humanist Pico della Mirandola translated the *Zohar* into Latin. And not until the seventeenth century did cabalism become a movement of consequence.

The cabalists held that reason alone could never penetrate the exalted mystical experience involved in their perception of God and His mysteries. Esoteric formulas, numerological acrobatics, theological mumbo jumbo went into the cabalists' efforts to apprehend God's will. And many a cabalistic omen or prophecy excitedly hailed the imminent appearance of the Messiah and the Day of Judgment. The fearful and the faithful found sustenance in a bizarre succession of self-proclaimed holy men and putative messiahs. (See Appendix: False Messiahs.)

The center of cabalistic teaching was Safed, in Palestine, which, in the sixteenth century, was the seat of a sizable community of mystics. Isaac Luria, the outstanding cabalist (he was known as the "Ari"—the "Lion"), a visionary who claimed to speak with the Prophet Elijah, presided over a circle of fervent disciples to whom he expounded arcane formulas and invocations; their prayers contained many secret, hidden Names of God, upon which the faithful were exhorted to meditate. Esoteric and minatory rituals were ordained. Elaborate number manipulations and abracadabras attended every conceivable interpretation of passages from the *Torah* and the names of prophets.

It is not so hard to understand why such supernatural and mystical doctrines attracted so many Jews for so many years. Given the wretchedness, the poverty, the abiding terror under which Jews lived, many devout souls became convinced that they would be delivered from the terrible tribulations of the *galut* only by the Messiah, who *would* come down to earth to usher in the Day of Judgment. One may ask: What else except the miraculous was there to place hope in? Heaven is the poor man's last hope—and reward.

See Appendix: Cabala, Gematria, Messiah; also Trevor-Roper's eloquent comments in Appendix: Sabbati Zvi.

canary

See KAYN AYNHOREH.

chachem
haham
chacham

> Pronounced KHAW-*khem* with two reverberating Scottish *kh*'s. The use of *two* uvular fricatives need not intimidate you: No word will more swiftly establish you as one who knows Yiddish. The plural is *chachamim*, pronounced *kha*-KHUM-*im*.
>
> Hebrew: "wise."

1. A clever, wise, or learned man—or woman.

A *chachem* is one who possesses or displays *chachma*, wisdom. A *chachem* is a savant, an expert, a brilliant mind, a man of learning and profundity. He need *not* be an intellectual: Many a cobbler or butcher, barber or vendor, was known as a *chachem*. Some *chachamim* were artisans *and* intellectuals. (The early sages almost invariably toiled in humble occupations.)

Atop the Jewish pyramid of respect stands the scholar—not, be it noted, the ruler. the conqueror, the prince, the millionaire, even the rabbi. but the scholar. (A rabbi can, of course, be a great scholar: but scholars were loftier than rabbis.) Power, wealth, honors, prizes, social status—none of these was as respected as learning, which meant learning in Talmud.

Jewish mothers sang a lullaby of hope that the little son in the cradle might become that most glorious of men: wise, learned, a—*mirabile dictu!*—*chachem*.

The first bright sayings of a child are hailed by ecstatic grandparents as *chachmas*. It is promptly forecast that the babe will grow up to be a real *chachem*—that is, profound, learned, virtuous.

The *Zohar*, a mystical thirteenth-century work, part of the cabalistic *Book of Creation*, defines the *chachem* this way: "What does a fool see? A man's clothes. What does the *chachem* see? A man's spirit."

The *Talmud*'s *Pirke Abot*, or "Sayings of the Fathers," says: "In whom wisdom is—in him is everything. In whom wisdom is not—what has he? And he who has acquired wisdom—what can he lack?"

A *chachem* is not the highest of *chachamim*, please notice. That paragon is a *talmid chachem*.

2. (Used sarcastically) A fool, a wise guy; one who tries to be clever but suffers a downfall.

Chachem is also used sarcastically, to indicate one who, pretending to astuteness, does something absurd, foolish, disastrous.

"Some *chachem!*" drips irony: it may be loosely rendered as "What a jerk."

A proud young *chachem* told his grandmother that he was going to become a doctor of philosophy. The *bubbe* smiled proudly: "Wonderful. But what kind of disease is 'philosophy'?"

Kessler was awakened from a deep sleep by his wife, who nudged him again and again, saying, "Get *up*, Max. I'm freezing, close the window. It's cold outside!"

"*Chachem!*" sighed Max. "And if I close the window, will it be warm outside?"

A Jewish merchant was returning to his small town, after having spent a week in the big city. Opposite him, in the train, sat a young stranger. The merchant, a gregarious soul, promptly introduced himself: "My name is Mandelbaum."

"My name," said the young man, "is Horowitz."

They shook hands.

"And where are you going, Mr. Horowitz?"

"To Glens Falls."

"Glens Falls? Well, what do you know? That's where I'm going. That's where I live!" Mandelbaum eyed the young man carefully. "Tell me, are you—married?"

"No," said Horowitz.

"Maybe—a salesman?"

"No."

"Are you going on business?"

"No," said Horowitz. "It's a social visit."

"Er—you have maybe relatives in Glens Falls?"

"No," said Horowitz.

Aha! thought Mandelbaum, every inch the *chachem*, and proceeded to reason thus-wise: He's going to Glens Falls, he's not married, he's not a salesman, and he has no relatives there. So why is he going? Obviously, to meet a girl—to meet her family, maybe to confirm an engagement. But who is the girl? To the Rabinowitzes this young man can't be going, because the Rabinowitzes have only one daughter, who was married six years ago. To the Plotniks? Nonsense! The Plotniks have two sons and no daughter. Perhaps the Arkins? But the Arkin girl is only seventeen: too young to get married, her father would never let her. Aha! The Mishnicks! No, because the Mishnick girl is already engaged to the son (the good-looking one) of Melnick, the tailor. Perhaps to the Bubricks? *Nya!* The Bubrick girl is at least thirty, has given up hopes of getting married, and anyway is visiting her aunt in Providence. The Shulmans! But the Shulmans' unmarried daughter is at college and doesn't come home until Passover, so she wouldn't be in Glens Falls now. The Feiffers? No, the Feiffers are rich and stuck-up; they would never let their daughter marry anyone but a rich young man—and this one, though very nice, is wearing an inexpensive suit and riding in the coach car, so he's not well off, so the Feiffers are out. . . . The Hollanders? The Hollander girl is getting married next week to that *shlemiel* of a dentist from White Plains. The Pincuses? Sure! The Pincuses have *three* girls, all marriageable: Shirley, Ruth, and Helen. . . . But Shirley is a good twenty pounds overweight and this young man is good-looking enough to be able to pick and choose. Ruth? Ruth is a widow—young, pretty, but still a widow, and with a two-year-old child! Helen? Helen! There's a gay young thing, with mischief in her eyes, and only last week she went to the city for a weekend——

With a broad grin, Mandelbaum stuck his hand out: "Horowitz, let me be the first to congratulate you!"

"Congratulate me?" Horowitz blinked.

"On your forthcoming marriage to Miss Helen Pincus!"

As Mandelbaum pumped his hand, the young man stammered, "But—we have told no one, not even her parents. How did you find out?"

"How did I find out?" echoed Mandelbaum. "It's obvious!"

chachma
hachma

Pronounced KHAWKH-*meh*, rattling those two *kh*'s with uvular abandon, the way an Edinburghian would. Hebrew: "Wisdom."

1. The divine spirit of Wisdom, which, according to the Midrash, existed long before the creation of the world and was the blueprint and ground plan for the creation. (This resembles the Christian mystical use of *Logos*, the word, as in John I: "In the beginning was the Word, and the Word was with God, and the Word was God.")
2. A wise, profound, or astute saying.
3. The reservoir of erudite, wise, philosophical knowledge. And, since Jews are fond of paradox, knowing life to be full of it.
4. A jocular or clever remark.
5. A tricky, wily, cleverly concealed ruse, tactic, or arrangement.
6. (Derisive) A foolish move or performance.

A *chachma* is the product of a *chachem*, obviously—though occasionally even an unlearned and unbrilliant man can come up with something so illuminating that one would call it a *chachma*.

In Jewish thought, wisdom is not the fruit of intellect or knowledge alone; wisdom involves basic moral and character attributes: The highest *chachma* lies in being righteous and spreading loving-kindness. Knowledge makes it possible for man to enter a state of grace in which true virtue, "doing good," can be practiced.

"Money can buy anything—except sense."

To the Jews, wisdom without love of man was a contradiction in terms. "The highest form of wisdom is kindness," goes an old proverb quoted by Jews.

Occasionally, *chachma* is used to describe tricks, subterfuges, clever evasions, unrevealed meanings, or wily, casuistic hocus-pocus. If you want to cut through legalisms and double-talk, if you want something said plainly, say, "Now let's have it without *chachma*."

Just as "wise" in English became the root for "wise guy," so *chachma* became a scathing name for a *gaffe*, a *faux pas*, a bit of folly or stupidity.

During a frightful storm at sea, the captain asked one of the passengers, a professional magician, to distract the frightened passengers. The magician gave a dazzling performance: made cards disappear, scarves turn into flags, and, for a desperate finale, presented a parrot who, he announced, "will now perform the greatest feat of magic in the history of prestidigitation!"

All eyes turned to the parrot. Drums rolled, trumpets blew —and suddenly a tremendous wave smashed the ship in two. The passengers found themselves thrashing in the water— including an old Jew who, hanging on to a plank for dear life, saw the parrot floating by. And to the parrot, the old man bitterly said, with a "Hoo-ha!" inflection: *"Chachma!"*

A Jew runs frantically into a railway station. Just as he gets to the track, the train pulls out. The Jew stops, looks after it, and sneers *"Chachma!"*

Chaim Yankel

Pronounced as one word, *Khym-*YONK-*'l* (not "chime," but with the throat-clearing *kh* of *ecch!*); rhymes with "dime jonquil."

Two masculine names, in common usage among Jews, pronounced as if one and used to describe:

1. A nonentity, a nobody, any "poor Joe."
2. A colloquial, somewhat condescending way of addressing a Jew whose name you do not know—just as "Joe" or "Mac" is sometimes used in English. "Hey, Mac, you dropped something." "Eh, Reb Yankel, look where you're going."

Yankel is the familiar form of Ya-acov (Jacob); *Chaim* (Hebrew for "life"), a common boy's name, was sometimes hastily acquired during a serious illness—as a talisman against death. It was actually believed that a changed name might confuse the Angel of Death, who would be looking for the victim under his original handle. It is doubtful that this had any effect upon the vital statistics.

See also NEBECH, SHLEMIEL, KUNI LEMMEL.

A *Chaim Yankel*, visiting a cemetery, beheld a magnificent marble mausoleum, on the portal of which was incised: ROTHSCHILD.

"Ai-ai-ai!" exclaimed the *Chaim Yankel*. "Now that's what I call living!"

chairlady

Pronounced as spelled. Yinglish.

A female chairman.

My mother was a prime mover in organizing one or another "group," women, to send clothing to Poland, and to raise funds to be sent there for shoes, milk, hot lunches for infants and schoolchildren. And it was at an "organizing meeting" of such ladies, held in our "front room," that I first heard the neologism *chairlady*. It was twenty years before I learned that un-Jews address a *chairlady* as "Madame Chairman," which is surely a contradiction in terms. I still think "chairlady" more sensible, to say nothing of sexually unconfusing.

As a child in Chicago, I was often taken by my parents to meetings of the Workmen's Circle (Lodzer Branch) and to endless "benefits," concerts, recitals, choral groups, Yiddish-theater parties. It was at the last that I first saw live theater, and first realized what passionate lovers of theater and recitals (of poetry no less than music) Jews are—and what enthusiastic and energetic audiences they constitute.

In an old theater on Blue Island Avenue I saw admirable performances by New York companies of the Yiddish theater, appearing in Chicago in such classics as *Yoshe Kalb, The Dybbuk, The Golem*. It was theater in the grand style and

European tradition, with full-bodied performances of exceptional power by artists of the rank of Boris Thomashevsky, Jacob Adler, Bertha Kalish, Maurice Schwartz, the sensitive Jacob Ben-Ami, young Muni Weisenfreund (later Paul Muni). Little did I then know that such orotund voices and grandiose gestures, such full-bodied tears and laughter, such outbursts of passion and fierce orchestrations of feeling—all, all were rigorously muted and repressed on the English stage.

I learned to love the baroque, unabashed expressionism in those marvelously eloquent matinees. I could also gain an advance sense of the nature of the play we were to attend by the sartorial preparations my mother made: a bright frock and only one handkerchief signaled a comedy; a somber dress and several handkerchiefs clearly foreshadowed a heart-rending, "true to life" tragedy or tearjerker. Years later, in Hollywood, I heard blasé friends characterize plays as "three-handkerchief" or "four-handkerchief" productions.

The *chairlady* said, "—and we must all learn to adjust to this fantastic new world, a world in which, only last week, an astronaut circled the world fifty times!"

"Humph!" humphed one of the ladies. "If you have money, you travel."

challa
challeh

Pronounced KHAHL-*leh*, with the rattling *kh*. Rhyme with "doll a." Hebrew: *challah*.

A braided loaf of white bread, glazed with egg white, very soft, delicate in flavor.

I, for one, consider *challa* a Jewish contribution to distinguished cuisine (there are not many), a bread to rank with the most exquisite productions of the baker's art.

Challa is a Sabbath and holiday delicacy. For *Shabbes* it is always made in a braided form. On holidays it may be kneaded into other shapes: circular, ladderlike, etc.

Children especially adore *challa*—for its almost-like-cake texture, its braided top, its crisp crust and ever-so-soft inside.

Two *challas*, uncut, are on the table of observing Jews on Sabbath eve; they are not cut until after the *broche* (blessing). This practice perpetuates the memory of the wilderness, where God dropped a double portion of manna on Friday (and none on the Sabbath); or, say some, it recalls the Temple, where two rows of bread were lined up before the altar. The home, which is of limitless importance in Jewish life, is in fact called in Hebrew *migdash mehad*—or "a small temple."

When a *challa* (or any Sabbath bread) is baked, a small piece of dough is, by tradition, tossed into the oven or fire—as a token of sacrifice. Why? Because *challa* is a Hebrew term used in Numbers 15 : 20 and Ezekiel 44 : 30, where it means "the priest's share" of the baking dough.

If you have never tasted *challa*, stop reading and repair to a Jewish bakery.

Some American Jews pronounce *challa* "holly," the younger ones not being able to manage the uvular *kh*, the rest thinking "holly" more genteel, more Americanized. This is deplorable.

How can one recognize a Reform Jew in a bakery on Friday? He orders a *challa* and says, "Slice it."

chaloshes
khaloshes

Pronounced *khol-LAW-shess* by Litvaks, to rhyme with "a cautious," and *kha-LOO-shess*, by Poles, to rhyme with "achoo, sis." From the Hebrew: *holosh*, "weak." Used in Yiddish to mean "faint."

A revolting, disgusting, or loathsome thing—whether in food, drink, or conduct, whether visible or ethical.

"A *chaloshes!*" is an eloquent way of describing revulsion, disgust or powerful umbrage. "The meal was a *chaloshes* to eat." "The movie? Sheer *chaloshes!*" "The speech he made? It was a *chaloshes* to listen to such tripe."

Mrs. Fleishman was checking out of Rosenbaum's Riviera Spa, in the Catskills.

"Did you enjoy your stay?" asked the owner.

"Well, to tell the truth, the food you serve here—it's terrible. A *chaloshes!* . . . And such small portions!"

chalutz
halutz
chalutzim (plural)

Pronounced KHA-*lootz* (with the guttural *kh*), to rhyme with "ma loots," or KHU-*lootz*, to rhyme with "the foots"; *kha*-LOOTZ-*im*. Hebrew: "pioneer."

1. Pioneer; a pioneer in any sphere of endeavor.
2. (More particularly) A young man or woman who went to Palestine (today, Israel) to settle the land.

The *chalutzim* lived under the most primitive conditions, built roads, drained swamps, planted trees, reclaimed soil and desert that had been uncultivated for centuries. Many of them lived cooperatively in *kibbutzim*.

Many *chalutzim* were well-educated Europeans who gave up professional careers in order to "live their ideal: to build Zion" with the sweat of their brow and the toil of their hands. In the early years of the twentieth century they were considered the elite of Palestine, and from their ranks came many of the leaders of the new state of Israel. Today, they enjoy a status equivalent to that of our Pilgrims, "Came over on the Mayflower," D.A.R.

See KIBBUTZ.

Chanukah
Channukah
Hanuka
Hanukkah

Pronounced KHON-*eh-keh*, with a Hebrew or Scottish *kh*, not an English *ch*; rhymes with "Monica." Hebrew: "Dedication."

"The Feast of Dedication," more colloquially known as "The Feast of Lights." One of the less solemn Jewish festivities.

This eight-day holiday usually falls in December. Unlike the festivals of *Succoth*, *Shevuoth*, *Pesach*, and *Rosh Hashana*, *Chanukah* does not have its origin in the Bible. It commemorates the victory of the Jewish Maccabees over Syrian despots (167 B.C.) in a fight for religious freedom that rescued Judaism, as a culture, from annihilation. The Apocrypha tells the story (Maccabees I and II).

The rebellion was led by a priest, Mattathias of the Hasmonean family, and his son, Judah the Maccabee (the Hammer). It continued for three years of guerrilla warfare against the armies of Antiochus IV, who was known to his minions as Epiphanes: "the risen god." Antiochus planned to convert the Jews by force to Greek polytheism, and he ordered them to build altars and shrines for idols, to stop circumcising male babies, etc. In 168 B.C. the great Temple was desecrated by a huge statue of Zeus, and Jewish courts were used for orgies. Thousands of Jews fled to caves; thousands wandered about in disguise.

The Maccabean uprising seemed hopeless. Guerrilla groups of Jews, unaccustomed to fighting and equipped with primitive weapons, fought the well-armed Seleucid soldiers—and won out at Emmaus. They returned to Jerusalem—to find a sacked, burned Temple, and they set about restoring it. On the twenty-fifth day of the Hebrew month of Kislev, in 165 B.C., Judah the Maccabee solemnly rededicated Zion's Temple—lighting the lamps of a great menorah—and celebrated the beginning of a week-long festival.

To this day, each *Chanukah*, Jews light candles for eight days—one the first evening, adding one light each night on the nine-branched menorah. A special ninth candle, called the *shammes* (servant), stands taller than the rest in the menorah and is used to light the others. This is interpreted to show that one can give love and light to others without losing any part of one's own radiance.

Chanukah is the only Jewish festival connected with a warring event, and it is a secular, not a religious, celebration. (So deeply ingrained is Jewish distaste for violence that King David himself was not permitted to build the Temple, because he had been "stained" by the blood of war.) Each *Chanukah*, the prophecy of Zechariah is read: "Not by strength, not by power, but by My spirit, sayeth the Lord of Hosts."

Chanukah is observed with parties, games, and gifts to the children. *Chanukah gelt*, a small gift of cash, is often distributed. A favorite food is *latkes*, potato pancakes.

A delightful *Chanukah* game is a put-and-take game played with a four-sided top (a *draydl* or *trendel*), using nuts for the betting. The *draydl* is marked with four Hebrew letters: *nun*, *gimel*, *hay*, and *shin*—the initial letters of the Hebrew words meaning "a great miracle took place there" (*nes gadol haya sham*). The letters also stand for the Yiddish words *nem* (take), *gib* (give), *halb* (half) and *shtell* (put)—which provide all the instructions needed.

I have it on indisputable authority that in Scarsdale, during a school celebration of Christmas, one of the children sang the carol as: "God rest ye, Jerry Mandelbaum."

chas vesholem
has vesholem

> Pronounced KHAHS *ve-SHO-lem*, to rhyme with "joss the tow men." Please clear your throat with that *kh*. Hebrew: "God forbid." Literally: Pity and peace.

> "God forbid."

This phrase is used as a magical invocation to ward off any evil spirit or undesired happenstance. "Be careful or you'll break a leg, *chas vesholem*."

The phrase also appears as *chas vechalila* (KHAHSS *ve-kha-LEE-la*); literally: "pity," and "far be it from coming to pass."

The simple *cholilleh* is a short synonym.

Chasid
Chasidim (plural)
Hassid
Hassidim

Pronounced KWAH-*sid,* to rhyme with "saw mid"; *Khah-*SEED-*em;* begin with the rattling-in-the-back-of-the-throat for a uvular *kh.* Hebrew: "pious," "pious one."

1. A most pious man; a disciple of a great rabbi.
2. A follower of the Chasidic philosophy and way of life.

The extraordinary Chasidic movement, opposed by many rabbis and pietists, raced through the Jewish communities of eastern and central Europe in the eighteenth century. It was founded by a simple man, a mystic, named Israel ben Eliezer (later called the *Baal Shem Tov*), who loved to wander about the open country where he felt he could best commune with God. He preached a folk gospel that had enormous appeal to small-town Jews because it opposed the rabbinical emphasis on formal learning, and derogated the endless Talmudic casuistry of the wise men.

Criticizing the pedantic reiterations of scholars, and the doom-ridden visions of the Orthodox, Israel ben Eliezer sang the praises of simple faith, joyous worship, everyday pleasures. God can be worshiped anywhere, said the *Baal Shem Tov,* directly and simply: God requires no synagogues, except "in the heart." Prayers should be spontaneous, personal, happy—not the formalized, automatic rote of the *shul.* (The parallel to Martin Luther's gospel of faith and anticlericalism is striking.)

The Chasidim preferred gay songs to magisterial invocations. They danced and clapped hands while singing out the Lord's praises, and they invited group expressions of religious rapture.

The Chasidic celebration of God offered poor Jews a new kind of communion—warm, intimate, personal—with a hitherto somber God; it also gave them precious catharsis. The Chasidim preached and evangelized with homely stories and

delightful parables, charming anecdotes and folk sayings anyone could understand. Their ecstatic songs and "frivolous"
dances angered many of Jewry's elders. The rabbis denounced
Israel ben Eliezer as ignorant and irreverent. Nonetheless, the
Chasidic movement spread through eastern Europe with gusto
—except in Lithuania, where the great Gaon of Vilna (i.e.,
the head of the rabbinical academy), Rabbi Elijah ben Solomon (1720–1797), publicly anathematized the *Baal Shem
Tov.*

A Chasid was treated by his followers with greater awe
than Jews customarily gave a rabbi. Disciples repeated a
Chasid's every phrase, imitated his every gesture. As is not
unusual in religious movements that begin with simple affirmations and oppose priestly protocol, the Chasidim were soon
elevated by their followers into holy men.

Chasidism's leaders became known as *tzaddikim*—seers,
near-saints, prophets believed to possess supernatural powers.
Ironically enough, the *tzaddik* became an ecclesiastical bridge
between man and God such as rabbis had never been. The
title *tzaddik* even became hereditary.

The *tzaddik* was often asked by his worshipful believers to
intervene with God during an illness or crisis, to speak directly
to the Almighty. Some *tzaddikim* used talismans and amulets
to ward off the evil eye. The faithful hung on a *tzaddik's* every
breath; every comment was invested with supernatural meaning.

Chasidism still has its passionate adherents, in small but
lively enclaves in New York, Chicago, Boston, and even in
some suburbs. (For a sensitive account, see Isaac Bashevis
Singer's "The Extreme Jews," in *Harper's* Magazine, April
1967.)

Chasidic tales and parables run into thousands. Many are
recounted in *The Hasidic Anthology,* by Louis I. Newman
and, more portentously, in two volumes by Martin Buber,
Tales of the Hasidim: Early Masters and *Later Masters.*

See also TZADDIK.

From Chasidic stories and sources:

Why do the wicked always form groups, whereas the righteous
do not? Because the wicked, walking in darkness, need com-

pany, but the righteous, who live in the light, do not fear being alone.

When a poor coach driver apologized to a Chasid because his work kept him from going to the synagogue, the Chasid asked: "And do you ever give free rides to the poor?"

"Often."

"Then you are already serving the Lord."

A king, visiting a prison, began to interview the inmates. Prisoner after prisoner insisted that he was innocent, that he had been framed, that a terrible injustice had been done.

The king asked the last prisoner, "And are you, too, as innocent as a lamb?"

"No, Your Majesty. I'm a thief. I was caught, fairly tried, sentenced."

"You admit you're a thief?" asked the king in surprise.

"Yes, Your Majesty."

The king said, "Throw this crook out of here!"

The thief was promptly ejected.

The other prisoners raised a fearful clamor. "Your Majesty, how can you do such a thing? How can you free a confessed criminal while we——"

"I was afraid," the king smiled, "that that wicked scoundrel would corrupt all you innocent souls."

On March 22, 1967, the following appeared in a two-column advertisement in *The New York Times,* page 29:

PURIM REMINDER

The Lubavitcher Rebbe, Rabbi Menachem M. Schneerson, has issued his annual call to world Jewry to observe the Purim festival, which is on Sunday, in full accord with its meaningful and inspirational message.

The Rebbe called upon Jewish spiritual leaders to inform their congregants, and educators and parents, to teach their students and children about the proper observance of the festival.

The Rebbe pointed out that in addition to reading the Megillah (Book of Esther) on the evening and morning of Purim, and reciting the "Al Hanissim" prayer, there are two special precepts incumbent upon all to observe on the morning or afternoon of Purim, namely *Mishloach Monos*—sending food gifts to friends, and *Mattonos LoEvyonim*—donating to the needy.

The mitzvos can easily be observed. In the case of *Mishloach Monos*, by giving a friend two kinds of edibles such as fruit, cake, beverages, etc., while the minimal requirement in observing *Mattonos LoEvyonim* is to give alms to at least two needy persons.

These mitzvos are very easy to observe and should not go unheeded simply because of unawareness.

The Rebbe also noted that youngsters, girls under 12 years of age and boys less than 13, should also be taught to observe the mitzvos. However, after this age, they are personally obligated to fulfill them.

MERCOS L'INYONEI CHINUCH
the educational arm of the Lubavitcher movement
770 Eastern Parkway—Brooklyn, N.Y. 11213

chassen
chaussen
chossen
hassen

Pronounced KHAW-*sen*, to rhyme with "Lawson," or KHU-*sen*, to rhyme with "You, son." From the Hebrew; originally: "celebrant," "bridegroom"; also "son-in-law."

1. Bridegroom.
2. The groom-to-be.
3. Son-in-law.
4. (Occasionally) Guest of honor; man of the hour.

Great pressure is exerted, in a religious Jewish community, for every young man to get married (in the old country, before the age of eighteen). An unmarried man is looked upon askance: such a one is selfish, insensitive to his duty, perhaps a bit *meshugge*, indubitably antisocial. He is even something of a sinner, for he is evading the responsibility to "multiply," as God commanded; he is failing to perpetuate life itself; he fails to honor the solemn debt that attends the gift of having been born; he misses the chance to provide himself with a *Kaddish* who will mourn his death and honor his name.

An unmarried man is also regarded as derelict in his duty to Jewry—for who knows what learned sons, what marvelous *talmid chachamim* he might have sired?

In so emphatic, consistent, and homogeneous a consensus was born the useful, if quixotic, institution of the professional matchmaker. (See SHADCHEN.)

Long, long before Freud, the Jews had this saying: "When a son gets married, he divorces his mother."

For months the rabbi had been urging the young man to become a *chassen*, to marry. And for months the energetic *shadchen* had been bringing the young man names, photographs, offers, dowries, of nubile maidens. All to no avail, it seemed.

"No, thanks," said the young man firmly. "I'm not interested. I just don't want to get married!"

"What? A Jewish lad? Not marry?"

"Certainly. I'm young. I'm free, I'm happy; why in the world do I need a wife?"

"Why do you need a *wife?*" echoed the *shadchen* incredulously. "My boy, you don't know! Let me tell you what a woman's love can mean, what a heaven on earth is connubial bliss. Take an old man like me, even. I am blessed with a wife, an angel, may she live to be a hundred and twenty! My home life is, every moment, a blessing. Just *visualize* it: I get up in the morning, my darling Rivkele has a wonderful breakfast ready for me. My clothes are laid out each day, clean, neat, not a button missing. I go off to work carrying the lunch she prepared for me with her own hands: a roast chicken, fine *kugel*, mouth-watering cakes. When I come home, my Rivkele is waiting for me at the door. She takes my things, takes off my shoes, puts on my slippers, sits me in my favorite chair, gives me a *shnaps*, diverts me by telling me what she did all day. She talks, I listen, the house is warm and cozy—a haven, a heaven. And my Rivkele talks, and talks and *talks* until—I tell you, that *yenta* is going to drive me right out of my mind!"

chasseneh

> Pronounced KHOSS-*se-neh*, with the Yiddish or Mac-Gregor *kh*, not the *ch* of "chocolate." Hebrew: "wedding."
>
> Wedding.

This is not the place to describe, discuss and analyze all of the ceremonies of a Jewish wedding, but a few aspects that please or impress me may interest you:

It is obligatory for wedding guests to praise the bride and extol her beauties to the groom: to avoid hypocrisy (and pain, to plain or homely girls) the *Talmud* rabbis decreed, with peerless sagacity: "Every bride is beautiful—and graceful."

Every Jewish bride, however poor, wore a wedding gown and had a trousseau: a collection in the community insured that.

During the marriage ceremony, the groom consecrates the bride with these words: "Thou art consecrated to me according to the law of Moses and Israel." Traditionally, the bride has nothing at all to say during the ceremony! (Is she speechless with joy, or panic?)

It is traditional for the groom to give the bride a simple ring, unadorned with stones and decorations; the rabbis wanted to minimize differences between the wealthy and the poor.

For a *chasseneh*, a rabbi and a formal religious service may be waived, by Talmudic dictum, under certain conditions: I have always loved the story of the Jew on a desert isle who wed himself to a woman and made Heaven and Earth his witnesses: "I call upon Heaven and Earth to witness that I consecrated you as my wife, according to the laws of Moses and of Israel."

"An old maid who gets married becomes a young wife."
"Parents can give a dowry, but not good luck."

"A groom and a bride have glass eyes. (They can see no faults in each other.)"

"Early to rise and early to wed does no harm."

"One can't dance with one behind at two weddings."

"Dance at every wedding and you'll cry at every funeral."

—FOLK SAYINGS

chaver
khaver

Pronounced KHAH-*ver*, with a strong, throat-clearing Germanic *kh* sound, as in *"Ach!"* *Chaver* rhymes with JOB-*ber*. From Hebrew: *chaver*, "comrade, friend." Plural: *chavarim*, pronounced *khah-*VAY-*rim*. The feminine form is *chaverta*, pronounced KHAH-*ver-ta*.

1. Friend, comrade, pal. "He's my closest *chaver.*"
2. The form of address used instead of "Mister" in many Jewish fraternal, trade union or political organizations. "The chair now recognizes *Chaver* Falstein."

I hear that some years ago, the presiding officer at a meeting of officials from several trade unions called upon "The head of the Steamfitters, *Chaver* O'Malley."

chazzen
hazzan
chazzonim (plural)

Pronounced KHOZZ'*n*, with the *ch* as in the Scottish *loch* and in a way that bears no relation whatsoever to the *ch* of "China" or "chipmunk." *Chazzen* rhymes with "rosin." The plural is *chazzonim*, pronounced *khah-*ZAW-*nim*. From Hebrew: "a seer."

A cantor—i.e., the trained professional singer who assists the rabbi in religious services.

The *chazzen* sings long passages of the liturgy. His recitation is not a chant or singsong, as is that of ordinary Jews in prayer: It is virtuoso singing, especially in the falsettoes, which are singularly sweet and soft.

The melodies that cantors trill out are not written down, but they are standardized; anyone familiar with the liturgy can enter a synagogue or temple and know from the cantor's melodic line whether it is an ordinary service, a Sabbath, Passover, or *Rosh Hashanah.*

The cantor (who can be any member of the congregation) sings out the opening words of a prayer, which the congregation takes up. The cantor sings the final verse and starts a new prayer by intoning its initial phrases. There were times when a cantor's *bravura* passages in a synagogue would be greeted by outbursts of applause.

Much Semitic music seems born in a wail and swathed in suffering; Jewish *chazzanut* (cantorial art) emphasizes the mournful and the lamentative. Emotion is expressed with intensity, because the cantor speaks for the congregation, as it were (he is known as the *shaleach tzibbur,* or "emissary of the congregation"), in intoning the emotions embedded in Hebrew texts: suffering, contrition, compassion, despair—and always gratitude to a benevolent (!) God.

For more than ten centuries, no device or instrument for the making of music was heard in any Jewish synagogue (although there were musical instruments in the Temple). Today, some Conservative congregations use an organ—but only Reform temples permit the use of other instruments.

Chazzonim were once widely admired for their art (e.g., Yossele Rosenblatt) but today they are not accorded the respect given a rabbi, nor the deference given any learned man. The intellectual status of *chazzonim* is, indeed, derided. "He has the brain of a *chazzen*" is not a compliment.

The *chazzen* is, by tradition, regarded as a simple man— even a simpleton. Away from the panoply of the pulpit, he is viewed as a gifted larynx. "Any Jew can be a *chazzen,*" goes the saying, "except that it just happens that at this moment, he's hoarse." Another folk saying is even more unkind: "All cantors are fools, but not all fools are cantors." It is even libeled that *chazzen* is an acronym, formed from the first letters of *"Chazzonim zenen naronim,"* a hallowed apothegm: "Cantors are fools." Poor chaps.

A familiar sideswipe, in Reform congregations, is found in the wisecrack: "When the *chazzen* knows no Hebrew, he is called a cantor."

Joseph Zabara, a thirteenth-century physician-poet of Barcelona, wrote that a cantor is a fool because "standing on a platform, he thinks he is on a pedestal." And it is said that "the song of fools" in Ecclesiastes 7 : 5 referred to cantors who, singing, interrupt the solemn ritual of prayer—so that the congregation may have a chance for some pleasant gossip.

Modern *chazzonim* are often university graduates and hold teaching certificates, combining *chazzanut* with Hebrew-school teaching in smaller congregations. See Appendix: Cantors.

It is said that when you inform a *chazzen* of a calamity, he whips a tuning fork out of his pocket, taps it, gets the right key, then cries, "Gevaaaalt!"

"Our new *chazzen!*" said one Jew. "What beautiful singing, no?"

"Eh!" scoffed the other. "If I had his voice, I'd sing just as good."

At the time of the creation, it is said, every living creature was told what his duties would be and was asked by the angels to suggest the length of its life span.

The horse, told that men would ride on his back, said, "In that case, please—twenty years of life will be enough for me!"

The donkey, told he would bear heavy burdens and hear many curses, said, "I'll be satisfied with twenty years, too."

The cantor, told he would do nothing but sing hymns, asked for sixty years. The angels felt that was too much, and suggested forty. The cantor protested, "I think I ought to get sixty years!"

So the angels took ten years from the life of the horse and ten from the life of the donkey, and added them to the forty of the cantor.

That's why, say the Jews, a cantor sings beautifully for the first forty years of his life, for the next ten sounds like a horse, and for the ten after that brays like a donkey.

Bahya, a second-century Spanish moralist (born Joseph ibn

Pakuda), tells us of a king who dismissed the dramatics of a *chazzen* thusly: "He prays to impress me, not God."

"A *chazzen* without a voice is like a sheep without wool." Note "sheep"; no one would dream of comparing *chazzonim* to lions, say, or tigers.

cheder
heder

> Pronounced KHAY-*der*, with a throat-clearing *kh;* rhymes with "raider." Hebrew for "room." Plural: *chedarim*, pronounced *cheh*-DAW-*rim* in Yiddish.
>
> The room or school where Hebrew is taught.

Jewish boys would begin studying as early as the age of three (!) and rarely remained illiterate past six. They would study six to ten hours a day, six days a week. Many Jewish boys received their early Hebrew education in a room *(cheder)* in the home of a paid *melamed* (teacher). In the larger *Talmud Torah* schools there were several rooms and more than one teacher. These schools customarily were supported by the synagogue, and charged no tuition.

The emphasis Jews give to education seems to be as old as the Jewish people. (See the Book of Joshua.) Jews held that the Jewish community must provide an education to every boy, no matter who or how poor. Virtually universal, democratic, elementary education (for males) existed among the Jews to a degree unknown, I think, among other people. Rabbinical authority even forbade a Jew to remain in any place that had no Hebrew teacher for the young.

To be sure, the *cheder* curriculum was narrowly limited, the pedagogical methods primitive: drill, repetition, and cracks across the knuckles with a pointer or ruler. But at a time when the overwhelming majority of mankind was illiterate, there was hardly a Jewish male over the age of five who could not read and write. The cultural impact and importance of this is for historians, sociologists, and educators to appraise.

The *Torah* (the Five Books of Moses) was the only elementary *cheder* text. Students would recite en masse, in a high singsong, swaying back and forth in a traditional rhythm, the tempo set by the teacher, the pace hastened or slowed by his appraisal of the students' comprehension of the passage they were droning out. (Advanced students learned the musical notations for the cantillation of religious texts.)

In the old country, before a boy entered a *cheder* he was carried into the synagogue by his father or *melamed* and placed in front of the *bema* (pulpit) to face the entire congregation; then the Scroll of the *Torah (Sefer Torah)* was unrolled and the Ten Commandments were read aloud, addressed to the little boy directly, reenacting the scene on Mount Sinai.

On his first day in *cheder*, the boy's mother and father would stand over him as the teacher pointed to the letters of the *aleph-bet* (alphabet). The lad repeated the names of the Hebrew letters *(aleph)* . . . *(bayz)* . . . *(gimel)* . . . *(daled)* . . . And for each name, his mother would give him a little honey cake or cookie, shaped in the form of that letter, or would put honey into his mouth, to eat with the cake—to show how sweet learning is.

At the end of this first lesson, the mother would enfold the boy and pray that her son fulfill his life with years of *Torah* study, marriage, and good deeds.*

A student of Abelard's wrote that "Christians educate their sons . . . for gain. . . . A Jew, however poor, had he ten sons would put them all to letters, not for gain . . . but to the understanding of God's laws; and not only his sons, but his daughters."**

The Jews are so often referred to as "the children of Israel" that a *cheder* boy once asked, "Didn't the grown-ups ever do anything?"

---

* For a survey of education among the Jews, see Simon Greenberg, "Jewish Educational Institutions," in *The Jews: Their History, Culture and Religion*, Vol. II, third edition, Louis Finkelstein, editor. Harper, 1960.

** *Great Jewish Personalities in Ancient and Medieval Times*, edited by Simon Noveck, B'nai Brith Publishers, p. 240.

Two *cheder* students were discussing how hard and tiring their studies had become, and impulsively one blurted: "Let's run away!"

"Run away? . . . Our fathers would catch up with us and give us a sound thrashing."

"So we'll hit them back!"

"*What?* Hit your *father?!* You must be mad. Have you forgotten the Commandment—always to honor your father and mother?"

"Mmh. . . . So you hit my father and I'll hit yours."

Chelm

Pronounced KHELM, with the guttural *kh.*

The name of a "legendary" town inhabited by befuddled, stupid, foolish, but endearing people.

Chelm is used as the name of a mythical place, but there is and was a real Chelm, some forty miles east of Lublin, with a population of around four thousand, the majority of whom were Jews. Another Chelm exists just east of Tarnow. How Chelm achieved its reputation for hilarious *non sequiturs* I do not know.

Chelm would enjoy no special name or fame, and surely no place in this lexicon, were it not that in Jewish folklore it has become the archetypical home of simpletons, an incubator of amiable fools, the Jewish equivalent of that Gotham from which "the wise men" came, Holland's Kampen, Italy's Cuneo, and Germany's "Schildburg"—all famous for fools.

There must be a thousand tall tales about Chelm and the unbelievable Chelmites; I give you but a handful.

The rabbi of Chelm visited the prison, and there he heard all but one of the inmates insist on their innocence. So he came back, held a council of wise men, and recommended that Chelm have *two* prisons: one for the guilty and another for the innocent.

The sages of Chelm began to argue about which was more important to the world: the moon or the sun. The community divided into two passionate camps. The reigning wise man then ruled: "The moon *must* be more important than the sun, because without the light of the moon our nights would be so dark we could not see anything. The sun, however, shines only by day—which is when we don't need it!"

A wise man of Chelm said, "What a crazy world this is. The rich, who have lots of money, buy on credit, but the poor, who don't have a cent, must pay cash. It should be the other way around: The rich, having money, should pay cash; and the poor, having none, should get credit."

"But if a storekeeper gives credit to the poor," objected another, "he can become poor himself."

"So fine!" said the idiot savant. "Then *he'll* be able to buy on credit, too!"

A farmer, riding home in his wagon, picked up a peddler from Chelm who was carrying a heavy bundle on his shoulder. The peddler sat down beside the farmer, but kept his bundle on his shoulders.

"Why don't you put your bundle down?" asked the farmer.

"It's nice enough your horse is *shlepping* me," said the peddler. "Do I have to add my bundle to his burden?"

cheppeh

See TCHEPPEH.

chevra

Pronounced KHEV-*ra*, with a German *kh* sound. From Hebrew: *chevara*, "comradeship."

A group of friends; one's pals or "gang." "He plays poker every Thursday night with his *chevra*."

In Israel, where the very religious rail against the modern dress and freer ways of the young people, a bitter joke goes: "She came back from the *kibbutz* pregnant, gave birth to a boy, and should name him after the father: *Chevra*."

chillul hashem
chillul ha-shem

> Pronounced KHILL-*el ha*-SHEM, to rhyme with "li'l o' them." Hebrew: "profaning God's name."

> A deed that leads or encourages others to disbelieve in, or withdraw from, God. A publicly performed transgression. The opposite is *kiddush hashem.*

A transgression against God's law is a desecration of God's name, hold the faithful, for every man is created in God's image, and man is only slightly less holy than the angels. Moreover, an act of immorality discredits all of Israel. God entered into a covenant with Israel: "Neither shall ye profane my holy name; but I will be hallowed among the children of Israel: I am the Lord which hallow you." (Leviticus 22 : 32.)

The more learned or influential a religious Jew is, the greater is his responsibility to serve as an example of honor. The concept of *noblesse oblige* is strong in Jewish life, but the aristocracy of Jews is one of knowledge plus morality in practice.

When the great Rab, who founded the Talmudic academy of Sura in Babylonia (two hundred years before the Christian era), was asked to give an example of what would be an act of *chillul hashem,* he replied, "In my case, if I bought meat and did not at once pay the butcher."

chloppeh

> Pronounced KHLYOP-*peh,* with the *ly* sound as in "million"—i.e., a Castilian *ll.* From Russian: "knock," "bang," "clap."

> To rain in torrents; to pour down "in buckets." "It's *chlopping* like a tropical storm." "She did not cry—she *chlopped.*"

chmallyeh

Pronounced with a strong opening Scottish *kh* sound: KHMOLL-*yeh*, to rhyme with "Kh-doll ya." From Slavic.

A severe blow; a clout with the hand. "Did he give me a *chmallyeh!*"

Chmallyeh usually conveys the idea that the force of the blow was excessive or unjust.

choleria

Pronounced *kha-*LEH-*ree-a*, with a rattling uvular *khah* to lead off; rhymes with "solaria." From Latin and Greek, into Hebrew: "plague." And *choleria* is related, I suspect, to "cholera."

1. (A curse) "To Hell with . . ."

One of the juicy curses, a *choleria* meant "A plague upon you" and whatever additional disasters the wisher could conjure up. "A *choleria* should possess him!" "A man like that— a *choleria* on him!"

2. A hellcat of a woman; a termagant; a hellion; a virago; a nag of a woman who is exceptionally mean. "He is married to a *choleria*." "That *choleria* will drive him to either suicide or murder."

cholilleh
chalileh

Pronounced *kholl-*ILL-*eh*, to rhyme with "Moll Willa." From the Hebrew: "May it not come to pass," or "God forbid." Literally, it means "Far be it . . ." and appears in Genesis 18 : 25, when Abraham was enjoining God not to destroy Sodom.

1. A common magical expression for "God forbid that should happen," uttered promptly before or after some dire prediction, fear, or possibility; an automatic incantation, descended from varieties of hocus-pocus, enlisted to circumvent the wrath of the gods, the malevolence of spooks, or the ubiquitous Evil Eye. "Be careful crossing the street you shouldn't *cholilleh* be hit by a car." "If a lunatic should *cholilleh* be elected President . . ." (My mother seemed to think "I hope he doesn't *cholilleh* get sick" was more efficacious, as a calamity-preventer, than "I hope he doesn't get sick *cholilleh*"—apparently because the *cholilleh* precedes the naming of the calamity; there's no accounting for abracadabra.)

2. A tongue-in-cheek expression affecting dismay over a possible and desired happenstance: "If I should *cholilleh* become a millionaire." "If my daughter *cholilleh* marries that wonderful boy . . ."

When the English and French governments opened the bidding for the digging of the great tunnel under the English Channel, engineering firms from all over the world placed their bids. And the lowest bid was from the firm of Marantz and Son.

Friends congratulated Marantz. "That's wonderful. How are you going to build the tunnel?"

"It's easy," said Marantz. "I'll start digging on the English side, and my son will start on the French side. And we'll dig and dig until we meet."

"But Marantz," an engineer protested. "Don't you realize that one of the hardest problems in all of engineering—one that has stumped some of our finest scientists—is the problem of getting two tunnels to meet!"

"What do you mean 'meet'?"

"I mean that the tunnel you start in England, and the tunnel your son starts in France—they start miles and miles apart, and they must come together exactly! What if *cholilleh* they don't?"

Marantz shrugged. "So the client will get two tunnels for the price of one."

Two Jews decided to kill Hitler. They bought revolvers and

concealed themselves in the doorway of a building they knew Hitler was due to visit. Hour after hour, with beating hearts, they waited. Finally, one assassin turned to the other and whispered, "I hope nothing happened to him, *cholilleh*."

chometzdik
hometzdik

Pronounced KHAW-*metz-dick*, with a fish-bone-stuck-in-the-roof-of-your-mouth *kh*, like a MacTavish's *ch*; rhymes with "Paw gets sick." From the Hebrew: *chametz*: "sour," "leavened," "fermented."

Something that is not eaten during Passover. "*A chometzdikeh Yideneh*" (a Jewish woman) means a sour old biddy, an unpleasant old nag.

See PESACH.

chotchke
chotchkeleh

Pronounced TCHOTCH-*keh*, to rhyme with "botch the," and TCHOTCH-*keh-leh*, to rhyme with "notch fella."

I prize these words, which are forms of *tsatske* and *tsatskeleh*, which I urge you to savor.

See TSATSKE.

A fur salesman, asked by a pretty young *chotchke* if the mink coat would be damaged if she were caught in the rain, replied, "Lady, did you ever see a mink carrying an umbrella?"

chozzer
chazzer

Pronounced KHAHZ-*zer*, with the emphatic Yiddish-

German-Scottish *kh* sound: rhymes with "Roz her."
Plural: *chozzerim*, pronounced *khahz-ZAY-rim*, rhymes
with "Cathay rim." Hebrew: "pig."

1. Pig, hog, or the meat thereof.
2. One who acts in an ungrateful way.
3. One who is uncouth.
4. One who is cheap, venal, selfish.
5. One who is stingy.
6. One who is greedy.
7. One who takes advantage of you, or tricks you
through sharp practices.

In Yiddish, oddly enough, one rarely says *chozzer* ("Pig!") to
describe someone dirty—as in English. *Chozzer* is used for
the ungrateful, the cheap, the selfish, greedy, stingy or fla-
grantly unfair.

Observing Jews do not eat ham, bacon, or pork, which are
forbidden to them by the Bible. (See KOSHER.)

The seemingly contradictory phrase *kosher chozzer fissel*
("kosher pig's feet") is used to describe someone who tries
to be holier-than-thou but has conspicuous defects.

Chozzerish (piglike) is used in an exuberant way to describe abandon, indulgence, pleasure. Thus, the phrase of
good wishes: "Go, live a *chozzerish tag*," which means "Go,
have yourself a ball—live it up."

The greenhorn in the Automat fed nickel after nickel into
the apple-pie slot.

His friend exclaimed, "Are you crazy, you *chozzer?* You
have already fifteen pies!"

Said the greenhorn: "Why should it bother you if I keep
winning?"

chozzerai

Pronounced *khoz-zair-EYE* to rhyme with "Roz her
eye." A Yiddish derivation from the Hebrew *chazir*,
"pig."

1. Food that is awful. "Who can eat such *chozzerai?*"
2. Junk, trash. "That movie was nothing but *chozzerai.*"
3. Anything disgusting, even loathsome. "A good deal of contemporary theater strikes me as *chozzerai.*" "I wish he would learn the difference between art and *chozzerai.*"

Chozzerai could do us all a great service, I think, if it replaced the now-popular "in" word, "crap."

This may be a gross libel on the innocent pig, I realize, since the pig, contrary to popular misconception, is a quite tidy creature; he wallows in mud because he likes to stay cool; mud is often the best barnyard medium for reducing body temperature. Mud looks filthy, but in fashionable spas the rich pay to bathe in it.

chuppa
chuppah
huppa

> Pronounced KHU-*peh*, to rhyme with "book-a"; make the *ch* a guttural *kh*. Hebrew: Originally, "chamber" or "covering."

> Wedding canopy.

The *chuppa* is used in all Orthodox and Conservative, and in some Reform, marriage ceremonies.

It is a fine canopy, usually made of white silk or satin, under which the bride and groom take their vows, and is held aloft by male relatives of the couple—one holding each of the wooden poles at the corners. The *chuppa* is often embroidered with some Biblical quotation, such as the one from Jeremiah: "The voice of mirth, and the voice of gladness, the voice of the bridegroom, and the voice of the bride" (16 : 9).

The *chuppa* suggests a royal canopy; the bride and groom are indeed considered "king and queen of this day."

It used to be that the bride left her father's house to go to her new husband's domain—which was symbolized by the *chuppa*. (One custom was to cut the poles from wood taken from trees that had been planted at the time of birth of the groom and bride.)

In some areas, Jews called the veil that covers the bride a *chuppa*, in others, the *chuppa* was the cloth or shawl that covered the heads of the marriage couple; in still others, bride and groom were wrapped in a large prayer shawl. In Poland, the *chuppa* became the canopy top used today. It was set up inside the synagogue, or in a courtyard, or out of doors.

In American synagogues, the *chuppa* is often a canopy of greens and flowers.

Of the *chuppa*, Sholom Aleichem once wrote: "You enter it living and come out a corpse."

Nuptial canopies are, of course, found in many cultures. The Greeks used a *thalamos* or bridal bower; the Brahmans use a twelve-pole canopy; in Spain and Scotland, newlyweds pass under a bower of leaves or boughs. In Sweden, bridesmaids hold a covering of shawls over the bride, to ward off the evil eye. (In many cultures, the wedding couple is protected from the evil eye by covers, cloths, enclosures.) In Tahiti, the couple is surrounded by, or rolled into, a mat.

The *chuppa*, in short, is not unique to Jews, nor was it invented by the Israelites. But it symbolizes the home and its very special, central meaning in Jewish life—as life's hub, life's refuge, life's temple.

See Appendix: Weddings.

chutzpa (noun)
chutspa
chutzpadik (adjective)

> Pronounced KHOOTS-*pah;* rattle that *kh* around with fervor; rhymes with "Foot spa." Do *not* pronounce the *ch* as in "choo-choo" or "Chippewa," but as the German *ch* in *Ach!* or the Scottish in *loch.* Hebrew: "insolence," "audacity."

Gall, brazen nerve, effrontery, incredible "guts"; presumption-plus-arrogance such as no other word, and no other language, can do justice to.

The classic definition of *chutzpa* is, of course, this:

Chutzpa is that quality enshrined in a man who, having killed his mother and father, throws himself on the mercy of the court because he is an orphan.

A *chutzpanik* may be defined as the man who shouts "Help! Help!" while beating you up.

In Paris, a plump Brooklyn *touristeh* entered a fine linen shop and, fingering a lace tablecloth, asked the proprietress the price thusly: *"Combien pour cette tishtoch* (tablecloth)?"

"Cinquante francs, madame."

"Cinquante francs?" echoed the American. *"Mais, c'est une shmatte* (rag)!"

The *baleboosteh* drew herself up in high dudgeon. *"Une shmatte, madame? Quelle chutzpa!"*

A woman, feeling sorry for a beggar who had come to her door, invited him in and offered him food. On the table was a pile of dark bread—and a few slices of *challa.* The *shnorrer* (beggar) promptly fell upon the *challa.*

"There's black bread, too," the woman hinted.

"I prefer *challa.*"

"But *challa* is much more expensive!"

"Lady," said the beggar, "it's worth it."

That, I think, is *chutzpa.*

And if you need one more example, *regardez* this:

A *chutzpanik,* having dined well in a restaurant, summoned the proprietor, to whom he said as follows, "My friend, I enjoyed your food, but to tell you the truth, I haven't a penny to my name. Wait: Don't be angry! Hear me out. I am, by profession, a beggar. I happen to be an extremely talented *shnorrer.* I can go out and within an hour *shnorr* the entire amount I owe you. But naturally, you can't trust me to come back. I understand. You'll be well-advised to come with me and not let me out of your sight for a minute, right? But can a man like you, a well-known restaurateur, be seen in the company of a man who is *shnorring?* Certainly not! So,

I have the perfect solution. I'll wait here—and you go out and *shnorr* until you have the cost of this dinner!"

That, certainly, is *chutzpa*.

"The bashful go to Paradise," said Judah ha-Nasi, twenty centuries ago, "and the brazen go to Purgatory."

A friend of mine swears that in a Jewish restaurant he once asked a passing waiter: "What time is it?"

Icily, the waiter said, "You aren't my table."

---

cockamamy

> Pronounced COCK-*a-may-me*, to rhyme with "lock a Mamie." Derivation: Ameridish, or children's argot.

> 1. Mixed-up, muddled; ridiculou*s*, implausible; not credible, foolishly complicated. "Did you ever hear such a *cockamamy* story?" "Of all the *cockamamy* excuses I ever heard."

This is not Hebrew and not Yiddish, but indigenous argot. H. L. Mencken's *Dictionary of American English*, surprisingly, does not list *cockamamy*. Neither does Eric Partridge's *Dictionary of Slang*. Nor, to my chagrin, does the comprehensive Berrey and Van den Bark *American Thesaurus of Slang*.

I never heard *cockamamy* used in Chicago, but have often encountered it in New York. It is a pungent adjective of disesteem.

> 2. Decalcomania: i.e., a picture or design left on the skin as a "transfer," from specially prepared paper which is wetted and rubbed.

I am informed by veterans of the Lower East Side that decalcomania pictures were called "cockamamies" because no one knew how to spell "decalcomania." That's not as *cockamamy* a feat of etymology as you might think. I have found none better.

In the movie *Teacher's Pet*, Clark Gable used *cockamamy* with scornful relish to dismiss an idea as totally absurd, desperately invented.

cohen

See KOHEN.

D

darshan
darshanim (plural)

See MAGGID.

An agnostic smiled, "But Darwin has proved that man is only another animal."

The *darshan* responded, "Then why has not a single breed of animal ever produced a Darwin?"

daven

> Pronounced DAH-*ven*, to rhyme with "robin." The origin of *daven* is unknown; it may be descended (remotely) from the French: *l'office divin*, "divine service." The word *daven*, incidentally, is used only by east European Jews, and those descended from them.

> To pray.

A traditional Jew *davens* three times a day *(shachris, min-chah,* and *mairev)* and adds supplementary prayers on the Sabbath and festivals. The main part of any prayer is the silent or whispered part, called *shemona esray,* always uttered while standing. The *shemona esray* originally contained eighteen benedictions; a nineteenth was added in the second century, but the name *shemona esray* (eighteen) was retained.

The cardinal role that *davening* has played in the life of the Jews will be seen in dozens of entries in this lexicon.

One of the most touching prayers is the one offered after rising: It thanks God for having "returned to me my soul, which was in Your keeping."

In the West, Jews face east when *davening,* for that is where Israel—nay, *Eretz Yisroel!*—is.

The Bible lists many examples of individual prayers of thanks (Moses after crossing the Red Sea, in Exodus; Deborah after her victory over Sisera, in Judges), or prayers in petition for help (Abraham requesting leniency for Sodom, in Genesis).

Most of the psalms originated as religious-philosophical-poetic affirmations, composed by individuals for use in public prayer. Communal prayer accompanied the bringing of sacrifices to the ancient Temple. When the Temple was destroyed, congregational prayers took the place of the Temple offerings.

A devout Jew will not read from the *Torah,* or recite the *Shema,* or pronounce the sacred Hebrew name of God, unless his head is covered; and the Orthodox never leave their heads uncovered by hat or *yarmulkah.*

No law in the Bible, or among the writings of the rabbis, seems to cover the custom of covering the head. This practice was, of course, not limited to the Jews: The use of a turban, fez, or other head-covering is considered a sign of respect in many parts of the Orient and the Middle East.

Why do Christians bare their heads in church and while praying? The practice originated with Paul (original name: Saul) who wrote (I Corinthians) that any who covered his head while "praying or prophesying . . . dishonoureth his head." I can only assume that Paul was overreacting against his early training.

See BROCHE.

———————————————

The extraordinary place and power of prayer among religious Jews is described by Maurice Samuel, in his sensitive and enchanting classic, *The World of Sholom Aleichem:*

> The God in whom he [Tevyeh, the dairyman] believes with all his heart, whom he loves and prays to at least three times daily . . . he addresses . . . with affection, irony, sympathy, reverence, impudence, and indestructible hope. . . .
>
> . . . every morning, at sunrise or shortly before, Tevyeh has to say his long morning prayers, the *Shachris,* and he has to say them, on week-days, with the prayer-shawl over his head, and the phylacteries on brow and arm. It's no good arguing with Tevyeh on this point. It is worse than useless to talk to him of superstition, mummery, and the opiate of the masses. He will have only one answer, delivered in a Talmudic singsong: "If all the persecutions of the ages, and all the bitterness of exploitation, could not prevent me from repeating the prayers of my fathers, shall I be made to fall away from them in a world of freedom?"
>
> But the *Shachris* is only a beginning. During the day Tevyeh must take time out—and he does it . . . under the most discouraging circumstances—for other prayers. Do what you like with Tevyeh, chain him to a galley, yoke him to a chariot, starve him, break him, he is going to say his three prayers daily.*

A Chasidic story:

A poor man, lost in the woods, found himself at nightfall without his prayer book. And he addressed this petition to the Almighty: "Dear God, I have done a stupid thing: I do not have my prayer book. And I have such a poor memory that I cannot recite the prayers by heart. . . . But You know all the prayers, Lord—so I'll just recite the letters of the alphabet, and You put them together in the right way."

And the Almighty regarded that prayer, because of its sincerity, more worthy than any of the others He heard that day.

* Maurice Samuel, *The World of Sholom Aleichem.* Knopf, 1943, pp. 14, 16–17.

dayan
dayyan
dayen
dayanim (plural)

> Pronounced DY-*en*, to rhyme with "Zion," or *die*-ON, to rhyme with "lie on"; pronounce the plural *die*-AW-*nim*. Hebrew: "Judge."

> A rabbinical judge.

In rabbinic literature, *dayan* meant "sage," a student of the Law, a rabbi of the community. (God is called *Dayan Emes*, "the righteous judge.")

The responsibilities of the rabbi and the *dayan* were often distinct and separate. Every *dayan* was a rabbi, trained in interpreting the *Torah* and *Talmud*, but not every rabbi was a *dayan*. In many communities, the *dayan* was more respected than the rabbi. His decision was known as a *Din Torah* (a verdict of the *Torah*).

The *Talmud* is full of instructions for the administration of justice: The judge may not listen to the arguments of one litigant in the absence of the other; equality before the law is underscored—no preference should be shown even to the learned; the first question put to litigants is, "Do you wish law or arbitration?"

In countries where Jewish communities were forced to live apart from the general population, the governments often granted judicial authority (in cases involving only Jews) to the *dayanim*. The general tendency was to submit to the law of the land except in matters affecting and within the confines of the Jewish community.*

My maternal grandfather was a *dayan* in Lodz, Poland, and to his home Jews came with a multitude of problems. He

---

* Yitzhak Baer wrote of the Jewish community in Spain: "In matters of jurisprudence, the laws of the Torah prevailed. The decisions of the Jewish judges were recognized, confirmed and executed by the Christian kings and their officials. . . . The *dayyan* wielded the same decisive authority in the *aljama* [Jewish community] as the *alcalde* did in the municipality." *A History of the Jews in Christian Spain*, Vol. I, Jewish Publication Society, 1961, p. 213.

held himself quite superior to rabbis, who came to him with their problems. He also preferred to conduct services in his home, regarding the synagogue as a place for less illustrious worshipers—hence, his followers would make up a *minyan*, over which he presided.*

See BES DIN.

The old *dayan* called before him the newest rabbi in town and, sighing heavily, said, "My heart is heavy. My words are like lead: for I have heard a rumor about you——"

"It's not true!" cried the young rabbi. "I know the rumor, *rebbe;* there's not a word of truth in it!"

The *dayan* drew himself up in horror. "*True* it should be yet? Isn't it bad enough there is a *rumor?!*"

A husband and wife came to the learned *dayan*, wrangling and fuming. The *dayan* first asked the woman into his study, where she plunged into a recitation of her husband's unkindnesses and inconsiderateness.

"——and I can't *stand* it any more, rabbi! I want to leave him! I want a divorce!"

The *dayan* nodded gravely. "You're right," he said and sent her out.

Now her husband entered, ranting: "She probably told you such a *megillah* of lies I wouldn't recognize them! The truth is she's a lazy, no-good *yenta*, a terrible *baleboosteh*, she's mean to me and my friends, I should throw her out of the house! I want a divorce!"

"You're right," said the *dayan*.

The man left.

One of the *dayan*'s students, who had observed all this with a puzzled air, inquired: "But *rebbe:* you told her *she* was right, and you told him *he* was right; I don't see how both of them can be——"

"You're *right!*" said the *dayan*.

Diaspora

See GALUT.

* For sensitive and haunting recollections of how a *dayan* li.... and worked, see Isaac Bashevis Singer's stories about his father, *In My Father's Court*. Farrar, Straus, Giroux, 1966.

donstairsikeh (feminine)
donstairsiker (masculine)

Pronounced *don-*STARE*-zi-keh*. Yinglish.

The neighbor who lives downstairs. "My *donstairsikeh* is an angel."

A *donstairsikeh* is doppelgänger to an *opstairsikeh*.

doppess

Pronounced DOP-*pess*, to rhyme with "mop-less."

Useless but commiserating bystander; ineffectual observer who is of little help.

This word thrived in the garment trade—possibly as a more scornful version of dope, *shlemiel, shmegegge*. It may come from *herum-tappen*, "to grope about, to fumble in the dark." Dutch and German Jews who heard no Yiddish used *doppess* for a clumsy groper.

Doppess served a need for those who wanted a word to convey, with both precision and subtlety, a character type known in all cultures: the useless observer who, in a crisis, does nothing more than offer obligatory sympathy.

My erudite friend Professor Daniel Bell tells me that a Thirty-seventh-Street Webster once defined *doppess* for him with picturesque precision: "The *shlemiel* is the pants-presser who always drops the hot iron off the ironing board. The *shlimazl* is the *shmo* on whose foot the iron always falls. And the *doppess* is the one who says, 'Tsk, tsk!' "

The man who habitually clucks "Tsk, tsk!" is also called a *tsitser*.

"One man chops the wood, the other does all the grunting."
　　　　　　　　　　　　　　　　　　—FOLK SAYING

draykop
draykopf

Pronounced DRAY-*kup*, to rhyme with "gray pup," or DRAY-*kawp*, to rhyme with "gray hawk." German: *drayen*: "to turn" or "twist"; *kopf*: "head."

1. A finagler who talks you into something, who "turns your head," who befuddles your good sense.
2. Someone who confuses you, bothers you, "talks off an arm and a leg."
3. An addlepate; one who is confused, whose head was turned.

The following involves two *draykops*, as far as I'm concerned:

The phone rang in the law offices. A voice answered, "Zucker, Zucker, Zucker, and Zucker."

"Hello, may I please speak to Mr. Zucker?"

"I'm sorry, but Mr. Zucker is in court."

"Well then, can I speak to Mr. *Zucker?*"

"Sorry, Mr. Zucker is in Washington."

"Well, how about connecting me with Mr. *Zucker?*"

"Mr. Zucker won't be in until two."

Sigh. "O.K., then I'll speak to Mr. Zucker."

"Speaking."

dreck

Rhymes with "fleck." From the German *Dreck:* "excrement," "dung."

1. Excrement.
2. Trash, junk, garbage.
3. Cheap or worthless things.
4. Plays, movies or performances, in any of the arts, of grossly inferior quality.

Dreck is forceful, but vulgar—like its English equivalent, "crap."

If you want to say "dirt," don't use *dreck*, but *shmutz* (rhymes with "puts").

I would not recommend your using *dreck* in front of my mother, much less yours, any more than I would approve of your using the sibilant four-letter English word for excrement.

Dreck is used for a wide variety of judgments of disapproval—from the condition of the streets to the caliber of a poem. I do not approve of careless usage: Both English and Yiddish have a rich enough vocabulary of disparagement. To say *dreck*, save in extreme cases, is *dreckish*. Better stick with *chozzerai*.

dresske

> Pronounced DRESS-*keh;* rhymes with "press the." Yinglish.
>
> Diminutive for "dress."

But stop! A *dresske* is not just a small dress, or a little dress, or even a bikini: *Those* would be called, in either fondness or ridicule, a *dresskeleh*—which is a diminutive, like "teeny-weeny."

A *dresske*, in classic Yinglish, means the kind of dress women dismiss as "a little nothing," or a garment for which the owner paid little.

Dresskes come from bargain basements, off racks labeled "Marked Down Drastically," and from certain emporia of notable values on Fourteenth Street. I do not think anyone ever found a *dresske* at Bergdorf's or Nieman-Marcus.

Note to the ladies: It is tactful to use *dresske* when your husband is complaining about expenses.

My favorite way of suggesting the true flavor of *dresske* involves the lady who, complimented on her new frock, replied with disdain: "This little *dresske?* It's nothing: I just use it for streetwalking."

dybbuk

Pronounced DIB-*book*, to rhyme with "rib hook." Hebrew: "evil spirit," "incubus."

1. An evil spirit—usually, the soul of a dead person that enters a living person on whom the dead one had some claim;
2. A demon who takes possession of someone and renders the mortal mad, irrational, vicious, sinful, corrupt.

When someone went mad, hysterical, or suffered an epileptic seizure, Jews would cry "A *dybbuk* has entered into him (or her)!"

The idea of the *dybbuk* is as old as demonology itself, and demonology is as old as man.

A prominent demon in Jewish lore, particularly associated with King Solomon (whom he dethroned for several years, according to legend) is *Ashmedai*, or Asmodeus.

Jews do not have a very vivid sense of the Devil, in the medieval Christian sense, as the incarnation of evil, the supreme, cunning tempter.

A *dybbuk* is the closest thing in Jewish folklore to a ghoul, vampire, incubus—a migrating spirit who has to find a living body to inhabit. To protect women in childbirth from such demons, superstitious Jews used odd amulets and fervent incantations.

Dybbuks, of course, can be exorcised. The approved method is offered here as a special service to my readers:

Get a holy man or wonder-worker, a *tzaddik* or even a *Baal Shem*, who will preside over a *minyan*. He reads the Ninety-first Psalm aloud, then, in a fearful voice, orders the damned *dybbuk* to vacate the body of the possessed person and, in God's name, go off to "eternal rest." This closely resembles the official rites recommended by the Roman Catholic Church. (See the manual: *De Ordinatione Exorcistarum*.)

If the *dybbuk* is stubborn and refuses to behave, as may be the case with such perverse critters, the *Baal Shem* orders a ram's horn (*shofar*) blown at once. That ought to do it.

One of the more charming details in the lore alleges that when a *dybbuk* flees a man or woman, a tiny, bloody spot, the size of a pinhead, appears on the pinky of the right foot. Either that, or a window develops a little crack.

S. Ansky (pen name of S. Z. Rapoport, 1863–1920) wrote a remarkable and compelling play, a classic of the Yiddish theater, called *The Dybbuk*, that has been performed around the world in many languages.

I own a little book written by Jacques-Albin-Simon Collin de Plancy (1793–1887), *A Dictionary of Demonology*, that has long beguiled me. It catalogues all sorts of spooky spirits, from a Neapolitan pig with the head of a man to Adrammelech, "grand chancellor of hell," whom the Assyrians worshiped with infant sacrifices and who, learned rabbis said, took the shape of either a mule or a peacock, which runs a gamut of pretty versatile disguises. Amduscias, a grand duke of hell, is shaped like a unicorn—and gives concerts.

My favorite in the boogeyman league is Tanchelin, a heretic who lived in the twelfth century. Tanchelin had such awesome powers that husbands begged him to sleep with their wives. I am not sure that Tanchelin was a demon so much as a *draykop*—which please see.*

dzhlob

See ZHLOB.

---

* A splendid compendium to consult on matters concerning angels, demons, spirits, spooks and allied supra-human powers and beings, both good and evil, is Gustav Davidson's *A Dictionary of Angels*, Free Press, 1967.

edel

Pronounced AY-*d'l*, to rhyme with "cradle." German: *edel:* "noble," "refined."

1. Gentle, sensitive, refined.
2. Shy, modest, humble.

"He is *edel*" is a compliment of the highest order.

edelkeit

1. Gentleness, sensitivity.
2. Modesty; sweetness of character.

We had a butcher on the West Side of Chicago who was revered by one and all because of the singular sweetness of his character. "Such *edelkeit!*" people said.

And yet, a saying goes: "Too humble is half-proud."

einredenish

Pronounced INE-*red-e-nish*, to rhyme with "Fine bed of fish." From the German *einreden*: "to make one believe"; literally, "to talk into." Yiddish adds the all-purpose *-ish* to convert the verb into a noun.

1. Something, usually wrong or unwarranted, that one has talked oneself into believing.
2. A delusion, an *idée-fixe*. "She has an *einredenish* that he hates tea."

You can't have a true or correct *einredenish*, please notice. If it's an *einredenish*, it partakes of the unrealistic or the insupportable.

"An *einredenish* is worse than a disease," goes a Yiddish apothegm. This anticipated Freud, and expresses the impressive popular insight that physical diseases are more readily cured than psychological delusions.

The history of the human race would have been far less monstrous had God substituted diseases for delusions. As between psychosis and sciatica, I'll take (or give) sciatica any day.

Einredenish might well be adopted in English, to mean "the incorrect, foolish, or fantastic things people talk themselves into believing."

My *einredenish* is that you can get Iowans to pronounce the *ch*'s in *chachem* the way Jews do—and Scots can.

"A man's worst enemies can't wish on him what he can think up himself."
—FOLK SAYING

At a mass meeting in Berlin, Adolf Hitler, victim of a most appalling *einredenish*, shrieked, "And who is responsible for all our troubles?!"

Ben Cohen shouted, "The bicycle riders!"

Hitler looked up, astonished. "Why the bicycle riders?"

"Why the Jews?" replied Cohen.

Poor Mr. Gittelman could not sleep. No pills from his doctor, no advice from his friends, helped his tormenting insomnia.

Mr. Gittelman began to look so haggard that his partner, Mr. Feigenbaum, said, "You'll end up in a loony ward!"

"So what can I *do?*" moaned Gittelman. "I drink hot milk. I take warm baths. I play soft music. I take every sleeping pill the doctor prescribes . . ."

"What about the oldest trick of all: counting sheep?"

Gittelman smote his forehead. "Harvey, so help me, I forgot that one. You're a lifesaver. Tonight, I'll count sheep and if I have to count up to ten thousand, I'll fall asleep at last!"

The next morning, the moment Gittelman entered the loft, Feigenbaum asked, "Did it work?"

"No," groaned Gittelman. "I counted sheep. Oh how I counted sheep. I counted up to two thousand without getting tired. So I sheared the sheep—all two thousand—and still I was wide awake. So I had an idea, and I made up two thousand overcoats. Do you *know* how tiring it is to make two thousand overcoats! I was exhausted and practically snoring—when it happened!"

"What happened?"

"All night I was up, worrying: where could I get two thousand linings?"

Epicoris

See APIKOROS.

Elohim

See ADONAI, JEHOVAH.

eppes

Pronounced EP-*pis*, to rhyme with "hep miss." From Middle High German: *eppes.*

1. Something; a little.
2. A somebody.
3. Quite; perhaps; maybe; for some inexplicable reason.
4. Debatable; unsatisfactory.

This delightful, resilient word has chameleon properties of a high order, and a surprising number of subtly shaded, shrewdly freighted connotations.

(a) "Eat *eppes*." (Eat something.)

(b) "*Eppes* I'm not hungry." (For some reason, I am not hungry.)

(c) "She served *eppes* a meal!" (She served quite some meal! But see (i) below; the tone is critical.)

(d) "Is that *eppes* a beauty!" (If uttered with enthusiasm: "Wow, is she a beauty!" Note the exclamation mark.) *But note:*

(e) "That is *eppes* a beauty?" (Uttered as a question, a hypothesis, with a frown or arched eyebrow, in hesitancy or oozing irony, this means: "You call *that* a beauty . . . ?" Note the absence of an exclamation mark.)

(f) "He thinks he's an *eppes*." (He thinks he's a somebody.)

(g) "There is *eppes* a painter!" (There, by God, is a painter! Here *eppes* is kin to the French *formidable*.)

(h) "Who has *eppes* an idea?" (Who has any kind of an idea, *please?*)

(i) "This is *eppes* some explanation!" (Sarcastic: "This is a most unsatisfactory explanation.")

An official brought the chief rabbi of a town before the Court of the Inquisition and told him, "We will leave the fate of your people to God. I'm putting two slips of paper in this box. On one is written 'Guilty.' On the other is written 'Innocent.' Draw."

Now this inquisitor was known to seek the slaughter of all the Jews, and he had written "Guilty" on both pieces of paper.

The rabbi put his hand inside the box, withdrew a slip of paper—and swallowed it.

"What are you doing?" cried the inquisitor. "How will the court know—"

"That's simple," said the rabbi. "Examine the slip that's in the box. If it reads 'Innocent,' then the paper I swallowed obviously must have read 'Guilty.' But if the paper in the box reads 'Guilty,' then the one I swallowed must have read 'Innocent.'"

That was *eppes* brilliant!

————————————

There is no truth in the allegation that on Halloween Jewish children ring doorbells and ask, *"Eppes* for *yontif?"*

Eretz Yisroel
Eretz Yisrael
Eretz Israel

> Pronounced EH-*retz* yis-ROY-*el*, to rhyme with "ferrets this toy El," or EH-*retz* yis-roe-AIL, to rhyme with "merits this tow rail." Hebrew: "The land of Israel."

> The land of Israel.

Eretz Yisroel has been the focus of Jewish dreams since the year 70 A.D. when the Second Temple was destroyed and the Jews were scattered throughout the world (see GALUT).

Eretz Yisroel is the believing Jews' "Promised Land," promised by God to Abraham and his descendants, the land of the kingdom of David and Solomon, the land in which the holy City of Jerusalem was built, the land where all Jews buried in the Diaspora will come to life again and where, in the very end of days, the Messiah will appear. Some Jewish prayers end, ". . . and next year, in Jerusalem."

During the long, long centuries of the Dispersion, *Eretz Yisroel* became to observing Jews more than a piece of land, or a place on the map: it became The Promised Land, Eldorado, a vision of a society free from prejudice, a utopia where Jews could live, study, and worship freely. It was literally the Holy Land; as such, it became the inspiration for a great body of Hebrew literature. (Under rabbinical law, if a man asked his wife to go with him to Israel to live and she refused, without some overriding reason, such as health, it was grounds for divorce.)

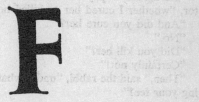

farbissen
farbissener (masculine)
farbisseneh (feminine)

> Pronounced *far-BIS-sen*, to rhyme with "car listen." From German *verbissen:* "obstinate, sullen."

> Embittered.

A *farbissener* is dour, mean, unpleasant, unlikable. So is a *farbisseneh*.

Farbissen carries the implication of psychologically distorted, crippled.

A *farbissener* doctor was called to the hut of a shoemaker whose wife was seriously ill.

"Please, doctor. Save her!" cried the husband. "I'll pay anything, even if I have to sell everything I own."

"But what if I can't cure her?" said the doctor shrewdly.

"I'll pay you whether you cure her or kill her!" cried the desperate husband.

A week later, the woman died. The doctor sent the shoemaker a huge bill. And now the poor man suggested they both go to the rabbi to discuss the fee.

The rabbi, who knew the doctor's reputation, said, "What was your agreement with this man?"

"He agreed to pay me for treating his wife," said the doctor, "whether I cured her or killed her."

"And did you cure her?"

"No."

"Did you kill her?"

"Certainly not!"

"Then," said the rabbi, "under what contract are you claiming your fee?"

farblondjet

> Pronounced *far*-BLAWN-*jit*, to rhyme with "car lawn kit."
> Slavic: "wander," "roam."

> Lost (but *really lost*), mixed-up, wandering about without any idea where you are.

I include *farblondjet* not because English lacks adequate words for what *farblondjet* describes, but because *farblondjet's* euphony exudes an aroma all its own. It refers not simply to being lost, but to having-gotten-way-the-*hell*-and-gone-off-the-track.

You can describe a meandering statement, a fouled-up presentation, a galloping *non sequitur*, a thoroughly confused *contretemps*, as one in which someone got really *farblondjet*. "He drove towards New Rochelle but got so *farblondjet* that he ended up in White Plains." "His appeal to the jury? Man, was he *farblondjet!*"

Professor Prescott asked a colleague in the philosophy department, Professor Minkus, "What does *farblondjet* mean?"

"Wandered way off course, lost, gone far astray," said Professor Minkus. "When I started my career, for instance, I was really *farblondjet:* I was a Reform rabbi for six years."

"Really?" said Professor Prescott. "Were you—unfrocked?"

"No," sighed Minkus, "just unsuited."

farchadat

Pronounced *far*-CHAH-*det*, to rhyme with "Car got it." Slavic: *chad*: "smoke," "daze."

1. Dizzy, confused, dopey, "punchy." "That guy walks around all *farchadat*."
2. Having a headache. "My head is really *farchadat*."
3. Smitten, charmed, beguiled. "He is *farchadat* by the girls."
4. Surprised, stunned, shocked. "When she heard the outrageous prices they were asking, she was positively *farchadat!*"

It's a good and useful word; it actually sounds *farchadat*. One says of a mixed-up person, "He has a *farchadster kop* (head)."

Misha and Grisha were discussing the wonderful life they would live come "The Revolution."

"Comes the revolution," said Misha, "we'll all eat strawberries and cream!"

"But I don't like strawberries and cream," said Grisha.

"Comes the revolution, you'll *have* to eat strawberries and cream!"

Was he *farchadat!*

farpotshket

Pronounced *far*-POTCH-*ket*, to rhyme with "car NOTCH let." From the German: *Patsche*: "slap."

1. Messed-up, sloppy, crossed-out-and-erased-and-written-ten-over-again.
2. Anything bollixed up, from a painting to a cause.

Farpotshket has an onomatopoetic splash to it I greatly enjoy. "His painting was certainly *farpotshket*." "Their statement to the press was really *farpotshket*." "He's famous for his *farpotshket* logic."

See POTSH.

farshtinkener

Pronounced *far*-SHTINK-*ener*. From the German: *verstinken*, "to stink up."

Stinking, all-stunk-up.

This uncouth word may be shunned by keepers of the flame, but expresses feeling forcefully.

"What a *farshtinkener* business!" has the edge on "What a stinking business," in my opinion, because the *sh* is more eloquent than the *s* in the communication of obloquious nuances. It is also more *chic* to enlist a foreign word when driven to coarse utterance.

At a dinner party, a *farshtinkener* anti-Semite, recounting his trip to central Africa, said, "It was wonderful. I didn't run into a single pig or Jew."

A hush fell over the table.

Then the voice of a Jewish guest was heard. "What a pity. The two of us could have corrected that so easily."

"Oh? How?"

"We could have gone there together."

fartootst (adjective)
fartootster (masculine)
fartootsteh (feminine)

Pronounced *far*-TUTST, to rhyme with "bar footst"; *far*-TUTS-*ter*, to rhyme with "car suits her," and *far*-TUTS-*teh*, to rhyme with "bar foots eh." From the German: *verdutzt*, "confused, mixed up."

The state of being bewildered, disoriented, discombobulated; slightly more intense than *tsedrayt*. "He's all *fartootst*."

When used as a modifier, or as a noun, *fartootst* becomes *fartootster* (masculine) and *fartootsteh* (feminine). "She's a *fartootsteh* hostess." "He's a *fartootster*."

Mr. Chamish called Mr. Nudelman indignantly: "Your bill is two months overdue already!"

"What?" said Nudelman. "Didn't you receive my check?"

"No."

"I'll put it in the mail immediately!"

(He was not *fartootst*.)

faygeleh

Pronounced FAY-*geh-leh*, to rhyme with "May bella." Diminutive of the German: *Vogel*: "bird." The German *Vögele* is pronounced FAY-*geh-leh*, too.

1. Little bird.
2. A girl's name.
3. A dear little, sweet little, tiny, helpless, innocent child. CAUTION: Use *faygeleh* for a little girl, not for a little boy, because *faygeleh* also means:
4. Homosexual. Quite common (the word, not the libidinal arrangement) in the American-Jewish vernacular. A synonym for the English "fairy" or "fag."

Jews use *faygeleh* as a discreet way of describing a homosexual—especially where they might be overheard.

feh!

Pronounced always with feeling, as FEH! Possibly from the German: *pfui*.

This juicy expletive cannot be enlisted without its exclamation point.

"*Feh!*" is the Yiddish replacement for exclamatory expressions of disgust such as "Phew!" "Pee-oo!" "Ugh!" "Phooey!" "Ecch!" and "Pfrr!" It strikes me as a crisp and exact delineation of distaste. In saying "Feh!," you may bare the teeth and wrinkle the nose, in visible reinforcement of the meaning.

Here are some circumstances in which "*Feh!*" may serve as the perfect utterance:

1. Smelling a rotten egg.
2. Passing an open sewer.

3. Inhaling Los Angeles smog.

4. Driving past the sulfur pits that fringe New York in New Jersey.

5. Whiffing a rotten fish.

6. Depicting a beatnik with mare's-nest hair.

7. Describing an old biddy (if you are young).

8. Describing a beautiful tart (if you are old).

9. Summarizing a political position you detest.

10. Appraising the honor or benevolence of an enemy.

11. Contemplating an operation for hemorrhoids.

12. Responding to an invitation to a bullfight.*

13. Reporting (the next day, to your loved ones) how the overripe grouse or pheasant smelled at the dinner last night, which, excuse the expression, was plain *chaloshes*.

14. Delineating the character of the *paskudnyak* who ran off with your wife.

15. Anticipating the *shloomp, shmendrick, kolyika,* or *shlemiel* of a nephew whom you had to take into the business because your wife insisted on "giving at least a *chance*" to her own flesh and blood.

16. Describing the *chutzpanik* who thinks he's going to marry your daughter.

17. Reporting a *klutz's* performance of Mozart.

18. Recounting how a soprano murdered an aria.

19. Depicting a hangover.

20. Portraying strongly negative feelings about any sight, event, person, crisis, experience or emotion.

Fehl, I salute you!

I once wrote an entire story to illustrate the puissance of this incomparable expletive: "Mr. K*A*P*L*A*N and the Unforgivable 'Fehl' "**

fifer

Pronounced FIE-*fer* to rhyme with "lifer." German: "whistler."

1. A whistler, a piper.

---

* There was a Jewish matador from Brooklyn, who fought in Spain as Sidney Franklin.
** In *The Return of H*Y*M*A*N K*A*P*L*A*N*, Harper, 1959.

2. A loud, shrill, noisy, aggressive or ill-mannered fellow.

3. A braggart.

A *fifer* is not quite *infra dig* enough to be a *graubyon;* he may *fife* without intending to mislead or misrepresent, the way a *fonfer* does.

4. A type who sets your teeth on edge. "She married a real *fifer*."

The phrase "I *fife* on you!" means "The heck with you!" or "Who cares about your opinion?"

––––––––––––––––

Mr. Rubin, who had just returned from his first trip to Europe, was regaling his friends with stories.

"And did you get to Rome?" one asked him.

"Naturally! Who doesn't go to Rome?"

"How did you like the Colosseum?"

Mr. Rubin made a regal gesture. "Very nice—if you like modern."

fin
finif
finiff
finnif

Pronounced to rhyme, respectively, with "tin," "lymph," "sin if." Yinglish. From German: *fünf*, "five."

1. Five.
2. A five-dollar bill; a five-pound note.
3. A five-year jail sentence.

"Fin" is the Anglicized and contracted form of *finif*, the Yiddish word for "five," and is widely used in colloquial English, especially by sports fans, gamblers, Broadway types, nightclub habitués, and newspaper columnists who memorialize these gaudy provinces of diversion. "Fin" is so much a part of American vernacular that I do not italicize it.

"Fin" and *finif* were used with his customary felicity by Damon Runyon, in his stories about that after-twilight world in which lived his "more than somewhat" unforgettable guys and dolls. "Fin" appears in John O'Hara's emphatically non-Jewish dialogue, going back to the early 1930's. It is standard argot among connoisseurs of boxing, racing, dice, poker, *et alia*.

H. L. Mencken attributes "fin" to German, not Yiddish.[*] I think this wrong. The word *fünf* is indubitably German; but the pronunciation *finif*, in two syllables, or *finf* (not *fünf*) in one, is just as indubitably Yiddish.

Wentworth and Flexner's excellent *Dictionary of American Slang*[**] attributes "fin" flatly to Yiddish, as do I.

flayshedig
flayshig

Pronounced FLAY-*sheh-dik*, to rhyme with "pay the sick," or FLAY-*shik*, to rhyme with "say Dick." From the German: *fleischig:* "meaty, fleshy."

Meats, poultry, or foods prepared with animal fats, which, according to the dietary rules *(kashruth)*, may not be eaten with dairy foods.

See KOSHER.

folks-mensh

Pronounced FOKES-*mentch*, to rhyme with "Folks bench." German: *Volksmensch;* "man of the people."

Jews are likely to harbor strong feelings about their "folk," meaning the Jewish people; in Yiddish, *folks-mensh* has come to mean more than a man of the people. Hence:

---

[*] *The American Language,* Knopf, 1962, p. 578.
[**] Crowell, 1967.

1. One who identifies himself with the masses, not the elite. You don't have to be Jewish to be a *folks-mensh*.

2. An honest, simple, unpretentious man or woman.

3. One who could, by virtue of achievement or wealth, be a snob—but is not. The opposite of Brahman. Franklin D. Roosevelt, my mother says, was at heart a *folks-mensh*.

4. One who is interested in Jewish life, values, experience, and wants to carry on the tradition.

5. A man or woman with a strong interest in popular culture, in the folk arts—whether Jewish or not.

6. One who displays a strong social conscience.

Jews refer to the collective body of Jews as "the *Yiddisher folk*," or people. Hence, a *folks-mensh* originally meant a man or woman interested in, and working for, Jewish causes.

Anyone who is affiliated with philanthropic organizations or worthy causes is a *folks-mensh*. Many Jews regard the present Rockefellers, surely no *parvenus*, as *folks-menshen*. They would not characterize Henry Adams or Henry James as *folks-menshen*.

I know a *folks-mensh* who wants the cabin notices in all El Al aircraft to read:

> FASTEN YOUR SEAT BELTS
> NO SMOKING
> EAT FRUIT

fonfer

Pronounced FUN-*fer*, to rhyme with "bun fur." Slavic: "to nasalize."

1. Someone who *fonfes*—i.e., talks through his nose, unclearly, or as if he has a bad cold. One of Sholom Aleichem's characters always pronounces "I am" as "I ab," and "You may" as "You bay." He was a *fonfer*.

2. A double-talker. "That *fonfer* can drive you out of your mind."

3. A man who is lazy, slow, "goofs off." "Don't be a *fonfer*—work!"

4. One who does not deliver what he promises: i.e., he *fonfes* promises.

5. A shady, petty deceiver. "That *fonfer* will make you think black is white."

6. One who cheats. "He's a *fonfer*; watch his addition." "Don't let him *fonfe* on the amount."

7. One who goes through the motions of a thing without intending to perform to his capacity, or your proper expectations. "It took him three hours to walk from here to Fourteenth Street to deliver that package. Did you ever hear of such a *fonfer?*"

8. A boaster, full of bravado. "He talks like a hero, but acts like a *fonfer*."

9. A specialist in hot air, baloney—a trumpeter of hollow promises. "He should be selling lots on the moon, that *fonfer*."

A friend tells me that his mother accompanied a neighbor to her citizenship hearing, years ago. The judge asked the neighbor, "Who was the first President of the United States?"

The poor soul's mind went blank.

"Do you know what she answered?" my friend exclaimed. "She turned to my mother for help, and after my mother *fonfet* aid into her, the neighbor said, 'Columbus.'"

fress (verb)
fresser (noun)

Rhymes with "dress." From German: *fress*, "devour."

1. To eat a great deal. "Did you ever see anyone *fress* like that?"

2. To eat quickly, noisily. "Don't act like a *fresser*." "Slow down; don't *fress*."

Gerry Blumenfeld writes that she once saw a restaurant in Mexico City whose menu, under "Sandwiches," read:

Pastrami por Fressers . . . 10 pesos
Pastrami (Double Decker) por Grandes Fressers . . . 15 pesos
Pastrami (Triple Decker) por Grandísimo Fressers . . . 20 pesos

frosk

Pronounced as it is spelled, with a short *o*.

A slap.

The beauty of its euphony, *frosk*, beguiles me—as I hope it will you.

"I gave him a *frosk in pisk*" is a splendid, sibilant way of saying "I gave him a slap in the puss."

"My father was so mad yesterday," said little Morris, "that five separate times he wanted to give me a *frosk*."

"How do you know it was exactly five times?"

"Because I counted."

"What did you count?"

"The number of times he hit me."

"I thought you said he *wanted* to hit you."

"I did. Would he have hit me if he hadn't wanted to?"

frum
frummer (masculine)
frummeh (feminine)

Pronounced with the short "u" or "oo" of "good," *not* to rhyme with "crumb" or "broom." German: *fromm:* "pious."

Religious, observant, orthodox. "He is *frum*." "He is a *frummer* Jew." "She is a *frummeh*."

It is said that when pious Jews left the old country, they would address God thusly: "And now, good-bye, O Lord; I am going to America."

Galitzianer

Pronounced *goll-itz-ee-ON-er,* to rhyme with "doll itsy on her."

A Jew from Galicia, a province of Poland/Austria. (When Poland was partitioned in 1772, Austria grabbed Galicia.)

Galicia, heavily populated by Jews (in the early twentieth century, they comprised over ten percent of the population), was a seat of Talmudic learning; it had several important *yeshivas* which produced prominent rabbis and scholars. The Jewish population of Galicia benefitted from Emperor Joseph II's decree of 1780, making education compulsory for his subjects.

The *Galitzianer* and the *Litvak* were often at odds, each claiming superiority over, and looking with a certain disdain upon, the other. The respective chauvinists viewed a marriage between a *Litvak* and a *Galitzianer* as almost exogamous, and wedding guests were fond of predicting that no good could come of such a strange misalliance.

My parents spoke with a certain prissiness about both *Galitzianers* and *Litvaks.* We were *Poylish* (Polish)—and were no doubt regarded, in turn, as *infra dig* by such *Galitzianers* and *Litvaks* as put on airs.

And Russian Jews, especially of the *intelligentsia,* looked down with cool impartiality upon all the rest. Among *Galitzianers,* a *Deutsch* or German Jew was regarded as modernized, probably unreligious, and certainly one who wore no beard, *payess,* hat. As for German Jews—! A self-appointed elite, they clearly disliked, snubbed or despised non-German *Jehudim;* and they were (if one must generalize) heartily disliked—and envied—by the poorer, less assimilated, much more religious kin to their east.

The *familiengefiel* (family feeling) of a common heritage, shared values, common problems, common threats, misfortunes and persecutions, was nevertheless exceedingly strong among European Jewry.

In the United States, the social-prestige scale was sensitive and exact: first-generation Jews envied second-generation Jews; and German Jewish families—Kuhns, Warburgs, Seligmans, Kahns, Schiffs, Lehmanns, Loebs, Ochses—became an elite of remarkable influence and social cohesiveness. The "pecking order" of this Establishment, its pride, philanthropy, snobbery, and Pecksniffian patronage of Russian and Polish Jews—all this is described by Stephen Birmingham in *Our Crowd: The Great Jewish Families of New York.** San Francisco's Jews became a distinguished, conspicuously civic-minded group of descendants of settlers dating back to the Gold Rush.***

See LITVAK.

---

* Harper & Row, 1967.
** For an illuminating inquiry into the identification patterns, social hierarchy, practices, values and conflicts within the conglomerate Jewish communities in America, see Nathan Glazer's excellent *American Judaism* in the Chicago History of American Civilization series, Daniel Boorstin, editor. University of Chicago Press, 1957; also Moses Rischin's *The Promised City: New York's Jews: 1870–1914.* Corinth Books, 1964; also, the articles by Nathan Glazer, Simon Kuznets, and Jacob Lestchinsky in *The Jews: Their History, Culture and Religion,* Vol. II, third edition, Louis Finkelstein, editor. Harper, 1960; and *The Jews; Social Patterns of an American Group,* Marshall Sklare, editor. The Free Press, 1960.

galut
galus

Pronounced GOLL-*us*, to rhyme with "call us." Hebrew: "exile."

1. Exile; the Diaspora; the dispersion of the Jews among the lands outside of Israel.
2. A state of alienation.
3. Residence among others and insubordinate status.

This is the Hebrew word for "exile"—especially *the* exile of Jews from the Holy Land.

Gan Eden

Pronounced *gon* AY-*din*, to rhyme with "wan maiden." Hebrew: "Garden of Eden."

The Garden of Eden.

"God planted a garden eastward, in Eden," says Genesis, and there Adam and Eve dwelt in innocent bliss—until their curiosity got the better of them, and all of us. This story was almost certainly borrowed from Babylonian mythology.

Where was Eden? Popular theory placed it between the Tigris and Euphrates rivers.

Now, the Talmudists and cabalists are persuaded that there were *two* gardens of Eden: the luxuriant garden on earth; and one in the heavens, the eternal abode of all the righteous after death. This celestial *Gan Eden* was (and is) synonymous with Paradise.

When a man dies, his good deeds are weighed against his bad deeds. The tipping scales indicate his fate—*Gan Eden*, or *Gehenna*.

Men's early images of Paradise were singularly simple—and naive. The celebrated Talmudic savant, Rab, said: "In *Gan Eden* there is no eating, no drinking, no cohabitation, no business, no envy, no hatred or ambition; but the righteous sit with crowned heads and enjoy the luster of the *Shekhinah*

(Divine Presence)." But Maimonides remarked, "To believe so is to be a schoolboy who expects nuts and sweetmeats as compensation for his studies. Celestial pleasures can neither be measured nor comprehended by a mortal being, any more than the blind man can distinguish colors or the deaf appreciate music."

See GEHENNA.

A rabbi once dreamed that he was in *Gan Eden*. There he saw all the sages, sitting and studying *Talmud*.

"Is this all there is to Paradise?" he exclaimed. "Why, we do this on earth!"

An angel answered, "Ah, you think the scholars are in *Gan Eden*, but you are wrong. It is the other way round: *Gan Eden* is in the scholars."

The Mezeritzer *Maggid* said: "A man's good deeds are used by the Lord as seeds for the planting of trees in the Garden of Eden. Thus each man creates his own Paradise. . . ."

gaon

Pronounced GUY-*awn*, or *guy*-AWN, to rhyme with "high lawn"; or GA-*own*. Hebrew: "genius," "learned." Plural: *geonim, guy*-AW-*nim*.

1. The head of a Talmudic academy.
2. A rabbi whose learning was so great that he was given the honorary title of *gaon*.
3. A genius.

The title *gaon* was held by the heads of the Talmudic academies of Babylonia from 589 to 1040. Then the title fell into disuse; it was later revived and again applied to a rabbi of exceptional learning.

The *geonim* judged religious questions. Questions were sent them from all parts of the Diaspora, and they provided the *responsa*.

Saadiah Gaon (892–942) translated the Bible into Arabic, wrote a Biblical commentary, defended the *Talmud* against the Karaite sect, and wrote a book that argues that Judaism rests on reason.

The *Gaon* of Vilna (1720–1797), Talmudic genius and implacable opponent of Chasidism, was one of the outstanding Jewish figures of eastern Europe. Aside from his extraordinary Talmudic studies, he recognized the need for secular learning; he wrote a book on mathematics and a Hebrew grammar.

The famous Duvner *maggid*, a *gaon*, was asked by an admiring student: "How is it that you always have the perfect parable for the topic under discussion?"

The *gaon* smiled. "I'll answer with a parable." And he told the following story:

A lieutenant of the Tsar's cavalry, riding through a small *shtetl*, drew his horse up in astonishment, for on the side of a barn he saw a hundred chalked circles—and in the center of each was a bullet hole! The lieutenant excitedly stopped the first passerby, crying. "Who is the astonishing marksman in this place? Look at all those bull's-eyes!"

The passerby sighed. "That's Shepsel, the shoemaker's son, who is a little peculiar."

"I don't care what he is," said the lieutenant. "Any man who can shoot that well—"

"Ah," the pedestrian said, "you don't understand. You see, first Shepsel shoots—*then* he draws the circle."

The *gaon* smiled. "That's the way it is with me. I don't search for a parable to fit the subject. I introduce the subject for which I have a perfect parable."

gefilte fish
gefulte fish

Pronounced ge-FILL-*teh fish*. From the German: "stuffed fish."

Fish cakes or fish loaf, made of various fishes which are chopped or ground and mixed with eggs, salt, and lots of onions and pepper. (Sometimes with sugar.) The traditional Friday night fish, served at the Sabbath dinner.

I find *gefilte fish* delicious, hot or cold, and recommend that red or white *chrayn* (horseradish) be handy, to dip the fish into, to suit your palate.

Recipes for *gefilte fish* can be found in many cookbooks.

A waiter brought a smoked fish to a customer, who studied it, sniffed at it, then leaned down and began to talk to the fish in a confidential whisper.

"Mister," asked the startled waiter, "what are you doing?"

"I'm talking to this fish."

"Talking to a *fish??*"

"Certainly. I happen to know seven fish languages."

"But what did you tell him?"

"I asked him where he was from, and he answered, 'From Peconic Bay.' So I asked him how things are in Peconic Bay, and he answered, 'How should I know? It's *years* since I was there!'"

Gehenna
Gehena

> Pronounced g'-HEN-*a* or gay-HEN-*a*, to rhyme with "say when a." Hebrew: *Gehinom:* "Hell." Literally: the Valley *(gay)* of Hinnom.

> Hell.

In the "valley of the sons of Hinnom" south of Jerusalem, says the Bible, children were sacrificed to the idol Moloch. For this reason, the valley was said to be accursed; *Gay-Hinnom*, or *Gehenna*, became synonymous with Hell. But Hell, according to early but "apocryphal" texts, is not located in the netherworld, but in "the third heaven!" (Lubricious angels who consort with human females are allocated to the second heaven, and are flogged each day.) The *Midrash Tannaim* locates Hell as "side by side" with Paradise.*

The *Talmud* pictures *Gehenna* as a dark place, filled with everlasting fire and sulfurous fumes. (The hot springs and

* See Gustav Davidson, *A Dictionary of Angels*, Free Press, 1967, p. xvii.

sulfuric smells of the medicinal waters of Tiberias were said to have their origin in *Gehenna*.)

Gehenna is the abode of the wicked after death. Some of the sins which lead to it are unchastity, adultery, idolatry, pride, mockery, and hypocrisy. (The *Talmud* contains a folk saying that Hell awaits one who always follows the advice of his wife.)

Gehenna may also exist on earth: "His life with her is a *Gehenna*." Conversely, it may be a *Gan Eden*.

Purgatory, incidentally, is nowhere named in the Bible, but was made official by Roman Church councils from the thirteenth century on. (Back in the third century, the celebrated scholar Origen had said that souls wait in a fearful place to be "purged of evil" so they may enter the Kingdom of Heaven "undefiled.") The Church of England scorned Purgatory as "grounded upon no warranty of Scripture, but rather repugnant to the Word of God."*

"Better to be in *Gehenna* with a wise man than in *Gan Eden* (Paradise) with a fool."

—FOLK SAYING

Jack Wishnograd was reading the obituaries in the morning paper when, to his astonishment, he read his own name! As his eyes raced down the column, his stupefaction rose: The entire obituary was his—every date, place, fact of his life! Wishnograd dashed to the phone and called his lawyer.

"Hello, Irwin? Did you read this morning's paper?"

"Sure. Who is this?"

"What do you mean 'Who is this?' It's me, Jack! I want you to sue——"

"*Jack?*" cried the lawyer.

"Certainly! I want you to——"

"Where are you calling from?"

gelt

Rhymes with "felt." From German: *Geld:* "money."

Money.

---

* Gustav Davidson, *ibid.*, p. xvii.

Gelt, like *shekels* or *mazuma,* has long been a part of American slang. (*See* SHEKEL, MAZUMA.) "Where did he stash the *gelt?*" "He'll do anything for *gelt.*"

George S. Kaufman, a prince of wit, once remarked that he liked to write with his collaborator, Moss Hart, because Hart was so lucky. "In my case," said Kaufman, "it's *gelt* by association."

Gemara

See MISHNAH and TALMUD.

Gematria

> Pronounced ge-MOT-*ree-a,* to rhyme with "the spot Rea." From the Greek: *geometria.*

> The use of letters as numerals; numerology.

In Hebrew, the letters of the alphabet also served the ancients as numbers (see Appendix: Gematria): *aleph* = 1, *bet* = 2, etc. Each letter, hence each word or phrase, possessed a numerical "value." Mystics converted the numerical values into supposed keys to the meanings of passages in the holy texts, and "equated" different words and phrases according to the total values of their letters: this naturally yielded startling coincidences. Where neither statistics nor probability theory existed, abracadabra could flourish uncontested.

Gematria starts with the premise, not uncommon to true believers, that the words in a holy text contain hidden and apocalyptic messages. (God, for reasons I have never understood, is often credited by His faithful with vast, calculated obscurity.) When one finds different phrases with the same numerical value, this presumably indicates a relationship in thought—which should reveal a new meaning or resolve an old ambiguity.

Here is a pretty example of *Gematria:* The Hebrew word for "pregnancy," *herayon,* turns out to have the numerical value of 270, which is also 30 times 9—"the number of days a woman carries a child." *Voilà!*

The manipulation of numbers for arcane purposes proliferated in the Middle Ages, when it became a popular mode of Biblical and Talmudic interpretation. Many scholars played with *Gematria* in the hope of discovering the exact date the Messiah was scheduled to arrive. Many extravagant hopes were raised and affixed to dates which were interpreted as foretelling when the heavenly Messiah would rescue the Jews from no-longer-endurable suffering and despair. Professor Hugh Trevor-Roper observes that "when Popes and Kings allied themselves with the blind prejudices of the Church and the mob . . . whither then were the persecuted remnant to turn for relief . . . but to that stock refuge of the oppressed: mysticism, the Messiah, the Millennium?"[*]

Nor were Jews alone in their preoccupation with miraculous deliverance. The Muslims, too, dreamed of supernatural salvation; seventeenth-century Anabaptists made their own mathematical hocus-pocus out of Holy Scripture to help along the Apocalypse; and otherwise sober Englishmen, the Millenarians, claimed to have found the exact date of the Second Coming.

The misterioso approach to Biblical exegesis was extensively followed in cabalistic literature, of course. Many ingenious, albeit ludicrous, rules were developed to govern the permutation of letters, words, and phrases in the quest for God's secrets.

For more examples, see Appendix: Gematria.

geshmat
geshmott

> Pronounced ge-SHMOTT, to rhyme with "the hot." From the Hebrew root *shemad*, from which are derived words meaning "destruction," "annihilation," and "apostasy." The connection between the two meanings is rooted in history.

1. Converted from one faith to another. *Geshmat* gen-

---

[*] Hugh Trevor-Roper, *Historical Essays*, Macmillan, 1963, p. 148.

erally describes a Jew who is converted to the Christian faith, rather than a Gentile who converts to Judaism.

2. A marked change in belief or conduct. (This usage is less common than the first.)

Jews are not proselytizers. Rabbis are required to make three separate efforts to discourage a would-be convert.

A Bulgarian (of all things) proverb goes: "When you baptize a Jew, hold him under water for five minutes."

". . . in converting Jews to Christians you raise the price of pork." *The Merchant of Venice*, Act III, Scene v.

Daniel Abramovich Chwolson (1819–1910), a Jewish professor under the Tsars, had been converted to the Greek Orthodox faith. When asked if he had done this out of conviction or expedience, he dryly replied, "I accepted baptism entirely out of conviction—the conviction that it is better to be a professor in the Imperial Academy in St. Petersburg than a teacher in a *cheder* in Vilna." (Another version goes ". . . than a *melamed* in Eyshishok.")

Daniel Abramovich Chwolson is an extraordinary figure, a noted scholar who, after his conversion, courageously defended the Jews during the odious Saratov trial, in which the ghastly canard that Jews drink Christian blood in religious services was once again dragged out. Chwolson taught Hebrew in a Roman Catholic seminary from 1858 to 1884 and often delivered lectures denouncing the heinous "blood accusation." He wrote several scholarly volumes about these libels and even persuaded the Tsar's brother to change his mind about "ritual murders."*

Heine dryly called a baptism certificate "the passport to European civilization."

Berele, the pickpocket, was brought before a judge who had been converted to Christianity.

---

* See David Gunzberg's brief "Daniel Chwolson; A Christian Jew," in the excellent anthology *The Golden Tradition*, Lucy S. Dawidowicz, editor. Holt, Rinehart and Winston, 1967.

"Your Honor," cried Berele, "I am confused!"

"Confused? Why?"

"I don't know whether to appeal to the quality of mercy that lives on in your Jewish heart, or to the Christian forgiveness you have recently adopted."

On a bitterly cold, snowy, dreadful night, in a Polish town, old Salkowitz, feeling his time had come, called to his wife: "Shurele, please, send someone to the priest and tell him to come right away—I am dying!"

"The priest? You must have a fever! You mean the rabbi."

"I mean the priest!" snapped Salkowitz.

"May God protect us! Are you secretly *geshmat?*"

"No, no; but why disturb the rabbi on a night like this?"

When Messrs. Ginsberg and Grabow, both *geshmat,* opened their new store, they decided, for tactical reasons, to call it "O'Neill and O'Neill."

On their very first day, a customer asked one of the salesmen, "I want to see Mr. O'Neill."

"Which Mr. O'Neill do you want?" replied the salesman. "Ginsberg or Grabow?"

gesundheit

Pronounced ge-ZUND-*hite,* to rhyme with "the Bund kite." German: "health."

1. Health.

Someone once said you can tell if a man is a Jew by how he answers the question: "How are you?" If he says, "Fine!" or "Couldn't be better," he's no Jew. For Jews, by tradition, fear that boasting (of good health or good luck) may attract some jealous and punishing evil spirit. The typical Jewish reply to "How do you feel?" is "Not bad," or "So-so."

2. The verbal amenity uttered when someone sneezes.

"Kerchoo!"

"Gesundheit!"

"Gesundheit!" is as obligatory a response to a heard sneeze as *"Aleichem sholem"* is to the greeting, *"Sholem aleichem."*

"Your health comes first; you can always hang yourself later."
——FOLK SAYING

Apocryphal, but not the less amusing:

When an El Al plane leaves New York, the pilot greets the passengers in these words: *"Sholem aleichem,* ladies and gentlemen, and welcome to El Al airlines. This is your pilot, Itzchak Levin, wishing you a happy, restful trip, which we certainly expect to have, God willing. And if by some remote chance we do run into trouble—God forbid!—do not panic, keep calm. Your life belt is under your seat. And if you must put it on, wear it in the best of health!"

get

Pronounced as in English. Hebrew: "divorce."

Divorce.

Rabbinical laws considered and ruled on divorces of every conceivable type, arising from almost every conceivable cause. The process and ritual entailed in a religious divorce was, and is, complex; only a small number of scholars, specially trained, can undertake the task.

A religious (as distinguished from a civil) divorce terminates a marriage among Orthodox Jews only if both husband and wife agree to it, and if the civil courts have already granted a civil divorce.

Reform rabbis do not, on the whole, ask for a religious divorce in addition to a civil divorce before husband or wife may remarry.

"To a wedding, walk; to a divorce, run."
——FOLK SAYING

gevalt!
gevald!

Pronounced ge-VOLLT!, the exclamation point being, at least psychologically, an inseparable part of the spelling. German: *Gewalt:* "powers," "force" (*höhere gewalt* is an "act of providence").

1. A cry of fear, astonishment, amazement. "*Gevalt!* What happened?"
2. A cry for help. "*Gevalt!* Help! Burglars!"
3. A desperate expression of protest: "*Gevalt,* Lord, enough already!"

Gevalt is a versatile, all-purpose word—used as both an explective and a noun. "She opened the door and cried, '*Gevalt!*'" "He took one look at her and let out a *gevalt!* you could hear in New Jersey." "Now take it easy, don't make a *gevalt.*"

"Man comes into the world with an *Oy!*—and leaves with a *gevalt!*"

—PROVERB

The special flavor of *gevalt!* is expressed in the story of the apocryphal Countess Misette de Rothschild, half-French, half-English, who lay in childbirth in the magnificent bedroom of her mansion off the *Champs-Elysées,* moaning and wailing. Downstairs, her husband, the Count, wrung his hands anxiously.

"Come, come," said the obstetrician. "She's not ready to deliver. Let's play cards. There's plenty of time."

They played cards for a while.

From above, came the shrill cry of the Countess: "*Mon Dieu! Mon Dieu!*"

The husband leaped up.

"No, no," said the doctor. "Not yet. Plenty of time. Play."

They played on.

Soon the Countess screamed: "Oh, God, oh *God!*"

Up leaped the haggard husband.

"No," said the doctor. "Not yet. Deal."
The husband dealt. . . . They played on.
Came a resonant: *"Ge-valt!"*
Up rose the obstetrician. "Now."

gilgul

Pronounced GILL-*g'l*, to rhyme with "sill pull." From Hebrew: *gilgul*, "rolling" (as of a wheel) or "turning" (as of a wheel). Plural: *gilgulim*, pronounced *gill*-GOO-*lim.*

1. (Literally) A turning or rolling, as of a wheel.
2. (More importantly) A reincarnation; someone with a reincarnated soul.
3. (Sarcastically) A person whose behavior, irrationality, stupidity, tactlessness, can only be explained by assuming that he is a *gilgul.* "That man is a *gilgul* of a horse!" "Such stubbornness you find only in the *gilgul* of a jackass." "Such crazy behavior comes only from a *gilgul* of a hyena."

Do not confuse a *gilgul* with a *dybbuk*, who is a demon. The idea of the *gilgul*, of the reincarnation of souls, of metempsychosis, plays an important role in Jewish cabalism and the writings of the *Chasidim.*

The idea of the transmigration of souls after death into the body of another mortal or animal is of course found in many "mystery religions" of the East. It was found among the Egyptians, in India and Persia, in certain Greek cults, among the Pythagoreans, and in the Mithraic and Zoroastrian creeds.

The history of medicine, and especially of efforts made to understand and alleviate mental disorders, is replete with the problems presented by evil demons who "possess" the unfortunate: spirits, devils, incubi, *et alia.*

See D. Atkinson, *Magic, Myth and Medicine*, World, 1956; G. Zilboorg and G. W. Henry, *A History of Medical Psychology*, Norton, 1951; and F. G. Alexander and S. T. Selesnick, *The History of Psychiatry*, Harper & Row, 1966.

See the entries: DYBBUK, CABALA, CHASID, ZOHAR.

glitch

Pronounced GLITCH, to rhyme with "pitch." German: *glitschen,* "slip."

1. A slide; to slide or skid on a slippery surface. "Be careful not to *glitch.*"
2. A risky undertaking or enterprise. "Be careful. It could be a *glitch.*"
3. A shady, not *kosher* or reputable affair.

The adjective is *glitchidig,* pronounced GLITCH-*i-dik.* To warn your child that the pavement is *glitchidig* seems to me delightful. Not, mind you, that "slippery" is any slouch as a word. *Glitchidig* just takes longer, and lingers in the ear.

goldeneh medina

Pronounced GOLD-*en-eh* m'-DEE-*nah. Goldeneh* is from German for "golden"; *medina* is Hebrew for "country," "land," "province."

(1) Literally, "golden country."

Goldeneh medina meant America: land of freedom, justice, opportunity—and protection against pogroms. Rarely did I hear such overtones of gratitude as went into the utterance of this compound noun.

That America's streets were "paved with gold" was more than a metaphor to the millions in Europe who dreamed of coming here.

(2) A fool's paradise.

In irony or sarcasm, *goldeneh medina* is used to mean a miraculous hope that ends in disappointment.

A poor tailor who lived in a cellar and slaved for a pittance once voiced his bitterness by describing New York as "Some *goldeneh medina!*"

A lady from Brooklyn was watching a parade on Fifth Avenue.

"Look!" someone cried. "There goes the Mayor of Dublin —and he's a Jew!"

"Ai-ai-ai," clucked the matron. "Where could such a thing happen? Only in this *goldeneh medina!"*

golem

Pronounced GO-*lem,* to rhyme with "dole 'em," or GOY-*lem,* to rhyme with "boil 'em." From Hebrew: "matter without shape," "a yet-unformed thing." (Psalms, 139 : 16)

1. A robot; a lifeless figure.
2. A simpleton, a fool.
3. A clumsy man or woman; a clod; someone who is all thumbs, poorly coordinated.
4. A slow-moving man or woman.
5. A graceless, tactless type.
6. Someone who is subnormal.

Typical phrases: "He looks like a *golem.* He walks like a *golem.* He is as slow-witted as a *golem.* He barely gets around, poor *golem."*

The *Talmud* poetically speculates: "How was Adam created? In the first hour, his dust was collected; in the second hour, his form was fashioned; in the third, he became a shapeless mass *(golem);* . . . in the sixth he received a soul; in the seventh hour, he rose and stood on his feet. . . ."

A *golem* can be virtuous, kind, just, said Maimonides, but his intellectual capacities are arrested.

The most famous of these imaginary creatures was the Golem of Prague. In the seventeenth century, a legend grew around Rabbi Judah Lowe (or Löw) of Prague, a renowned scholar who was supposed to have created a *golem* to help protect the Jews from many calamities the anti-Semites attempted. The *golem* helped Rabbi Lowe bring criminals to justice; he exposed spreaders of anti-Semitic canards; he saved an innocent girl from apostasy by force; he even discovered in the nick of time that the Passover *matzos* had been poisoned! Rabbi Lowe, the story went, removed all life from the *golem* every Friday, for he would not allow the creature any mobility that might desecrate the Sabbath.

A well-known play, *Der Goilem*, modeled on *Faust*, sensitively written in Yiddish, in 1921, by the Jewish poet Leivick Halpern (1888–1962), who wrote as H. Leivick, was performed for years all over Europe and America. The story of the *golem* was made into a movie several times: in French, German, Yiddish.

Perhaps the most famous literary treatment of a *golem* is Meyrink's, in German, translated by Pemberton.

Mary Shelley, who wrote *Frankenstein*, may have gotten the idea from the *golem* legends.

Would you believe that volume IV (F–G) of the great *Oxford English Dictionary* has no entry for *golem*? Nor the *Encyclopaedia Britannica*? Nor the *Encyclopedia Americana*? Heavens.

When the scientists at the great Weizmann Institute in Rehovoth, Israel, built their first large electronic computer, they dubbed it "Golem I."

gonif
gonef
gonov

Pronounced GON-*iff*, to rhyme with "Don if." Hebrew: *ganov:* "thief."

1. Thief, crook.
2. A clever person.
3. An ingenious child.
4. A dishonest businessman.
5. A shady, tricky character it would be wise (a) not to trust, (b) to watch every minute he's in the store.
6. A mischievous, fun-loving prankster.

The particular meaning depends, of course, on context, tone of voice, inflection, accompanying gestures.

(A) If uttered with a beam, a grin, an accompanying "Tchk! Tchk!" or an admiring raise of the hands, *gonif* is clearly laudatory. Thus, a proud grandparent will say of a child, metaphorically, "Oh, is that a *gonif!*" (God forbid you should think a grandparent is lauding a child's criminal characteristics.)

(B) If uttered with pulled-down mouth, in a lugubrious tone, or with heartfelt dismay ("A *gonif* like that shouldn't be allowed among respectable citizens"), the meaning is derogatory.

(C) Uttered in steely detachment ("That one is, plain and simple, a *gonif*"), the word describes a crook, thief, purloiner, trickster.

(D) Said in admiration, with a wink, cluck, or shake of the head ("I tell you, there is a *gonif!*"), the phrasing is equivalent to: "What a man!" or "There's a clever cookie."

(E) The usage I find most interesting is the one I often heard as a child, and sorely puzzled over: "America *gonif!*"

In that phrase was (and is) wrapped admiration, awe, gratitude, and a declaration of possibilities beyond belief and without limit. To say "America *gonif*" was to say: "Anything is possible in this wonderful land." "America is a miracle!" "America? Inventiveness, resourcefulness, ingenuity—and that's what it rewards." "Where but in America could such a thing happen?"

If you wish to express some of these sentiments *vis-à-vis* a person, try *genavish* (pronounced ge-NAY-vish), which is simply *gonif* turned into an adjective. Thus: "He has a *genavish* (clever, diabolic) mind." "That lad has *genavish* (remarkable) ingenuity." "Take my advice, stay away from those *genavish* (clever, but tricky) ideas."

You can also say *genavisher*, which prolongs the descriptive titilation.

See GOZLIN.

Eric Partridge* avers that *gonif* has been used in England since 1835.

H. L. Mencken, in *The American Language,*** spells *gonif* as *ganov* and *gonov*, and attributes *gun* (to mean a gunman)

---

* *A Dictionary of Slang and Unconventional English,* Macmillan, 1961.

** Knopf, 1962.

and other peculiar derivatives to it. Absurd. A *gonif* is hardly a gunman.

"Carny" (carnival) folk use *gonov* to mean a fool, says Mencken, not a smart, sharp fellow. David Maurer* cites a similar meaning. I am surprised.

In the *American Thesaurus of Slang,*** compiled by Berrey and Van den Bark, *gonif* is cited with these variant spellings: *gonef, gonof, gonoph.* All I can say to such improvisations is that only a *gonif* would dream up such orthography.

The first day home from school, little Milton's mother ran out eagerly to meet him.

"So what did you learn?"

"I learned to write," said Milton.

"On the first day already you learned to *write*? America *gonif!* So what did you write?"

"How should I know?" said Milton. "I can't read."

"A man is not honest simply because he never had a chance to steal."

—FOLK SAYING

Gott

Pronounced *GAWT*, to rhyme with "taught." From German: *Gott:* "God."

God.

(But see ADONAI, ADOSHEM, GOTTENYU.)

Gottenyu!

Pronounced GAWT-*en-yew!* (*Gott* rhymes with "caught," not "cot.") From German: *Gott:* "God."

"Dear God," "Oh, dear God," or "How-else-can-I-describe-my-feelings!"

---

* *American Speech*, 1931.
** Crowell, 1943.

Gottenyu! is an exclamation that is uttered with affection, despair, or irony, to lend force to a sentence by adding fervor to sentiment.

It is a warm, informal, personal way of enlisting God's attention, *not* invoking his aid. Nor does it describe the Lord in any way.

It is a colloquial epithet used, for the most part, without really meaning God, *per Se* (I guess I must capitalize *Se* here). "Were we happy! *Gottenyu!*" "*Gottenyu!*—you never saw such a mess!" "Was I scared? Miserable? Oh, *Gottenyu!*" A common phrase is "*Zeeser Gottenyu,*" "Sweet God."

A charming dictum has it that, under stress, Jews exclaim, "*Oy, Mamanyu!*" When stress becomes fear they cry, "*Oy, Tatenyu!*" (*tata* being "father"). And when things *really* get tough, Jews cry, "*Oy, Gottenyu!*" Note the realistic stratification of power.

goy
goyish (adjective)
goyim (plural)

Rhymes with "boy," "boyish," "doyen." The plural is pronounced GOY-*im*. The adjective is *goyish* (neuter), *goyisher* (masculine), or *goyisheh* (feminine). From the Hebrew: *goy*: "nation."

1. A Gentile, i.e., anyone who is not a Jew. (This covers an enormous amount of ground.) A young male Gentile is a *shaygets*, the female a *shikseh*.

(a) It is important to note that the idea of respect for others and the values of a pluralistic society form an old, integral part of Judaism and Jewish tradition. The rabbis taught that all men are equal in the eyes of God if they do the will of God: "Whether Jew or Gentile, man or woman, rich or poor—according to a man's *deeds* does God's presence rest on him."

(b) Mormons call any non-Mormon a Gentile; Jews are therefore Gentiles to Mormons; I have never met a Jew who quite knows how to adjust to this startling idea.

I once spent three happy days in Utah without observing any noticeable change in my disposition.

2. Someone who is dull, insensitive, heartless.

Just as some Gentiles use "Jew" as a contemptuous synonym for too-shrewd, sly bargaining ("He tried to Jew the price down," is about as unappetizing an idiom as I know), so some Jews use *goy* in a pejorative sense.

Relentless persecution of Jews, century after century, in nation after nation, left a legacy of bitter sayings: *"Dos ken nor a goy."* ("That, only a *goy* is capable of doing"); *"A goy bleibt a goy."* ("A Gentile remains a Gentile," or, less literally, "What did you expect? Once an anti-Semite, always an anti-Semite.")

Experience made many Jews feel that Gentiles are not gentle.

"Goyisher" or *"goyisheh kop"* means "Gentile brains" or "Gentile ways." It is not, alas, complimentary.

When endurance is exhausted, kindliness depleted, the effort to understand useless, the epithet, "A *goy!*" is used—just as, I suppose, Armenians say "Turk!" or Mexicans say "Gringo!" or Frenchmen "Boche!" or—but there is no end to the catalogue of xenophobic depreciation.

The rabbis long tried to moderate the bitterness of their flock: "A Gentile who observes the *Torah* is as good as a High Priest," wrote a fourth-century sage.

The *Sefer Hasidim,* a thirteenth-century work, says: "If a Jew attempts to kill a non-Jew, help the non-Jew."

The great Rashi, eleventh-century French rabbi, reminded Jews that Gentiles "of the present age are not heathens."

And in *Tosefta Baba Kamma* it is solemnly noted that to rob a non-Jew is more heinous than to rob a Jew—because such robbery "involves the desecration of the Name."

"Gentiles are not used to Jewish problems."

—FOLK SAYING

A London Jew became so prosperous that he changed his name from Nate Greenberg to Noel Greenhill, bought a fine home on Park Lane, and proceeded to acquire various *objets d'art*—including a beautiful painting by Rubens.

The following year, his affluence having increased, he exchanged the Rubens—for a Goya. . . .

On Houston Street, a young priest saw a large sign over a hardware store: PINCUS AND O'TOOLE.

The priest went in, to be greeted by a man with a beard and *yarmulkah*.

The priest smiled, "I just wanted to come in to tell you how wonderful it is to see that your people and mine have become such good friends—even partners. That's a surprise!"

"I've got a bigger surprise," sighed the old man. "I'm O'Toole."

Mr. O'Neill and Mr. Pinsky were chatting. O'Neill said, "Did you hear about the fight between Cooley and McGraw?"

"How could I miss it?" said Pinsky. "Wasn't it in front of my eyes?"

"I didn't know you were there."

"What then? I was maybe in the White House?"

"Whose fault was it: Cooley's?"

"Who else?"

O'Neill sighed, "Pinsky, *why* do Jews answer every question with another question?"

Pinsky pondered. "Why not?"

gozlin
gozlen

> Pronounced GOZ-*lin*, to rhyme with "Roslyn." Hebrew: *gozlon*: "one who deprives others of their rightful possessions by force."
>
> 1. A thief—but not a professional; a professional is a *gonif*.
> 2. A swindler, one who outwits others.
> 3. A merciless, rapacious, unethical person. "Who would have believed that he would turn into such a *gozlin*?"

"Not only did he break the commandment not to steal, he also stole the Bible."

—FOLK SAYING

graub
grauber
graubyon

Pronounced GRUB or GRAWB, to rhyme with "daub," and GRAW-*ber*. From the German *grob*, "coarse, uncouth, rough."

1. Coarse, crude, uncouth, vulgar; ill-mannered.
2. Ignorant; insensitive.

"A *grauber yung*" (exactly as "Jung") means a coarse young man, a crude fellow, an uneducated poltroon. Jews tend to equate education with gentleness, knowledge with considerateness.

In our house, *graub* was used as an expletive of forceful contempt: "He's *graub!*" meant the mortal under discussion was a goon, a vulgarian, one of low sensibility. "What a *graub* thing to do!" conveyed an ocean of scorn and dismay.

A *graubyon* is a person who is *graub*.

A rabbi came to the notoriously brutal governor of a province in Poland and pleaded for help for the many who were starving.

The *grauber* governor struck the rabbi across the face. "Jew, take that!"

The rabbi nodded. "That, sir, is for me. Now what will you give to my people?"

gridzheh

Pronounced GRID-*zheh*, to rhyme with "Ridge-ya." Slavic: "to gnaw."

Literally, to chew or to gnaw, the way an animal does, with sloppy, slobbering sounds; to grind one's teeth.

As used, *gridzheh* conveys the idea of carping, beefing, complaining, nagging. The grating sound of the word is itself unpleasant. "Stop *gridzhing*." "All she does is *gridzheh*." *"Es gridzhet mir"* means "It gripes me."

See also NUDZH, TCHEPPEH.

H

H

Habdala
Habdalah
Havdala

Pronounced, in Yiddish, *hahv-DOL-lah,* to rhyme with
"Bob lolla." Hebrew: "separation."

The ceremony that signalizes the ending of the Sabbath.

The sweet-sad rite that each week says farewell to "Queen
Sabbath" is performed by the male head of the family when
he comes home from the evening service *(mairev)* in the synagogue. He lights a braided candle and a saucer of alcohol, by
which he warms his hands with certain traditional gestures,
and, his family close to and around him, over a wine glass
he recites this solemn benediction: "Blessed art Thou, O Lord
our God, King of the Universe, who makes a distinction
between holy and profane, between light and darkness, between Israel and the nations, between the seventh day and
the six days of work." It is customary to sing a melody, to
either Hebrew or Yiddish words, asking God's grace for the
week ahead.

146

Then an ornamental box, in which spices are kept, is raised, its sweet aroma sniffed—to revive the spirit saddened by Sabbath's end.

The *Chasidim* used to celebrate the *Habdala* with rhapsodic dances in a circle, to which cabalistic significances were assigned.

Hadassah

Pronounced *ha-DAH-sah*, to rhyme with *"La casa."* Hebrew: "myrtle." *Hadassah* is the Hebrew and Yiddish form of the Biblical Esther.

1. Esther.
2. The Women's Zionist Organization of America.

Founded in 1912 by the remarkable Henrietta Szold, the *Hadassah* organization today has over 300,000 members in some 1200 chapters. It was originally organized to raise the standards of health, hygiene, and public medicine in Palestine, which was ridden by diseases; and to widen and deepen the awareness, among Jews in America, of Jewish traditions and ideals.

In Israel, *Hadassah*'s hospitals and services have made striking contributions to medicine. The Hadassah Medical School, the only one in Israel, is part of Hebrew University.

Haftarah
Haftorah

Pronounced *hoff-TOE-reh*, to rhyme with "doff Mona," or *hoff-TOY-reh*, to rhyme with "doff Moira." Hebrew: "end," "conclusion."

A chapter from the Prophets, read in the synagogue (after the portion from the Pentateuch) on Sabbaths and festivals.

The practice of reading a passage from the Prophets, after the *Torah* reading, has been observed since the first century. Each portion of the *Torah* has a specific *Haftarah* of its own.

The *Haftarah* is chanted with a special system of cantillation. A Jewish boy learns this cantillation and on his *Bar Mitzva* chants the *Haftarah* assigned to that Sabbath.

Haggadah
Agada

Pronounced *ha-GOD-da*, to rhyme with the way an Englishman pronounces "Nevada." Hebrew: "tale" or "telling."

1. The enormous repository of Jewish allegorical material, including historical episodes, theology, folklore, fable, prayers, parables, witticisms, anecdotes, ruminations, sermons, etc., etc., found in the *Talmud*. Scholars classify the material as exegetical and nonexegetical; history; religion and ethics; mysticism; eschatology—and even superstition.

The *Haggadah* appealed to the common people, for it contains a wealth of enchanting episodes and marvelous stories about scholars and saints and martyrs. Four qualities distinguish it, says Professor Judah Goldin: charm, extraordinary piety, ethical fervor, and affirmations of God's love for the children of Israel.*

2. The narrative that is read aloud at the Passover *Seder* piecing together, from many sources, the story of Israel's bondage in, and flight from, Egypt.

The *Haggadah* draws material from the book of Exodus and from the *Talmud*. It contains psalms, prayers, hymns—even several amusing jingles at the end to hold the interest of the children, who must sit through a very long ceremony and feast. When the youngest child asks "The Four Questions" on

---

* *The Jews: Their History, Culture and Religion*, Vol. I, pp. 163–164.

Passover, the father responds from the *Haggadah:* "Slaves were we unto Pharaoh in Egypt."

The *Haggadah* has grown down the centuries. Some of its contents trace back to ancient liturgy, but most of it is a creation of laymen throughout the years. The basic form seems to have been set in the second century; the first *Haggadah,* as a separate collection of prayers, appeared around the thirteenth century.

Prior to Gutenberg, the *Haggadahs* were, obviously, written out by copyists and calligraphers; some are as magnificent as only medieval illuminated manuscripts can be—with exquisitely ornamented Hebrew letters and lavish illustrations of Biblical events, the coming of the Messiah, the restoration of Zion. The library of the Jewish Theological Seminary in New York contains some marvelous old *Haggadahs.*

See PESACH.

haimish
haimisher (masculine)
haimisheh (feminine)

Pronounced HAME-*ish,* to rhyme with "Danish" or "Jameish." From German: *Heim:* "home."

1. Informal, cozy, warm.
2. Having the friendly characteristics, or kind of rapport, that exist inside a happy home.
3. Without "side," unpretentious; putting on no airs; unspoiled by office or honors.

The last usage is the most frequent. President Truman was ever so *haimish.* No one in his right mind would call Generals de Gaulle or MacArthur *haimish.*

Haimish is the opposite of snobbish, supercilious, or to get fancy about it, charismatic.

"A *haimisher mensh*" means someone with whom you can take your shoes off, or let your hair down.

Jews put a high value on being *haimish.*

Halakah
Halakha

Pronounced ha-LOKH-a, with the guttural kh sound of "Loch Lomond," for the second spelling, which is Yiddish; the first is Hebrew. Hebrew: "law."

Jewish Law—and accumulated jurisprudence: that is, the decisions of the sages, but without Biblical citations, notes, references. The Halakah simply states the laws crisply, as in a code.

The great rabbis did not "create" Halakah: What the rabbis did was to codify and clarify the legal teachings, adapting them to changed social conditions. "The Rabbinic Halakah," writes Judah Goldin, "protected legislation from inflexibility and society from fundamentalism."*

The Talmud is composed of Halakah and Haggadah. Note the difference between the Haggadah of the Talmud and the Haggadah used as part of the Passover Seder.

halava
halavah

See HALVAH.

halevai
alevai

Pronounced hah-liv-EYE, to rhyme with "dollify." An Aramaic word, found quite frequently in the Talmud.

"Would that," "Oh that . . ." meaning I hope, I wish, I hope so, I wish I had, if only I had, etc.

---

* Judah Goldin, "The Period of the Talmud," in The Jews: Their History, Culture and Religion, Vol. I, third edition, Louis Finkelstein, editor. Harper, 1960, p. 159.

Jewish women sprinkle *halevai* around generously in conversation: *"Halevai* (if only) she should meet a nice boy!" "Sick? He's dying, the poor man—*halevai* (I hope) I am wrong." "Next year could be better, *halevai.*" "He has a chance of getting into Harvard. *Halevai!*" "They warned me a hundred times. I should have listened. *Halevai.*"

He sat there, sighing and moaning and ruminating thusly: "Oh, if only the Holy One, blessed be His name, would give me $10,000, I promise I would give a thousand to the poor. *Halevai!* . . . And if the Holy One doesn't trust me, He can deduct the thousand in advance and just give me the balance."

halla

See CHALLA.

halvah
halavah

Pronounced *holl*-VAH, to rhyme with "solve uh," or *holl-a*-VAH, to rhyme with "doll of uh," or *khal*-VAH, with the German *ch*. From Turkish: *helva,* and Arabic: *halva.*

A very sweet, flaky confection of distinctive texture made of honey and ground-up sesame seeds; streaks of chocolate are sometimes mixed in.

Halvah, which crumbles into sticky flakes in the mouth, is a "treat," *nosh* or dessert prized by those with a more-than-average sweet tooth. It is found in Turkish, Syrian and Armenian food stores, and in many delicatessens in Jewish neighborhoods in the United States. *Halvah* is a particular favorite of children.

The confection is made up in oblong blocks, about 12 inches × 3, from which a portion is sliced off according to the size requested by the customer.

Contrary to demotic mythology, *halvah* is not a "Jewish" goody and is not typical of Jewish comestibles. It was un-

known to the Jews of eastern Europe (perhaps Jews in some
Balkan areas knew it) who first encountered it in New York
where it was sold by Turkish, Syrian, Armenian vendors. Its
popularity spread swiftly, because it was sweet and cheap,
but today seems to have lost a good deal of its appeal. It is
almost impossible to eat very much of it.

Hanuka
Hannuka

See CHANUKA.

hasseneh

See CHASSENEH.

Hasid
Hasidim
Hassid
Hassidic
Hassidim

See CHASID.

hazzen

See CHAZZEN.

hamantash

Pronounced HAW-*men-tosh*, to rhyme with "Jaw men

bosh." Presumably named after Haman (see below); *tasch* is German for "pocket."

A special cake: a triangular "pocket" of dough filled with poppy seed or prune jelly. The plural is *hamantashen*, and children love them.

Hamantashen are the triangular little cakes that are special treats during the Feast of *Purim*, a happy day that celebrates the foiling of the plot of Haman, first minister to King Ahasuerus, who wanted to destroy all the Jews in Persia.

See PURIM.

Haskala
Haskalah

Pronounced *has*-KOL-*la*, to rhyme with "La Scala." Hebrew: "knowledge," "education," "erudition."

The movement of enlightenment, intellectual emancipation, libertarian and secular education among Jews, like the European Enlightenment of the eighteenth century.

Haskala was bitterly denounced and resisted by many rabbis, by Orthodox Jews, by fundamentalists—all of whom recognized the grave threat that secular education, and Western rationalism and philosophy, posed to traditional faith and orthodoxy.

Those who followed and furthered the *Haskala* called themselves "enlightened ones" or *Maskilim* (singular: *Maskil*).

The founder of the *Haskala* was the philosopher Moses Mendelssohn (1729–1786; he was the model for Lessing's *Nathan the Wise*), who was determined to end the superstition, the intellectual conformity, the poverty and social backwardness, of ghetto and *shtetl* life. He attracted collaborators and students from all over Europe. Mendelssohn inveighed against Judaism's "narrow labyrinth of ritual—theological casuistry." He opened the first school of Jews to include courses in German, French, geography, mathematics. Mendelssohn's disciples published a Hebrew magazine (*Ha-Me'-*

assef) that served to channel to Jewry the whole ferment of ideas, literature, and political liberalism that swept Europe after the French Revolution. The *Haskala* transformed Hebrew itself into a living, changing language—a Hebrew that came to be used by poets, novelists, journalists, and the man in the street.

It laid the groundwork for the strong social-democratic movement that captured the imagination of young Jews; it served to encourage the entry of Jews into politics; it spurred interest in agriculture and manual labor. It also aroused strong nationalism amongst some Jews, just as the Napoleonic era galvanized nationalist feelings among Germans, Italians, Poles. The *Haskala* was the forerunner of Reform Judaism in religion, and Zionism in politics.

Hashem

Pronounced *ha*-SHEM, to rhyme with "bosh hem." Hebrew: "The Name."

One of the words used in referring to God.

See ADOSHEM.

Hatikvah
Hatikva

Pronounced *ha*-TICK-*vuh*, to rhyme with "a kick huh." Hebrew: "the hope."

The national anthem of Israel.

The song *Hatikvah* was written in 1878 by Naftali Herz Imber, and set to music by Samuel Cohen. It was adopted as the Jewish national anthem at the first Zionist Congress in Basel, 1897.

When the state of Israel was established in 1948 *Hatikvah*, with a slight change in its wording, became the national anthem.

Hillul Hashem
Hillul ha-Shem

See CHILLUL HASHEM.

hok a tchynik
hak a chainik

> Pronounced TCHY-*nik*, to rhyme with "Guy Nick" (with the *tch* as in "church"). *Hok* is "strike," *tchynik* is "teapot," "tea kettle," from the Slavic: *tchay*, "tea."

> I would not dream of burdening your mind with *hok a tchynik*, "knock a kettle," or "beat a tea kettle," if that's all it meant. To "knock a teapot" means:
> 1. To talk a great deal; to yammer, to yak.
> 2. To talk nonsense or "bushwa."

This is a widely used phrase in the conversational badminton of Jews. "Please, *hok nit kain tchynik!*" ("Please, stop talking so much"; "Stop spouting all that nonsense"; "Stop talking my ear off.")

The expression may have come from the meaningless rattling of a cover of a boiling pot, or from the noisy whistling of steam in a kettle. Or it may have come from the improvised toys of children at play. Since toys were a rarity among the poor in the *shtetl,* children made use of ordinary objects. To simulate a drummer or a band, it was easy enough to bang away on a pot or kettle.

In any case, "knocking a teapot" has become a picturesque phrase for constant chatter.

holdupnik
holdupnick

> Pronounced *hold*-UP-*nick.* Yinglish.

One with a penchant for robbing—i.e., holding up—people.*

hoo-ha!

Pronounced WHO HAH!, to rhyme with "Poo Bah."

An immensely impressive Yiddishism for the expression of:
1. Admiration. "His new house? *Hoo-ha!*"
2. Astonishment. "*She* ran away? *Hoo-ha!*"
3. Envy. "Did he marry a pretty girl? *Hoo-ha!*"
4. Skepticism. "I can't lose? *Hoo-ha?!*"
5. Deflation. "He calls himself a singer—*hoo-ha!*"
6. Scorn. "Some friend. *Hoo-ha!*"

Also used, depending on vocal emphasis and accompanying facial expression, to convey the meaning of:

1. "Imagine that!" ("Left his wife? *Hoo-ha!*")
2. "You don't mean it!" ("Her, *hoo-ha?!*")
3. "Well, whaddaya know!" or "I'll be damned." ("Right in the middle of the lecture, *hoo-ha!*, he stood up and left!")
4. "Wow!" ("What a party! *Hoo-ha!*")
5. "Who do you think you're fooling?" ("Sure, I believe every word, *hoo-ha!*")
6. "That'll be the day!" ("He wants to be President, *hoo-ha!*")
7. "Like hell!" ("I'll give him a present, *hoo-ha!*")

Hotzeplotz

Pronounced HOTS-*eh-plotz*, to rhyme with "lots o' cots."

1. A town in Silesia.
2. "Way to hell-and-gone," "Way out in the sticks," "God only knows where." "I went from here to *Hotzeplotz* looking for you!" "They sent him to a new post

---

* See Bernard Malamud, *The Magic Barrel*, p. 206.

all the way in *Hotzeplotz*. . . ." "Lost? We could have been in *Hotzeplotz!*"

Hotzeplotz is recommended as a ploy, for use with hitch-hikers, drunks, obnoxious colleagues, or people who latch on to you during a taxi strike and ask could you just drop them off, it's only forty-three blocks out of your way. Thus: "Sorry, but we're going to *Hotzeplotz*," or "Where do I live? In *Hotzeplotz*."

See also SHNIPPISHOK.

hozzer

See CHOZZER.

huppe

See CHUPPA.

hutspa
hutzpah

See CHUTZPA.

in mitn derinnen

> Pronounced *in* MIT-*ten* *d'*RIN-*nen*. German: "in the middle of the thing"; Hebrew: *ilian* (?) *inen:* "subject," "idea."

> Out of the blue; all of a sudden; for no reason.

I happen to be fond of this phrase. Tossed into an English sentence, it underlines the inexplicable, stresses the illogic of an act, or calls attention to the insufficiency of a cause.

"We were discussing the concert when, *in mitn derinnen,* he starts to criticize the President!"

"She was telling me about their trip to Europe when, *in mitn derinnen,* her husband brought up his cavities!"

"What makes you say that, *in mitn derinnen?*"

in mitske derinnen

> A popular and potent variation of *in mitn derinnen.*

Little Benny was watching his mother bake cookies. He stood

there for a long time, then said, "Mamma, why don't you ask me something?"

"What should I ask you, *in mitske derinnen?*"

"You could ask me, 'You want a cookie, Benny?'"

J

Jehovah

Pronounced (in English) *Jee*-HO-*vah*. Not a Yiddish
word. It is not a Hebrew word. It is some scribe's Latin
transliteration of *YHVH*, to which the vowel marks for
"Adonai" had been added. The word appeared for the
first time in an English text in 1530.

God.

Yahveh, which was mistranslated into *Jehovah*, is the word
formed by adding vowel sounds to the Tetragrammaton, the
four Hebrew letters that stand for the Mystical and Ineffable
Name of God. The English equivalents of the Hebrew letters
are *YHVH* (called *yud, hay, vav, hay*).

These letters were the Unutterable Name, so the Masoretes
(who observed the tradition of *Masorah*, interpretive notes
for the "correct" spelling and meaning of ancient Hebrew
texts) added vowel marks to *YHVH* as a signal to readers to
say "Adonai" instead; and this *combination* was mistakenly
transliterated into Latin as JeHoVa(H)—or Jehova(h)—so

used for the first time in the year 1516, says the *Oxford English Dictionary*. This is as clear as I can make it.

See ADONAI, and Appendix: The Names of God.

An aging Jew, crossing the street in front of a church, was knocked down by a hit-and-run driver. As he lay there, half conscious, a priest hurried out, knelt, and prepared to administer the last rites. "Do you believe in God the Father, God the Son, and God the Holy Ghost?"

Cried the old man, "I'm dying and he asks me riddles!"

Judesmo

See LADINO.

K

kabala
kabbala

See CABALA.

kabtzen
koptzen
kabtzonim (plural)

> Pronounced KOP-*tz'n*, to rhyme with "Hopson." Hebrew: *kabotz:* "to collect." The plural is *kabtzonim* (kop-TZU-nim), and they will always be among us.

> 1. A pauper (literally; but the word is used as much for disdain as for description).
> 2. One who does not amount to anything and never will.

"Kabtzen!" is often uttered with a sneer, and is clearly a judgment about someone inferior or ineffectual. "Him pick

up a check? He's a *kabtzen*." "God forbid you should even think of marrying such a *kabtzen!*"

"Poverty is no disgrace—which is the only good thing you can say about it."

—FOLK SAYING

An ebullient *shadchen* (matchmaker) brought his young male prospect to the home of a potential bride.

When they started homeward, the *shadchen* said, "Well, was I exaggerating? Isn't that a doll of a girl? And can you imagine what a *dowry* she'll bring you! Did you see the furnishings in that house? The fine hangings? That collection of fine silver?!"

"But the father seemed awfully eager . . ." said the young man uneasily.

"She has a dozen suitors!"

"The mother kept pushing, hinting . . ."

"She *likes* you!"

"For all I know, they even borrowed all that silver just to impress me!"

"*Borrowed* it?" cried the *shadchen*. "Who would lend a nickel to such *kabtzonim?*"

Mendele Mocher Seforim, "Mendele the Bookseller," penname of Solomon J. Abramovich (1836–1917), whom Sholom Aleichem dubbed *"Der Zayde,"* the "grandfather," of Yiddish literature, called one of his imaginary towns "Kabtzansk," or Pauperville.

"A poor man has few enemies, but a rich one fewer friends."

"It's no disgrace to be poor, but it's no honor either."

"A full purse is not half as good as an empty one is bad."

—FOLK SAYINGS

A poor man found a wallet with ninety rubles in it. In the wallet was a name and address and this notice: "If found, return. Ten rubles reward."

The poor man rushed to the address, a fine home, where the *baleboss* thanked him, counted the money and said, "I see you have already removed ten rubles for your reward."

"I? No! Never! I swear it!"

The rich man sneered, "There were one hundred rubles in that wallet."

"I swear to you, on my mother's grave. . . ."

At this point, a rabbi entered. The poor man appealed to him, telling his tale. The rich man then told his and, slyly, ended: "—so whom will you believe, *rebbe*, that *kabtzen* or me?"

"You, of course." And the rabbi took the wallet from the rich man and gave it to the *kabtzen*.

"Rabbi, what are you doing?" cried the rich man.

"I'm taking you at your word," said the rabbi. "You said your wallet contained one hundred rubles. This man says the wallet he found contained only ninety. Therefore, this wallet can't be yours."

"But I—what of my money?"

"We must wait," smiled the rabbi, "until someone finds a wallet with one hundred rubles in it."

Kaddish

Pronounced KOD-*dish* or "cod dish." Aramaic: *kadosh*, "holy."

1. A prayer glorifying God's name, recited at the close of synagogue prayers; this is the most solemn and one of the most ancient of all Jewish prayers.
2. The mourner's prayer.
3. A son is sometimes called, affectionately, *"Kaddishel,"* or *"My Kaddish."*

The *Kaddish* (originally recited after completing a reading from the Bible, a religious discourse, or a lesson) is a doxology that glorifies God's name, affirms faith in the establishment of His kingdom, and expresses hope for peace within Israel. The language of the prayer is not Hebrew but Aramaic, which was the vernacular spoken by the Jews in their Babylonian exile and during the days of the Second Temple or Commonwealth.

In time, a belief arose among the Jews that the praises of God in the *Kaddish* would help the souls of the dead find lasting peace—and the prayer became known as the Mourner's Prayer, even though it contains not one reference to death or resurrection.

The *Kaddish* is recited at the grave, for eleven months after a death, by the children of the deceased, and each year on the anniversary of death. (See YORTZEIT.)

Couples who had no son would sometimes adopt an orphan (a relative, if possible) and raise him as their own. He was called their *Kaddish*, and guaranteed there would be someone to recite the prayer for them after their death.

Judaic law forbids any form of display or ostentation at a funeral. The rabbis of yore instituted simple burial rites, and this served to enforce a "democracy in death" in which no family, however poor, would be shamed by the simplicity of coffin or shroud.

Cremation, incidentally, is expressly forbidden to Jews; the Bible says, "Dust returneth unto dust," and Jews have always felt a profound obligation to, and respect for, the body—which God created.

Mr. Morton Wishengrad wrote a television program, for the admirable *Eternal Light* series, in which he imagined a genesis for the *Kaddish* (as a mourner's prayer) that deserves to be repeated:

A great scholar died, deeply mourned by the community and his disciples, one of whom mused: "When we end our reading of a chapter from *Torah*, we pronounce a *Kaddish* in praise of the Lord. Why not then utter a *Kaddish* when a chapter of a man's life is ended?"

Sholom Aleichem has left us this delightful memory of the *Kaddish* that he and his five brothers recited in mourning for their mother:

> You should have heard us deliver that *Kaddish!* A pleasure! All our relatives beamed with pride, and strangers envied us. One of our relatives . . . exclaimed, When a woman has six sons like that to say *Kaddish* after her, she will surely go straight to paradise. Either that or the world is coming to an end! *

* Maurice Samuel, *op. cit.*, p. 37.

kalikeh
kolyika

Pronounced KOL-*li-keh* or KOLL-*yi-keh,* to rhyme with "doll yucca." Russian: "cripple."

1. Cripple.
2. Someone who is sickly.
3. A clumsy person.
4. A stupid, ignorant man.
5. An inept performer: a singer off-key, a pianist who hits wrong notes, a waiter who spills the soup. "As a dancer (skater, laundress, barber, baritone, etc.), is he/she a *kalikeh!"*

A *kalikeh* is often blood-brother to a *shlemiel.*

Mrs. Rabinowitz was walking along Fifty-seventh Street with six-year-old Genevieve. At the corner of Fifth Avenue Genevieve sneezed.

"Gesundheit," said her mother.

At the corner of Madison Avenue, Genevieve sneezed again.

"God bless you, sweetheart," said Mrs. Rabinowitz.

At the corner of Park Avenue, Genevieve sneezed twice.

"Wham!" went Mrs. Rabinowitz's palm against Genevieve's rear. "With all my other troubles, a *kalikeh* I've got!"

Mr. Katz fitted on the made-to-order suit and cried in dismay: "Look at this sleeve! It's two inches too long!"

"So stick out your elbow," said the tailor, "which bends your arm—and the sleeve is just right!"

"The collar! It's half way up my head!"

"So raise your head up and back—and the collar goes down."

"But the left shoulder is two inches wider than the right!"

"So *bend,* this way, and it'll even out."

Mr. Katz left the tailor in this fantastic posture: right elbow stuck out wide, head far up and back, left shoulder tilted. A stranger accosted him.

"Excuse me, but would you mind giving me the name of your tailor?"

"*My* tailor?" Katz cried. "Are you mad? Why would anyone want my tailor?"

"Because any man who can fit a *kalikeh* like you is a genius!"

kalleh
kolleh

Pronounced KOLL-*eh*, the way a southerner might pronounce "collar," or to rhyme with either Walla in "Walla Walla."

Hebrew: "bride."

1. A bride; a recently married female.
2. A young married woman.
3. Your daughter-in-law (when you want to tease her.)

A girl who is not yet married, or is ready to be married, is called a *kalleh moid*—a "bride girl."

It is interesting to note that in old Babylonia, where *kalleh* meant "months of study," scholars would withdraw from the world for "a *kalleh* month"—i.e., a month in which they would "remarry" the *Torah*.

See also CHASSENEH.

A follower of the great Hillel wrote: "Every bride is beautiful and graceful." (That's in the *Talmud*.)

"A bride with beautiful eyes need not worry about her figure." Hoshaia Zeera (died 350) said that.

When something is exceptionally fortunate or felicitous, toogood-to-be-true, or when someone can't believe a stroke of great luck, a delightful comment is to be found in the saying: "What's wrong? The *kalleh is tzu shayn?*" ("Is the bride too beautiful?")

"The best horse needs a whip; the wisest man—advice; the best woman—a man." —FOLK SAYING

_____

"A wise man, looking for a bride, should take an ignoramus along to advise him." —PROVERB

kaporeh
kapora

Pronounced _ka-POOR-eh_, to rhyme with "La Moora." Hebrew: "forgiveness."

1. No good. "It is _oyf kapores_" means "It's good for nothing," or "It's a mess."
2. In a parlous state; in difficulties; sick. "He is _oyf kapores_" means "He is in trouble" or "He faces grave trouble."
3. "The devil with . . ." "The hell with . . ." "A _kaporeh_ on the car; just so no one was hurt!"
4. Atonement by vicarious methods (the original meaning in Hebrew).

Very Orthodox Jews practice a ceremony known as _shlogn_ ("beating") _kapores_ on the day before _Yom Kippur_. A fowl or (more often these days) a sum of money is offered to the poor, as a symbolic form of redemption for the life of the individual, and this prayer is said three times: "This be my substitute, my vicarious offering, my atonement. This (cock, hen) shall meet death, but I shall find a long and pleasant life of peace."

I have never seen the ceremony of _shlogn kapores_, which involves waving a rooster (!) over the head of someone whose sins are presumably passed on to the "scapegoat" fowl. My parents sighed and shook their heads over such "superstitious nonsense," such clearly "medieval _mishegoss_."

Rabbinical authorities in the Middle Ages opposed the practice, calling it pagan and foolish, but they were unsuccessful in their disapproval—for the frightened and the superstitious prevailed, as they, alas, so often do.

_____

An old Jew was walking down the street muttering oaths with great gusto: "A plague should attack his head! Beets should grow in his belly! A *kaporeh* should possess his soul!"

"Mister," cried a passerby. "Whom are you cursing so early in the morning?"

"Who?" echoed the old man. "I don't know—but don't worry: Someone will turn up."

Kapoyr

See MOISHE KAPOYR.

kasheh

Pronounced KOSH-*eh*, to rhyme with "pasha."

This word has two distinct derivations, and two distinct families of meanings.

1. From Russian: *kasha*, "porridge."

In Yiddish, *kasheh* can mean a cooked cereal; but—it also means a mixed-up, difficult, irksome confusion: a "rhubarb" (in sports lingo). Anyone who causes confusion is said to have "cooked up a *kasheh*."

2. From Hebrew: *kasheh*, "difficult."

This has come to mean, by extension, a difficult problem, a troublesome question, and, finally, any question at all.

A woman may come to a rabbi with a *kasheh* about some aspect of keeping a *kosher* kitchen.

A child in the "why" stage will ask *kashes* until Papa loses his mind.

A young Talmudist may try to stump his teacher with a casuistic challenge to an argument. "That's quite a *kasheh*," might be the reply; or "What kind of a *kasheh* is that?" (not so good-humored).

On *Pesach* the youngest child at the *Seder* asks the *Fier Kashes,* the "Four Questions."

Weinstein and his son were taking a walk.

"Papa," asked the boy, "what's the highest mountain on earth?"

"I don't know."

A little later, the boy asked, "Who was the king who followed Napoleon?"

Weinstein scratched his head. "I don't know."

And a little later, the boy asked, "Why does the moon always have the same side facing us?"

"Oy," sighed Weinstein. "I don't know . . ." Then, seeing the expression on the boy's face, he quickly added, "Ask, ask *kashes!* How else will you learn?"

kashrut

See KOSHER.

kayn aynhoreh
kineahora
kine-ahora

Pronounced *kane-ane-*HAW-*reh,* or *kine-ine-*HAW-*reh,* or, more quickly, *kine-a-*HAW-*reh,* rhyming respectively with "lame Dame Dora," "fine line Laura," "Dinah Cora." From German: *kein,* "no," "not one"; and Hebrew: *ayin ha-rah:* "the evil eye." The *kein* and *ayin* have blended into one Yiddish word,· *kein* or *kayn.*

1. The magical phrase uttered to ward off the evil eye, a reflex of mumbo jumbo employed to protect a child or loved one.
2. The phrase uttered to show that one's praises are genuine and not contaminated by envy—i.e., "I cast no evil eye. . . ." "That man is an angel, *kayn aynhoreh* (or *kineahora*)."

Our ancestors, Jew and *goy* alike, were constantly fearful of tempting the gods to anger; man's *hubris,* his boastings, his very successes, ran the risk of offending some god—and boomeranging into disaster. An envious, jealous mortal could cast an evil spell on another's luck—or health. *Kayn aynhoreh* or *kineahora* was articulated to thwart such demons.

Jewish women, especially, employed the rubric *kayn aynhoreh* in contexts such as these: "My child? In perfect health, *kayn aynhoreh.*" (Thank God.) "We should only live, *kineahora,* to see that day." "My son? First in his class, *kayn aynhoreh.*"

Virtually all people, and all religions, hold uneasy ideas about the cacodemons who operate through the "evil eye." Demonic spirits, diabolic ghouls, evil sprites, abound everywhere—and are thought to "come out" through the eyes. So mothers would drop a little salt and a crumb into a child's pocket, to protect it—presumably to feed any goblins who came along. Little girls sometimes wore beads, as a necklace or bracelet, to ward off evil spirits.

Not all evil eyers were malevolent, incidentally; some were believed to be virtuous mortals to whom the powers of the supernatural had been given. (Simeon bar Yochai was believed to have the awesome power of reducing evil people to instant bones with one mordant look. Other learned men were credited with incendiary—"blazing"—eyesight.)

Back in the fourth century, a Catholic ecclesiastical council in Spain issued a canon announcing that no Jew would be allowed to stand in a field that belonged to a Christian—because a Jew's mere glance was so fiendish that it could wither an entire crop. Of such madness is the story of the human race compounded.*

See Appendix: Evil Eye.

In the Bronx, if you overpraise someone, or call attention to his good fortune, the recipient may blurt: "Don't give me a canary!"

Originally, this ran, "Don't put the *kayn aynhoreh* (evil eye) on me."

---

* For an analysis of medieval conceptions of the Jew, and their influence on later anti-Semitism, see Joshua Trachtenberg, *The Devil and the Jews,* Harper, Torchbook paperback, 1966.

A Jewish patriarch was on the witness stand.

"How old are you?" asked the District Attorney.

"I am, *kayn aynhoreh*, eighty-one."

"What was that?"

"I said, 'I am, *kayn aynhoreh*, eighty-one.'"

"Just answer the question!" said the D.A. sharply. "Nothing else. Now, how old are you?"

"*Kayn aynhoreh* eighty-one," said the old man.

Now the judge said, "The witness will answer the question and *only* the question, without additional comment, or be held in contempt of court."

Up rose the counsel for the defense. "Your Honor, may I ask the question? . . ." He turned to the old man. "*Kayn aynhoreh*, how old are you?"

Said the old man, "Eighty-one."

khaloshes

See CHALOSHES.

khasseneh

See CHASSENEH.

khaukhem

See CHACHEM.

khaukhma

See CHACHMA.

khaver

See CHAVER.

kibbutz
kibbutzim (plural)

> Pronounced *kib*-BUTZ, with the *u* as in "puts," not "cuts."
> Hebrew: "collective," "group." Plural: *kibbutzim* (*kibbutz*-IM).

> A cooperative settlement of farmers in Israel. (Do not confuse *kibbutz* with *kibitz*, even though every *kibbutz* probably has its *kibitzers*.)

Under the leadership of Edmond de Rothschild and Maurice de Hirsch a Jewish Colonization Association was organized in 1899, to establish *kvutżoth* in Palestine—the predecessors of the *kibbutzim*.

The *kibbutzim* of Israel have won international respect for the courage, idealism, and perseverance of their members, Jews from all parts of the world, who elect to live the extremely hard and dangerous life of settlers, in pioneer conditions, in Palestine. The *kibbutzim* play a central part in Israel's defenses, for many were established near the frontiers of the surrounding Arab states.

Kibbutzim are farm collectives based on the ideals of Zionism, mutual aid, individual labor, and socialism. They vary greatly in size, degree of mechanization, details of authority, ownership, profit sharing. They have been intensively studied by economists, agronomists, social psychologists, and educators from all over the world; their structure has been adopted in many of the underdeveloped countries of Africa and (less often) Asia. There is a Japanese Kibbutz Association, and some eighty Japanese students have worked on *kibbutzim* in Israel.

The pioneers who live on the *kibbutz* are called *chalutzim*.

Kibbutzim are no longer increasing in number. As living standards in Israel rise, there has been a decline of enthusiasm for the extremely hard and simple life of the *kibbutzim*. There is also an increasing desire on the part of young Israelis to leave the *kibbutz* for cities, superior schools, and broader opportunities.[*]

---

[*] An excellent book about the *kibbutzim* is Melford Spiro's *Kibbutz: Venture in Utopia.* Harvard University Press, 1956.

kibitz
kibbitz

Pronounced KIB-*its*, to rhyme with "Tibbets." From German: *Kiebitz:* "lapwing," and "spectator at card game." (Do not confuse with *kibbutz*.)

1. To comment while watching a game. "I was *kibitzing*, not playing." (I was watching, with comments.)
2. To joke, fool around, wisecrack; to socialize aimlessly. "We were *kibitzing* around."
3. To tease, needle, gibe, second-guess. "Don't *kibitz*: he's sensitive." (Don't needle, tease, or "ride" him.)
4. To carry on a running commentary while another is working. "He was *kibitzing* us all the way." (He was advising, second-guessing, criticizing.) "He's not employed there, he just *kibitzes*."

See KIBITZER.

It has been said that when you tell a joke to a German, he laughs. When you tell it to an Englishman, he laughs twice: when he hears it, and when he understands it. When you tell it to a Frenchman, he laughs three times: when you tell it, when he recalls it, and when he repeats it.

But when you tell a joke to a Jew, he interrupts to say he's heard it before—then he tells it to you, in an "improved" (i.e., his) version.

It has also been said that in this sense, at least, every Jew likes to *kibitz*.

kibitzer
kibbitzer

Pronounced KIB-*itz-er*, to rhyme with "Lib hits 'er." From the German name for a bird, the *Kiebitz* (Latin name: *vanellus*), a lapwing or peewit, reputed to be especially noisy and inquisitive, and called, colloquially, *Kibitzer*. Staunch Yiddishists seem to forget that in

German *kiebitzen* means to look over the shoulder of a card player.

1. Someone who *kibitzes*—that is, gives unasked-for advice or suggestions, especially as a bystander-observer at a game (bridge, poker, checkers, chess).
2. Someone who butts into the affairs of others, sticks in his nose or his "two-cents."
3. Someone who joshes or teases.
4. Someone who flatters.
5. Someone who humors one along.

Kibitzers are rarely knowledgeable or respected; if they were, they would be advisers, not *kibitzers*. "What are you—a *kibitzer?*" (a wise guy who doesn't participate but offers easy advice). "As a poker player, he's a good *kibitzer*." (He second-guesses better than he plays; he's better as a cocky bystander than as a player.) "As a worker, he's a fine *kibitzer*." (He talks more than he works; he puts on airs.) "I'm afraid it's a slipped disk, and that *kibitzer* tells me one good cha-cha will get me back in shape." "Oh, stop your *kibitzing!*" (He has carried flattery beyond credibility.)

———————————

Jablonsky sent up a cry of rapture when he won first prize at a lottery.

A *kibitzer* asked him, "What made you pick a number like 63, anyway?"

"It came to me in a dream!" cried Jablonsky. "I dreamed I was in a theater, and on the stage was a chorus of sevens —each dancer a number 7, in a line, exactly eight 7's long! So I chose 63."

"But eight times seven is 56, not 63!"

Jablonsky chortled, "So O.K., *you* be the mathematician!"

———————————

The play, *The Kibitzer*, by Jo Swerling (1929), made both the title and its star, Edward G. Robinson, famous overnight.

———————————

The sign on the door read:

DR. JOSEPH KIPNIS—PSYCHIATRIST
DR. ELI LOWITZ—PROCTOLOGIST

Under this, a *kibitzer* had written:

"Specialists in Odds and Ends."

With great pride, Benjamin Bernstein painted himself a sign to hang over his store:

FRESH FISH
SOLD HERE
DAILY

As Bernstein placed the ladder, to hang up the sign, a *kibitzer* sang out, "What kind of *cockamamy* sign is that?"

"Why? What's wrong with it?"

" '*Fresh* fish,' Bernstein? It would never occur to your customers that you sell fish that *aren't* fresh—unless you advertise it!"

"You're right." Bernstein took his brush and painted out "Fresh."

"Wait!" said the *kibitzer*. "What about 'Sold'? Obviously you sell fish; you don't give them away free."

Mr. Bernstein painted out "Sold," and said, "O.K.?"

"No, why 'Here'? Obviously, you don't sell fish over *there* . . .'

"You're right!" And Bernstein painted out "Here."

"That leaves 'Daily,' " said the *kibitzer*. "I ask you, is that smart? If fish are fresh they *must* come in and go out daily. Right?"

"Absolutely!" Bernstein crossed out "Daily," leaving a sign that read only:

FISH

"Perfect," said the *kibitzer*.

Now Bernstein started up the ladder, when along came another *kibitzer*.

"Why are you putting up that ridiculous sign?"

"What's wrong with it?"

"You don't have to put up any sign, Bernstein, *your* fish everyone smells a mile away!"

So Bernstein put up no sign at all, thinking how lucky he was to have friends of such uncommon acumen.

kibosh

Pronounced KY-*bosh*, to rhyme with "my gosh." Derivation: mysterious.

1. Nonsense, "bosh" (when used as a noun; this was the nineteenth-century usage); but
2. "To put the *kibosh* on," which is the way the word is used today, means to arrange things so that something will not occur; to put an end to something; to "jinx" something so that it will fail or not take place; to spoil; to impair; to squelch; to veto. "His decision put the *kibosh* on all our hopes and plans."

Is *kibosh* of Yiddish extraction? Good question.

(A) The *Oxford Dictionary of English Etymology*, edited by C. T. Onions,* says *kibosh* is of uncertain origin. Dickens used *kibosh* back in 1856, the word at that time meaning "nonsense" or "bosh."

(B) *Webster's Unabridged Dictionary*, third edition,** says that *kibosh*'s ancestry is unknown.

(C) The *Oxford English Dictionary* says that *kibosh* is of "heraldic" origin, which, put that laconically, is no help.

(D) Eric Partridge, in his *Dictionary of Slang and Unconventional English*,*** agrees with the O.E.D. (above) but says that "to put the *kibosh* on," meaning to seal the doom of, comes from Yiddish. Why, I don't know; he offers no evidence.

(E) Padraic Colum, the Irish poet, asserts that *kibosh* comes from Irish Gaelic *cie báis*, meaning "cap of death." (*Bais* is pronounced "bawsh" in Gaelic.)

(F) In *Phrase and Word Origins*, Alfred H. Holt says that a "Mr. Loewe, who ought to know," traces *kibosh* to a Yiddish word "formed from four consonants, representing eighteen-pence. When, at a small auction, an eager bidder jumped his offer to eighteen-pence, he was said to have 'put the *kibosh*' on his fellow-bidders."

But I have not the faintest notion what those "four con-

* Oxford, 1966.
** G. & C. Merriam, 1966.
***Macmillan, 1961.

sonants" could be, or why they represented "eighteen-pence."

[One suggestion is that *kibosh* is an acronym composed of the initial letters of three Yiddish words for "18 British coins." In Hebrew, *chai* was often used to signify 18; the *sh* might be the initial sound of the word *shekel;* but this linguistic reconstruction falls down on the "b" sound. (It might stand for "British," but would not the acronym then be "ki*brosh?*") The number 18 possessed magical properties, since the letter equivalents (see Appendix: Gematria) formed the word "life." Thus, by extension, its use could presumably put the "hex" on an opponent.]

(G) *Webster's New World Dictionary of the American Language* says of *kibosh:* "earlier . . . *kybosh*, prob. Yid.?" which puts it indecisively, and proceeds to cite Germanic possibilities I find no more impressive. (Why should *kiebe*, which means "carrion" in Middle High German, lead to *kibosh?*)

(H) H. L. Mencken records the fact that *kibosh* was included in a glossary of about one hundred and twenty-five Americanisms that were added to Sinclair Lewis's *Babbitt* when it was published in England in 1922. But Mencken did not stick his neck out anent *kibosh's* parentage.*

(I) William and Mary Morris, in their *Dictionary of Word and Phrase Origins*,** repeat the Yiddish-origin and Gaelic-origin attributions of this tantalizing word, and conclude that *kibosh* has "according to H. L. Mencken, been widely used in America for more than a century."

(J) The admirably comprehensive *American Thesaurus of Slang*, by Berry and Van den Bark,*** includes several uses of *kibosh*, and even gives us a noun I never heard of, *kiboshery*, meaning "nonsense."

(K) Julian Franklyn, author of *A Dictionary of Rhyming Slang*,**** suggests that *kibosh* originated in the heraldic *caboshed* or *caboched*.

Now, why do I bother you with this *megillah*, for a word that may not come from Yiddish at all?

(1) Because I always assumed that *kibosh* has a Jewish mother or father: it sounds mighty close to the name of a

---

* See *The American Language*. Knopf, 1962, pp. 263, 573.
** Harper & Row, 1962.
*** Crowell, 1943.
**** Hillary House, 1960.

Hungarian or Rumanian card game, *Kalabriasz* (mispronounced *Klabiotch* by Jews) I used to see old men play when I was a boy.

(2) I want to give you one little example of the prolonged, irksome, frustrating and unbelievable *tsuris* to which a writer subjects himself when he rashly undertakes to write a book such as this.

kichel

Pronounced KIKH-*el*, with a Germanic *kh*. German.

A small, plain cookie.

This unpretentious little biscuit has been present at Jewish celebrations for hundreds of years. The current style of elaborate *Bar Mitzvas* and weddings has upstaged the *kichel*, but at less pretentious festivities guests still wish the hosts well with a glass of wine or *shnapps*, and a *kichel*.

Kichelach are made of unsweetened dough with a high egg content which makes the little cookies puff up. They may be baked plain, or with a sprinkling of sugar.

Kiddush

Pronounced KID-*ish*, to rhyme with "Yiddish." Hebrew: "sanctification." (Do not confuse with *Kaddish*.)

The prayer and ceremony that sanctifies the Sabbath and Jewish holy days.

The father recites the *Kiddush* before the Friday-night Sabbath dinner begins, over a goblet or cup of wine. He begins with a recitation of Genesis 2 : 1–3, which tells how God rested on the seventh day of Creation and made it holy. Two *broches* (blessings) follow: the first praising God for having created wine; the second thanking the Lord for having created the holy Sabbath "as an inheritance, a memorial of the Creation" and "in remembrance of the departure from Egypt."

All those at the table share in the *Kiddush* wine.

Some Jews recite the *Kiddush* without wine, using the *challa* loaf instead—for the rabbis long ago realized that thousands of Jews were too poor to afford wine, albeit a sip, each Friday.

The *Kiddush* ceremony predates the Christian Communion and Eucharist. The first Christians were Jews, and adapted and adopted the ritual of a communion (or "love feast") that was used among the sect of Jews called *Essenes.*

Kiddush Hashem
Kiddush ha-Shem

> Pronounced KID-*dish* ha-SHEM, to rhyme with "Yiddish posh hen." Hebrew: "sanctification of God's name."

> The concept that God needs mortal men to hallow His name, and that men become sanctified by following God's commandments.

The Book of Leviticus (22 : 32) has God say: "I will be hallowed among the children of Israel; I am the Lord which hallows you."

The opposite of *Kiddush Hashem* is *Chillul Hashem*—or "the profaning of God's name."

It is important to note that *Kiddush Hashem* involves any generous, noble, altruistic, considerate deed *that honors all Jews.* This comes from the old idea that the Jews are "a kingdom of priests," and that each Jew therefore bears perpetual responsibility to act to all other men in such a way as to honor all Jewry. The *Talmud* cites as a case of true *Kiddush Hashem* a Jew's returning to an Arab, from whom he had purchased a camel, a jewel that he had found around the camel's neck: "I bought a camel, not a precious gem." And the Arab cried, "Blessed be [your] God; blessed be the God of Israel."

Being a martyr is the highest form of *Kiddush Hashem*—that is, enduring torture and accepting death because of faith in God, or to prevent a profanation or desecration of God's name. (The idea of martyrdom as the ultimate testimonial to God arose during the Jewish wars against the Romans.)

The extraordinary importance, even magic, Orthodox Jews associated with the Name of God fascinated and puzzled me when I was a boy.

kike

(Vulgarism); pronounced to rhyme with "like." Yinglish. From Yiddish: *kikel:* "circle."

A thoroughly offensive, obnoxious way of referring to a Jew.

Kike is meant to be contemptuous and to suggest a cheap, low-class, ill-mannered, or ugly Jew.

Eric Partridge cites 1935 as the probable date of *kike*'s "adoption" into English* but that date is much too late. *Kike* was used in New York as early as 1914, and is included in H. L. Mencken's *American Language* (1919) as one common term of disparagement, akin to "sheeny"; or to "dago" or "wop" for an Italian.

The *Oxford English Dictionary* includes *kike* in its supplement volume, No. XIII (1961). In earlier editions, *kike* does not appear except as an obsolete form of *kick* or *keek*, a Scottish/North England dialect word, also spelled *kyke*, *keke*, *kike*, that means "to peep, to glance." The German *kieken* means "to peep"; the Yiddish version, *kick*, means "look."

Why, in the United States, was *kike* coined as an epithet for "Jew"? Assimilated German Jews, in the later decades of the nineteenth century, referred to the poorer, "pushy" immigrants from eastern Europe as "kikey" or "kikes." One reason today advanced for this is that many Ashkenazic names ended in *-sky* or *-ski;* presumably the taunt "ki-kis" led to "kikes."** I find this quite unconvincing: The letters *ski* or *sky* were always pronounced *skee*, and repetition-play would surely have given the neologism "kee-kees," or "keeks," not *kikes*.

My researches have led me to the following conclusions:

---

* Eric Partridge, *A Dictionary of Slang and Unconventional English.* Macmillan, 1961, p. 1158.

** See Stephen Birmingham, *Our Crowd: The Great Jewish Families of New York.* Harper & Row, 1967, pp. 291 ff.

1. The word *kike* was born on Ellis Island, when Jewish immigrants who were illiterate (or could not use Roman-English letters), when asked to sign the entry-forms with the customary "X," refused—and instead made a circle. The Yiddish word for "circle" is *kikel* (pronounced KY-*kel*), and for "little circle," *kikeleh*. Before long the immigration inspectors were calling anyone who signed with an "O" instead of an "X" a *kikel* or *kikeleh* or *kikee* or, finally and succinctly, *kike*.*

2. Jewish storekeepers on the Lower East Side, and peddlers who went far out into the hinterlands with their wares, conducted much of their trade on credit; and these early merchants, many of whom could not read or write English, would check off a payment from a customer, in their own or the customer's account book, with a little circle ("I'll make you a *kikeleh*")—never an "X" or a cross.

Why did Jews make an "O," never an "X"? Because of the profound fear, not to say revulsion, felt for the symbol of the cross—which to them represented not only a barbaric form of execution (see Appendix: Crucifixion), but the very sign under which they had themselves been persecuted, and their ancestors brutalized and slaughtered.

And so those who drew *kikelehs*, whether on Ellis Island or Avenue B, in Ohio or Kansas or wherever the hardy peddlers traveled into the Mid- and far West, came to be known as "*kike* men" or "*kikes*." Dr. Shlomo Noble informs me that the miners of northeastern Pennsylvania would say, "I bought it from the *kike* man," or "The *kike* man will be coming around soon."

Some say that the word *sheeny* began, in a similar way, as a strictly descriptive, nonpejorative word.

See SHEENY.

kinder

Pronounced KIN-*der*, to rhyme with "tinder." German: "children."

---

* I obtained this information through the courtesy of Stephen Birmingham, who shared with me a letter sent to him by Mr. Sidney Berry. Mr. Berry's authority for this illuminating observation was the late Philip Cowen, "dean of immigration inspectors" at Ellis Island, later the founder and first editor of *The American Hebrew*.

Children.

—But how little does "children" convey that bursting sentiment, *naches,* and pride with which Jews say *"kinder."*
Sometimes this parental feeling is carried to startling extremes. My wife remembers a neighbor who was so fierce in her maternal affections that when her *no-goodnik* son was arrested, for some petty infraction of the law, she returned from visiting him in jail to announce, "You never *saw* such a beautiful jail as my Morris is in!"

kinderlach (diminutive)

Pronounced KIN-*dair-lach,* making the *ch* a Scottish *kh.*

Little children.

To express special affection to friends, a gathering, a dinner party, a committee, one may say, "Well, *kinderlach . . .*"

kineahora
kine-ahora

See KAYN AYNHOREH.

kishka

Pronounced KISH-*keh,* to rhyme with "shishke" as in "shish kebab." Russian: "intestines," "entrails."

1. Intestines.
2. A sausagelike comestible of meat, flour, and spices stuffed into intestine casing, and baked.
3. A water hose (colloquial, and vivid enough).

Kishka is a delicacy of Jewish cuisine (which, to tell the truth, is not noted for range). It is made according to housewives' ancestry, palate, spices, and patience.

Aside from food, the words *kishka* and *kishkas* are used to mean intestine, "innards," belly. Genteel Jews hesitate to do so. My father and mother never would use, or approve, the following: "His accusation hit me right in the *kishka*." "I laughed until my *kishkas* were sore." "Oh, my full *kishkas!*" (I think this less offensive, in post-prandial praisings, than "Oh, my stuffed stomach.")

> 4. Plural: *kishkas*—even though the same intestine is being described. To hit someone "in the *kishkas*" means to hit him in the stomach or, in indelicate parlance, "in the guts."

A man with an undiscriminating palate is said to possess *"a trayfeneh kishka"*—an un-*kosher* intestine. To say *"a Yiddishe kishka,"* or "You can't describe a *Yiddishe kishka,"* is to say that no one can gauge the prodigious appetite of a hungry Jew.

Mrs. Gershenbaum, in Moscow, sent a telegram to her husband, in Kiev: "SAYS TO OPERATE OPERATE."

Mr. Gershenbaum replied: "SAYS TO OPERATE OPERATE."

The police promptly arrested Gershenbaum: "What secret code are you using?"

"No code," said Gershenbaum.

"Do you take us for fools? Just read these telegrams!"

"Well, my wife is sick in the *kishkas*. So she went to Moscow to see a famous surgeon, and she wired me: 'SAYS TO OPERATE. OPERATE?' So I replied, 'SAYS TO OPERATE? OPERATE!' "

kittel

Pronounced KIT-*t'l*, to rhyme with "little." German: *Kittel*, "smock, overall."

The white robe worn by the cantor (and some other men) at services on High Holy days and at major festivals.

Among the Jews of eastern Europe, most men wore a linen

kittel during the High Holy days: The simple, spotless white robe signified purity and simplicity.

klezmer

Pronounced KLEZ-*mer* or KLETS-*mer*, to rhyme with "Mesmer" or "gets her." Plural: *klezmorim (klez-*MOR-*im).* From the Hebrew: *klei-zemer:* "musical instruments."

An informal group of musicians; many were itinerants who went from village to village, in eastern Europe, playing traditional music, folk songs, folk dances, solemn hymns before prayer.

These musicians rarely knew how to read music (what Jews could afford music lessons, and who in the *shtetl* would teach them?) and passed their skill down from father to son. They earned very little and had to keep moving, seeking out country fairs, weddings, synagogue dedications, *Purim* festivities, etc.

As characters, the shabby *klezmorim* were familiar to all Ashkenazic Jews; they were regarded as drifters, odd types, itinerant minstrels. They are a recurrent theme in the paintings of Marc Chagall and Chaim Gross.

Klezmer music was played on trumpets, bugles, flutes, clarinets, fifes, violins, cellos, drums. A typical group would contain three to six members.

In some ways *klezmer* music was like the music of jazz "combos" in that it grew out of improvisation, ingenious harmonizations, solo innovations. It reflected the patchwork quilt of national cultures in which Jewish life was lived; Hebraic themes were embroidered with motifs from the folk music of Russians, Poles, Czechs, Germans, Hungarians, Rumanians, Slovenes, Greeks, Arabs.

During the Middle Ages, the making of music was a recognized profession among both Oriental and European Jews. In many places Jewish musicians played at Christian religious ceremonies. They were, indeed, often preferred to other minstrels because of their reputation for "modesty and sobriety"

—and once they came into demand, punitive taxes were imposed to discourage them.*

klop
klap

Rhymes with "slop." German: "blow," "hit."

1. A blow; to strike a blow; to hit. "Give him a *klop;* you're closer."
2. More colorfully, to *klop* is to yammer, to yak, to blab on at great length and without mercy. "He *klopped* me in *kop*" means either "He knocked me in the head," or, better, "He talked my ears off." "All day long, he *klops* about his troubles." *"Klop der kop in der vant"* means "Beat your head against the wall."

See CHMALLYEH.

klutz
klotz

Rhymes with "butts." From German: (a) log, or block of wood, (b) a heavy person, (c) a strong man or giant.

1. A clod; a clumsy, slow-witted, graceless person; an inept blockhead.
2. A congenital bungler.

The word even sounds *klutz*-like.

A *"klutz-kasheh"* is a silly question which brings up irrelevant problems or rests upon foolish premises.

To Mr. Meyers, in the hospital, came Mr. Glotz, secretary of the synagogue, who said: "I bring you the good wishes of our Board of Trustees, that you should get well and live to be

* See Abraham Z. Idelsohn, *Jewish Music.* Tudor Publishing Co., 1944, pp. 453 ff.

a hundred and ten years old! That's an official resolution, passed by a vote of 14 to 7!"

Glotz was a *klutz*.

The men sat sipping their tea in silence. After a while the *klutz* said, "Life is like a bowl of sour cream."

"Like a bowl of sour cream?" asked the other. "Why?"

"How should I know. What am I, a philosopher?"

Two *klutzes* were discussing their wives. "My wife drives me crazy: every night she dreams she married a millionaire!"

"That drives you crazy? You're lucky. *My* wife dreams she's married to a millionaire in the daytime."

knaydl

Pronounced K-NAY-*dl*, to rhyme with "ladle." The plural, *knaydlach*, is pronounced K-NAY-*dlakh*. From German.

A dumpling—usually made of matzo meal, usually served in chicken soup, usually on Friday night, generally at the Passover *Seder*.

Knaydl is used affectionately for a child, as we say "my little dumpling," or to describe a round, fat, chubby woman.

knippl
knippel

Pronounced KNIP-*p'l*, to rhyme with "ripple."

See PUSHKE.

knish
knishes (plural)

Pronounce the "k" as well as the "n." From Ukrainian.

1. Little dumplings filled with groats, grated potatoes, onions, chopped liver, or cheese. The *knish* has become an American *nosh* through the efforts of celebrated *knish*-makers on the Lower East Side. (A famed *knish* bakery was established on Houston Street in 1910. It has flourished ever since.*)

2. A term of abuse. "He has the brains of a *knish*."

3. When you say you hit someone "with a *knish*" you mean you reward, instead of punish, him. Don't ask me why.

4. A crease. (As a verb, to *knish* means to crease.)

5. Vagina (vulgarism).

k'nocker

Pronounced *not* "nocker," but κ'NOCK-*er*, with the *k* a separate sound, as in "Canute." (I make the apostrophe part of the spelling to make sure you pronounce both the *k* and the *n*.) From German: *knacken:* "to crack or snap." A *knacker* meant someone who cracked a whip, was a doer, a big shot. In Yiddish, *k'nocker* is derisive.

1. A big shot—who knows it and acts that way.
2. A boastful, cocky, self-advertising fellow; a "show-off."

The braggadocio aspect is important: a successful but modest man is ordinarily not called a *k'nocker*.

A *k'nocker* is someone who works crossword puzzles with —a pen (especially if someone is watching).

During the *Yom Kippur* services, a *k'nocker* was beating his breast, praying loudly; and, carried away, cried out, "I am the lowliest of men, Lord, unworthy of Your goodness! I am a *no-goodnik*, a nobody, a nothing!"

Next to the *k'nocker*, the poor *shammes* (sexton), too, was beating his breast and chanting his deficiencies. "Forgive me, O Lord, I'm a nothing."

* See Glaser and Snyder, "Yonah Shimmel vs. the Mock Knish," in the *New York World-Journal Tribune*, April 16, 1967.

The *k'nocker* promptly protested: "Look who claims he's a nothing!"

Two Jewish *k'nockers*, approaching Honolulu, got into an argument about the correct pronunciation of Hawaii: One was sure it was "Hawaii," the other positive it was "Havaii." They made a bet.

When they got off the plane, they hurried over to the first native they saw and said, "Aloha! How do you pronounce the name of this island: Hawaii or Havaii?"

"Havaii," said the native.

"Thank you."

"You're velcome," said the native.

kobtzen

See KABTZEN.

kochalayn
koch alayn

> Pronounced KOKH-*a-layn* or KOKH-*a-line;* be sure to make the uvular *kh* as bonnie as a Scot's. Strictly Ameridish. From German: *koch:* "to cook"; *allein:* "alone."

> A room or bungalow, in a summer colony, with cooking facilities.

This gorgeous specimen of Ameridish comes to us from the language crucible of the Catskill Mountains, the hallowed center and El Dorado of Jewish summer resorts.

The culture of the Catskills distinguishes hotels, which are for *alrightniks,* from *kochalayns,* which are for *balbatish* "singles," couples, or families.

I first heard this indispensable word used thusly: "Who can *affoder* (afford) a fancy hotel? I take a *kochalayn.*"

In the Catskills, it is claimed that an ingenious gentleman crossbred a Guernsey with a Holstein—to get a Goldstein.

This cow does not moan "Moo," but "Nu?"

kochleffl

Pronounced KOKH-*lef-fl*, with a Glaswegian *kh*, as in "loch." From German: *koch:* "to cook"; *leffl:* "spoon."

1. A cooking spoon. The *kochleffl* was the long wooden spoon used for stirring a pot.
2. A busybody; a gadabout. What word is better than *kochleffl* to describe someone who butts into everyone else's business?
3. A live wire, go-getter, organizer, activist, promoter; someone who stirs things and people up.
4. A bright, inquisitive, energetic toddler. "That little girl—a regular *kochleffl!*"

Kohen
Cohen

Pronounced CO-*en*, to rhyme with "go when" or CANE to rhyme with "Dane." Hebrew: *kohen:* "priest." Plural: *kohanim,* pronounced *ko-HA-nim.*

Priest—i.e., a Hebrew priest of yore.

Family names such as Cohen, Cohn, Cahn, Kahn, Kagen, Cahana, and even Echt and Katz (formed from the initials of *kohen tzedek,* "a priest of justice") often claim descent from the priests of ancient Israel—as do some Germans named Köhne, Schiff (a pun on *Kahn:* "boat") and even Bloch.

Aaron, brother of Moses, was the first high priest, the ancestor of all Hebrew priests, the *kohanim,* who conducted sacrifices and services in the desert sanctuary, and later in the great Temple in Jerusalem.

After the Jews went into exile, the title of *kohen* was passed down, even though the priestly prerogatives and responsibilities no longer existed.

Many proscriptive laws circumscribed the actions of a *kohen;* a few are still followed by traditional Jews:

A *kohen* may not marry a divorcee.

A *kohen* may enter a cemetery only for the funeral of a member of his immediate family.

A *kohen* is the first one called to the *Torah*-reading in the synagogue.

I know of no sound historical evidence that links the Cohanes of Ireland to the Cohens of Tel Aviv.

The firm of Farnsworth, Sullivan, and Cohen was one of the largest and finest in the city. A friend of Cohen's asked, "Why is your name last? Everyone knows that Farnsworth spends all of his time in the country and Sullivan most of it at the race track. Your name should be first!"

"Well," smiled Cohen, *"my* clients read from right to left."

There is no truth in the observation that after Robert Briscoe, a Jew, was elected Lord Mayor of Dublin, the Irish began to see leprecohens.

Kol Nidre

Pronounced *Cawl* NID-*reh*, to rhyme with "Paul Sidra." Hebrew: "all vows."

The plaintive prayer that ushers in *Yom Kippur*. The words are not Hebrew, but Aramaic.

In synagogues and temples all around the globe, the cantor chants the *Kol Nidre* just before sunset, on the eve of *Yom Kippur*. He sings it three times, first softly, then louder, then *fortissimo*—and the congregation responds antiphonally, reciting the prayer as a recitative. Throughout this, the *Torah* scrolls are held aloft by three worshipers.

The *Kol Nidre* is chanted very solemnly, with more anguish than any other prayer, for it seems to recapitulate, in each worshiper's memory, the long history of violence and humiliation to which Jews have been subjected. The melody, as sung by the cantor in the falling twilight, is immensely moving. (Beethoven included a piece of it in his *Quartet in C sharp Minor*. Tolstoy said it "echoes the story of the martyrdom of a grief-stricken nation.")

But the text of the *Kol Nidre*, surprisingly, is that of a legal document, not a paean to God.

> *Kol Nidre* (all vows), obligations, oaths, anathemas, be they called *konam* or *konas* or by any other name, which we may vow or swear or pledge . . . from this Day of Atonement until the next . . . we do repent. May they be deemed to be forgiven, absolved, annulled or void—and made of no effect. They shall not bind us nor have power over us [and] the vows shall not be considered vows nor the obligations obligatory, nor the oaths oaths.

Kol Nidre was originally *opposed* by the rabbis, because it suggested that vows could be taken not too seriously, since they could be negated on *Yom Kippur*. But the chant/prayer became popular nevertheless—I think for three basic reasons:

(1) Jews attach singular importance to a promise. Judaic law demands that every vow be fulfilled even, according to Rabbi Louis Finkelstein, if the fulfillment entails severe sacrifices. (*The Jews: Their History, Culture and Religion,* Vol. II, pp. 1739–1802.)

(2) Charlemagne forbade the Jews, when in a court, to swear by their own religious oath; instead, Jews were forced to use the repellent *More Judaico*. Oaths were "administered" to Jews in brutal ways: a Jewish witness had to kneel, or was forced to don a wreath of thorns; he was made to stand in water (since he had declined baptism) or on a pigskin; he was instructed to repeat the oath while teetering on a low stool from which one leg had been removed. . . . It is no wonder to me that Jews asked God to exempt them from the performance of vows undertaken under such circumstances.

(3) Many Jews were forcibly converted during the Inquisition. One can understand why these hapless "renegades" to their faith would want God to absolve them from guilt in having taken vows they were forced to take, and to remit in advance any sin occasioned by vows they might have to take in the year ahead.

The rabbis taught that the dispensation allowed in *Kol Nidre* applies only to those vows that involve the vower alone

—not any that entailed the interests of another. So a man might be absolved of responsibility for a vow of conscience, to God, but not of a promise made to another man. *That* had to be fulfilled.

For other remarks, see Appendix: Kol Nidre.

kopdrayenish

Pronounced KAWP-*dray-eh-nish*, to rhyme with "hawk bray a fish." German: *drehen:* "to turn"; *Kopf:* "head."

1. Something that makes one's head spin with its difficulty.
2. Something that confuses one because of its noise; a tumult.
3. Something that turns one's head; flattery, a compliment.

"Who needs a *kopdrayenish* like that?" "He had so much *kopdrayenish* he didn't know what he was doing." "Stop *draying* me a *kop*." "That's enough *kopdrayenish*."

See also TSEDRAYT, TSEDOODELT.

kosher

Pronounced KO-*sher*, to rhyme with "no sir." From the Hebrew: *kasher:* "fit," "proper," "appropriate," "permissible."

Kosher is probably the Hebrew word most widely encountered in English. (Its multifarious meanings in American slang, and as a form of Yinglish, will be explored below.)

(A) As a Hebrew-Yiddish word, *kosher* generally means only one thing:

(1) Fit to eat, because ritually clean according to the dietary laws.

Many a meat store in a Jewish neighborhood carries two Hebrew words on the window; they look alike but are not.

They read, from right to left: *basar kasher* (pronounced, in Yiddish, BAW-*ser* KO-*sher*). *Basar* means "meat."

A *kosher* meat store or restaurant serves no un-*kosher* meats.

Eating and drinking, to the ancient Jews, involved grave religious obligations, and strongly reinforced the idea of the Jews as a people "set apart," chosen by the Lord as "Mine . . ." "holy unto Me" (Leviticus). The strict observanee of dietary rules was believed to strengthen the dedication of a Jew to his role as one of God's instruments for the redemption of mankind. (Some scholars think *kosher* practices were designed as acts of moral self-discipline, to resist the influence of the Greeks and Romans, who were given to prodigious self-indulgence and sensuality.) The strict observance of *kosher* laws has declined drastically among Western Jews.

(B) In Yiddish, *kosher* is used to describe anything:

(2) Pertaining to Orthodox Jewry. "He is a *kosher* Jew" means he observes the dietary laws.

(3) Pious, devout. "He is a *kosherer* Jew" means he is very pious; a female would be "a *koshereh* Jew."

(4) Sympathetic. "He is a *kosher* kind of man." He is kind, understanding.

(5) Dear, sweet, lovable. "She has a *koshereh* soul."

(C) In American slang (extensively documented by H. L. Mencken, Eric Partridge, Berrey and Van den Bark), *kosher* comes in a gorgeous array of flavors:

(6) Authentic; the real McCoy. "That's *kosher*" can mean 14-karat gold, sterling silver, genuine antique.

(7) Trustworthy, reliable. "Is he *kosher?*" which once meant "Is he Jewish?" is now taken to mean "Can I trust him?" or "Is he part of the group?" or even (as I heard it used in the Pentagon) "Has he been cleared for classified information?"

(8) Legitimate, legal, lawful. "Is this deal *kosher?*" means "Is this deal on the up-and-up?" "Everything is *kosher*" means "Everything is proper."

(9) Approved by a higher source; bearing the stamp of approval. "It's *kosher*," uttered by a company V.P., can mean that the president has approved it; uttered by a lieutenant, it means it has the sanction of a superior.

(10) Fair, fair and square, ethical. Eric Partridge says this usage came into English from London's East End, around 1860.

All in all, *kosher* is, I suppose, the most resourceful Yiddish word in the English language.

Kosher: Dietary Data (in brief)

Meat and milk may not be eaten simultaneously. (Orthodox Jews allow six hours to pass between a meat and a dairy meal, but less if vice-versa.) Separate cooking utensils and vessels for the service and storage of foods are used for dairy and meat products—viz., Moses' thrice-uttered warning (Exodus, Deuteronomy) not to seethe a kid in its mother's milk.

"Clean" and "unclean" animals are listed in Leviticus (11) and Deuteronomy (14). Precisely forty-two animals are named as taboo.

Only those four-footed animals that chew their cud *and* possess a cloven hoof are *kosher*. (This includes goat, gazelle, pygarg and antelope, though I have yet to hear of a Jew going that far.) An animal that chews its cud but is not cloven-hoofed is *trayf* (non-*kosher*)—e.g., the camel, the rabbit. It grieves me to inform the pious reader that the camel, Bible notwithstanding, is cloven-hoofed, and that the rabbit does not chew the cud. Creatures that crawl, like lizards and snakes, are forbidden. So is the mouse. So is the weasel. Only fish having both scales and fins are *kosher*. Shellfish are taboo. (What a pity.) Birds of prey (vultures, owls, hawks, eagles) are taboo, as are nearly all wild fowl. Any animal that has not been slaughtered according to ritual—even a chicken, a cow—is unclean and *verboten*.

The *shochet*, a religious slaughterer, must examine each individual animal for signs of infection, disease, or abnormality: he must dispatch an animal by slashing the throat with one stroke. If the knife binds or sticks, even for an instant, the animal is no longer *kosher*. *Kosher* meat must be stamped or sealed by a *mashgiach* (supervisor).

An excellent, lucid account of dietary laws will be found in Rabbi Seymour Siegel's *Jewish Dietary Laws*.*

---

* Burning Bush Press, 1961, 1967.

For more extensive notes on the food aspects of *kashruth*, and its history, see Appendix: Kosher.

The jokes Jews tell about matters *kosher* are endless. Here is one of the briefest:

Late one rainy afternoon, when he saw no other customers inside, Mr. Finkelstein walked into an elegant but not *kosher* delicatessen. He bought some tomatoes, and, with elaborate insouciance, asked (for the first time in his life) "By the way, eh, how much costs that—bacon?"

Came a terrific flash of lightning and clap of thunder. Finkelstein looked up to the heavens, protesting, "I was only *asking!*"

koved
kovid

Pronounced KAW-*vid*, to rhyme with "law lid." Hebrew: "honor."

Honor, glory.

"A man who pursues *koved*, from him glory runs away."
—TALMUD

And I have heard a clause tacked on: "But he who does good and does not pursue *koved*, him *koved* overtakes."

krechtz

Pronounced KREKHTZ, to rhyme with "Brecht's." German: *krächzen:* "croak," "craw."

1. To grunt-groan-croak-moan-or-wheeze in minor pain or discomfort.
2. To fuss or complain—with audible sound effects.
3. To make cranky, gasping, ambiguous noises.
4. A sound of complaint, discontent or minor sadness.

Krechtzing (in Yiddish, *krechtzen*) is reserved for secondary discontents or minor ailments. You would never say *krechtz* for a sound of real pain, or genuine tragedy.

A *krechtz* is not a scream, which is a *kvitch*, nor a full-throated cry, which is a *geshrei*. Moreover, *krechtz* is neither a deep-throated moan nor a subtle sigh, which is a *ziftz*. You moan a bit and sigh quite often whilst *krechtzing*. A confined gasp-sigh-moan is best.

People who are hypochondriacs *krechtz* a good deal; so do middle-aged women in the menopause—and Jewish men losing at pinochle; so do chronic gripers. Old people *krechtz* a good deal, especially when their children are around.

Note that *krechtz* describes the sounds one makes, not the cause thereof. You may *krechtz* about something, never *at* someone. And it is much more common to use *krechtz* about someone else than about one's self. "Are you in pain? You've been *krechtzing* for an hour." "Why are you *krechtzing* so much? Is the stock down?" "All he does is read and *krechtz*." The savor of *krechtzing* can be enhanced by liberal doses of "*Oy!*" In fact, "*Oy!*" is itself a *krechtz*.

Two men met on the street. Said the first: "How's business?"

Krechtzed the second, "Eh."

"Well, for this time of year, that's not bad!"

In the old days, when trains welcomed customers, when there were few bedrooms and one slept in an upper or a lower berth, a Mr. Fortescue, tossing and turning in an upper, could not get to sleep because, from the berth below, came a woman's constant, mournful *krechtzing*: "*Oy* . . . am I toisty . . . *Oy* . . . am I toisty!*"

On and on went the murmurous lament, until Mr. Fortescue got out, crawled down the ladder, padded the length of the car, filled two paper cups with water, brought them back and handed them in through the curtains to the passenger in the lower berth.

"Madame, here. Water!"

"God bless you, gentleman; thank you."

Fortescue crawled up into his berth, and he was on the very edge of sweet somnolence when, from below, came the suspiration: "*Oy* . . . vas I toisty. . . .*"

krenk

Pronounced exactly as it is spelled, with the *e* as in "bent." From German: *krank:* "sick."

1. An illness. To be *kronk* (sick) is to have some *krenk*.

I would not include so pedestrian a noun except that *krenk* adorns some dire curses old Jews used to resort to: "He should only come down with a *krenk!*"

2. Nothing. Used ironically: "He asked me for ten dollars; a *krenk* (nothing) I'll give him!"

Mrs. Kaminsky telephoned a well-known psychiatrist. "Are you the crazy-doctor?"

"Well—I'm a psychiatrist."

"I want to come see you. I think maybe I have a psychological *krenk*. But first, how much do you charge?"

"Thirty dollars an hour."

"Thirty dollars an *hour?*" gasped Mrs. Kaminsky. "Goodbye. That crazy, I'm not."

kreplach
kreplech

Pronounced KREP-*lokh* or KREP-*lekh*, as a German would render the *kh*. From German: *kreppel;* note French *crêpes.*

A triangular or square dumpling, not unlike Italian ravioli, that contains chopped meat or cheese, etc. Usually served in soup.

Kreplach are traditionally eaten on *Purim* and *Rosh Hoshanah*, and the day before *Yom Kippur*.

Mrs. Kushner was so upset about her little Sidney that she went to the school psychiatrist. "All of sudden, my Sidney developed this thing: He just won't eat *kreplach*. The minute he sees them, he throws a temper tantrum!"

"When did this start?" asked the psychiatrist, and when she finished, said, "Show your little boy exactly what *kreplach* are, make him familiar with each ingredient, the entire process by which you cook them. And if you explain each step gently, patiently, whatever is causing his anxiety will disappear."

So Mrs. Kushner took little Sidney into the kitchen with many soothing sounds, and set him on a high stool, and smiled reassuringly. "So look, Sidneleh darling, here on the table I put a little square piece of dough. Dough. Right? Like I use in making the bread you love. Good? And in the middle of this tasty little square of dough I put some nice, chopped-up meat. *Oh*, such delicious meat! . . . Then I fold over one corner of the little square of dough—like this, nice, easy—then I fold the second corner over, just like the first—and then the third corner—my! Isn't that pretty? Just like a little hat. And now, the last thing I do is fold over the last corner and you see—"

"*Kreplach!*" screamed Sidney. "*Kreplach! Kreplach! Kreplach!*"

krich arein in di bayner

Pronounced KRICKH (Scottish *kh* sound) *ah*-RINE *in dee* BAY-*nair*. German: *kriechen*, "to crawl," *Bein*, "bone."

(Literally) "Crawl into the bones"; to get under one's skin. To trespass on one's innermost and sensitive areas.

Er kricht arein in di bayner. He crawls into your very bones.

Krich nit arein in di bayner! Don't crawl into my very bones.

Zi kricht arein in di bayner. She worms her way into your most private affairs.

kugel

Rhymes with "good'l." Also pronounced KIGL, to rhyme with "big'l." German.

Pudding of noodles or potatoes.

The name comes from the pan in which the pudding was baked and kept over the Sabbath.

A *kugel* is traditionally found on the Sabbath table because it can be prepared before *Shabbes* begins and be kept in the warm oven. (Injunctions against working on the Sabbath prohibit cooking or even lighting a fire.)

I feel obliged to tell you of an old saying: "If a woman can't make a *kugel*—divorce her." I disapprove of this.

Kuni Lemmel

Pronounced KOO-*ni* LEM-*mel*, the first word rhyming with "loony." From German: *Lümmel:* "bumpkin."

A yokel; a simpleton; a Simple Simon.

Avrom Goldfaden (1840–1908), Yiddish playwright, producer, director, and composer, wrote a well-known operetta, *Di Tzvei Kuni-Lemell*, with a confusion-of-identities plot that became popular.

See CHAIM YANKEL, SHLEMIEL.

A *Kuni Lemmel* may be defined according to an old folk saying: "He is the kind who looks for a notch in the saw."

kurveh

Pronounced KUR-*veh*, to rhyme with "purdah." From Hebrew: *karove:* "a strange woman who comes very close."

Prostitute.

Around our house, *kurveh* was absolutely, unequivocally taboo. I never heard my father or mother use the word when I was a boy; not until I was twenty did my father—apologetically—utter it.

When some news story, some discussion of an event, simply

demanded that a prostitute be mentioned, my parents would say "a bad woman," or "an *oysvorf* of a woman."

See NAFKA.

kvell

Pronounced exactly as it's spelled. From German: *quellen:* "to gush," "to swell."

1. To beam-with-immense-pride-and-pleasure, most commonly over an achievement of a child or grandchild; to be so proudly happy "your buttons can bust"; doting—with a grin, conspicuous pride, uncontainable delight. "At their boy's Bar Mitzva, naturally, they *kvelled*." "Watch her *kvell* when she reads his report card." "Let me *kvell* with you over such an honor."

Jewish parents are most energetic in *kvell*ing over their children's endowments (real or illusory), achievements (major or minor), or praise from others (sincere or obligatory).

One authority I consulted put it this way: "Only from your children can anyone *shep* (derive) such *naches* (prideful pleasure) as makes you *kvell*—know what I mean?"

2. To enjoy, gloat, or crow over someone's defeat or humiliation. "All right, be charitable, don't *kvell* over his mistake." "Every decent man will *kvell* when that sadist goes to jail."

The ladies met on the Grand Concourse, Mrs. Blumenfeld carrying her groceries, Mrs. Kovarsky pushing a pram with two little boys in it.

"Good morning, Mrs. Kovarsky. Such darling little boys! So how old are they?"

"The doctor," said Mrs. Kovarsky, "is three, and the lawyer is two."

kvetch
kvetcher (masculine)
kvetcherkeh (feminine)

> Pronounced KVETCH, to rhyme with "fetch"; KVETCH-*er*, to rhyme with "stretcher"; KVETCH-*er-eh*, to rhyme with "fetch 'er a." (Do not confuse with *kvitch* or *krechtz*.) From German: *quetschen*: "to squeeze," "to press."

> *Kvetch* is a verb and a noun; *kvetcher* is a man who *kvetches; kvetcherkeh* is a female complainer.

A. *As a verb.*

1. To squeeze, pinch, eke out. "Don't *kvetch* the peaches." "He manages to *kvetch* out a living." "He'll *kvetch* the deal out to its last decimal point." "No one knows how someone else's shoe *kvetches*."

2. To fuss around, to be ineffectual. "She *kvetches* all day long."

3. To fret, complain, gripe, grunt, sigh. "What's she *kvetching* about now?" (An excellent companion to *kvetch*, in this usage, is *krechtz*. "All she does is *kvetch* and *krechtz!*" can hardly be improved upon for descriptive precision and power.)

4. To delay, stall, show reluctance. "He's still *kvetching* around."

5. To shrug. "He *kvetches* his shoulders."

B. *As a reflexive verb.*
Kvetchen zich.
To exert or push oneself.

This can be used to describe a soprano straining to hit a high note, a stammerer bulling through a sound barrier, a woman in labor trying to hasten birth by squeezing, grunting, forcing.

C. *As a noun.*
Kvetch, kvetcher or *kvetcherkeh* describes:

1. Anyone, male or female, who complains, frets, gripes.

A "sad sack" who magnifies minor aches and pains. A chronic complainer. "What a congenital *kvetcher!*"

To be strictly grammatical, a female *kvetcher* should certainly be called a *kvetcherkeh,* which, through the lilt of euphony, enhances the characterization.

2. One who works slowly, inefficiently or pedantically. "It will take forever, he's such a *kvetch.*"

3. One who constantly alibis for poor or lazy performance. "That *kvetch* comes up with a different excuse every Monday and Thursday." (The phrase "Mondays and Thursdays" is Yiddish for constantly, repetitively. It derives from the fact that a small portion of the Torah is read in the synagogue on Monday and Thursday mornings, every week, every year, and has been repeated as ritual for generations.)

4. A "wet blanket," one who diminishes the pleasures of others. "Don't invite them to the party; he's a *kvetch.*"

There is a prized lapel button that reads:

FRANZ KAFKA

IS A

KVETCH

kvitch

Rhymes with "snitch." From German: *quietschen,* "to squeal."

Do not confuse *kvitch* with *kvetch.* Do not confuse *kvitch* with *krechtz. Kvitch, kvetch,* and *krechtz* often work beautifully in tandem, but are not synonyms.

A. *As a verb:*

To scream—but not a scream of real terror. It is, rather, a yelp. A woman will *kvitch* or "give a *kvitch*" on sighting a mouse, singing a finger, or meeting a long-lost friend. (In a moment of real fear or tragedy, Jewish women do not *kvitch,* but give a *geshrei,* which rhymes with "fresh fry.")

I think it correct to state that 95 percent of all the *kvitching* in the world is done by women. "Don't *kvitch* when you see the bill." "When she stuck herself with the needle, she *kvitched*" (or, better, "gave a *kvitch*"). "*Kvitch* day, *kvitch*

night, he won't change his ways!" "Please, no more or I'll
kvitch!"

B. As a noun:

A scream—but a special, not-to-be-taken-too-seriously exclamation.

A *kvitch* is no wise a *geshrei;* nor is it a substitute for
gevalt. A *kvitch* is midway between a squeal and a scream. It
is not prolonged or cacophonous; it is a small, unpretentious,
often obligatory exclamation of dismay, surprise, or not-exces-
sive alarm.

Approved or standard forms of *kvitching:*

Surprise: "When I walked in, she gave a *kvitch* you could
hear in Canarsie."

Distaste: "When she saw the wound, she let out a *kvitch.*"

Pleasure: "When they called her to the platform, she gave
out with a *kvitch.*"

Minor pain: "She stubbed her toe and gave a *kvitch.*"

Discombobulation: "Everyone was running around; the
kvitching could drive you crazy."

Dismay: "Please, no more *kvitching* or you'll disturb the
neighbors."

Disapproval: "She took one look at her son's girl and let
out a *kvitch.* No one could blame her, least of all me."

NOTE: To help you distinguish *kvitch* from *kvetch* from
krechtz (a salubrious set of niceties) I offer these observations:

You can *kvitch* sedately, charmingly, out of happiness; to
kvetch is always negative, bilious, complaining; and to *krechtz*
is to utter grating noises of physical discomfort or spiritual
woe—possibly spurious.

Kvitching may be hard on the ears, but *kvetching* is hard
on the nerves. As for *krechtzing,* it should be reserved for a
hospital room.

Some families produce personality types who are adept,
even effusive, in their *kvitching;* other families specialize in
kvetching—communal grousings drenched in self-pity; and
some *krechtz* so loudly and so often that they sound like a
convention of hypochondriacs.

If you take the trouble to familiarize yourself with the
nuances of *kvitching, kvetching,* and *krechtzing,* you may zest-

fully add them to your arsenal of exclamatory locutions. Connoisseurs should enlist them for the relief of English words that are becoming exhausted from overwork.

To the widow, who was shrieking and wailing over her dear departed's body, a friend said, "Please, restrain yourself, enough *kvitching*."

To which the widow retorted, "This you call 'enough'? Wait until we get to the cemetery! *Then* you'll hear *kvitching!*"

Ladino

Pronounced *lah-*DEE*-no,* to rhyme with "casino." Spanish: "familiar with several languages."

The vernacular used by Sephardic ("Spanioli") Jews, in Spain, Portugal, Turkey, the Balkans, Morocco; and by Spanish- and Portuguese-speaking Jews in Central and South America.

Ladino is a form of fifteenth-century Castilian Spanish, profusely sprinkled with Talmudic expressions and Hebrew words, and with borrowed Arabic, Turkish, and Greek words and phrases. It is also called *Judesmo* or *Judaeo-Spanish.*

In Ladino, Spanish words are often given Hebrew prefixes or suffixes; Hebrew words are Spaniolized by using them as roots and forming Spanish verb conjugations from them.

Some Spaniolized Hebrew words have become part of modern Spanish and Portuguese: *malsin,* for example, meaning "slanderer" or "informer" (from Hebrew *malshin*), which dates back to the Inquisition.

Ladino is often called by Spaniards *idioma castellano,* or

lengua vulgar. Wry Ashkenazim called it "a Sephardic substitute for Yiddish."

See Appendix: Ladino.

lag baomer

See SEFIRAH.

landsman

> Pronounced LONTS-*mon*, to rhyme with "nonce don." The plural is *landsleit,* to rhyme with "Don's height." German: *Landsmann,* "a fellow countryman."
>
> Someone who comes from the same home town—i.e., in Europe.

This usage was borrowed from the German immigrants in America, who quickly organized clubs, societies, "circles" of acquaintances from their native areas.

Though *landsman* is purely descriptive, and describes one you do not necessarily like or admire, it did acquire warm, friendly overtones.

"He is a *landsman*" often means "He is our kind of person," or "He is Jewish."

A newly arrived immigrant could expect to find a bed and a bowl of soup in the home of a *landsman,* and he might be passed along from one home to another until he got a start in the New World. A man who had established a toehold in America would often help a *landsman* find a job.

"My friend," said the owner of the men's clothing shop, "you are my *landsman*—and to a *landsman* I offer special bargain prices! Here is the best suit in the house. Will I ask you the one hundred dollars which, as you can see, is clearly marked on the label? No! A hundred I ask an ordinary customer, not a *landsman.* I also don't ask you ninety dollars. I don't even ask eighty! I ask seventy-five dollars, and not a penny more!"

"Ah," said the customer, "why should you lose money on me, just because we happen to come from the same place?

You are my *landsman* no less than I yours. So what should I offer for this suit? Thirty dollars? Never. Thirty I would offer a stranger, not a *landsman*. Forty? That would be an insult. To you, my *landsman*, I offer fifty dollars, and not a cent less!"

"It's a deal."

Two *landsleit* met in Brooklyn. "So how is it going with you, Glickman?"

"Not so good," *krechtzed* Glickman. "Last month I spent on doctors and medicines—forty-five dollars!"

"Forty-five dollars?! In one month! Back in the old country you could have been sick two *years* for that kind of money!"

latke

Pronounced LOT-*keh*, like "vodka." Slavic: "pancake"— usually:

A potato pancake.

Latkes were traditionally served at Chanukah, but now are served anytime. I love them.

Jewish cooks (which means Jewish women; who ever heard of a Jewish male cooking?) pride themselves on their *latkes*, which vary in taste and texture.

Long before medical research caught up with her, my mother decreed that anything fried is bad for the digestion, and discouraged my craving for the golden-brown, crisp *latkes* she would, from time to time, make.

A common phrase is *flat vi a latke*, "flat as a pancake."

L'chayim

Pronounced *l*-KHY-*im*, with a resounding German *kh*, to rhyme with "to fry 'em." Hebrew: "To life."

The toast offered, with raised glass, before sipping wine or liquor: "To your health."

Some innocents confuse *L'chayim* with *mazel tov*, using one when the other would be appropriate. There is no reason to err. *L'chayim* is used whenever one would say "Your health," "Cheers!" or (I shudder to say) "Here's mud in your eye."

Mazel tov! is used as "congratulations."

See MAZEL TOV for a surprising number of variations on this theme.

An interesting practice grew up in connection with the Hebrew word *chai* ("life"). Each letter of the Hebrew alphabet also serves as a number. (This alphabet predated the Arabic numeral system.) Thus, the first letter of the Hebrew alphabet, *alef*, serves as a one; *bet*, as two, and so on through *yud*, which is ten. The next letter, *kaf*, is 20; *lamed* is 30; through *taddi*, which is 90. *Koof* is 100; *resh* is 200; *shin* is 300; and the last letter of the alphabet, *taf*, is 400. Combinations of letters form the intermediate numbers, just as they do in the Roman numeral system.

A favorite pastime of the rabbis was to read meaning into words or phrases in the *Torah* or Prophets, by adding the numerical value of their letters, totaling them, and then breaking that total down into other combinations of letters. (See Appendix: Gematria.) Another game equated the letters of a word with a date, and thus predicted the coming of the Messiah—or, *ex post facto*, discovered that a catastrophe had been "predicted" in the holy books.

Since the Hebrew letters forming the word *chai* ("hope for life") add up to the number 18 (*ches* serves as 8; *yud* as 10), this number became charged with special attributes. Tradition-observing Jews give money to charity in amounts which are multiples of 18—in gratitude for a relative's recovery from illness, in honor of a child's birth, *Bar Mitzva*, or graduation, or as a gentle reminder to the heavenly tribunal when someone is sick.

In time of either stress or rejoicing, the Jew had one automatic response: Give to charity.

lendler

Pronounced LEND-*ler*. Yinglish.

The Jewish immigrants' pronunciation of the word for that repository of heartlessness and indifference to human suffering: the landlord. (Landlords suffer unpopularity in all cultures.)

Lendler has come down through the decades to enjoy a place of its own in the distinctive argot of Manhattan, Brooklyn, the Bronx and Queens.

When you rented rooms from a *lendler,* you became his *tenor.* Singing had nothing to do with it.

I once worked for a *lendler* who owned an apartment house that contained thirty *tenors.* The superintendent was called Mr. Janitor. (In Chicago, we had janitors, not "supers.") The janitor complained that the *tenors* were insufficiently appreciative of his stellar "soivices." The tenants considered the janitor a "Mister Loafer-who-is-so-lazy-a-person-can-bust-from aggravation-before-he-answers-a-polite-'Please-attend-to-the-radiator!'"

It was a full, rich life.

letz

Pronounced LETS, to rhyme with "gets"; plural LAY-*tsim,* to rhyme with "baits 'im." From Hebrew: *letz:* "a cynic."

A wit; a teasing, scornful jokester.

In the Middle Ages, *laytsim* referred to spirits who imitate and mock humans in order to torment them. Later, *letz* was used to describe any witty tease, a funmaker with a strain of scorn in his humor, a tart "card," the "life of the party."

Dr. M. J. Kornblum and Dr. Albert Steinhoff, both obstetricians, share an office. On the door, under their office hours, some *letz* printed:

24 HOUR SERVICE . . . WE DELIVER

levaya

Pronounced *le-vy-a*, to rhyme with "deny ya." Hebrew: "funeral." Literally: "accompanying" or "escort."

Funeral.

Jewish law requires that burial take place as soon as possible after death, and forbids any display or ostentation at a funeral. The rabbis insisted on simple burial rites, which served to enforce the egalitarianism of death. By tradition, a Jew is buried in a plain white shroud, and an unadorned pine box. (Cremation is foreign to the Jewish tradition; Judaism stresses respect for the holiness of the body, God's creation.)

It is considered both a MITZVA and a duty to attend a funeral, a mark of respect to the deceased and to the mourners. Since Jews have always taken this injunction seriously, a Jewish funeral is generally well attended. In a small community, everyone was expected to attend—except the teacher (*melamed*) who must not interrupt instructing the children!

Pious Jews sometimes have a little bag of soil from the Holy Land placed in their coffin.

It is not uncommon to hear a mourner, just returned from a funeral, comment on the size of the turnout, the beauty of the rabbi's eulogy, the attractive appearance of the cemetery. "O, *a shayneh levaya!*" ("A beautiful funeral").

At Orthodox funerals, collectors for charity pass among the mourners, rattling their little boxes as they chant, "*Isodoh tatzel mimovess*" ("Charity saves from death"). This minatory message to the living must surely strike some as a reflection (albeit unconscious) on the deceased.

How perceptive is the old folk saying, "All things grow with time—except grief."

The mourners filed past the coffin, some sobbing, some sighing, and Mrs. Mittelman murmured, "Look at him. How peaceful he looks . . . how relaxed . . . so tan . . . so healthy!"

"Why not?" replied Mittelman. "He just spent three weeks in Miami."

l'havdil

Pronounced *l'HOV-d'l*, to rhyme with "m'cobble." Hebrew: "to separate."

1. The special ceremony that "separates" the holy Sabbath from the other days of the week. See SHABBES.
2. The expression used to distinguish sacred from nonsacred discourse.
3. An expression of modesty, to show one's respect for, and inferiority to, another. "True, I am a composer, but *l'havdil*, how can you compare me to Mozart?"
4. An ironic expression to indicate one's patent superiority over another.

"Rabbi, you speak as beautifully as that rabbi over on Thirteenth Street."

"*L'havdil.*"

Litvak

Pronounced LIT-*vok*, to rhyme with "bit lock."

1. A Jew from Lithuania, or neighboring regions.
2. An erudite but pedantic type—thin, dry, humorless.
3. A learned but skeptical sort. A *Litvak* is sometimes called a *tsaylem kop* (a *tsaylem* is a cross, but in this case the phrase means "death's head") because of the reputation for learning plus skepticism (in the eyes of the *Chasidim*) enjoyed by Jews from Lithuania.
4. A shrewd, clever fellow.
5. (Derogatorily, by *Galitzianer* Jews) A sharp trader, a corner cutting type—and one whose piety is shallow.

In some circles, *Litvak* is used not only to describe, but to deride. "What can you expect from a *Litvak?*" "He's as clever as a *Litvak.*"

(I have no doubt that a *Litvak* would refer to me as "a Poylisher *gonif.*")

Sholom Aleichem once said, "A Litvak is so clever that he repents before he sins."

See GALITZIANER.

loch in kop

Pronounced LAWKH-*in-kawp* or *-kup*, with a Scottish or German *kh* sound; rhymes with "hawk in taut" or "talk in pup." German: "hole in the head."

(Literally) Hole in the head.

This delectable phrase is used to characterize anything you definitely do not need. "That I need like a *loch in kop!*"
    For a related and splendid phrase see "*. . . toyten bankes.*"

loksh

Pronounced LUCK-*sh* (yes, I know I'm breaking up one syllable), to rhyme with the way a drunkard would pronounce "ducks."

1. A noodle.
2. A thin person.
3. A tall, thin person.
4. A dollar (don't ask me why).
5. An Italian. Why an Italian? Because Italians eat spaghetti, noodles, i.e., *lokshen* (plural of *loksh*).

The phrase "*a langer* (LAHNG-*er*) *loksh*" is like "a long drink of water."

A beggar came to Mrs. Gimpel's back door. "Lady, I'm starved. You have maybe something to eat?"
    "Much, I haven't got," sighed Mrs. Gimpel. "Would you like—some *lokshen* left over from last night?"
    "Certainly!"
    "Then come back tomorrow."

lox

You can't mispronounce this; it rhymes with "box." German: *Lachs*; Scandinavian: *lax*: "salmon."

Smoked salmon.

Lox is highly salted; "Nova Scotia" salmon is more delicate, more bland and more costly. *Lox* has become a Sunday-brunch delicacy. I have had it served me from Bel Air to Park Avenue, by bohemian cartoonists and investment bankers.

Usually, *lox* is served on a *bagel* (plain or toasted), coated with butter and lathered with cream cheese.

It may startle you to know that the luxurious practice of eating *lox*, thought to be so typical of East European Jews, actually began for them in New York. *Lox* was almost unknown among European Jews and is rare to this day there—and in Israel.

Lox, incidentally, is distant cousin to *leax*, the Anglo-Saxon for "salmon." And, though I hate to admit this, the finest salmon in the world is Scottish salmon; the most exquisite *lox* I ever tasted was at the Prince Connaught Hotel, London.

A beggar mooched half a dollar and raced into a delicatessen for a *bagel* and *lox*.

The donor followed him in angrily. "I didn't give you money to throw away on luxuries!"

To which the beggar replied: "When I'm broke, I can't afford *lox*. When I *have* money, you tell me not to spend it on *lox*. So tell me, Mr. Philosopher, when *can* I eat *lox?*"

luftmensh

Pronounced LOOFT-*mensh*. German: *Luft:* "air"; *Mensch:* "man."

1. Someone with his head in the clouds.
2. An impractical fellow, but optimistic.
3. A dreamy, sensitive, poetic type.
4. One without an occupation, who lives or works *ad libitum*.

The prototype of the *luftmensh* was one Leone da Modena, a sixteenth-century Venetian Jew, who listed his skills and cited no fewer than twenty-six professions. His talents ranged from preaching to composing epitaphs. Why would so accomplished a man be classified as a *luftmensh?* Because out of all twenty-six professions (plus assiduous alchemy on the side), he barely made a living.

Israel Zangwill wrote an amusing story, *The Luftmensch,* about a gentleman whose business cards read, "Dentist and Restaurateur."

Perhaps the best-known *luftmensh* in Yiddish literature is Sholom Aleichem's "Menachem Mendel"—a luckless dreamer, a meek *shlimazl,* fate's perpetual patsy.

lump

Pronounced so that the *u* rhymes with the *oo* in "oomph" and not with the *oo* in loom. From German: *Lump:* "scoundrel."

1. A no-good.
2. A low-life, a bum.
3. A man who makes unpleasant advances to a lady.
4. A coarse, unrefined, boorish fellow.
5. A scoundrel.

"He's a *lump*" is also used the way we say in English, "He's a bastard."

maarev

See MAIREV.

macher

Pronounced MOKH-*er;* be sure to use the German *kh,* as in "Ach!" German: *Macher:* "maker," "do-er."

1. Someone who arranges, fixes, has connections; a big wheel; an "operator."
2. Someone who is active in an organization, like the zealous president of the Sisterhood or the P.T.A.; on campus, a "B.M.O.C."

The man who could miraculously produce a visa, or provide immigration papers, or get an exit permit for a Jew, was known as a *macher.*

A *"gontser macher"* means a real operator, a real big shot.

Machers can be *k'nockers,* if they boast about their exploits (real *machers* don't).

Most *k'nockers* are tenth-rate *machers*—if, indeed, *machers* at all.

See also K'NOCKER.

During a convention in Miami, two female delegates, *machers*, met in the lobby. Sadelle* fell upon Shirley's neck and they embraced and chattered away.

"Darling, you look wonderful," said Sadelle. "A regular new woman! Tell me, what do you do to look so good?"

"Ssh. I'll tell you a secret. I'm having an affair!"

"Really? That's marvelous! Who's catering?"

machetayneste
machetuneste

Pronounced *mokh-e-TANE-es-teh,* to rhyme with "Maritaine Esta," or *mokh-e-TUN-es-teh;* be sure to rattle the *kh* in the back of your throat. Hebrew: *mechutan, mechutenet:* "relative (m. and f.) by marriage."

Female relative. The variety of relationships defined by *machetayneste* requires first-person illustration: "My *machetayneste*" can mean:

1. The mother of the girl I'm going to marry; or
2. The mother of the girl my son is going to marry; or
3. The mother of the boy I'm going to marry; or
4. The mother of the boy my daughter is going to marry; or
5. My daughter's or my son's mother-in-law. This is the original and remains the most common and exact meaning.

* When Jewish matrons became "classy," they changed "Sadie" to "Sadelle" and "Sarah" to "Shirley." It was considered chic to change the "i" in a name to a "y" and use as many double letters as possible: Cheryll, Shirlee, Dyanne.

Among males it was common, in the 1920's and '30's, for Isadores to become Irvings, Irvings to become Irwins, Irwins to become Erwins; Sidneys became Sydneys, and Morris underwent Gallicization to Maurice. These fandangos in nomenclature are but a brief sampling of a larger body of transformations that began in Europe, long ago, in the efforts Jews made to become assimilated, to break out of the ghetto, to evade discriminatory reactions to stereotyped Semitic names.

Of special value is meaning 5, which describes a relationship for which there is no word at all in English.

The masculine form is *machuten*.

___

One of the oldest of Jewish stories concerns the poor man who came to his rabbi and complained that he was living in one room with his wife and four children and *machetayneste* —and the congestion was impossible to bear any longer.

"Do you have a goat?" asked the rabbi.

"Yes."

"Take it into the room."

"*What?*"

"Do as I say."

So the poor man went home and brought the goat into his house.

A week later he hurried to the rabbi, sputtering: "I did what you asked. I took the goat in, and things are even worse than before! Rabbi, what shall I *do?*"

"Do you have any chickens?" asked the rabbi.

"Yes. Three——"

"Bring them into your house."

"Rabbi!"

"Do as I say."

So the poor man brought the three chickens into the house, and a week later returned to the rabbi, wringing his hands.

"It's terrible! I can't stand it any more!"

"Put out the goat," said the rabbi.

The poor man did as he was told and came back. "It's a little better, rabbi, but three chickens in a room with seven people . . ."

"Throw out the chickens," said the rabbi.

And finally the man stood before the rabbi, overjoyed: "Rabbi, there's no one as wise as you! My house now is a paradise!"

machetunim

Pronounced *mokh-eh-TU-nim*, with a crumb-expelling *kh*, to rhyme with "Bach attune him." Yiddish variation and transformation of Hebrew *mechutan:* "relative by marriage."

1. The members of one's wife's extended family.
2. The members of one's husband's extended family.
"His wife comes from a large family: she must have fifty *machetunim*." "I like her husband, but not all her *machetunim*."

The definitive explication of *machetunim* is to be found in this sardonic conundrum:

Q.: "Why did Adam and Eve live so long?"

A.: "Because their lives were not shortened by *machetunim*."

machuten
machutin

Pronounced *m'*KHOOT-*n*, to rhyme with "m'tootin." Note the larynx-seated *kh*. Derives from the Hebrew: *hatan:* "bridegroom." The masculine of *machetayneste*.

1. Father-in-law.
2. Father-in-law to be; that is:
   (a) the father of the girl I'm going to marry;
   (b) the father of the boy I'm going to marry.
3. My son's or daughter's father-in-law.

English could heave a great sigh of relief if it adopted *machuten* and *machetayneste*. Think of the improvement over the awkward phrasings above.

maggid

Pronounced MA-*gid*, to rhyme with "Pa did." Hebrew: "preacher." The plural is *maggidim* (ma-GID-*im*).

A teacher-preacher, usually itinerant.

The *maggid* played a significant role in holding together the religious and cultural strands of life in the Jewish communities in eastern Europe. A humble, often untidy, shabbily clothed "country preacher," he wandered about on foot, by cart, by wagon, from *shtetl* to *shtetl*—teaching, preaching, comforting, an evangelist concerned with the poorest among the tribes of Israel.

Please remember that rabbis were not expected to preach sermons; they were much more occupied with advanced study, with teaching, with interpreting the law, with stimulating study and discussion of the *Torah*. The *darshan* was the one paid to deliver sermons in the synagogue on *Shabbes* afternoons. The *darshan* was a learned man, a Talmudist, a rabbi himself. The *darshanim's* preachings were, of course, in Hebrew, erudite, technical, and often pedantic.

And because of the rabbis' aloofness from the pains and problems of ordinary people, which was akin to the remoteness of professors from peasants, intellectuals from housewives, the *maggidim* came to play a cherished role among the laity.

The *maggid* was much more of a *folksmensh* than either the rabbi or the *darshan*. He generally used Yiddish, for instance, instead of Hebrew, in his informal sermons. With no set base, no home pulpit, no official status, he lived off the contributions made to him by his usually poor, unsophisticated listeners.

To be sure, some *maggidim* were messianic, fulminating orators of the fire-and-brimstone school, fundamentalists who hammered away at sin and its fearful punishment, like the revivalists of the American "Bible Belt." But the most beloved *maggidim* were the homey-philosopher types—good-natured, humane, tolerant of human frailty, skillful in mixing jokes, stories, and parables into their sermons.

The lore of Jews from eastern Europe was vastly enriched by the *maggidim*, and by the delightful fables and moralistic tales they circulated.

See also TZADDIK, CHASID, REBBE.

A most learned *maggid* used to ride from town to town to preach, and he loved to invite questions—questions of any sort—from the groups to whom he held forth.

Now the *maggid's* driver always listened to the sermons, and to the questions and the answers, observing and admiring his *maggid*.

This went on for many years, until one day the driver said,

"*Rebbe*, I have listened to you deliver sermons and answer questions for twenty years. I can recite them in my sleep. . . . Just once, before I die, I'd like to have the experience of being a *maggid*, as revered as you are. Tomorrow—forgive me—we're going to a village neither of us has ever seen before. Why can't we—just this once—change places? I'll wear your broad hat and caftan, and they'll ask *me* the questions, and I'll answer every one—exactly the way you would!"

The *maggid* thought this so interesting an idea that he agreed. And so the *maggid* and the driver changed clothes, and the driver delivered a fine sermon and then the congregation began to ask him questions, all of which he answered with the greatest of ease. But the last question was asked by a *yeshiva bucher*, and was so new, so technical, so profound, that the poor driver had not the faintest notion of how to answer it. So he drew himself up and thundered,

"I am amazed anyone should ask me a question as simple as that! Why, even my driver back there, a poor, hard-working Jew who never even set foot in a *yeshiva*, can answer it. Driver!" he sang out to the *maggid*. "Stand up so all can see you! You heard the question. Answer it!"

mah nishtana
mah nishtannah
mah nishtanu

Pronounced *ma nish-TAH-nah* or *ma nish-TAH-noo*, to rhyme respectively with "polish Donna" and "polish Baloo." Hebrew—*mah:* "what" and *nishtana:* "distinguishes."

The words that begin the Four Questions asked at the Passover *Seder*. The full text is: *"Mah nishtana ha-leila ha-zeh mikol ha-laillos?"* meaning, "What makes this night different from all other nights?"

A Jew may exclaim *"Mah nishtana!"* when he means "How on earth can you explain that?!" or "Who would have anticipated that?"

See SEDER, HAGGADA.

mairev
maarev
maariv

> Pronounced MY-rev, to rhyme with "tire of." Hebrew: *maariv*: "the evening prayer."

> The daily evening religious service.

The first Jewish astronaut returned from a 100-orbit voyage around the earth. When reporters asked him how he felt, he said, "Exhausted! Do you know how many times I had to say *shachris*, *mincha*, and *mairev*?"

Maariv is the name of an evening newspaper in Israel.

makkes

> Pronounced MOCK-*ess*, to rhyme with "Ho(tch)kiss." From Hebrew: *makot*: "plagues, blows, visitations. . . ."

> Nothing. (I mean that's what *makkes* means: "nothing.") "You'll get *makkes*" means you'll get nothing.

Makkes and *bubkes* are distantly related, *makkes* being "nothing," and *bubkes* being a paltry, ludicrous, unworthy amount —almost nothing.

I once coined the phrase: "from *bubkes* to *makkes*" (out of the frying pan into the fire; from bad to worse; from little to nothing) but it never caught on. I'd like to try once more.

mama-loshen

> Pronounced *ma-meh* LAW-*shen*, to rhyme with "Mama Caution." Hebrew: *loshn*: "tongue."

> 1. "Mother language" or "mother's tongue."
> 2. Yiddish itself.

"Can I talk *mama-loshen?*" means "Will you understand if I speak Yiddish?"

To say "Let's talk *mama-loshen,*" means "Let's cut out the formal talk (or double talk)," "Get to the heart of it," "Let's talk man-to-man," "Lay it on the line."

"Mama's language" has an interesting background: Hebrew was the father's language, since the holy books were in Hebrew, and only Jewish males were taught to read. Yiddish became known as "the mother's tongue," the language of the home.

See YIDDISH.

Marrano

Pronounced *m'*-RAH-*no* to rhyme with "Milano." Spanish: "pig." Plural: *Marranos.* (Derivations other than Spanish are sometimes suggested.)

The contemptuous name used by Spanish and Portuguese Catholics, five hundred years ago, for converted Jews—such conversions being by force and *en masse*—who remained "secret Jews."

It was said that the tears of the Jews blended with the waters of the baptism they were forced to undergo.

Conversions were effected, in the name of a sweet and gentle Savior, on the rack, in the pyre, on a torture wheel; via hot lead poured into bodily orifices, branding irons, blinding rods; during a process of de-tonguing, de-nailing, skin-stripping, limb-separation through literal horsepower.

Several popes, in different periods—Clement VI, Boniface IX, Nicholas V—were horrified by such persecutions, and expressly forbade conversions by force; but the Church in Spain, Portugal, France, Mexico, Peru managed to carry on an effective Inquisition. Most of the forcibly made Christians practiced their Judaism in secret.

The story of the *Marranos*—from Portugal and England to Turkey and Persia—is unfailingly fascinating.

In Spain, before the expulsion of the Jews, many *Marrano* families, probably known to be *pro forma* converts, rose to positions of great influence and enjoyed high status. Many *Marranos* merged into the rarefied ranks of Spanish aristocracy. "It was not long before the majority [!] of distinguished Spanish families married into newly converted Christian families,"* writes Poul Borchsenius; he cites the record of one family alone, the Caballerios of Saragossa, which came to include in its *mishpoche* a minister of finance in the kingdom of Navarre, a vice-chancellor of the Kingdom of Aragon, the Speaker of the Cortes (Parliament), a bishop, a vice-rector at the University of Saragossa, a judge of the high court—and a fanatical anti-Semite. "The example is by no means unique."

In the fifteenth century, Spain became a vast bonfire in which the unholy *auto-da-fé* (how ironically titled) burned "new Christians" by the hundreds, and pious fanatics devised ever more hideous tortures. Torquemada, the Chief Inquisitor, persuaded Isabella and Ferdinand to expel all Jews. Between one hundred and fifty thousand and five hundred thousand human beings, including men at the very heart and mind center of Spanish life and culture, were driven out. About one hundred thousand found their first sanctuary in Portugal (whence they were soon expelled). A few thousand went to Italy, a like number to North African cities, and some went as far as Poland and Turkey, which accepted refugees in those days. And many *Marrano* families wandered, wretched and harassed, around the world, seeking shelter. To them, Pope Alexander VI, a Borgia, father of Cesare and Lucrezia, who flaunted his venality and licentiousness, hardly seemed Christ's Vicar—for he gave Ferdinand and Isabella the title of "Catholic sovereigns" and cited, among their most appreciated services to the Church and civilization, their expulsion of the Jews. Spain never recovered from the disastrous excision.

Marrano Jews founded the modern Jewish communities in Amsterdam and London. Other "crypto-Jews" existed in Majorca (the *chuetas*), in Persia (the *Jedid-al-Islam*), in South Italy (the *Neofiti*), in Salonica (the *Donmeh*).**

---

* Poul Borchsenius, *History of the Jews*, Vol. III. Simon & Schuster, 1966, pp. 212–213.

** See Professor Cecil Roth's *History of the Marranos*, third edition. Oxford, 1959; also B. Netanyahu, "The Marranos of Spain," in *Proceedings of the American Academy for Jewish Research*, Vol. XXXI, 1963.

Mashiach

See MESHIACH.

maskilin

See HASKALA.

matmid

See YESHIVA BUCHER.

matzo
matzoh

> Pronounced MOTT-*seh* (not MOTT-*so*) to rhyme with "lotsa." Hebrew: The plural in Hebrew is *matzoth*, pronounced MOTT-*sez*, in Yiddish.

> Unleavened bread (it comes in thin, flat, ridgy oblongs, and is semiperforated to facilitate neat breaking).

During Passover, no bread, no yeast or leavened products are eaten. *Matzos* commemorate the kind of unleavened bread the Jews, fleeing from Egypt in the thirteenth century B.C., ate because they could not pause in their perilous flight long enough to wait for the dough to rise. Exodus 12 : 15: "Seven days shall ye eat unleavened bread. . . ."

Today, *matzos* are enjoyed all year round, and are served in many restaurants.

The following story has nothing to do with *matzos* but may give you an irreverent slant on Exodus. It is Hollywood's version of the flight from Egypt:

Moses, racing his harassed people across the desert, came to the Red Sea and, snapping his fingers, called: "Manny!"

Up, breathless, ran Manny, publicity man. "Yes, sir?"

"The boats!"

"What?"

"The *boats*," said Moses. "Where are the boats—to get us across the Red Sea?!"

"Oh, my God! Moses, what with all the news items and human-interest stories—I forgot!"

"You *what?*"

"I forgot!"

"You forgot the *boats?!*" cried Moses. "You idiot! You moron! The Egyptians will be here any minute! What do you expect me to do—talk to God, ask Him to part the waters, let all of us Jews across and drown the pursuing Egyptians? Is *that* what you think——"

"Boss," said Manny, "you do that and I'll get you two pages in the Old Testament!"

mavin

> Pronounced MAY-vin, to rhyme with "raven." Hebrew: "understanding."

> An expert; a really knowledgeable person; a good judge of quality; a connoisseur. "He's a *mavin* on Mozart." "Are you a real *mavin?*" "Don't buy it until you get the advice of a *mavin.*"

Mavin was recently given considerable publicity in a series of newspaper advertisements for herring tidbits. "The Herring *Mavin* Strikes Again!" proclaimed the caption. The picture showed an empty jar.

A real advertising *mavin* must have thought that up.

"Don't ask the doctor, ask the patient."　　　　——PROVERB

mazel

> Pronounced MOZ-z'l, to rhyme with "nozzle." Hebrew: "luck."

> Luck; good luck.

See also MAZEL TOV.

A buxom blonde wore, at a charity ball, an enormous diamond. "It happens to be the third most famous diamond in the whole world," she boasted. "The first is the Hope diamond, then comes the Kohinoor, and then comes this one, which is called the Lipshitz."

"What a diamond!"

"How lucky you are!"

"Wait, wait, nothing in life is all *mazel*," said the diamonded dame. "Unfortunately, with this famous Lipshitz diamond you must take the famous Lipshitz curse!"

The ladies buzzed and *tskd*. "And what's the Lipshitz curse?"

"Lipshitz," sighed the lady.

"When a man has *mazel*, even his ox calves."

One Jew said to another, "They say a poor man has no *mazel*. Do you believe that?"

"Absolutely! If he had *mazel* would he be poor?"

mazel tov!

> Pronounced MOZ-z'l, to rhyme with "schnozzle"; *tov* is pronounced TUV, TUFF, or TAWF. Hebrew: *mazel:* "luck"; *tov:* "good."

> "Congratulations!" or "Thank God!" rather than its literal meaning: "Good luck." The distinction is as important as it is subtle.

Don't *"mazel tov!"* a man going into the hospital; say *"mazel tov!"* when he comes out.

Do not say *"mazel tov!"* to a fighter entering a ring (it suggests you are congratulating him for having made it to the arena), or a girl about to have her nose bobbed (which would mean "and about time, too!")

Say *"mazel tov!"* to an Israeli ship captain when he first takes command: this congratulates him on his promotion;

don't say *"mazel tov!"* when the ship reaches port: this suggests you're surprised he got you there.

At all Jewish celebrations—a *brith*, wedding, graduation, *Bar Mitzva*—you will hear *"mazel tov!"*'s resounding like buckshot in a tin shed.

The ancient Hebrews, like the ancient Babylonians, Egyptians, and Greeks, fiddled around with astrology. In the Bible, *mazel* referred to a planet, a constellation of the zodiac, and the word was invoked when "fate" was involved. Later, Talmudic sages sternly warned the Jews to eschew soothsaying and diviners. (Poor believing Jews had a hard time knowing what to think: The Bible, after all, talks of the "signs of heaven"—Jeremiah, for instance, and Isaiah. But the *Midrash* teaches: "The Holy One forbade astrology in Israel"; and it is said that God made Abraham "a prophet, not an astrologer." The great Maimonides called astrology "a disease, not a science.") Nonetheless, Jews continued to utter *"mazel tov!"* Soon the supernatural or divinational aspects were forgotten (just as "God be with you" became "good-bye") and *mazel* became simply "luck," *"mazel tovl,"* "Congratulations."

Mournfully, Mr. Lefkowitz entered the offices of his burial society. "I've come to make the funeral arrangements for my dear wife."

"Your wife?" asked the astonished secretary. "But we buried her last year!"

"That was my first wife," sighed lugubrious Lefkowitz. "I'm talking about my second."

"Second? I didn't know you remarried. *Mazel tov!"*

"How am I doing?" the writer answered his friend. "You have no idea how popular my writing has become. Why, since I last saw you, my readers have doubled!"

"Well, *mazel tov!* I didn't know you got married."

Mr. Grossman entered the third-class compartment, found every seat occupied; and saw an old woman sprawled out over two seats, ready to doze off.

"Mazel tov!" said Grossman.

"Thank you," said the old woman, sitting up and moving over. "But—what's the occasion?"

"This is the first time I've seen you since your wedding," said Grossman, sitting down.

mazik

Pronounced MOZZ-*ik*, to rhyme with "Fosdick." Hebrew: "one who causes injury." The plural is *mazikim*, pronounced *mozz*-IK-*im*.

1. **A bright, swift, mischievous, clever, or ingenious child.** *Mazik* is used most frequently in this admiring or doting way. And in this usage *mazik* and MOMZER have much in common. But *mazik* treads on no sensitive ground, whereas *momzer* does. "He's a little *momzer*" can mean "He's a clever little rogue," or "He's a little bastard." "He's a *mazik*" describes a little devil, not a diabolic child.

2. A quick, able, skillful person.
3. Someone ready to gamble or take a risk.
4. A mischievous fellow, a prankster.
5. A restless, happy-go-lucky type.

Used about an adult, *mazik* usually means "a hell of a fellow, happy-go-lucky, a live wire"—*not* a sinister or malevolent *mazik*. (See below.)

When used about an adult, *mazik* often has slightly ironic overtones; it suggests achievement "no one dreamed that *mazik* capable of."

By now you have probably guessed that shadings of sarcasm and condescension are exceptionally subtle (and ubiquitous) in Yiddish.

6. A destructive person (rarely used today).
7. A demon or devil (rare).

The last two uses, which are much older than the first five, are infrequently employed today. And the user should offer ample indications in the context that he means the sinister type of *mazik*, not the pleasant kind.

Sidney and his little sister were visiting their grandmother, who placed two apples on the table—one large and red, the other, small and withered.

"Now, darlings," she said, "I want to see which of you has the better manners."

"She does," said Sidney, taking the bigger apple.

He was a *mazik*.

mazuma

Pronounced *m'-ZOOM-a*, to rhyme with "bazooka." From the Hebrew, originally meaning "prepared" or "ready."

(Slang) Money, particularly ready cash.

I always heard *mazuma*, clearly a vulgarism, used to mean money (*gelt*). *Mazuma* was used rather than *gelt* when a lingering, amusing effect was desired. Just as we say, "Man, is he loaded!" (to mean rich, not drunk) some say, "Has he got *mazuma!*"

Mazuma and/or *mezuma* do not appear in the Bible or the *Talmud*, authorities aver, but *mezumen*, meaning term-loan, appears in legal discussions.

This synonym for money ("scratch," "wampum," "the green") may come from the Chaldean *m'zumon*, according to H. Hishin.*

Eric Partridge says *mazuma* came into Canadian parlance around 1914, and it is cited in Brophy and Partridge's *Songs and Slang of the British Soldier.*

"It's not that money makes everything good; it's that no money makes everything bad."   —FOLK SAYING

It is said of a couple in CHELM that the parsimonious husband always made his wife tell him exactly how she had spent the household *gelt*. One day, after she returned from shopping, he said, "I gave you five rubles when you left. How did you spend them?"

* *American Speech*, May, 1926, p. 456.

"Well," said his wife, "I bought a little this and a little that."

"That's two rubles," said the husband.

"Then I spent a ruble here——"

"That's three."

"—and a ruble there."

"Four," said the husband.

"Four?" His wife frowned. "Now what did I do with that fifth ruble?"

"See!" cried the husband. "You send a woman shopping and she wastes your money without knowing on what."

mechaieh

Pronounced *m'-KHY-eh*, to rhyme with "Messiah." The *kh* sound is, of course, the way a MacTavish would roll it out. From Hebrew.

Pleasure, great enjoyment, a real joy.

Mechaieh is invariably uttered with a smile, a grin, a patting of the stomach, a pleased cluck or shake of the head.

When you take off your shoes and stretch out in front of a fire, that's a *mechaieh*.

When you hear a great virtuoso sing, it's a *mechaieh*.

I suggest you preface *mechaieh* with a blissful "Oh!" "Oy!" or "Ah": "Oh, this is a *mechaieh!*" *Oy* adds flavor to the utterance, but "Ah" is not to be sneezed at in this connection.

Mechaieh comes from the Hebrew *chay*, meaning "life." Technically, a *mechaieh* is one who gives life. (*Mechaieh* also meant God.)

Yiddish-speaking Jews converted the word into "putting life into" or "giving pleasure." That in itself was a *mechaieh*.

Finsterwald stumbled along the street, limping, moaning, groaning, leaving a trail of *"Oy vay!"*s in his wake. A stranger stopped him. "What is the matter?"

"What's the *matter?* My shoes are absolutely killing me!"

"So why do you wear them?"

"I'll tell you. My business couldn't be worse. I owe the

butcher, the baker, the grocer, the landlord. I have two daughters so ugly who knows if I'll ever be able to get them married? My son is a *zhlob* and my wife nags, nags, nags until I can go crazy. I come home each night from a fruitless day's work, and I look at the bills and at my family and at that point I could kill myself. So I take off my shoes—and mister, the minute these shoes are off my feet, it's such a *mechaieh* it's the only thing that makes life worth living!"

mechuleh

Pronounced *m'*-KHOOL-*eh,* to rhyme with "a pull a." Hebrew: "finished," "destroyed."

Finished unsuccessfully, ended unhappily. "He went *mechuleh*" means he went bankrupt. "That marriage? *Mechuleh!*" means they're not living together any more—at least.

Mechuleh is like "*Fini!*" in French, or "Pfft!" in Winchell-ese, if that's any help to you.

In the Bible, *mechuleh* was used to mean "to end" or "to exterminate." Later, the word came to mean "spoiled" or "damaged."

That's all I know about *mechuleh.*
Mechuleh.

medina

Pronounced *m'*-DEE-*na;* rhymes with "farina." Hebrew: "country," "state."

Province, area, country, land. In Yiddish it means, as well:
1. Domain.
2. Area of involvement.

"That's his *medina*" means "That's his problem, his headache."

The United States was known as the *"goldeneh medina"*—Eldorado—to the Jews who came here.

A poor, undernourished tailor, working in a basement, once said ironically, "Observe the glory and the grandeur of my *medina.*"

But one of his sons became a professor, another became an editor, his daughter a concert pianist.

His children became, as with millions of immigrants, his *goldeneh medina.*

megillah

Pronounced *meh-GILL-eh*, to rhyme with "guerrilla." Hebrew: "scroll."

1. *Megillah* usually describes the Book of Esther, which is read in the synagogue during the Purim holiday; also the book of Ruth. (There are five *megillahs* in all.)

2. Anything very long, prolix; a rigmarole. The Book of Esther wanders through a crushing concatenation of detail, and the devout sit through the long, long reading after a day of fasting.

3. In popular parlance: anything complicated, boring, overly extended, fouled up. "He'll put you to sleep with that *megillah.*" "Don't give me a *megillah*" means "Spare me the full, dull details."

In show business, *megillah* has become a much-favored word and I have heard it, not without surprise, on many a television program: the *Tonight* show's chit-chat; dramas where shady characters employ their special argot, not criminal but certainly *infra dig;* scenes between lawyers; in comedy routines, by Jewish and non-Jewish entertainers alike, instead of "all that jazz," or "all that malarkey." Thus: "Cut the *megillah.*" "He gave me a real *megillah.*" "Who needs a *megillah* like that?"

Night-club habitués and jet-set jokers, in Hollywood, New York, and Miami, use *megillah* as matter-of-factly as if they were in the synagogue during Purim, just as many Italians say *"una Iliade"* who have never read the *Iliad.*

A gontzeh megillah, meaning "a whole *megillah*," is a common phrase; it simply adds a note of dismissal via emphasis.

Two men sat opposite each other in the train. After a while, the first man said, "Uh—where are you from?"

"Newark," said the second, "and I'm going to Philadelphia. My business is insurance. My name is Boris Mishkin, I'm not rich, I have a son at Rutgers and a daughter who's married. My wife's maiden name was Kowalsky and she comes from Paterson. I'm a Democrat. I don't fish or play golf. I spend my summers in the Catskills and go to Miami for two weeks every December, where I stay in a motel. I go to a Reform temple and contribute to the UJA, B'nai Brith, and the Community Chest. I don't have a brother of the same name because I don't have a brother, and my sister you couldn't possibly have known because she died thirty years ago in Cracow. Now, if I've forgotten anything in this *megillah*, please ask me right now, because I want to take a nap until we reach Philadelphia!"

melamed

Pronounced *m-LAH-med*, to rhyme with "Muhammad." Plural: *melamdim*, pronounced *m-LAHM-dim*. Hebrew: "teacher."

1. A teacher—of elementary Hebrew, more exactly. Hebrew teachers were not rabbis or sages, but an unworldly, impecunious lot whose social status was respectable, but not enviable. The *melamed*'s work was teaching-by-rote. (My father used to say, "If they were smarter, they'd be rabbis.")

2. An incompetent. To call someone a *melamed* who does not earn his living as a *melamed* is to speak with condescension. ("Those who can, do," said Shaw. "Those who can't, teach.")

3. A *shlemiel*, a well-meaning, innocuous drip.

4. An unworldly, unsophisticated, impractical type. There is a saying: "A *melamed* remains a *melamed*." It means "He'll never get anywhere," or "What did you expect?"

It always puzzled me that the Jews, who so revere learning, should speak patronizingly of a teacher. The reason, I suppose, is that the *melamed* is the teacher of elementary Hebrew to young boys—teaching-by-sheer-repetition—and every Jewish community seemed to contain a great many elders, perambulating repositories of lore and wisdom, compared to whom the *melamed* lacked luster. Besides, *melamdim* were considered rather poor teachers, and a Jew who had no way of making a living, or who had failed in what he had undertaken, could become a *melamed* as a last resort.

Among the *melamdim* were many deeply pious men, dedicated to teaching—but their teaching could not help becoming repetitious and boring.

A Jewish saying goes: "He has no luck—like a *melamed*."

Pitying, even derogatory, tales about *melamdim* abound among Jews. In all of them, the *melamed* is not the hero but the goat—hapless, unlucky, unresourceful.

Sholom Aleichem defined a *melamed* as "a Jew who deals with *goyim*"—meaning that a *melamed*'s students, being little boys, know about as much Hebrew as do Gentiles.

"Ah," sighed a *melamed*, "if I were Rockefeller, I'd be *richer* than Rockefeller."

"How could that be?"

"I would do a little teaching on the side."

A *melamed* was given to taking a little nip while his pupils droned on. And when this became known, parents began to withdraw their boys from his class.

His wife pleaded with him to change his ways. "Give up drinking and you'll get the pupils back."

Sighed the *melamed*, "You tell me to stop drinking so I should be able to teach, but I have been teaching so I should be able to drink."

The *melamed* asked one of his young students, "Yussele, do you say your prayers before each meal?"

"No, *melamed*."

"*What?* You don't pray before each meal?!"

"I don't have to. My mother's a good cook."

Melech Ham'lochim

Pronounced MEH-*lekh* ha-*meh*-LAW-*khim*, to rhyme with "derrick papa saw him," using the guttural *kh* twice. Hebrew: "King of Kings."

One of the titles used to avoid uttering the Name of God (see ADONAI, ADOSHEM).

Since God is the King of kings, all men, whether princes or paupers, are His servants. Hence, the rabbis taught that no man should serve another, for all are servants of God alone.

A sign in a café in Jerusalem reads: "Self-service. 'For you are servants unto Me,' saith the Lord."

menorah

Pronounced men-AW-ra, to rhyme with "aurora." Hebrew: "candelabrum."

The *menorah* most commonly referred to is the eight-branched candelabrum lit on *Chanukah,* the Feast of Lights.

The word first occurs in Exodus 37, where you can find a detailed description of the seven-branched gold candelabrum made by Bezalel, the artisan, for the Tabernacle in the wilderness. The *Menorah* was later placed in the Temple in Jerusalem.

The Arch of Titus in Rome, which commemorates the conquest of Judea by the Romans, has a *menorah* depicted on it.

Originally, it was an oil lamp that was lighted on Sabbath eve, with a flax wick soaked in eight or nine separate spouts arranged in a line or in a circle. Oil lamps gave way to brass or silver candlesticks in the eighteenth century.

When candles replaced oil lamps, the charming custom arose of lighting one candle for each child in the family. In lighting these, the mother would close her eyes and pass her hands quickly across the candle flame, toward herself, as if to inhale divine spirit. "The soul," says Proverbs, "is the Lord's candle."

mensh
mench

Rhymes with "bench." From German: *Mensch:* "person." Plural: *menshen.*

1. A human being. "After all, he is a *mensh,* not an animal."
2. An upright, honorable, decent person. "Come on, act like a *mensh!*"
3. Someone of consequence; someone to admire and emulate; someone of noble character. "Now, there is a real *mensh!*"

It is hard to convey the special sense of respect, dignity, approbation, that can be conveyed by calling someone "a real *mensh!*"

As a child, I often heard it said: "The finest thing you can say about a man is that he is a *mensh!*" Jewish children often hear the admonition: "Behave like a *mensh!*" or "Be a *mensh!*" This use of the word is uniquely Yiddish in its overtones.

The most withering comment one might make on someone's character or conduct is: "He is not (did not act like) a *mensh.*"

To be a *mensh* has nothing to do with success, wealth, status. A judge can be a *zhlob;* a millionaire can be a *momzer;* a professor can be a *shlemiel,* a doctor a *klutz,* a lawyer a *bulvon.* The key to being "a real *mensh*" is nothing less than —character: rectitude, dignity, a sense of what is right, responsible, decorous. Many a poor man, many an ignorant man, is a *mensh.*

See also BALBATISH.

"Ten lands are more easily known than one man."

—PROVERB

meshiach
mashiach

Pronounced *m'-*SHEE-*ach*, with a rattling *kh* sound at the end; rhyme it with "Marie, *ach!*" From Hebrew: *ha-mashiah:* "the anointed." The Hebrew *mashiah* became, in Greek, *messias,* or, in translation, *christos;* hence, *messias* = messiah; *christos* = Christ—and both denote "the anointed one."

Messiah.

1. Originally, in the Old Testament, *meshiach* was the title for kings ("God's anointed") and priests, who were initiated into sacerdotal status by being anointed with sacred oil.

2. Later, *meshiach* meant a prophet, or anyone with a special mission from God.

3. Then, *meshiach* came to mean the awaited Deliverer of the Jews from their bondage and oppression, who will restore the kingdom of Israel.

4. Finally, *meshiach* means the Savior who will make the world acknowledge God's sovereignty, thus ushering in the Day of Judgment.

English translations of the Bible tend to separate the idea of "the anointed" from the "Messiah"—the first used for the living, the second for the expected. The Jewish concept needs to be understood historically. The Old Testament uses the term *mashiach,* anointed king, for Saul, David, Zedekiah, and Cyrus of Persia (no Jew). David, "the anointed of Yahweh," established the dynastic principle among the Jews.

From this seems to have developed, across many years, the idea that some man, blessed by God with superior virtues, would come from the House of David to end Israel's tribulations and torment, to enforce justice and establish peace. A spiritual leader, a Messiah, would establish that new messianic age—on earth, be it noted—which the great prophets Isaiah and Micah foretold. And in the new Age of Righteousness *all* of mankind would be redeemed.

Jews distinguished the earthly Messiah from a heavenly Messiah: The earthly Messiah, a dreamed-of deliverer of the Jews, was to be a man born of the line of David; but the heavenly Messiah lives in heaven "under the wings of the Lord" (Enoch, 39) and existed before the sun and the stars were made. And his mystical Name existed before the sun. The idea of a divine Son of Man was not understood by Jews in the later messianic sense.

The doctrine of the Messiah has been one of the most powerful elements in the history of Judaism—and, of course, Christianity. Whenever epidemics, starvation, pogroms, wars, expulsions, or any of the thousand torments visited upon the Jews seemed unendurable, the faithful and desperate looked once more into their holy books for some hidden sign, some new revelation, some miraculous harbinger of hope; pious mystics, numerologists, astrologers, cabalists, and, later, *Chasidim* predicted the exact time when the glorious Messiah would usher in the Kingdom of God.

The Romans, who could make no sense out of the Jews' concept of a Messiah, feared messianic claims and predictions for political reasons, because they considered them a camouflage for rebellion against Rome's rule. And messianic hopes often did lead to political militancy; messianic ideas buttressed protests against a sense of resignation, an utterly passive acceptance of Israel's lot that, some Jews felt, was encouraged by Talmudic law.

Around 60 A.D., and especially after the destruction of the Second Temple in 70 A.D., messianic fevers raged among Jewry. Daniel's book of prophecies was seized upon and quoted to prove the imminence of the Messiah's arrival. And when, in the year 115, the Jews, led by the remarkable Bar Kochba, rose in armed rebellion against Rome, and for years held off superior forces, Bar Kochba was acclaimed "the Messiah."

It is hardly surprising that the history of the Jews is studded with pseudo-prophets and false Messiahs, all self-proclaimed: mystagogues, adventurers, some sincere but paranoidal visionaries, some charlatans—each claiming to be fulfilling a divine mission, or claiming to have received a revelation directly from God. They fanned the fires of hope for miraculous deliverance in hundreds of thousands of desperate hearts. These mountebank Messiahs were as colorful and brazen a company of crackpots and *saltimbanques* as ever paraded across the pages of history.

I admire the passage, in *Antiquities of the Jews*, in which Josephus writes: ". . . they were deceivers and deluders of the people, and under [the] pretense of divine illumination . . . prevailed upon the multitude to act like madmen."

One man's *meshiach* may be another's *meshuggener*.

A group of ultraorthodox zealots, called *Neturei Karta*, who today live in Israel, refuse to recognize Israel as an independent state because, they maintain, such a holy sovereignty could only have been established by the *Meshiach*—and the *Meshiach* has, clearly, not yet arrived.

See Appendix: False Messiahs, Sabbatai Zvi.

meshugge

Pronounced *m'*-SHU-*geh*, to rhyme with "Paducah." Hebrew: "crazy."

Is there anyone who does not know that *meshugge* means crazy? Crazy, nuts, wildly extravagant, absurd.

The potent *sh* and muscular *ug* unite to give *meshugge* a ripe combination of sounds that may account for the word's increasing popularity in English.

A crazy man is a *meshuggener*.

A crazy woman is a *meshuggeneh*.

Note: "That's *meshugge*," but "that's a *meshuggeneh* idea."

Also see MISHEGOSS.

"Every man has his own *mishegoss*."   —FOLK SAYING

Old Mr. Yonklowitz could not sleep. For nights on end, week after week, the old man complained of insomnia. His children had brought in doctors; they had given the old man pills, syrups, tranquilizers—all to no avail.

The frantic children finally decided to call in a hypnotist. They did not decide this lightly, mind you, but in desperation. And to find a reliable hypnotist, they consulted a psychiatrist.

When the hypnotist arrived, the children introduced him to the old man. "Papa, a wonderful doctor, a man who works miracles, a *specialist* who makes people sleep!"

The hypnotist said, "Mr. Yonklowitz, if you'll have just a

little faith in me, you'll fall asleep like a child." He held up a watch and said, "Keep your eyes here. That's right. . . . Good." The hypnotist now swung the watch back and forth, slowly intoning: "Left . . . right . . . Your eyes are getting tired . . . tired . . . Your eyelids are heavy . . . heavy . . . sleep . . . sleep . . . sleep."

The old man's head hung low, his eyes were shut, his breathing was as rhythmic as a babe's.

The hypnotist placed his finger on his lips, cautioning the children to remain silent, and stole out.

Whereupon the old man opened one eye. "That *meshuggener!* Has he gone yet?"

meshumad

Pronounced *m'*-SHU-*med*, to rhyme with "diluted." Hebrew: "apostate." Plural: *meshumadim*.

A willing convert from Judaism; an apostate.

Note the word "willing." Jewish history is full of so many mass conversions, by hair-raising tortures and threats of death, that Jews distinguished forced converts, or *anusim*, from those who joined another faith of their own volition, *meshumadim*.

The most famous and important of Jewish *anusim*, of course, were the *Marranos* of Spain.

See MARRANO.

metsieh

Pronounced *meh*-TSEE-*eh*, to rhyme with "Let's see a." Hebrew: "find."

1. A bargain, a lucky break. "Believe me, that's a *metsieh.*"
2. No bargain (used bitterly), nothing to brag about. "He married some *metsieh.*" "Oh, thank you for such a *metsieh!*"

Today, *metsieh* is used mostly in this dry, disillusioned, sarcastic way.

Metsieh originally meant something valuable that was found. The *Talmud* expresses this lovely thought: "God found the Jews as one finds grapes in the desert."

I know of no English word with quite the bouquet of *metsieh*, and commend it to you. It's a *metsieh* in itself.

The *Baba Metsia* ("Middle Gate") is a tractate of the *Talmud* that deals with laws of possession, obligations of guardianship, and so on.

mezuzah
mezzuza

> Pronounced *meh-*ZU-*zah*, with a short "*u*" as in "put." Rhyme it with "kazoo's a." In Hebrew, *mezuzah* means "doorpost"; but don't use it that way, unless you're in Israel.

> The little oblong container (about the size of two cigarettes) that is affixed to the right of the front door-jamb of his home, in a slanting position, by a Jew who believes in putting up a *mezuzah*.

An Orthodox Jew touches his fingers to his lips, then to the *mezuzah*, each time he enters or leaves his home.

Inside the *mezuzah* is a tiny, rolled-up paper or parchment on which are printed verses from Deuteronomy: 6 : 4–9, 11 : 13–21. The first sentence is Israel's great, resounding watchword: "Hear, O Israel, the Lord our God is one." The inscribed passages contain the command to "love the Lord your God, and to serve Him with all your heart and with all your soul"; they end with an inscription reminding the faithful that God's laws are to be observed away from, as well as at, home, and that children must have a respect for God's laws instilled in them. (The enclosed material also includes the injunction to inscribe these words "upon the doorposts of thine house.")

The *mezuzah* consecrates the home, which is so very important in the life and the ethos of Jews; the home is, in fact, a temple; it is known, in Hebrew, as *migdash mehad*.

Some scholars say that the *mezuzah* carries on the Egyptian practice of writing "lucky" sentences over the entrances to their houses. Muslims inscribe "Allah," and verses from the Koran, over their doors and windows.

An old Brooklyn Jew, after much cajoling from his children, took the train to Florida for the winter. His children had arranged for him to stay in one of the nicest hotels on the ocean. The hotel, they assured Grampa a hundred times, was strictly *kosher*. That was, indeed, the only kind of hotel the old man could be coaxed into entering.

The manager took the old man up to his room, expatiating on the hotel's features: "Pinochle every afternoon; movies twice a week; a TV set in every room . . ."

"But your kitchen," asked the *zayde*. "It it strictly *kosher?*"

"Absolutely!" said the manager. "We serve only *kosher* meat; everything is cooked in a strictly *kosher* manner."

At the door of his new room, the *zayde* automatically reached up to touch the *mezuzah*. There was no *mezuzah*.

The old man recoiled. "No *mezuzah?*"

"Don't get excited," said the manager, smiling. "On the roof, we have a master *mezuzah!*"

midrash

> Pronounced MID-*rash*, to rhyme with "bid posh." Hebrew: "commentary," "interpretation." From the root verb meaning "to study," "to investigate." Plural: *midrashim*.

> The very highly developed analysis, exposition, and exegesis of the Holy Scriptures.

The scholars of the period of the Second Temple (fifth century B.C. to 70 A.D.), convinced that the words of the Bible lent themselves to many interpretations and could be applied to all ages, to varied social conditions, and to all types of men, initiated complex midrashic interpretations of the Bible. These savants read involved ideas into simple verses, and found esoteric meanings in every jot and tittle of the holy texts.

After the dispersion of the Jews, the rabbis, their leaders, carried on the hermeneutic tradition; their sermons, based on Biblical texts, included a great deal of homiletic material—parables, allegories, illustrative stories, inspirational and edifying interpretations, that spoke directly to the common people. And beginning in the fourth century many of these curious sermons were written down and collected. There are over one hundred books of *midrashim* extant.

What is the difference between a *midrash* and any other analysis of, say, a verse? The *midrash* purports to penetrate the "spirit" of the verse and derive an interpretation which is not obvious. (It is often also not persuasive.) In the *midrash* there is total amnesty for *non sequiturs*, and poetic license—greatly inflated—becomes philosophy or, at least, theology.

See Appendix: Talmud.

miesse meshina

> Pronounced ME-*sa* m'-SHE-*na*, to rhyme with "Lisa Farina." Hebrew: *meshuna*, "unusual, abnormal," *m'ess*, "death."

An ugly or unfortunate fate or death.

The phrase is widely used by Jews either as a lament ("What a *miesse meshina* befell him!") or as a curse ("May he suffer a *miesse meshina!*").

mikva
mikvah
mikveh

> Pronounced MICK-*va*, to rhyme with "pick the." Hebrew: "a pool of water."

> The bath, prescribed by ritual, which a Jewish bride took before her wedding, and which religious Jewish women took (a) at the end of their menstrual period, (b) after bearing a child.

Under rabbinical law, a husband and wife were not permitted to come into close physical contact, much less cohabit, throughout the time of her menstruation, or for seven days afterward. On the seventh day, the wife was required to take a bath in running water, or in a bath expressly built for that purpose: a *mikva*.

A community of Jews was obligated to have and maintain a community *mikva*.

The rules and regulations governing the *mikva* are quite detailed; in fact, a whole section of the *Mishnah* explores this recondite subject. The woman recites a benediction while in the water.

Today, only very religious Jewish women observe the *mikva* custom—or attend a bathhouse for *mikvas* such as were found in Europe and on the Lower East Side.

Gentiles sometimes remarked on the unusual emphasis Jews placed upon cleanliness and hygiene; some said this amounted to a veritable "cult of purity." Such a "cult" was of immense value in keeping Jewish women cleaner, and the Jewish family healthier, than might otherwise have been the case. Bathing frequently must also have created and intensified a sense of self-respect. This seems all the more significant if one observes the differences in hygiene and sanitation, even today, between Jewish and Arab families/communities throughout North Africa and the Middle East.

See also SHVITZBUD.

I am told that pious American Jews refer to a *mikva* as a "ritualarium." No comment.

milchedig
milchik

Pronounce MILL-*kheh-dik*, to rhyme with "bill the sick," with a throat-clearing *kh*, or MILL-*khik*, to rhyme with "fill Dick." From German: *Milch*: "milk"; *milchig*: "milky."

1. Dairy foods which, according to the dietary laws (*kashruth*), may not be eaten with or immediately after

meat. Such foods are those that contain milk, butter, cream, cheese.

2. Pale, sickly-looking. "She's been sick for a week and looks *milchedig*."

3. A colorless, ineffectual personality, a Caspar Milquetoast. "She married a real *milchediker*."

mincha
minhah

Pronounced MIN-*kha*, with a Caledonian *kh*. Hebrew: "an offering."

The daily late-afternoon religious service.

By tradition, pious Jews pray at least thrice a day: *shachris*, in the morning; *mincha*, in the afternoon; *mairev*, in the evening.

minyan
minyon

Pronounced MIN-*yon*; rhyme it with "Binyon." Hebrew: "number," or "counting."

1. Quorum. (Sometimes used in a jocular way.)

2. The ten male Jews required for religious services. No congregational prayers or rites can begin "until we have a *minyan*."

To have ten men is to have a "synagogue." Children do not count, because children are not mature enough to understand the prayers. Since one cannot always find ten adult male Jews, exceptions to the *minyan* are permitted for a wedding, for instance, or a circumcision.

Solitary prayer is laudable, but a *minyan* possesses special merit to the observant, who have held from antiquity that when ten male Jews assemble, for either study or worship, God's Presence or *Shechinah* dwells among them.

You will remember that Abraham asked the Lord to save the righteous in Sodom, and God said He would spare Sodom if at least ten truly righteous men could be discovered in that sink of corruption. *Mishna* says that since God exempted Caleb and Joshua from his denunciation of the spies returned from Canaan (in Numbers), a congregation is twelve minus two—or ten.

It is worth remarking on the number of times the magical number ten (which is the normal number of fingers we are allotted on hands and feet) appears in Judaic law, lore, and history:

(1) The Ten Commandments

(2) The ten plagues visited on Pharaoh

(3) The ten days of penitence

(4) The ten generations cited in the Bible from Adam to Noah, and from Noah to Abraham

(5) The ten tests of faith God gave Abraham

(6) The unit of ten, in the clan structure, established by Moses (Exodus 18 : 25)

Minyan is often used in a jocular way, to mean "Do we have a quorum (or a majority)?" or "Have most of those we expected arrived?"

"Nine wise men don't make a *minyan*, but ten cobblers do."

"Nine saints do not make a *minyan*, but one ordinary man can—by joining them."

—FOLK SAYINGS

---

mishegoss
mishegaas

> Pronounced *mish-eh-*GOSS, to rhyme with "dish o' Joss."
> Hebrew: *meshuga*: "insane."

> Literally: insanity, madness.

But *mishegoss* is more often used in a lighter vein to describe not mental disease, but

(1) A wacky, irrational, absurd belief; nonsense; hallucinations. "Did you ever hear such a piece of *mishegoss?*"

(2) A state of affairs so silly or unreal that it defies explanation. "No one can figure it out; it's plain *mishegoss.*" "How can you cope with such a *mishegoss?*"

(3) A piece of tomfoolery, clowning, "horsing around." "He's the life of the party with his jokes and *mishegoss.*" "Please, cut out all the *mishegoss!*"

(4) A fixation, an *idée fixe.* "She has a new *mishegoss*— that the neighbors are trying to ruin her."

Note that *meshugge* can be used both seriously ("The psychiatrists declare him *meshugge*") and playfully ("Oh, he's hilarious, he acts *meshugge*") but *mishegoss* is nearly always used in an amused, indulgent way.

See MESHUGGE.

Mr. Samuel Goldwyn once remarked, during a dinner-table argument about psychiatry: "Anyone who goes to a psychiatrist ought to have his head examined."

The office of three psychoanalysts is alleged, by a malicious wit, to carry this shingle:

S. M. SPERO, M.D.

J. MELNICK, M.D.

R. GABRILOWITZ, M.D.

6 COUCHES—NO WAITING

And since we're on the subject, you may be interested in this definition of a psychoanalyst: "A Jewish doctor who hates the sight of blood."

When Mr. Klein returned from a visit to his friend Teitlebaum, in the psychiatric ward, Mrs. Klein bombarded him with questions.

"Poor Teitlebaum," sighed Mr. Klein. "Sick in the head. He rants, he raves, he talks *mishegoss.*"

"So how could you even talk to him?"

"I tried to bring him down to earth. I talked of simple everyday things: the weather; did he need warm clothes; the ten dollars he owes us. . . ."

"Aha! Did he remember?"

"That *meshugge,*" said Klein, "he isn't."

mish-mosh
mish-mash

Pronounced MISH-MOSH, to rhyme with "pish-posh." I prefer to spell this delicious word *mish-mosh*, as it is pronounced, but the 13-volume *Oxford English Dictionary* spells it *mish-mash*, and traces it to the German *mischmasch* and the Danish (!) *misk-mask*. It is unnerving to learn that *Junius' Nomenclator* called it *mishmash* as far back as 1585.

1. A mixup, a mess, a hodge-podge, a fouled-up state of things.
2. Confusion galore. "What a *mish-mosh!*" "You never heard such a *mish-mosh* of ideas."

No Jew pronounces this "mish-mash." In fact, when a Congressman on one of Groucho Marx's *You Bet Your Life* television shows did say "mish-mash," Groucho gave him a startled stare and remarked: "You'll never get votes in the Bronx if you go on saying *mish-mash* instead of *mish-mosh*." (Mr. Marx later wrote the same advice to Governor Scranton of Pennsylvania.)

I consider *mish-mosh* a triumph of onomatopoeia—and a word unlike any I know to suggest flagrant disorder.

Mishnah

Pronounced MISH-*neh*, to rhyme with "wish the." Hebrew: Literally, "to repeat one's learning," "review."

One of the two basic parts of the *Talmud;* the other (and much later) part is the *Gemara.* The *Mishnah* is the codified core of the Oral Law—that vast body of analysis and intepretations that was originally not written down for fear of affecting the sanctity of the *Torah.*

The *Mishnah,* which is written in Hebrew (the *Gemara* was

written in Aramaic), is divided into six "orders" (sedarim) and, in turn, into sixty-three massekhtoth or tractates. (Only thirty-six and one-half of these, incidentally, have a gemara appended.) Each tractate or treatise is divided into perakim, or "chapters," and each chapter into paragraphs. There are 523 "chapters."

The Mishnah's six "orders" are:

(1) Seeds, which discusses agricultural problems and laws, the products of orchards and fields, the rituals attending each;

(2) Festivals, which sets forth the halakah (law, rules) for fast days, festivals, the Sabbath;

(3) Women, which covers relations between men and women, betrothals, nuptials—and divorce (the Jews very early reconciled themselves to human incompatibilities);

(4) Damages, a detailed code of civil and criminal law, with cases;

(5) Sacred things, rituals, offerings, sacrifices, services;

(6) Purities or Purifications, matters of personal hygiene, clean and unclean foods, etc.

The Mishnah had its origin after the return of the Jews to Judea from their Babylonian exile (537 B.C.), when the scholars of the Great Assembly, the Jews' religious and legislative body, established basic rules for the interpretation of Jewish law. The Great Assembly produced a group of scribes (soferim) who were the official copyists and teachers of the Bible. They were followed by the tannaim, sages who continued to interpret Biblical laws and apply them to changing historical circumstances. Their discussions, ordinances and interpretations were, by tradition, transmitted orally, lest they diminish the sanctity of the Bible, i.e., the Written Law. Finally, their sheer accumulated bulk and breadth impelled some scholars to codify and transcribe them.

Hillel (c. 30 B.C.–20 A.D.), the greatest Pharisee, a tower of wisdom, a model of humility and benevolence (Jesus of Nazareth was clearly influenced by Hillel's teachings), made one of the earliest attempts to codify the vast, tangled body of oral teachings. No one knows what happened to his effort.

The illustrious Rabbi Akiba initiated the pioneer work of collecting and classifying the oral traditions, legal decisions and precedents, into a mishnah, or "review," and Akiba's work was continued by Judah ha-Nasi, "the Prince." (He was said to have been born on the day Rabbi Akiba suffered a martyr's death.) Rabbi Judah, known also simply as "Rabbi," was head of the *Sanhedrin*, the high court (see Appendix), that compiled, edited and codified the accumulated body of oral law, and around 200 A.D. declared the canonical labor closed. (It was Judah ha-Nasi who said, "Much have I learned from my teachers, more from my colleagues, but most from my students.")

Soon after Rabbi Judah completed the *Mishnah*, collections of additional material appeared: the *Tosefta* ("supplement"), *Baraitas* ("excluded traditions") and material pertaining to the Pentateuch. But Judah's *Mishnah* remained the central authority.

See Appendix: Talmud.

Judah Goldin offers an excellent and concise account of the *Talmud*'s history.*

mishpocheh
meshpocheh

> Pronounced *mish-PAW-kheh*, to rhyme with "fish locheh." Hebrew: "family."

> 1. Family, including relatives far, near, remote and numerous.
> 2. Ancestors, lineage.

The closest thing in English to *mishpocheh* is "clan."

Parents, grandparents, siblings, uncles, aunts, cousins (first, second, once removed), all form part of that extended family Jews call *mishpocheh*.

Nothing is more flattering than to say someone comes from a fine or distinguished *mishpocheh*.

"All Jews are *mishpocheh*" means that all Israel is one family. This intense feeling of a common heritage, common obligations, common values, has led the state of Israel to

---

* Judah Goldin, "The Period of the Talmud," in *The Jews: Their History, Culture and Religion*, Vol. I, third edition, Louis Finkelstein, editor, Harper, 1960.

accept, without exception, Jewish immigrants of the widest, sharpest cultural differences.

The Chase Manhattan Bank's memorable advertising campaign is built around the slogan "You have a friend at Chase Manhattan." 'Tis said that a sign in the window of the Bank of Israel reads:

"—BUT HERE YOU HAVE MISHPOCHEH!"

mitzva
mitzvah
mitzvoth (plural)

Pronounced MITZ-*veh*, to rhyme with "fits a"; the plural, *mitzvoth*, is pronounced MITZ-*vas*. Hebrew: "commandment."

1. Commandment; divine commandment.
2. A meritorious act, one that expresses God's will; a "good work," a truly virtuous, kind, considerate, ethical deed.

Mitzva is second only to *Torah* in the vocabulary of Judaism. The *Talmud* elaborates the concept in many places. *Mitzvoth* are of various kinds: those of positive performance (caring for the widow and orphan) and those of negative resolve (not accepting a bribe); those between man and God (fasting on *Yom Kippur*) and those between man and man (paying a servant promptly); those that specify the duties required of rabbis, and those that state the special sympathy for suffering required of any Jew.

Mitzvoth are regarded as profound obligations, as inescapable burdens, yet they must be performed not from a sense of duty but with "a joyous heart."

There are 613 (!) separate *mitzvoth* listed in the *Sefer Mitzvoth Gadel*, of which 248 are positive (the first being: "be fruitful and multiply"), and 365 negative. Maimonides, who listed all the *mitzvoth* in his *Book of the Mitzvoth* (written in Arabic, incidentally), remarked that a man who performed in accordance with only one out of the 613 deserved salvation—*if* he did so not out of self-interest, or to win credit, but entirely out of love and for its own sake.

The rabbis often used the phrase *simcha shel mitzva* ("the joy of fulfilling a pious act, a commandment") to hammer home the notion that good deeds performed out of a sense of requirement are not as meaningful as those performed out of desire—and with enjoyment.

One sage has said that God prefers the joy to the *mitzva*. (How he found this out, I do not know.)

It has been said that the basic principle of Jewish ethics lies in the idea of mandatory *mitzvoth*. Said Eleazar ben Simeon: "The world is judged by the majority of its people [and] an individual by the majority of his deeds. Happy is he who performs a good deed: *that may tip the scale for him and the world* [italics mine]."

Israel Zangwill called the *mitzvoth* the Jews' "sacred sociology."

————————————

If you do something honorable, especially kind or considerate, a Jew may beam, "Oh, that was a *mitzva!*" or "You performed a real *mitzva!*"

————————————

"One *mitzva* leads to another."
"The reward of a *mitzva?* Another *mitzva.*"

—FOLK SAYINGS

At the end of a pier in Tel Aviv, a man was about to jump into the sea when a policeman came running up to him. "No, no!" he cried. "How can a man like you, in the prime of life, think of jumping into the water?"

"Because I can't stand it any more! I don't want to live!"

"But listen, mister, *please*. If you jump in the water, I'll have to jump in after you, to save you. Right? Well, it so happens *I* can't swim. Do you know what that means? I have a wife and four children, and in the line of duty I would drown! Would you want to have such a terrible thing on your conscience? No, I'm sure. So be a good Jew, and do a real *mitzva*. Go home. And in the privacy and comfort of your own home, hang yourself."

————————————

Mr. Berkowitz stood before the angels in heaven anxiously,

as they examined the record of his deeds on earth. And the Chief Admitting Angel exclaimed, "But this is fantastic! This is unprecedented! In your entire lifetime did you not commit even *one* little sin?"

"I did try to live in virtue," faltered Mr. Berkowitz, "as a good Jew and a God-fearing man. . . ."

"But not one—little—*averah* in a whole lifetime!" sputtered the Admitting Angel. "You performed nothing but *mitzvas?!* . . . We can't let you into heaven: You are practically an Angel. No, no, you must be like other men—fallible, subject to temptation, prone to transgress . . . at least *once*. So, I will send you back to earth for twenty-four hours, during which time you must commit a sin—*one little sin*. Then appear before us again, at least *human!*"

The sinless and bewildered Mr. Berkowitz found himself back on earth, unhappy and uneasy, determined to try to take one step off the impeccable path of his righteousness. An hour passed, then two, then three; poor Mr. Berkowitz had found no opportunity to commit an *averah*. And then a buxom woman gave him a wink. . . . Mr. Berkowitz responded with alacrity. The lady was neither young nor beautiful—but she was willing! And when she blushingly hinted that he might indeed spend the night with her, Mr. Berkowitz was in sixth heaven (the seventh was yet to come).

In the dark, wee hours, Mr. Berkowitz looked at his watch: only one more hour before he would be whisked back to heaven. . . . Only half an hour . . . And as he quickly put on his clothes, prepared for his return to the celestial region, his blood froze—as the old maid in the bed sighed, "Oh, Mr. Berkowitz, what a *mitzva* you performed this night!"

mizrach
mizrachi

Pronounced MIZZ-*rokh*, with the Germanic *kh* sound as in *Ach;* rhymes with "Fizz loch." *Mizrach:* Hebrew: "east," "sunrise." (For *Mizrachi*, see below.)

A framed picture hung on the wall of every House of Study (or *Bes Midrash*) and in front of the synagogue lectern from which the readings are made.

The *mizrach*, which is often beautifully appliquéd and embroidered, is intended simply to show the congregation in which direction to face while praying—the direction always being where Jerusalem is. Thus, Jews in Persia or China or India (see Appendix: Cochin) turn to the west when praying.

Fifty years ago, a *mizrach* adorned many a Jewish home; not so today.

Mizrachi is the name of an organization of Orthodox Jews, staunch Zionists, who conduct much fund raising for Israel; the *Mizrachi* were important in Hebrew education in America, and very important in working for the creation of an independent Jewish state in Palestine.

Mogen David
Magen David

> Pronounced MAW-*ghen* DU-*vid* in Yiddish, to rhyme with "Fog in tumid." Hebrew: "Shield of David."

> Star of David; the six-pointed star that is the national symbol of Israel.

No one is sure how and when the Star of David first came into use as a symbol of Jewry. The first Zionist Congress adopted it in 1897.

No reference to the *Mogen David* is found in rabbinical writings until the thirteenth century, and the first explicitly Jewish association did not occur, it seems, until the seventeenth century. More I cannot tell you.

mohel
moel

> Pronounced MOY-*l*, to rhyme with "Doyle" (though I never heard of a *mohel* named Doyle), or "goil" (though that would be a startling combination, given *mohel*'s meaning). The English pronunciation is *mole*. Hebrew: a circumciser.

The man who circumcises the male baby in the ritual of *Brith Milah* eight days after birth.

See BRITH.

Circumcision is performed mostly by physicians today, but historically the *mohel* was a specialist in this quite unique, not to say narrow, field.

The knife a *mohel* uses must be double-edged—not for symbolic reasons, but to make sure the baby gets a swift, clean cut. If the knife were not double-edged, reasoned the rabbis, the blunt side might be used by mistake and the baby hurt (That always struck me as a good example of how closely those old sages reasoned.) The *mohel* usually comes prepared with two knives, each double-edged, in case one turns out to be dull.

In Europe and the United States, the circumcision is conducted in the home—or if the child is still at the hospital, there. Oriental Jews perform circumcisions in the synagogue.

The *mohel* holds no hallowed spot in the Jewish hierarchy of respect. He is regarded as a technician; God forbid he should perform any other type of surgery.

Like *chazzanim*, *mohels* are often the butt of jokes.

One of the first puns I ever heard was this: "The rabbi gets the fees, but it's the *mohel* who gets all the tips." I puzzled over that one for years.

A man passed a store window with nothing in it but a clock, stepped inside, and asked, "How long would it take to fix my watch?"

"How should I know?" shrugged the *baleboss*. "I don't fix watches. I'm a *mohel*."

"But—in your window—you have a clock!"

"So what would *you* put in the window?"

moichel

Pronounced MOY-*khel*, to rhyme with "joyful." Hebrew: *mochel*: "pardoner," "forgiver."

1. Forgive. Literally, "I forgive you."
2. (Ironically) "No, thanks."

"*Ich bin dir* (or *ihm*) *moichel*," an exquisitely dry, ironic phrase, is used to mean: "Thanks a *lot;* you (or he) can keep it"; "Don't do me any favors"; "Oh, *dandy!*"

Moishe Kapoyr

Pronounced MOY-*sheh* ka-POYR. *Moishe* is the Yiddish pronunciation of "Moses"; *kapoyr* means "backwards," "reverse," "the other way around," from Russian *kubaryom.*

Anyone who persists in being contrary, opposing, contradicting, putting things exactly opposite to what others do. "He has a streak of *Moishe Kapoyr* in him." "Don't argue; don't be a *Moishe Kapoyr.*" "He gets things so balled up, so topsy-turvy, his name could be *Moishe Kapoyr.*"

A *Moishe Kapoyr* must have a strong streak of perversity in him. With little effort he can be a *nudnik.*

In the 1920's, the *Jewish Daily Forward* ran a continuing series of single-frame cartoons about a contumacious character named *Moishe Kapoyr*, who delighted a nationwide public with his comic absurdities and "upside-down" comments.

momzer
mamzarim (plural)

Pronounced MOM-*zer;* rhymes with "bombs her." Hebrew: "bastard." Plural: pronounced *mom-ZAY-rim.*

1. A bastard. illegitimate. "She left home and gave birth to a *momzer.*"
2. An untrustworthy person. "I wouldn't trust that *momzer.*" "He may gyp you, that *momzer.*"
3. A stubborn, difficult man. "She married a real *mom-*

zer." "How can you get anywhere with such a bull-headed *momzer?*"

4. A clever, quick, skillful fellow (said admiringly). "Oh, is he a *momzer!*" "He has the wit of a *momzer.*"

5. An impudent sort. "Imagine such nerve: what a *momzer!*"

6. An irreverent (but not offensive) character; a scala-wag.

7. A detestable man, like the colloquial English "He's a bastard."

Momzer is often used with affection and admiration to describe a very bright child, a clever or ingenious person, a resourceful, gets-things-done, corner-cutting type.

"Most bastards are bright," said Abba Saul. And the *Midrash* observes that no one is as bold as a bastard.

A proud grandfather may beam, "My grandson, smart? A little *momzer!*"

Mothers are less likely to employ the word—at least about their own—and consider *momzer* a vulgar word, not to be used in "mixed company," or without blushing. Perhaps they remember the criticism: "When a mother calls her child a *momzer,* you can believe her."

CAUTION: Don't call anyone a *momzer* to his face unless you are on friendly terms; and don't call a child a *momzer* unless you're sure Papa or Mamma will not be offended.

The Biblical meaning of *momzer* is not merely "a child born out of wedlock," but a child born of a man and a woman between whom there could be no lawful marriage (e.g., the child of an incestuous relationship, or a married woman and a man not her husband). This was the *momzer* who could not "enter into the congregation of the Lord" (Deuteronomy 23 : 3). The rabbis considered this law harsh, and sought to limit the definition.

Under Jewish law, the illegitimate child of Jewish parents inherits from his natural father.

The Jews' reverence for learning is seen in the *Mishnah*'s judgment: "A learned bastard stands higher than an ignorant high priest" (*Horayot,* 3.8).

See OYSVORF.

He kept trying to persuade her to come to his apartment. She kept refusing.

"Why *not?*" he persisted.

"Well, I just know I'd—hate myself in the morning."

"So sleep late," he said.

(He was a *momzer.*)

motzi

Pronounced MOE-*tzee*, to rhyme with "goat sea." Hebrew: "provide," "bring forth."

The blessing over bread, recited before each meal.

This benediction goes: "Blessed art Thou, O Lord our God, King of the universe, who brings forth *(hamotzi)* bread from the earth."

This brief blessing is one of the most common in Jewish observance.

See BROCHE, DAVEN.

mutche

Pronounced MU-*cheh*, rhymes with "putsch-eh." Russian: *mutchit:* "to torture," "to torment."

1. To nag. "She *mutches* him day and night about his appearance."
2. To harass.
3. To struggle along, barely making ends meet. "How are things?" "Oh, I *mutche* (he *mutches*) along."

The most common usage is the last: "One *mutches* oneself to make a living."

This is so common that a typical conversation in Yiddish will run:

"*Sholem aleichem* (Hello). How are things?"

"Eh! One *mutches* oneself. And with you?"

"Likewise."

"*Nu*, stay healthy. I'll see you soon."

A most pious old Jew had prayed in the synagogue thrice every day of his adult life. His worldly business partner had not once set foot therein. And in his seventieth year the old Jew addressed the Lord thusly: "Oh, God, Blessed be Thy Name, have I not every day since my *Bar Mitzva* celebrated Your Glory? Have I ever made a move, named a child, taken a trip, without consulting You first? Is there a more devout, humble, observing soul in all Your fold? . . . And now I'm old, I can't sleep, I'm poor. . . . But my partner! That no-good! That *apikoros!* Not *once* has he even made a prayer! Not a penny has he given to the synagogue! He drinks, he gambles, he runs around with loose women—and he's worth a *fortune!* . . . Dear God, King of All the Universe, I am not asking You to punish him, but please tell me: why, why, *why* have You treated me this way?"

The synagogue rumbled as The Voice intoned: "Because all you do, day after day, is *mutche* me!"

N

naches
nakhes

Pronounced NOKH-*ess*, to rhyme with "Loch Ness"—with the *kh* sound a Scot would use in pronouncing "loch." Hebrew: *nachat:* "contentment."

1. **Proud pleasure, special joy—particularly from the achievements of a child.**

Jews use *naches* to describe the glow of pleasure-plus-pride that only a child can give to its parents: "I have such *naches:* My son was voted president of his play group." "Are you *shepping* (getting) *naches* from your daughter's career?"

2. **Psychological reward or gratification.**

I am getting *naches* from writing this book, since a new book is indeed a brainchild.

See also KVELL.

A very proud woman said to her friend, "My son, the doctor, is such a marvelous doctor—you *must* go to him."

"But why? There's nothing wrong with me."

"Believe me, with my son, go only once and he's sure to find *some*thing!"

Two old friends meet (in Jewish anecdotes, old friends are always meeting).

"I haven't seen you in twenty-five years. Tell me, how is your boy Harry?"

"Harry? *There's* a son! He's a doctor, with a wonderful office, with patients from all over the United States!"

"Marvelous. And what about Benny?"

"Benny? A lawyer. A *big* lawyer. He takes cases all the way up to the Supreme Court!"

"My! And your third boy, Izzy?"

"Izzy's still Izzy. Still a tailor," sighed the father. "And I tell you, if not for Izzy, we'd all be starving!"

nadan

Pronounced NOD-'n, to rhyme with "sodden." Hebrew: *nadan:* "dowry."

Dowry.

In the *shtetl*, even the poorest of brides had a dowry—collected by the community.

"Sell even the Holy Scrolls," goes an old saying of the Jews, "to make sure a poor girl has a dowry."

nafka

Pronounced NOFF-*keh*. Aramaic: *nafka:* "streetwalker."

Prostitute.

See KURVEH.

narr
naar

Pronounced NAHR, to rhyme with "far." From German: *Narr:* "fool," "buffoon."

1. Fool.
2. Clown, buffoon. "He acts like a *narr.*" "Don't be a *narr!*"

Two Israeli spies, caught in Cairo, were put up against the wall. The firing squad marched in. The Egyptian captain asked the first spy, "Do you have any last wish?"

"A cigarette."

The captain gave him a cigarette, lighted it, and asked the second spy, "Do you have a last request?"

Without a word, the second spy spit in the captain's face.

"Harry!" cried the first spy. "Please! Don't make trouble."

He was a real *narr.*

A *narr* said, "We have a rabbi, he gets paid so little, I don't know how he keeps alive. In fact, he would starve to death except for one thing: every Monday and Thursday—he fasts."

narrishkeit
naarishkeit

Pronounced NAHR-*ish-kite,* to rhyme with "Carr is right." German: *Närrischkeit:* "foolishness."

1. Foolishness.
2. A triviality; trivia. "The movie? A piece of *narrishkeit.*"

nayfish
nafish
nefish

Pronounced NAY-*fish*, to rhyme with "bay dish." From Hebrew: "a being," "person," "soul."

1. An innocent.
2. A person of no consequence—weak, ineffectual, pathetic.
3. A contemptible or cowardly sort.

A *nayfish* is clearly related to a *shlemiel*.

A *nayfish* handed the druggist a prescription. The druggist gave him three little bottles of pills.

"All these?" asked the *nayfish*. "What are they for?"

"The red ones calm your nerves; the white ones relieve your headaches; the blue ones are for asthma."

"Amazing. Such little pills and each one knows exactly what to do."

nebech
nebbech
nebish
nebbish

Pronounced NEB-*ekh* or NEB-*ikh*, with the *ch* as sounded by Scots or Germans, not the *ch* of "choo-choo." From Czech: *neboky*.

In recent years, no doubt to help the laryngeally unagile, the pronunciation NEB-*bish* (note the *sh*) has gained currency. The word is even spelled *nebbish*, notably in a collection of cartoons on cocktail napkins, matchbooks, ashtrays and, for all I know, Cape Cod lighters. My feeling is that *nebbish* should be used only by people unable to clear their throats.

As an interjection, *nebech* means:

1. Alas, too bad, unfortunately, "the poor thing." "He went to the doctor, *nebech*." "She, *nebech*, didn't have a dime."

In this usage, *nebech* expresses:

(a) Sympathy. "He lost his job, *nebech*."

(b) Regret. "They asked me, *nebech*, to break the sad news."

(c) Dismay. "He looked, *nebech*, like a ghost!"

(d) "Poor thing." "His wife, *nebech*, has to put up with him."

Never say *nebech* about something you welcome, enjoy, are happy to report, or are glad happened. Hence the irony of this: "What would make me the happiest man in the world? To be sitting on a park bench in the sun, saying to my best friend, 'Look! There, *nebech*, goes Hitler.'"

As a noun, *nebech* means:

2. An innocuous, ineffectual, weak, helpless or hapless unfortunate. A Sad Sack. A "loser." First cousin to a *shlemiel*. "He's a *nebech*." "Once a *nebech*, always a *nebech*." "Whom did she marry? A real *nebech!*"

3. A nonentity; "a nothing of a person."

To define a *nebech* simply as an unlucky man is to miss the many nuances, from pity to contempt, the word affords.

Nebech is one of the most distinctive Yiddish words; it describes a universal character type.

A *nebech* is sometimes defined as the kind of person who always picks up—what a *shlemiel* knocks over.

A *nebech* is more to be pitied than a *shlemiel*. You feel sorry for a *nebech*; you *can* dislike a *shlemiel*.

There is a well-known wisecrack: "When a *nebech* leaves the room, you feel as if someone came in."

Stories, jokes, and wisecracks about the *nebech* are, by careful count, countless.

As the apothegm has it: "A man is, *nebech*, only a man."

A *nebech* went into a store to buy a little hand fan for his wife, who liked to fan herself while rocking on the porch.

He examined a hundred fans, unable to make up his mind. The *baleboss,* disgusted, exclaimed, "What's so hard?"

"I can't decide between the fans that cost a nickel and the fans that cost a dime. . . . What's the difference?"

"The difference is this," said the owner. "With a ten-cent fan, you make like this"——he waved a fan vigorously in front of his face; then he lifted a five-cent fan——"and with the five-cent model, you do like this." He held the fan still——and waved his head.

This mordant reprimand went for naught.

Said the *nebech:* "I wonder if my wife will think it's worth it."

———————————

"Better ten enemies than one *nebech.*"

———PROVERB

———————————

A *nebech* pulled into a parking place on a busy street in Tel Aviv. Along came a policeman.

"Is it all right to park here?" asked the *nebech.*

"No," said the cop.

"*No?* But look at all those other parked cars! How come?"

"They didn't ask."

———————————

A seventh-grader was so late coming home from his suburban school that his mother was frantic.

"What happened to you?" she cried.

"I was made traffic guard today, Mamma, and all the kids have to wait for my signal, after I stop a car, before they cross the street."

"But you were due home two *hours* ago!"

"Mamma, you'd be surprised how long I had to wait before a car came along I could stop!"

He had the makings of a *nebech*—maybe even a *shlemiel.*

———————————

nebechel
nebechl

The Jewish love of affectionate diminutives is seen in this variant, which means an even more pitiful specimen or *shmatte* of a *nebech.*

nechtiger tog, a

Pronounced *a* NEKH-*tig-er* TAWG, to rhyme with "a
Brecht bigger dog." From German: *nächtiger:* "nightly";
Tag: "day."

1. Literally, "a nightly day"; hence an impossibility, an
absurdity, a self-contradiction; unfounded.
A nechtiger tog is also used as a sarcastic exclamation of
denial.
2. Don't believe it. "Did he return the book? *A nechtiger
tog!*"
3. Not on your life. "Would I go on such a mission? *A
nechtiger tog!*"
4. Whom is he trying to kid? "He said they netted ten
percent. *A nechtiger tog!*"
5. Like hell, or "Tell it to Sweeney." "It will be finished
by Thursday? *A nechtiger tog!*"

neshoma
neshuma

Pronounced *ne-*SHAW-*ma*, to rhyme with "the fauna," or
*ne-*SHU-*ma*, to rhyme with "Petluma." Hebrew: *neshamah:* "soul."

1. Soul.
2. The source and breath of life.
3. A "soul" in the sense of a man, a mortal being. "He is
a tortured *neshoma*."

No precise distinction existed between body and soul until
rabbinical times (i.e., post-Biblical days) when the Hebrew
neshamah came to mean that aspect of man that is spirit,
spiritual, noncorporeal—and immortal. Jews were probably
influenced in these theological and metaphysical niceties by
Greek thought.

In the *Talmud* it is said that God created individual souls
when He created the world; empirically, when a child is born,

his or her preassigned *neshoma* joins the body. Evidence for this is lacking.

In Orthodox Judaism, the idea of resurrection plays an important part—and the conception of bodily resurrection is often closely linked to the immortality of the soul or *neshoma*.

Judaism has no serious problems about the "evil," "impurity," or carnality of the body. Man's body is holy, being God's creation, God's gift, God's design. How, then, can man's natural needs and functions—if moderately, properly, not harmfully expressed—be immoral? Sex is treated with surprising ease and "modernity" in rabbinical thinking.

Jews never made "vile bodies" the culprit in that lamentable carnival of life called Sin. Body and soul form a unity; neither is purer or wickeder than the other; when a mortal commits a sin the soul is as responsible as the body.

nexdoorekeh (feminine)
nexdooreker (masculine)

Pronounced *neks-*DOOR*-eh-keh.* Pure Yinglish.

The female neighbor who lives next door. "My *nexdoorekeh* is very friendly." The masculine form, for a male neighbor, is *nexdooreker.*

Maurice Samuel tells me he never heard the masculine form used "because the man next door was never at home: he was working."

But I once had a *nexdooreker* who told me this memorable story:

Two *shlemiels* were discussing the meaning of life and death. Finally, one sighed: "Considering how many heartaches life holds, death is really no misfortune. In fact, I think sometimes it's better for a man not to have been born at all!"

"True," the other nodded. "But how many men are that lucky? Maybe one in ten thousand!"

-nik
-nick

Pronounced NICK. A suffix, from Slavic languages.

This multipurpose syllable converts a verb, noun or adjective into a word for an ardent practitioner, believer, lover, cultist or devotee of something.

Thus, a *nudnik* is someone who *nudzhes* or pesters. An *alrightnik* is someone who has done so well that he is prosperous.

We are familiar, of course, with "beatnik" and "peacenik." *The New York Times* recently referred to "Bachniks," and a friend of mine, dieting, wailed it was especially hard for her because at heart she was a *noshnik.*

-Nik lends itself to delightful *ad hoc* inventions: A *sicknik* would be one who fancies "sick" or "black" humor. A *Freudnik* would be an uncritical acolyte of the father of psychoanalysis. And recently homosexuals began to refer to heterosexuals, with some amusement, as "straightniks."

noch

Pronounced NAWKH; rhyme this with the Glasgow rendition of *loch.* German: *noch:* "another."

1. Another. "Give me *noch* an example."
2. Else, more. "What *noch* did he tell you?" "I'll give him *noch* a chance."
3. Yet—but a "yet" of surprise. "Did you tell him more, *noch?*" "You expected praise, *noch?*" "For such cowardly conduct did you think he'd get a medal, *noch?*"

The last is the most subtle and distinctive usage, emphatically and characteristically Yiddish.

An elderly Jew, riding in the subway, saw a Negro reading the *Jewish Daily Forward.*

The Jew watched, spellbound, as the Negro read sedately

on. Finally, unable to contain himself, the old man asked, "Excuse me, mister. I don't want to be rude—but I have to ask it: Are you Jewish?"

The Negro lowered the paper in disgust: "That's all I need *noch!*"

no-goodnik

Pronounced no-GOOD-*nik,* to rhyme with "so good, Nick." Yinglish. This mutation borrows the phrase, "no-good," and adds the stalwart suffix *-nik.*

1. Someone who is "no good"—unethical, irresponsible, undependable. A man who does not keep his word or honor his obligations.
2. One who does not earn an honest living; a wastrel; a drifter.
3. A shady character; a bum; a lowlife; a be-careful-you-shouldn't-get-involved-with-that-type type.
4. A petty lawbreaker; a trickster; a cheat.

"Remember Mrs. Plotnick, she had three sons? *Nu,* the oldest became an *alrightnik,* he lives in Scarsdale; the second went to Columbia, he became a Ph.D.; but the *boychik,* who does who-knows-*what*-for-a-living, turned out a *no-goodnik!* From him, be sure, Mrs. Plotnick will never get *naches.*"

nosh
nosher
noshen

Rhyme respectively with "gosh," "josher," "joshin'." German: *nachen,* "to eat on the sly."

(A) *Nosh:*
1. A snack, a tidbit, a "bite," a small portion.
2. Anything eaten between meals and, presumably, in small quantity: fruit, a cookie, "a piece cake," a candy.

Jews loved to *nosh* long before they ever went to a cocktail party or tasted tidbits.

(B) *Nosher:*

1. One who eats between meals.
2. One who has a sweet tooth.
3. One who is weak-willed about food and dieting.

(C) *Noshen* (verb):

To *nosh* is to "have a little bite to eat before dinner is ready," or to "have a little something between meals." "I came in to find her *noshing*." "He's used to *noshing* after midnight."

Many delicatessen counters display plates with small slices of salami, or pieces of halvah, with a legend affixed to a toothpick: "Have a *nosh*." The *nosh* is not free, but cheap. In some Jewish delicatessens a lucky customer sees a little "flag" stuck into an open plate of goodies: *"Nem* (take) a *nosh* a nickel."

New York is full of the most extraordinary items and opportunities for *noshing*.

nu
nu?
nu!
nu-nu?
noo-ooo ...

All pronounced NOO, to rhyme with "coo," but with various intonations and meanings. From Russian: *nu:* "well," "well now," etc.; cognates are common in Indo-European languages.

"Nu" is a remarkably versatile interjection, interrogation, expletive.

Nu is the word most frequently used (aside from *"oy"* and the articles) in speaking Yiddish. And with good reason: *Nu* is the verbal equivalent of a sigh, a frown, a grin, a grunt, a sneer. It is an expression of amusement or recognition or uncertainty or disapproval. It can be used fondly, acidly, tritely, belligerently.

Nu is a qualification, an emphasizer, an interrogation, a caster of doubt, an arrow of ire. It can convey pride, deliver scorn, demand response. When used in tandem, as *nu-nu*, it carries another cargo of nuances.

Here are a score of shadings of this two-lettered miracle:

(1) *"Nu?"* (Well?)

(2) "I saw you come out of her apartment." *"Noo-oo?"* (So-o?)

(3) *"Nu,* after such a plea, what could I do?" (Well, then.)

(4) *"Nu?"* (How are things with you?)

(5) *"Nu?"* (What's new?)

(6) "I need the money. . . . *Nu?"* (How about it?)

(7) "—and he walked right out. *Nu?!"* (How do you like that!! Imagine!)

(8) "I'm going to the dentist." *"Nu?"* (What's the hurry?)

(9) *"Nu,* I guess that's all." (I'll be finishing or going along now.)

(10) "—and you're supposed to be there by noon. *Nu?!"* (What are you waiting for?)

(11) "—and signed the contract. *Nu!"* (That's that!)

(12) *"Nu-nu?"* (Come on, open up, tell me.)

(13) "My wife was wondering what happened to the cof-feepot she lent you. . . . *Nu?"* (I hate to mention it, but——.)

(14) "They doubled the rent! *Nu?"* (What can one do?)

(15) "Did you or didn't you tell him? *Nu?"* (I challenge you.)

(16) *"Nu-nu,* my friend?" (One must resign oneself.)

(17) "They all agreed with him. But I—*nu?"* (I, for one, am dubious.)

(18) "They waited and waited. *Nu,* he finally showed up." (And so, in the course of time.)

(19) "She accused him, he blamed her. *Nu,* it ended in court." (One thing led to another, and . . .)

Nu is so very Yiddish an interjection that it has become the one word which can identify a Jew. In fact, it is sometimes used just that way, i.e., instead of asking, "Are you Jewish?" one can say, *"Nu?"* (The answer is likely to be *"Nu-nu."*)

Movie producer: "Sam, I'm going to buy the most terrific book you ever read: *The Well of Loneliness.*"

"Harry, you must be out of your mind! You can't make that into a movie."

"Why not?"

"It's about two Lesbians!"

"Nu? So I'll change them to Austrians."

How dated such a joke must seem to those who were not raised under the Hays Office movie code.

nuchshlepper

Pronounced NUKH-*shlep-per*, with the *kh* guttural and far back in the throat, as if trying to clear out a crumb; to rhyme with a Berliner's rendition of "Hoch leper." German: *Nachshlepper:* "a dragger after," "a straggler."

1. One who drags along after someone; a toady; a fawner; a tolerated supernumerary. "A Hollywood actor can't take a walk without at least one *nuchshlepper.*" "She got in on someone else's ticket, the *nuchshlepper.*" (She was also a *trombenik.*) "He doesn't work for us; he's just a *nuchshlepper.*"
2. A dependent. "A successful man's family always provides him with at least one *nuchshlepper.*"

See also TSUTCHEPPENISH.

nudnik
nudnick

Pronounced NUD-*nick*, to rhyme with "could pick." *Nudnik* may come from the Russian *nudna,* but it has become as uniquely Yiddish a word as there is. It is sometimes pronounced NUD-*nyik*, just as *paskudnak* is often pronounced *poss-kood*-NYOK, by those who wish to add a vocal prolongation of distaste.

A pest, a nag, an annoyer, a monumental bore.

A *nudnik* is not just a nuisance; to merit the status of *nudnik*, a nuisance must be a most persistent, talkative, obnoxious, indomitable, and indefatigable nag. I regard *nudnik* as a peerless word for the characterization of a universal type.

A mother often says to a child, "Stop bothering me. Don't be a *nudnik!*"

Morris Rosenfeld, the poet, wrote an entire essay on the *nudnik*, whom he defined as a man "whose purpose in life is to bore the rest of humanity."

See NUDZH.

A derivative of *nudnik*, recently coined, covers the special category of pedantic or pedagogical bores: *phudnik*. What is a *phudnik?*: "A *nudnik* with a Ph.D."

Mr. Polanski complained to his doctor, "Something terrible has happened to me. I try to stop it, but I can't. . . . Morning, noon, and night—I keep talking to myself!"

"Now, now," the doctor crooned, "that isn't such a bad habit. Why, thousands of people do it."

"But, doctor," protested Polanski, "you don't know what a *nudnik* I am!"

nudzh (noun)
nudzheh (verb)
nudzhedik (adjective)
nudzhik (adjective)

Nudzh is pronounced NUD-*jeh*, to rhyme with "could ya," NUDJ-*eh-dig*, to rhyme with "would ya dig," and NUDJ-*ik*, to rhyme with "could ya" plus a wisp of a hiccup. From the Russian: "to fret," "to ache dully."

As a verb:
Nudzheh means to bore, to pester, to nag. A person who *nudzhes* you is a *nudnik*. If he annoys you long enough, you can say, "Stop *nudzhing* me!"

As a noun:
Nudzh is a Yinglish word, descended from "nudge."

But where a nudge is open a *nudzh* is surreptitious, a kick under the table, a widening-of-the-eyes-accompanied-by-a-slight-tilt-of-the-head to indicate that the recipient of the *nudzh* is being reminded: of a job to be done, or a nicety that has been overlooked, or a *gaucherie* committed by a third party, or the impossibility of swallowing what was just said.

As adjectives:

Nudzhedik and *nudzhik* are adjectives, and mean unsettled, queasy, upset, nauseated. "I can't settle down today; I feel so *nudzhedik*." "Whenever I take a bus, I get *nudzhedik*."

See MUTCHE.

In the movie *You're a Big Boy Now* (1967), the actress snaps at the stage-struck adolescent: "Don't be a *nudzh!*"

O

ongepotchket

Pronounced AWN-*ge-potch-ket*, to rhyme with "Fonda
Lodge kit." From Russian: *pachkat:* "to soil, to sully."

1. Slapped together or assembled without form or sense.
2. Messed up; excessively and unesthetically decorated;
overly baroque. "She wore her new diamond earrings, a
necklace, bracelet, two rings and a brooch. *Oy*, was she
ongepotchket."

A suggested connection between the German *Patsch* and the
Yiddish *ongepotchket* derives from the fact that overhandling
spoils an article. In cooking, the less it has been handled the
lighter the pastry; hamburgers will be more tender if *potched*
less.

Mr. Fleishman, a new art collector, bought a painting which
was much admired by his friend Meyerson, a self-proclaimed
expert: The painting was one large square of black, with a
dot of white in the center.

A year later, Mr. Fleishman bought another painting by
the same modernist genius: A large square with *two* white
dots.

Proudly, Fleishman hung the picture over his fireplace and telephoned his *mavin* friend Meyerson to come right over. Meyerson took one look at the picture and wrinkled his nose: "I don't like it. Too *ongepotchket*."

opstairsikeh (feminine)
opstairsiker (masculine)

Pronounced *op*-STARE-*zi-keh*. The male who lives upstairs is an *op*-STARE-*zi-kair*. Pure Ameridish.

The neighbor who lives upstairs. "My *opstairsikeh* is a music teacher." "My *opstairsiker*—a man, an angel—is moving out."

oy
oy!
oy oy!
oy-oy-oy!

Pronounced—well how else can you pronounce it? The exclamation point is part of the spelling when *"oy!"* has a full head of steam.

Oy is not a word; it is a vocabulary. It is uttered in as many ways as the utterer's histrionic ability permits. It is a lament, a protest, a cry of dismay, a reflex of delight. But however sighed, cried, howled, or moaned, *oy!* is the most expressive and ubiquitous exclamation in Yiddish.

Oy is an expletive, an ejaculation, a threnody, a monologue. It may be employed to express anything from ecstasy to horror, depending on (a) the catharsis desired by the utterer, (b) the effect intended on the listener, (c) the protocol of affect that governs the intensity and duration of emotion required (by tradition) for the given occasion or crisis.

Oy is often used as lead-off for *"oy vay!"* which means, literally, "oh, pain," but is used as an all-purpose ejaculation to express anything from trivial delight to abysmal woe. *Oy vay!* is the short form of *"oy vay iz mir!"* (pronounced *"oy* VAY *iz meer"*), an omnibus phrase for everything from personal pain to emphatic condolences. (*Vay* comes from the German *Weh*, meaning "woe.")

Oy is also used in duet form, *oy-oy!* or in a resourceful trio: *oy-oy-oy!* The individual *oy!*s can play varying solo roles, to embellish subtleties of feeling: thus *OY!—oy—oy*, or *oy, oy, OY! OY-oy!* can mean "And how!"

It is worth noting that *oy!* is not *ai!*, and runs a decidedly different gamut of sensibilities. *Ai!* is also used in tandem (*"ai-ai!"*) and *à trois*, as the French, no novitiates in the *"ai—ai—ai!"* league, would put it.

As for the difference between *oy!* and *"ah!"*, there is (naturally) a saying to illustrate the distinction:

"When you jump into cold water you cry '*oy!*' then, enjoying it, say 'a-aah.' When you commit a sin, you revel in the pleasure, 'a-aah'; then, realizing what you've done, you cry '*oy!*' " *Oy*, accordingly, can be used to express:

1. Simple surprise. "When she saw me there, she said, '*Oy*, I didn't expect you!' "
2. Startledness. "She heard a noise and exclaimed, '*Oy!* Who's there?' "
3. Small fear. "*Oy!* It could be a mouse!"
4. Minor sadness (sighed). "When I think of what she went through, all I can say is *o-oy*." (Note the *oy* prolonged, to indicate how sensitive one is to the troubles of others.)
5. Contentment. "*Oy*, was that a delicious dinner!"
6. Joy. "*Oy*, what a party!"
7. Euphoria. "Was I *happy*? *Oy!* I was dancing on air!"
8. Relief; reassurance. "*Oy*, now I can sleep."
9. Uncertainty. "What should I do? *Oy*, I wish I knew."
10. Apprehension. "Maybe he's sick? *Oy!*"
11. Awe. "He came back alive yet? *Oy!*"
12. Astonishment. "*Oy gevalt*, how he had changed."
13. Indignation. "Take it away from me. *Oy!*"
14. Irritation. "*Oy*, is that some *metsieh!*"
15. Irony. "*Oy*, have you got the wrong party!"
16. Pain (moderate). "*Oy*, it hurts."
17. Pain (serious). "*Oy, Gottenyu!*"
18. Revulsion. "*Feh!* Who could eat that? *O-oy!*"
19. Anguish. "I beg you, *tell* me! *Oy!*"
20. Dismay. "*Oy*, I gained ten pounds!"

21. Despair. "It's hopeless, I tell you! *Oy!*"

22. Regret. "*Him* we have to invite? *Oy!*"

23. Lamentation. "*Oy,* we cried our eyes out."

24. Shock. "What? Her? Here? *Oy!*"

25. Outrage. "That man will never set foot in this house so long as I live. *Oy!*"

26. Horror. "——married a dwarf? *Oy gevalt!*"

27. Stupefaction. "My own partner . . . *o-o-oy.*"

28. Flabbergastation. "Who ever *heard* such a thing? *Oy!* I could *plotz!*"

29. At-the-end-of-one's-wittedness, or I-can't-*stand*-any-more. "Get out! Leave me alone! *O-O-O-o-o-oy!*"

———————————

Mrs. Fishbein's phone rang.

"Hul-lo," a cultivated voice intoned, "I'm telephoning to ask whether you and your husband can come to a tea for Lady Windermere——"

"*Oy,*" cut in Mrs. Fishbein, "have *you* got a wrong number!"

oyrech

> Pronounced oy-*rekh* (note the guttural *kh*); rhymes with nothing I can think of. From the Hebrew: *oreach:* "guest."

> Guest.

The word is mostly used in the phrase "*On oyrech auf Shabbes,*" "a guest for the Sabbath."

It was customary for the head of a Jewish household to try to bring a stranger home, usually from the synagogue, to share the Sabbath dinner. A Jewish stranger in any *shtetl* or community on a Friday night was fairly certain to receive an invitation to "come home and make *Shabbes* with us."

Jews placed great emphasis on such hospitality; to be alone, far from the bosom of one's own, on a Friday night—that was just too sad to contemplate, or permit.

An *oyrech* for *Shabbes* was not simply welcome; he supplied others with the coveted opportunity of doing a good deed.

One of the outstanding *mitzvas* and virtues, among Jews, is hospitality. It was drilled into me, as a child, how wonderful it is to be a host, and how alert and attentive one must be to the needs and "good time" of anyone who enters one's home. The food offered a guest must be as abundant and as costly as one can possibly make it—even if (as was often true) a family had to "go without" for many a day to come. *Hachnoses orchim,* an important, recurrent Hebrew phrase for hospitality, was Abraham's salient virtue.

The wildest story I ever heard about hospitality deals with a Mr. Ostrovsky, let us say, a traveling salesman, who found himself in the synagogue in a little *shtetl* in Galicia one Friday night. After the prayers, as the Jews turned right, turned left, in the traditional manner, smiling, shaking hands, uttering the *"Gut Shabbes!"* greeting, Mr. Ostrovsky, sighing and melancholy, set off in search of a place to sleep.

"Where are you going?" exclaimed a man. "A Jew, alone, on *Shabbes?* Come, man. Come home with me! Have dinner in my house, spend the night with us. No, no; no excuses! My name is Glantz. Come along. My wife is a marvelous cook, and you'll have a dinner you'll never forget!"

Off went the grateful Ostrovsky with his exuberant host.

Mr. Glantz's promises were not empty: No host and hostess could have been warmer, kinder, more considerate. Ostrovsky was given a fine bedroom, urged to soak in a hot tub, given fluffy towels and scented soap—and fed a superlative dinner. He slept, that night, between fine linen sheets, and next morning ate a sumptuous breakfast.

As he made his heartfelt farewells to his host, Ostrovsky said, "How can I ever thank you?"

Said his host, "Just attend to this." And Glantz handed Ostrovsky a piece of paper. The incredulous Ostrovsky read:

1 Bath hot water		10 kopecks
1 Cake scented soap		20 kopecks
1 Large towel		10 kopecks
1 Sabbath dinner (complete)		2.50 rubles
2 Fresh sheets		20 kopecks
1 Fresh pillow case		10 kopecks
1 Breakfast		75 kopecks
	Total	3.95 rubles

"But—what's this?" asked Ostrovsky.

"Your bill," said Glantz.

"You expect me to *pay* this?!"

"Certainly," said Glantz. "Are you denying that you bathed here, slept here, ate like a king——"

"Deny it? I'm flabbergasted!" exclaimed Ostrovsky. "You *invited* me here! You *asked* me to be your *Shabbes oyrech!* I've never heard a more outrageous——"

"Stop!" Glantz held up his hand peremptorily. "Let's not argue, my friend. Will you agree to come to our rabbi and tell him everything, and abide by his decision?"

"Will I?" cried Ostrovsky. "I can't *wait* to hear what the rabbi tells you about such disgusting behavior!"

Off went the two men to the rabbi, who, seeing their expressions, said, "Well, my friends, what happened so to spoil your Sabbath?"

Ostrovsky told his tale to the rabbi, pouring the words out with fervor.

The rabbi turned to Glantz. "And what do you, the host, have to say?"

"Nothing," said Glantz. "Everything he said is accurate, just as it happened."

"There you are, rabbi!" cried Ostrovsky. "You see?"

The rabbi nodded. "After hearing you both, and considering all the delicate ethical problems involved, and based on the wisdom—on just such problems—I have studied for years in the *Talmud*, my decision is clear: Ostrovsky, pay the bill."

Ostrovsky could hardly believe his ears. He was speechless. He was shocked. He was discombobulated. And yet . . . a rabbi had pondered; a rabbi had spoken . . .

With a heavy heart, Ostrovsky sighed, "Very well."

Ostrovsky and his host left the rabbi's house, and Ostrovsky started to count out money.

"What are you doing?" asked Glantz.

"Paying your bill," said Ostrovsky.

"*Paying* me? For my hospitality? You must be crazy. Do you think I would accept money from you, my honored guest, my *oyrech auf Shabbes?*"

Ostrovsky sputtered: "*You* gave me the bill! You *asked* for money! *You* made me come here! *You*——"

"Oh, that," scoffed Glantz. "I just wanted you to see what a dope we have here for a rabbi."

oysgematert

Pronounced *oyss-ge-*MOT-*tert*, to rhyme with "Royce besotted." From German: *matt:* "exhausted."

To be utterly exhausted, worn out. "I'm *oysgematert!*" "After what she went through, who can blame her for being *oysgematert?*"

oysvorf

Pronounced OYSS-*voorf*, to rhyme with "Royce woof." From German: *Auswurf:* "trash."

1. A dissolute person, a scoundrel, a bum.
2. An outcast, an antisocial type. "Sure he's a Bohemian; even as a child, he was an *oysvorf.*"
3. A mean, meddlesome, ungrateful person. "I can't understand an *oysvorf* like that one!" "One *oysvorf* can paralyze the work of a whole committee."

See PARECH, GOZLIN, NO-GOODNIK.

oytser

Pronounced OY-*tser*, to rhyme with "Roy, sir." From Hebrew: *o-tsar:* "treasure."

1. Treasure. "My child? An angel, an *oytser* to us both." "Our maid is an *oytser.*"
But again, as with so many Yiddish words, *oytser* is employed to mean exactly its opposite:
2. (Ironically) By no stretch of the imagination a treasure. "Her son? God save you from such an *oytser!*" "He almost ruined me, that *oytser!*" "Such an *oytser* I wish my worst enemies."
The ironic meaning is heard as often as the straight one.

Spitzer, who sold hot dogs, was accosted by a friend. "How's business?"

"Not bad," said Spitzer. "I've already put away $1,000 in the bank."

"In that case," said the friend, "maybe you can lend me five dollars."

"I'm not allowed to."

"What do you mean you're not '*allowed*' to?"

"I made an agreement with the bank. They agreed not to sell hot dogs if I promised not to make loans."

Spitzer was some *oytser*.

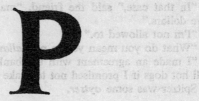

parech

Pronounced PARR-*ekh*, with a Germanic *kh*. Hebrew: *parach*: "sprout."

1. An unpleasant, sly, low-grade person.
2. Someone unreliable and to be avoided. "Don't confide in that *parech*."
3. Someone ungrateful and presumptuous, who takes advantage of the probity of others.

In the Bible, *parech* means to sprout—referring especially to scabs in the scalp, which were considered contagious. In time, *parech* came to mean a scabrous person.

pareveh

Pronounced PAAR-*eh-va*, to rhyme with "jar of a," or (more often) PAAR-*va*, to rhyme with "larva." The origin of *pareveh* is unknown.

Neutral dietetically.

Foods, to be *pareveh*, include neither animal nor dairy products, and can therefore be eaten with either. (Jewish dietary laws require that meat and dairy foods not be consumed at the same meal. See KOSHER.) To be *pareveh*, a cake, for instance, can be made with coffee or fruit juice instead of milk, and with vegetable fat or oil substituted for butter.

The marvels of modern technology have expanded the roster of *pareveh* foods to include margarine made without milk solids or butter fat (often sold as "diet" margarine), as well as *pareveh* milk, cream, and even ice cream, which is made with hydrogenated soy bean oil.

paskudne
paskudneh

Pronounced *poss*-KOOD-*neh*, to rhyme with "Joss would na"; or (as I much prefer) *poss*-KOOD-*nyeh*, with the *ny* as rippling as in "canyon," to rhyme with "Joss could knee a." From the Polish/Ukrainian word for "nasty," "dirty," "sloppy."

1. Nasty, dirty, sloppy. "What a *paskudne* experience!" "The weather? *Paskudne!*" "He is cursed with that *paskudne* mouth of his." "They served us a *paskudne* dinner."
2. Mean, unkind, disgusting. "Such *paskudne* treatment I never got anywhere else." "She is a *paskudne* type."
3. Contemptible, odious, the opposite of *simpático* (which, in Yiddish, is *sympatish*). "That whole family is *eppes paskudne*." "What drives a man to such *paskudne* conduct?"

paskudnyak
paskudnak

Pronounced with full fruitiness: *poss-kood-*NYOK, slurring the *n* into the *y* as in "canyon"; to rhyme with "Joss would 'nyok.'" From Polish/Ukrainian. Spelled with or without a *y*, the use of which adds to the effect of acute distaste.

A man or woman who is *paskudne* (though purists prefer to say *paskudnika* for the female of this species), hence nasty, mean, odious, contemptible, rotten, vulgar, insensitive, petty and—in general—opprobrious. "I wouldn't say 'Hello' to a *paskudnyak* like that!" "Did you ever hear of such a *paskudnyak?*" "That whole family is a collection of *paskudnyaks.*"

This word is one of the most greasily graphic, I think, in Yiddish. It offers the connoisseur three nice, long syllables, starting with a sibilant of reprehension and ending with a nasality of scorn. It adds cadence to contempt.

———————

A Jew, crossing the street, bumped into an anti-Semite.
   "Swine!" bellowed the *paskudnyak.*
   "Goldberg," bowed the Jew.

paskustva

Pronounced *poss-*KOOSS-*tva*, to rhyme with "Las puss tva."

1. Feminine form of *paskudnyak.*
2. A *paskudne* act. "That was a piece of *paskustva*" means "That was a disgusting thing to do."

Passover

See PESACH.

patch

See POTCH.

payess

Pronounced PAY-*ess*. From Hebrew: *pe'ah* (singular) and *pe'ot* (plural): "side earlocks," "curls."

The long, unshorn ear-ringlet hair and sideburn-locks worn by very Orthodox Jewish males.

The custom among Orthodox Jews of letting their ear curls grow, and wearing a full beard, comes from an instruction in Leviticus 19 : 27: "Ye shall not round the corners of your heads, neither shalt thou mar the corners of thy beard." (A learned friend informs me that *payess* are regarded as symbolizing the uncut corners of the field at harvest time, which were by tradition left to be gleaned by the widow, the orphan, the stranger.)

In the Middle Ages, church and secular powers often *forbade* Jews to trim their beards in any way. Why? To be certain that a Jew could be identified.

Payess were savagely resented, in many Gentile areas, and were forbidden by law for a time, in Tsarist Russia.

To wear or to cut the *payess* became an important question among Jews—especially where an exit from the ghetto was possible: e.g., in the U.S. after 1880, during the great immigration movements from eastern Europe. To cut the *payess* was an open and defiant sign of departure from Orthodoxy, a desire to become Americanized as soon as possible. Families were split asunder over *payess*.

In that section of Brooklyn which is an enclave of Chasidic Jews, the main street is sometimes called *Rue de la Payess*. . . .

The bearded beatnik confronted his girl's father arrogantly: "Man, how come you treat me so nasty—when *your* old man always gives me the big Hello?"

"My 'old man,' " scowled the father, "thinks you're studying at the *Yeshiva*."

pekl
pekel
peckel

Pronounced PECK-'*l*, to rhyme with "freckle." From the Bavarian dialect of German: *Päckl*, "little package."

1. Bundle, parcel, little package.
2. A knapsack or bundle carried on the back or shoulders (see below.)
3. "To send a *pekl*": to send food and gifts, for a holiday or (with clothing) to relatives overseas.
4. "To have a *pekl*" means to be in trouble, to have a "passel" of problems.
5. "He left her a *pekl*" is an idiomatic expression for "He got her pregnant."
6. "He always carries his *pekl* with him" is a way of describing a hunchback.

Pekl evokes special and warm associations among Jews, for it was from the little *peklech* of wares—containing ribbons, needles, thread, pins, buttons, hooks-and-eyes, laces, scissors, etc.—that many Jews made their living, in Europe no less than in the New World to which they came. (The first peddlers in America, incidentally, were not Jews, but "Connecticut Yankees.") From the *pekl* of the Jewish peddler and itinerant merchant in America in time came a wagon of wares, then a little store, then an "emporium," then a department store, and in future generations a retail chain. . . .

The adventures and adversities of the peddler who set off on foot, crossing strange new land and hills and even mountains, bringing his commodities to farmers' and miners' wives; the dietary difficulties he endured; the prejudices and *popularity* he encountered (in New England and the South, Jews were welcomed by many pious folk as "people of the Book," "living witnesses" of the Word, authorities on Hebrew and the Old Testament)—all this forms one of the sagas of the aliens who made America what it is.

Interesting material about the Jewish peddlers will be found in Harry Golden's brief *Forgotten Pioneer*, World, 1963, which re-creates several life stories most vividly, in the words of his informants; and in Stephen Birmingham's *Our Crowd: The Great Jewish Families of New York*, Harper & Row, 1967.

Pesach

Pronounced PAY-*sokh*, with a guttural *kh*, to rhyme with "bays loch." Hebrew: "to pass over," "to spare."

The Passover holiday and celebration.

This is the most cherished of Jewish holidays, the Festival of Freedom. It lasts eight days.* The first two and last two days are full holidays; the intermediate days are semiholidays, known as *chol hamo'ed* (rhymes with "ol'man NOAH'd").

Pesach commemorates Israel's dramatic deliverance from enslavement in Egypt over 3200 years ago, as recounted in Exodus.

On the evenings preceding the first and second nights of Passover (Israeli Jews and Reform Jews in the Diaspora celebrate only the first), a great family *Seder* (SAY-*der*) is held. (*Seder* means order of procedure.) This combination banquet and religious service is the highlight of the holiday—and, to many, of the year. Since nothing containing leavening, or which has come in contact with a leavening agent, may be used during the festival, special china and utensils are set aside for the Passover week.

On the table are symbolic foods commemorating events connected with Passover: the *matzo*, or unleavened bread, a

---

* In Israel the holiday is observed for seven days. The three major festivals of the Jewish year, Passover (*Pesach*), Pentecost (*Shevuoth*), and the Feast of Booths (*Succoth*) were originally marked by pilgrimages to the Temple in Jerusalem. As the Jewish year is based on a lunar calendar, the dates for these festivals were determined by the authorities after observing the previous new moon. They then sent messengers to the distant communities where Jews dwelled, establishing the date of the festival. In order to allow for a possible delay in receiving the message, or for any inaccuracy in the report, an additional day of observance for these festivals was added in the communities outside of Israel.

reminder of the haste in which the Israelites left Egypt, without waiting for their bread to rise; bitter herbs, marking the bitterness of slavery; a roasted egg and bone, symbolic of the offerings brought to the Temple on this festival; *charoseth* (*kha-RO-ses*), a mixture of chopped nuts, apples, cinnamon, and wine, representing the clay from which the Israelites made bricks while in slavery. Each setting has a wine glass. The father half-reclines at the head of the table, propped up on pillows or on a sofa: this dramatizes freedom and ease (perhaps in imitation of Roman patricians at a banquet).

By custom, guests are sought for a family *Seder:* friends, a student living away from home, a traveler, a neighbor, a soldier.

The grandfather, father, or oldest son is the leader of the service. He opens the *Seder* with an Aramaic prayer. (Aramaic was the vernacular of the post-Exilic Jews from the sixth century B.C.) He raises a tray with three *matzos* on it, displays them to the company, and intones the ancient litany:

> This is the bread of affliction that our fathers ate in the land of Egypt. All who are hungry, let them come and eat—all who are needy, let them come and celebrate Passover with us. Now we are here: next year may we be in Israel. Now we are slaves: in the year ahead may we be free men.

The prayer was probably composed shortly after 70 A.D., when the Romans crushed Judea and the Jews went into *galut*—exile. The use of the present tense stresses the underlying significance of the *Seder* as the re-creation of a living experience. The rabbis of old taught that "every man in every generation must look upon himself as if he personally had come forth out of Egypt. It was not our fathers alone that the Holy One redeemed, but ourselves also did He redeem with them." Every generation can know slavery in one form or another; and every generation can be redeemed.

The leader then raises his wine goblet: "Not only once have they risen to destroy us, but in every generation. . . . But the Holy One, blessed be He, always delivers us from their hands."

A favorite moment of the *Seder* arrives when the younges

child at the table asks why this night is different from all other nights of the year, and poses "Four Questions" (the *Fier Kashehs*) to the father: Why do we eat unleavened bread? Why do we use bitter herbs? Why do we dip the herbs in salt water? Why do we recline at the table?

The father replies with the phrase, "Slaves were we unto Pharaoh in Egypt," and continues retelling the ancient story of the Pharaoh's refusal to let the children of Israel go, the plagues visited upon the Egyptians, the miraculous salvation at the Red Sea, and the arrival at Mount Sinai, where the *Torah* was given to the children of Israel. (The name of Moses occurs but once, oddly enough!)

The *Haggadah*, the narrative read at the *Seder*, also includes many rabbinic comments, hymns, prayers, stylized questions and answers—the whole constituting a ceremony of celebration and praise to the Lord.

When the *Haggadah* reaches the story of the Ten Plagues that afflicted the Egyptians, everyone at the table spills a little wine from his or her glass as each plague is named. Why? So that their cup of joy, even when celebrating a moment of deliverance, should not be full. The sages taught the Jews not to rejoice over another's misfortune. "Rejoice not when thine enemy falleth" (Proverbs 24 : 17).

(I must confess that *I* have always enjoyed gloating over the come-uppance suffered by the detestable, regardless of race, color, or creed.)

A story in the *Talmud* relates that after the Israelites had safely crossed the Red Sea, they sang a song of praise to God, but when the angels sought to join in the triumphant paean, God thundered: "You shall not sing while my other children (the Egyptians) are drowning."

Late in the *Seder* ritual, a large goblet of wine is poured for the Prophet Elijah, and the front door is opened, while all sing a hymn welcoming him in—Elijah being the herald of the Messiah. (For more somber explanations of why the door is opened, see Appendix: Passover.)

See also HAGGADAH.

Sholom Aleichem dryly remarks somewhere that even though *Pesach* comes only once a year, Jews insist on asking questions all year long.

pilpul

Pronounced PILL-*pull*, to rhyme with "fill full." Hebrew: "debate," "dialectics."

1. An inflated form of analysis and debate used in Talmudic study: i.e., unproductive hair-splitting that is employed not so much to advance clarity or reveal meaning as to display one's own cleverness.
2. (Colloquially) Any hair-splitting or logic-chopping that leaves the main boulevard of a problem to bog down in the side streets.

"If you insist long enough that you're right, you'll be wrong."
" 'For instance' is not proof."

—FOLK SAYINGS

pisha paysha

Pronounced PISH-*eh* PAY-*sheh* (or PEH-*sheh*), to rhyme with "dish acacia." Yinglish.

A card game, played by two—one of whom is usually a child.

It is a very simple game, often one of the first taught to children, particularly useful in whiling away the hours of convalescence after an illness. It was a good game to play with a child because a child could easily win; only luck is involved. (Jewish parents preferred to say that *pisha paysha* is "educational" because it helps teach the young the sequence of numbers.)

The game is played this way: The deck is placed face down; one card is placed face upward; the players draw from the deck, in turn, and seek to build upward or downward upon the open card; i.e., if a 5 is exposed, you may place upon it either a 4 or a 6. The player with the fewest cards in his hand when the deck is exhausted, wins.

I was taught to play *pisha paysha* by my father, when I was six or seven. I have spent many an idle moment since then wondering what on earth *pisha paysha* means, and where on earth it originated. By a feat of uncanny bookmanship (happening to open a published-in-England book on games) I am at last able to dispel the world's ignorance: *pisha paysha* is some Jew's corruption of the name of a card game known in England as "Pitch and Patience." Some called it "Peace and Patience." In my memory, it will remain imperishably inscribed as *pisha paysha.*

pisher
pisherkeh (diminutive)

> Rhymes with "fisher." From German: *pissen:* "to urinate."

> (Vulgarism)
> 1. A bed-wetter.
> 2. A young, inexperienced person; a "young squirt."
> 3. An insignificant or inconsequential person; a "nobody."

Literally, a *pisher* is one who urinates; but that is a far cry from present and popular usage. "He's a mere *pisher*," means "He's very young," or "He's still wet behind the ears" (excuse the misleading metaphor). "You can't let him decide: He's only a *pisher!*" means he's too young or inexperienced to be given such responsibility. "He's just a *pisher*," means "He's a nobody," has no influence.

A common saying (common in both senses) is: "So call me *pisher*," or "So let him call me *pisher*," which means, "I don't care," "What does that matter?" or "Sticks and stones may break my bones but names can never harm me."

In France, an elderly Jew, tired of hearing a young man boast of his ancestry, finally said, "Listen, La Fontaine: I knew your grandfather, who changed his name to La Fontaine from

Schpritzwasser (Squirtwater). And he told me that *his* father changed his name to Schpritzwasser from what everyone called him, which was Moishe the *Pisher!* So please, don't put on airs, 'La Fontaine.' "

pishke
pishkeh

See PUSHKE.

pisk

Pronounced PISK, to rhyme with "risk." Polish: "mouth."

1. The mouth of an animal or a human.
2. (Colloquialism) An eloquent or garrulous speaker.
3. A brusque slang word for "mouth," used in expressions such as "Shut your trap."

To say that someone has a *pisk* can mean that he speaks eloquently, brilliantly—or without decorum or restraint. "I heard him lecture. There is a *pisk!*" or "She had to open her big fat *pisk!*"

The diminutive, *piskel* or *piskeleh*, is often applied admiringly to a child who speaks precociously. "Does he have a *piskeleh*."

A meaningless folk saw goes: "A fox runs from Brisk to Trisk carrying a rifle in his *pisk*."

pitsel
pitseleh (diminutive)

Pronounced PITS'*l* and PIT-*seh-leh*, to rhyme with "Fritzl" and "Fit Sulla." From German: *Bissel*, "a little piece," "a bit."

1. A small piece; a morsel; a bit of something.
2. A baby; an infant.

"And how is your darling *pitseleh?*"
"I think she's carrying a *pitseleh.*" (I think she's pregnant.)

platke-macher

Pronounced PLAWT-*keh* MA-*kher*, to rhyme with "Maude k' Bach'er," or PLYOT-*keh* MA-*kher*. Slavic: *platke:* "gossip"; and German: *Macher:* "maker."

1. A malicious, trouble-making carrier of rumors or animadversions, who enjoys creating suspicion or animosity among friends. "The minute you tell that *platke-macher* something personal, she (or he) can't wait to tell it to your friends."
2. A gossipy intriguer, who deliberately repeats confidences and spreads unpleasant tales. "God spare me from the wiles of that *platke-macher.*"

See also YENTA, YACHNE.

pletsl

Pronounced PLETS'*l*, to rhyme with "Edsel."

A thin, flat, crisp roll, often garnished with poppy seeds or onion.

plosher

Pronounced PLOB-*sh'r*, to rhyme with "*kosher.*" From German: *Plauschen*, chat (dialect).

1. A braggart, a blow-hard, a "hot air" artist.
2. An indiscreet and unreliable gossip.

3. One who inflates and exaggerates his own talents or resources.

See FONFER, TROMBENIK.

The *nouveaux riches* Nathansons had gone to Europe and visited Israel and were now home, boasting about their trip to their friends.

"And in Rome we had an audience with the Pope!" said Mr. Nathanson.

"With the *Pope?*" echoed an astonished friend. "So how did you like him?"

"*He* was marvelous. Her, I didn't care for."

What a *plosher!*

In the plane headed for Arizona, two of Abraham's progeny were chatting.

"I can't wait to get to the hotel," said the first, "and change and rush out to the golf course! . . . Are you a golfer?"

The other replied, "Me? Golf is practically my whole life! I'd rather play than eat! I belong to the finest country club in Cleveland! I play every chance I can!"

"Really? . . . Well, I play in the low 70's. . . ."

"So do I," exclaimed the *plosher,* "but if it gets one degree colder I go right back to the hotel!"

plotz
platz
plotst

Pronounced PLOTZ to rhyme with "Watts." From the German: *Platz:* "place"; *platzen:* "to burst."

1. A place, a seat. "Save my *plotz.*" (But this is not why I include *plotz,* a word with another ambience, one all its own.)

2. To split, to burst, to explode. "From so much pleasure, one could *plotz!*" "What they went through would make a person *plotz.*" "I can't laugh any more or I'll *plotz!*"

3. To be aggravated beyond bearing; to be infuriated; to be outraged. "His heart will *plotz* from such suffering." "He makes me so angry I could *plotz*." "From such conduct, one can *plotz*." "I wish he would *plotz* from frustration!"

Plotst is the Yinglish past tense of *plotz*. "He laughed so hard he practically *plotst*." "What did he do? He *plotst*!" "Is he a comedian? Why, the whole theater *plotst*!"

Pincus and Bernstein were walking down a street in Berlin when they saw an SS cop approaching. Only Pincus had an identity card. Bernstein said, "Quick, run! He'll chase *you*, and I'll get away."

So Pincus broke into a run, and he ran and he ran until he thought his heart would *plotz*.

"Stop! Stop!" cried the policeman, who finally caught up. "Jew!" he roared. "Show me your papers."

The gasping Pincus produced his papers.

The Nazi examined them and saw they were in order. "But why did you run away?"

"Eh—my doctor told me to run half a mile after each meal!"

"But you saw me chasing after you and yelling! Why didn't you stop?"

"I—thought maybe you go to the same doctor!"

potch
patch

Rhymes with "botch." Both noun and verb. From German: *Patsch*: a "smack," a "blow."

1. A slap, a smack. "Man, did she give him a *potch*!" "Don't be fresh or I'll *potch* you."
2. An insult, a blow to one's pride. "To me, his words were a terrible *potch*." "When I read it, it was like a *potch*."
3. A reverse or setback to one's hopes. "Last season gave me a *potch*."

There is a saying: *"A potch fargeyt, a vort bashteyt,"* "A slap passes, but a word (i.e., an insult) remains."

potchkeh
potchkee

Pronounced POTCH-*ka*, to rhyme with "notch k'"; or rendered as POTCH-*kee*, to rhyme with "watch me," for playful phonetic effect. From German: *Patsch:* a "slap."

1. A slap, usually playful.
2. To fuss or "mess around" inefficiently and inexpertly. "I spent all day in the kitchen *potchkeeing* around." "He *potchkees* around with paint and they call him a painter." "When you *potchkee* around, your work is *ongepotchket.*"
3. To dawdle, to waste time. "Let's go; don't *potchkee.*"

See ONGEPOTCHKET.

prost

Pronounced PRAWST, to rhyme with "lost," or PRUST, to rhyme with "crust." Possibly from Slavic.

1. Common, vulgar.
2. Unlearned.
3. Ill-mannered, boorish.

No more cutting or scornful adjective existed, in my home, than *prost.* To call someone *"proster* Jew" or "a *proster mensh"* was to dismiss him as hopelessly deserving of disrespect. Money, success, influence, had nothing to do with it: *"Prost is prost!"*

A *proster* Jew can redeem himself by applying himself to learning and good deeds, and by adopting the gentle, modest demeanor that distinguishes "a man of *yiches.*"

See YICHES, GRAUB.

pupik

> Pronounced PU (the *u* of "put") -*pik*, to rhyme with "look it." Slavic.

> Navel.

Pupik is used in a variety of broad, colorful expressions—ironic, maledictory, and ribald.

"*A shaynim donk in pupik*," "A pretty thanks in the navel," means "Thanks for nothing."

"*Zoll vaksen tsibiliss in zein pupik!*" "Onions should grow in his navel!"

"What does he do? He sits around all day looking at his *pupik*."

A classic definition of an unrealistic, impractical type is this: "He's the kind who worries whether a flea has a *pupik*."

Purim

> Pronounced POOR-*im* (not PURE-*im*); rhymes with "tour 'em." Hebrew: *pur:* "lot."

> The Feast of Lots, commemorating the rescue of the Jews of Persia from Haman's plot to exterminate every man, woman, and child of them.

Lots had been drawn or cast by Haman, first Minister of King Ahasuerus (possibly Artaxerxes II), to determine the date on which the Jews of Persia would be slaughtered. A miraculous deliverance was effected by the heroism of beautiful Queen Esther, who was Jewish, and the sagacity of Mordecai, her uncle and guardian. Haman ended up being executed on the gallows he had erected to dispatch Mordecai. The story is told in the Book of Esther. (See Appendix: Purim.)

Purim is a day which Jews regard fondly, because it tells them that tyrants and fanatics *can* be defeated. In a larger sense, it signifies that evil cannot prevail forever. Since the Middle Ages, an enemy of the Jewish people has been known as a "Haman." Deliverances from other calamitous events have been celebrated and called *Purim* by Jewish communities in Saragossa, Frankfurt, Egypt, and Tiberias. There is a saying, of rueful sagacity: "There are so many Hamans, but only one *Purim*."

In synagogues and temples, the *Megillah* (Scroll of Esther) is read on the eve and morning of *Purim*. Whenever the name of Haman is uttered, the children set up a racket of boos and jeers, and spin ratchety noisemakers around and around. In some communities, Haman's name is written upon the soles of one's shoes, so that his name may literally be wiped out.

Among the customs associated with *Purim* are the sending of gifts (food and money) to the poor, and the exchanging of gifts of food with friends. Feasts, dances, and masquerades are held. *Purim* is the closest thing to the carnival in Jewish life; in Israel, it is celebrated with public processions, complete with floats and costumes, and private masquerade parties.

The symbolic food of *Purim* is the *hamantash*, a three-cornered sweet pastry filled with prunes or poppy seeds.

On *Purim* Eve in Tokyo, Harry Siegel, far, far from his home in Staten Island, asked the Japanese hotel clerk: "Excuse me. Would you happen to know if there is—a Jewish synagogue—here—in Tokyo?"

"Synagogue?" replied the clerk. "Ah, so, Siegel-san. Ah, yes! *Is* synagogue! Reave hotel—ralk down street straight two brocks, turn reft—*banzai!*—is synagogue!"

So Mr. Siegel left the hotel, walked two blocks, turned left, and there—lo and behold!—was a synagogue. He entered. All of the worshipers were Japanese, as was the rabbi, and the *Purim* services had begun, and Mr. Siegel happily joined in.

When the services were over, he went up to the rabbi and said, "My name is Siegel. I'm from America. I just want to tell you, Rabbi, how very happy I was to be with you tonight."

The Japanese rabbi beamed. "Is honor! But excuse. You Jewish?"

"Certainly."

"That's funny," said the rabbi. "You don't rook Jewish."

pushke
pishke

Pronounced PUSH-*keh*, PUSH-*key*, or PISH-*key*. From the Polish: *puszka*—and a darling of a word, if you ask me.

1. The little can or container kept in the home, often in the kitchen, in which money to be donated to charity is accumulated.

Each charitable organization would provide its own *pushke*. (Jewish housewives customarily put a few coins in the *pushke* every Friday night, before lighting the Sabbath candles.) Collectors for the various charities would come around at regular intervals, and the *baleboosteh* (housewife) would empty her *pushke*.

The *pushkes*, set out on a shelf or the kitchen windowsill, carried labels that read like a catalogue of human misery—and benevolence:

For Orphans

For Widows

For the Anshe ———— Synagogue

For Trees to be Planted in Palestine

For Victims of Persecution

For the Blind

For the Lame

For the Hebrew Home for the Aged

For a Rabbinical Trip to the Holy Land

For Milk for Jewish Children in Hospitals in the Old Country

For a Library Wing for the *Yeshiva*

For the Importation of a Noted Cantor from Poland for Rosh Hashanah Services

For Meetings to Protest Pogroms in the Ukraine

For Men Maimed while Returning from Religious Services

For the Rumanian Brotherhood

For the Galician Brotherhood

For the Hungarian Brotherhood

For the Lithuanian Brotherhood

For the Training of Newly Arrived Immigrants

For Resettlement of Jewish Refugees from Turkey in the Land of Israel

For Machinery and Farm Equipment to be Sent to Jewish Farmers in Indiana

For the Jewish Chicken Raisers in Kankakee Recently Bankrupted by the Ravages of Red Tick among Rhode Island Roosters

I can't, offhand, remember *all* the titles.

NOTE: There is no Hebrew or Yiddish word for charity. The word used for charity is *tzedaka*, which means justice. Charity was, and is, considered a duty, an obligation, a necessity, a God-forbid-you-should-ever-forget-to-give-to-the-poor-and-orphaned-and-needy-or-any-other-worthy-cause.

2. The money saved up by a married woman, out of the household funds her husband gave her; a nest-egg. In this usage, a *pushke* is often known as a *knippl*.

Women fiercely guarded as earnings the small amounts their careful management of the household made it possible for them to divert to personal, undisclosed causes.

The woman would spend her "little *pushke*" as she saw fit: for a charity, a treat for the children, a special holiday delicacy, a small luxury for herself. Often the *pushke* was the family's only emergency fund for doctor bills, operations, etc.

My wife claims that when I married her she had already saved up her own little *pushke*, which I was *not* to consider "divvies," which is not Yiddish but Chicagoese for anything to be divided up. (When we saw a pal pick up a coin or other object, we would scream "Fen dibs!" "Fen dibby!" or "Fen divvies!" That established, the finder had to cut in the caller for half the spoils. I have no idea where this custom originated, but it always gave me romantic images of the Klondike, where bearded, desperate miners hoarsely croaked *"Fen dibs!"* to establish their claim to a stake in the Cornucopia Lode. . . . I have wandered pretty far from *pushke*, but I'm entitled to some fun, too.)

putz

Rhymes with "nuts."

Literally, *putz* is vulgar slang for "penis." But the vulgarism is rarely used to designate the member; the word *shmuck* does that.

As used, *putz* is a term of contempt for:
1. A fool, an ass, a jerk.
2. A simpleton or yokel; an easy mark.

CAUTION: *Putz* is not to be used lightly, or when women or children are around. It is more offensive than *shmuck*; the latter may be used in a teasing and affectionate way, vulgar though it is, but *putz* has a pejorative ambience.

See SHMUCK.

rabbi

See REBBE.

rachmones

> Pronounced *rokh*-MAW-*ness*, to rhyme with "loch (as a Scot pronounces it) lawless." Hebrew: "compassion," "pity."

> Pity, compassion.

This quintessential word lies at the heart of Jewish thought and feeling. All of Judaism's philosophy, ethics, ethos, learning, education, hierarchy of values, are saturated with a sense of, and heightened sensitivity to, *rachmones*.

God is often called the God of Mercy and Compassion: *Adonai El Rachum Ve-Chanum.*

The writings of the prophets are permeated with appeals for *rachmones*, a divine attribute. (So, too, are the words of Jesus, and the books of the New Testament.)

Note that the Hebrew root *rechem*, from which *rachmones* is derived, means "a mother's womb." The rabbis taught that a Jew should look upon others with the same love and feeling that a mother feels for the issue of her womb. "He is in such straits one can only have *rachmones* on him." "The least one can show is *rachmones*."

reb
Reb

See REBBE.

rebbe

Pronounced REB-*ba*, to rhyme with "jeb-a." From the Hebrew: *rabi*, pronounced *rah*-BEE, meaning "my teacher."

1. Rabbi.

The title "rabbi" does not have the same connotation as does "priest" or "minister." A rabbi is not an intermediary between God and man, as is, say, a Catholic priest. A rabbi is not even or always a spiritual arbiter, as is a Protestant minister. A rabbi is—a rabbi. His position traditionally gives him no power, no hierarchical status. This may be hard to believe, but it is so. The authority of a rabbi rests on his learning, his character, his personal qualities: ordination, although it has ancient roots, did not become institutionalized until modern times. Even now a rabbi may be ordained by another rabbi.*

A rabbi enjoys no priestly privileges. In Orthodox worship, in fact, the rabbi rarely leads the services: the *chazzen* (cantor) usually does, but any respected, learned layman may take the pulpit to lead the prayers. (Only in modern times, incidentally, did rabbis become Sabbath preachers. See MAGGID.)

* Cecil Roth, editor, *The Standard Jewish Encyclopedia*, Doubleday, 1966, p. 1457.

The title "rabbi" was given to those men learned in Jewish law who taught in the academies, large and small. The title was not used until the beginning of the Christian era. To Jews, Moses is the exemplar of a rabbi, for he was the most important teacher of all. Pious Jews call Moses *Moishe Rabbenu* (MOY-*sheh* rab-BAY-*noo*), which means "Our Teacher, Moses."

Traditionally, a rabbi is a teacher of the *Torah* (in the broad sense, the Bible, *Talmud* and later rabbinic works), and seeks to apply it to daily life.

Down the centuries, the sages stressed that scholars must share their knowledge with the less learned, and their insights with the less spiritually sensitive; hence, rabbis were enjoined to spread instruction and enlightenment, to uplift the moral, ethical, and religious life of their congregations. (One of the loveliest of Yiddish songs, *"Oyfn Pripetchok,"* mentions how the *rebbe* teaches little boys their ABC's.)

What does a rabbi do? Today, pretty much what a clergyman does: He performs the ceremonials that attend birth, confirmation, marriage, death; interprets the tenets of Judaism; is responsible for teaching and overseeing religious instruction in the synagogue or temple school; preaches sermons; offers comfort and consolation; visits hospitals; counsels families; tries to "guide the perplexed"; advises members of his congregation about problems ranging from the connubial to the collegiate; comments on the social scene; ventures into psychotherapy. A rabbi today combines the functions of minister, lecturer, counselor, social worker, psychiatrist. He is also the representative of the Jewish community vis-à-vis the public.

Rabbis are graduates of a *yeshiva* or seminary. In addition, Reform, Conservative, and a growing number of Orthodox rabbis hold degrees (often more than one) from secular universities.

The rabbi is not imposed upon the congregation by an ecclesiastical hierarchy. He is freely engaged—and disengaged—by the members of the community.

2. The spiritual leader of a Chasidic group or sect, not necessarily ordained.

A Chasidic *rebbe*, though well-grounded in Jewish learning, does not necessarily have formal ordination from a seminary or *yeshiva*. He may have inherited his position from his father, or he may have been invited to assume the leadership of a group of *Chasidim* because of his personal qualities.

The relationship of the Chasidic *rebbe* to his followers is very close. He is often the object of a veneration that gives rise to stories of mystical abilities.

(See CHASID.)

"It was hard for Satan alone to mislead the whole world, so he appointed prominent rabbis in different localities."

—A CHASIDIC SAYING ATTRIBUTED TO
NAHMAN OF BRATZLAV, EARLY NINETEENTH CENTURY
EARLY NINETEENTH CENTURY

Three women were discussing their sons, with the customary pride and *naches*.

"*My* boy," said the first, "is a famous surgeon, and president of his medical association!"

"*My* son," said the second, "is a professor in the Law School!"

"*My* son," said the third, "is a rabbi."

"A *rabbi?* What kind of career is that for a Jewish boy?"

"A rabbi whose congregation does not want to drive him out of town isn't a rabbi; and a rabbi they do drive out isn't a man."

—FOLK SAYING, BASED ON A SAYING IN THE *Talmud*.

"Unless you can play baseball, you'll never get to be a rabbi in America."

Solomon Schechter (former head of the Jewish Theological Seminary of America), to Louis Finkelstein (current Chancellor), quoted in *Time*, October 15, 1951.

Glickman came to a rabbi to confess his sins, but he was so shame-stricken that he said, "I'm not here for myself, rabbi, but—for a friend."

"What sins did he commit?"

"Oh, my friend often takes the name of the Lord in vain; and he has cast envying eyes on his neighbor's wife; and he——"

"Stop," sighed the rabbi. "Your friend is foolish: Why did he not come here himself? He could have told me that *he* had come for a friend, and saved you this embarrassment."

rebbitsin
rebbetsen

Pronounced REB-*bi-tzin*, to rhyme with "debits in."

The wife of a rabbi.

The *rebbitsin* played an important role in the Jewish community of yesteryear. She often served as mother-surrogate to her husband's students. Like Caesar's wife, she was supposed to be a model of probity, and like a *rebbitsin* she was expected to be a strong right arm to the rabbi, and a ministering angel to the community.

There is a saying (*naturally*, there's a saying): "Better close to the *rebbitsin* than to the rabbi."

The modern *rebbitsin* often teaches in the congregational school, lectures on Jewish customs to women's organizations, helps guide the Sisterhood, visits the sick, comforts the bereaved, serves as hostess for many occasions. And like the wife of a college president, or any modern corporation executive, she is carefully "looked over" by the board of a new congregation before her husband is engaged as spiritual cicerone.

"All *rebbitsins* are magicians, for how else can they raise a family on a rabbi's salary?"

There was a rabbi who was known for his absolute fairness.

One day, his *rebbitsin* accused their maid of having stolen a candlestick. The wretched maid wailed that she was innocent.

"Very well," said the *rebbitsin*, "let us go to the rabbinical court and let them decide!"

The rabbi said, "I'll come along."

"You don't need to," said his wife. "I can plead the case against this wretched girl."

"I'm sure you can," said the rabbi. "But who will plead her defense?"

Riboyne Shel O'lem

Pronounced ri-BOY-neh shel OY-lem, to rhyme with "Le-moyna shall boil 'em." Hebrew: *Ribono Shel Olam:* "Master of the World."

1. **Oh, God in heaven!**

A ringing, rhetorical ejaculation that appeals to God to witness:

(a) Some remarkable thing. "*Riboyne Shel O'lem*, just look at that rain come down!"

(b) Some unexpected development. "We were finishing when—*Riboyne Shel O'lem*, in walked their lawyer!"

(c) Something disgraceful, unfair, brazen. "It was a scandal, *Riboyne Shel O'lem!*"

(d) Anything that leaves one speechless, from the sublime to the unforgivable. "*Riboyne Shel O'lem*, what could I say?!"

Although God is being addressed directly, the phrase is not religious, strictly speaking. It is a synonym for "Oh, God!" "God in heaven!" "This you have to see for yourself!" "I don't *believe* it!" "Holy Moses!" et cetera.

2. **God willing; if only God will help me; if only God will do it; dear God, *please*.** "If only she would recover, *Riboyne Shel O'lem!*" "The day he comes home—*Riboyne Shel O'lem*—will we celebrate!" "I just want to get through these next weeks, *Riboyne Shel O'lem*."

Mr. Abraham, driven to desperation by the endless delayings of the tailor who was making him a pair of trousers, finally cried, "Tailor, in the name of heaven, it has already taken you six *weeks!*"

"So?"

"*So*, you ask? Six weeks for a pair of pants? *Riboyne Shel O'lem!* It took God only six days to create the *universe!*"

"*Nu*," shrugged the tailor, "look at it . . ."

Paris, 1939.

Three weary German refugees stood in line, in the offices of a Relocation Committee.

"Where would you like to go?" an official asked the first refugee.

"London."

"And you?" the official asked the second.

"Switzerland."

"And you?" he asked the third.

"Australia."

"Australia?" echoed the official. "Why so far?"

The refugee said, "Far from where?"

Riboyne Shel O'lem!

Rosh Hashanah
Rosh Hashonah
Rosh Hashona
Rosh Hoshanah

Pronounced *rawsh ha-*SHAW*-neh* (rhyme with "cautious fauna"); or *rosh ha-*SHO*-na* (rhyme with "cautious Mona"); or *rawsh ha-*SHAH*-na* (rhyme with "cautious Donna"). Hebrew: "beginning (of the) year."

Rosh Hashanah commemorates the birthday of—the world.

So said the rabbis, in the *Talmud* and *Midrash*, who held that *Rosh Hashanah* celebrates the anniversary of creation itself.

Rosh Hashanah begins the Ten Days of Penitence (also known as the Days of Awe) which end with the most solemn of religious days in the Jewish calendar, *Yom Kippur*. During these days of penitence and prayer, all mankind presumably passes before the Heavenly Throne, and God looks into their deeds and hearts. Judgment will be passed on *Yom Kippur*, the devout aver, but "prayer, penitence, and charity may avert the evil decree."

The dominant and recurring theme throughout *Rosh*

Hashanah services is the sovereignty of God. The *Shofar* (ram's horn) is blown several times, in a prescribed pattern of notes, the first to celebrate God's kinship, the second to stress the role of the individual, the third to remind the congregation of all the events associated with the blowing of the ram's horn. (In ancient Judea, the ram's horn was used as a communications device, to send signals from one mountain peak to another.) In the *Talmud*, it is ventured that the *shofar* helps confuse Satan and his hosts, those cunning spirits of perdition who try to influence God when He judges us sinners.

Rosh Hashanah is a solemn yet very happy time; entire families gather from everywhere for the holiday, and for the feast; bread or apple is dipped in honey to symbolize a hoped-for sweetness in the year ahead. A blessing thanks the Lord for having "sustained us to this day."

The traditional *Rosh Hashanah* greeting is *"Leshana tova tikosevu,"* le-SHAH-*nah* TOE-*vah tee-kah*-SAY-*vu*—"may you be inscribed for a good year."

Orthodox and Conservative Jews observe two days of *Rosh Hashanah:* Reform Jews celebrate only one.

Rosh Hashanah, like all Jewish holidays, is determined by the lunar calendar, and falls in late September or early October.

For other facts see Appendix: Rosh Hashanah.

rov

> Pronounced RUV, to rhyme with "dove," or RAWV, to rhyme with "mauve." Hebrew: "rabbi."

> Rabbi.
> (See REBBE.)

A great king, grown old and eccentric, called before him the chief rabbi of his realm. "Before I die, there's something I want you to do, Rabbi. Teach my pet monkey how to talk!"

"What?"

"That's a command: Teach my monkey how to talk, within one year, or your head will be chopped off!"

"But Your Majesty, to carry out a request like that, I need more than a year—I need at least ten."

"I'll allow you five and not a day more!"

The rabbi returned to his flock and told them what had happened. And they all cried out in sympathy. "But what will you *do*, *rov*?"

"Well," said the *rov*, "in five years, many things can happen. For instance, the king could die. Or, I could die. Or—the monkey could die. And besides, in five years, who knows—maybe I can teach that monkey how to talk!"

S

Sabbath

See SHABBES.

Sabbati Zvi
Shabbatsi Zvi
Shabtsi Zvi

See Appendix: Sabbati Zvi.

sachel

Pronounced SAY-*kh'l*; rhymes with "playful." Hebrew: "understanding."

Native good sense, common sense, judgment.

_____

1948. Jerusalem was under tight Arab siege. Food and water were running low. The spirits of the Jews ran abysmally low

—except for one jolly, wrinkled storekeeper who was known for his fund of stories and his inexhaustible *sachel*. The old man hopped around with a cheerful smile, repeating the refrain, "Don't worry, don't worry, everything will be all right, we'll all be saved."

"We're on the threshold of starvation, of defeat, of death!" a neighbor protested.

"So what?" came the answer. "*Ei*ther we'll be saved by natural means, or we'll be saved through a miracle!"

"Explain yourself."

"It's this way: Either we'll be saved by natural means—that is, God will come to our aid, as He has done throughout history. Or, we'll be saved by a real miracle—our army will break through the siege." _____

"Many complain of their looks, but none complain of their brains."

—PROVERB

Sanhedrin

Pronounced *san*-HED-*rin*, to rhyme with "tan red bin." From Greek: *synedrion:* "assembly."

The seventy elders, plus a Patriarch or President *(Nasi)*, who sat in Jerusalem, until 70 A.D., as a combination of Supreme Court and College of Cardinals, ruling on certain theological, ethical, civil, and political matters.

An extraordinary amount of nonsense and demagoguery has come down through history to make the name *Sanhedrin* appear far more mysterious than it ever was, or need be. Bigots have exploited the myth of a supposed "international council," or "Elders of Zion," who allegedly rule over all Jews in secret, and plot dire deeds for them to perform in a worldwide conspiracy.

· The *Sanhedrin* was simply a court, combining ecclesiastical and civil authority, in ancient Jerusalem. It was originally a lofty academic *collegium*, composed of learned men and priests, who interpreted Scripture.

Many modern scholars think that there must later have

been two *Sanhedrins:* one of aristocrats and priests, with jurisdiction over certain civil and criminal matters, the other a court of Pharisees who attended to matters of ritual, the calendar, rules and regulations concerning the priesthood, etc.

When Titus destroyed the Great Temple in 70 A.D., the *Sanhedrin* lost all political powers and moved to Tiberias, there to lay the foundation for later rabbinical scholarship. Its functions were replaced by those of the *Beth Din,* or "court of law."

After Israel was founded (1948) there were requests for the revival of the *Sanhedrin.* This was not done because of legal and constitutional problems.

See Appendix: Sanhedrin.

schatchen

See SHADCHEN.

schlack
schlag

See SHLOCK.

shlemiehl
schlemiel
schlemihl

See SHLEMIEL.

schlep

See SHLEP.

schlok
See SHLOCK.

schloomp
schlump

See SHLUMP.

schmaltz

See SHMALTZ. Both spellings have become acceptable.

schmo

See SHMO.

schmuck

See SHMUCK.

schneider

Pronounced SHNY-*der*, to rhyme with "wider." From German: *Schneider:* "tailor."

1. Tailor.
2. (In gin rummy) To win a number of games before your opponent has won one.
3. To shut out an opponent.

The spelling with *sch-* is so well established as a family name that it is retained here, even though it is an exception to my general rule, which would dictate *shneider*.

schnook

See SHNOOK.

Seder

> Pronounced SAY-*der*, to rhyme with "nadir" or "paid her." Hebrew for "order," or "order of the service."

See PESACH.

Sefer Torah

> Pronounced SAY-*fer* TOE-*reh* or TOY-*rah*, to rhyme with "wafer bow rah" or "caper Moira." Hebrew: "Book of the *Torah*."

> The scroll containing the Five Books of Moses that is kept in the Ark at the front of a synagogue or temple.

The *Sefer Torah* is read from on each Sabbath and festival. The scroll is of parchment and is hand lettered, in Hebrew, by specially trained scribes who must be punctilious in their copy work. The scroll is covered with a mantle of silk or velvet and is often adorned with a silver breastplate and crown.

See TORAH.

Sefirah
Sefiras Haomer

> Pronounced *se*-VER-*ah*, to rhyme with "let's see, ma"; *ha*-OHM-*er*. Hebrew: "counting."

> The forty-nine-day period that begins with the second day of Passover, when the *omer* (a sheaf of new barley)

was traditionally brought to the Temple in Jerusalem as an offering, and ends on *Shevuoth*, the feast of the wheat harvest.

Beginning with the second day of Passover, the *"omer* is counted" during daily prayers, according to a prescribed ritual, and is followed by the recitation of Psalm 67, which includes the verse "Then shall the earth yield her increase; and God, even our own God, shall bless us."

The forty-nine days of *Sefirah* have become a period of mourning, because of the many misfortunes which, tradition holds, have overtaken the Jews at this period: persecutions suffered under Roman rule, the martyrdom of saints such as Rabbi Akiba, the slaughter of Jews by the Crusaders.

The famous revolt of the Warsaw Ghetto occurred during *Sefirah*.

Traditionally, Jews do not participate in festivities during this period. Weddings are not scheduled. These restrictions are lifted for *Lag Baomer*, the thirty-third day of the *Sefirah*, which is a minor festival.

In recent years, Israel's Independence Day, which falls during this period, has been excepted from *Sefirah* rulings and is celebrated.

Sephardi
Sephardic (adjective)
Sephardim (plural)

Pronounced *seh-FAR-dee*, to rhyme with "Bacardi." Hebrew: "Spanish." (Spain, in Hebrew, is *Sepharad*.)

Spanish and Portuguese Jews, and the descendants of the Jews of Spain and Portugal. (In modern Israel, *Sephardim* has been somewhat extended to include Jews of the Middle East.)

Spain was thought, by the rabbis of the Middle Ages, to be the *Sepharad* mentioned in the Bible (in Obadiah's prophecy), where the Jews exiled from Jerusalem found refuge. In time, all of the Jews in Spain and Portugal came to be called *Sephardim*.

Sephardic Judaism, which dominated Jewish culture from around 600 A.D. until the expulsion of the Jews from Spain at the end of the fifteenth century, was an exceptionally sophisticated blend of Talmudic thought, Greek philosophy, Aristotelianism, such science as then existed, and the ideas of Averröes, the great Islamic scholar whom medieval Christians were not permitted to read because of Church prohibition. Sephardic Jews were not unacquainted with Latin, Spanish, French. They widened Judaic thought with secular knowledge from geometry, algebra, astronomy, medicine, metaphysics, music, mechanics.

Sephardic Jews rose to positions of eminence in Spain, Portugal, North Africa—as physicians, philosophers, poets, financiers, advisers to kings and courts. The Sephardic writers wrote mostly in Arabic, even when writing about *Torah* and *Talmud!* They were aristocratic; their religious services, no less than their style of living, were invested with a splendor such as Ashkenazic (eastern European) Jews did not know.

When the Sephardic Jews were expelled from the Iberian countries they moved on to settle along the coastline of the Mediterranean, and in Holland and England—and their colonies.

Communities of Sephardic Jews are today found throughout Asia Minor, in Israel, Turkey, Greece, England, Holland, Latin America, and, of course, the United States—where Sephardic Jews were the first Jewish immigrants. The earliest synagogues in America were Sephardic.

Sephardic Jews differ from Ashkenazic Jews in many customs, in the order and text of their prayers, in the intonation of the chants used in the synagogues. (The *Sephardim* claim that their liturgy stems from the Talmudic academies of Babylonia; *Ashkenazim* follow the Palestinian ritual.)

The vernacular used by Sephardic Jews, as opposed to the Yiddish of Ashkenazic Jews, is Ladino. Many *Sephardim* cannot make head or tail out of Yiddish, and an *Ashkenazi* could not understand a conversation in Ladino.

But much more basic than these differences are the ways in which the *Sephardim* differ from the *Ashkenazim* in their style of thought and living. These I have tried to describe in several entries in this lexicon: see ASHKENAZI, SHTETL.

Sephardim are the least numerous of Jewry's three main groups. The *Encyclopedia Britannica* (vol. 20, p. 228, 1968 ed.) estimates for 1960: 11,000,000 Ashkenazim; 1,500,000 Oriental Jews; 500,000 Sephardim.

This story has nothing to do with Sephardic Jews—or *Ashkenazim,* for that matter; but how can I withhold it from you any longer?

An American, visiting Israel, was invited to the ceremonies dedicating the Tomb of the Unknown Soldier.

Speeches were made by the president of Israel, by Ben-Gurion, by the commanding general of the army, and at last the tarpaulin that covered the monument was pulled aside— to reveal a simple, marble plinth, on the front of which was engraved:

> CHAIM ISADORE COHN
> BORN: POLAND, 1903
> DIED: ISRAEL, 1955

"I thought this was a tomb to the unknown soldier!" exclaimed the American.

"Oh, it *is*," said an Israeli.

"But how? 'Unknown?' They've inscribed his name, his birthdate, his——"

"Ah," said the Israeli, "you don't understand. As a *tailor,* he was known; but as a soldier—*mneh!*"

sh-
shm-

Not words, but prefatory sounds, of mockery or dismissal, that "pooh-pooh" the word they prefix.

1. To negate or deride the meaning of a word, the word is repeated—but with *shm-* prefixed to the repetition. "The doctor says she has a serious virus? Virus-shmirus, as long as she's O.K." (This is, of course, a variation

of the classic "Cancer-shmancer, as long as you're healthy.") "The mayor? Mayor-shmayor, it's his wife who runs the show." "Exams-shmexams, relax!" "Girls-shmirls, *anything* to keep him from working!" "Who said that? Charley? Charley-shmarley, what does *he* know?"

2. *Sh-* is the introductory signal to a rich symphony of disesteem. A great many words of mockery and asper-sion, words that jeer, sneer and scorn (Jeer, Sneer, & Scorn could be the name of a real-estate firm) begin with *sh-*: shlemiel, shlimazl, shloomp, shmegegge, shmo, shmuck, shnook, shnorrer.

If you eschew the *sh-* and *shm-* sounds, you rob Yinglish of two of its phonetic glories.

Mrs. Siegel confided to her neighbor that her son had gone through so miserable a phase that he was now seeing a psychoanalyst. "And the doctor says my Marvin is suffering from an Oedipus complex!"

"Oedipus-Shmoedipus," scoffed her neighbor, "so long as he loves his mother."

Shabbes

Pronounced SHAH-*biss*, to rhyme with "novice." Hebrew: *shabbat:* "rest," or "cessation of labor."

Sabbath.

The life of Jews was so very hard, for so very long, that the Sabbath became more than a weekly respite from servi-tude, from bone-wearying labor—and anxiety, if not terror. *Shabbes* is called "the Queen of the week," "the Bride," and, in however bitter a time and place, the Sabbath was the miraculous time when even the lowliest, poorest, least conse-quential of men could feel himself in kingly communion with the Almighty, favored by God's special concern: "It is a sign between me and the children of Israel" (Exodus 31 : 17).

To "make *Shabbes*" means to be festive, to celebrate.

The Fourth Commandment says: "Remember the Sabbath

day to keep it holy. Six days shalt thou labor, and do all thy work: But the seventh day is the Sabbath of the Lord thy God."

And so, for Sabbath, down the generations, in every land, Jews have scrubbed every nook of their dwelling, bathed themselves with the utmost care, donned fresh garments, laid out (however poor) their best linens, glasses, utensils. *Shabbes* brought—each week, throughout a lifetime—a sense of personal splendor, cleanliness, devotion, exaltation.

"No doubt it calls for an effort," writes Maurice Samuel, "to understand how a wretched little householder—a Jew, a pauper, an exile, an object of persecution—could sit down to the Passover ceremonies at home and feel that he was a king, his wife a queen, and his children princes and princesses, yet come out of the Passover cheerfully free from delusions of grandeur. (Delusions of persecution . . . the Jew has never had: he has not needed them.)"*

Mystics believed that the *Shechinah*, or Divine Presence, descends each Friday when the sun sets.

In the *shtetl, Shabbes* was redolent with intimations of divinity, the hint of angels and arcane secrets, visions of heaven with all the blessed seated on golden thrones under the sparkling stars. "[Our] house was filled with the odor of burning wax, blessed spices," writes Isaac Bashevis Singer, "and with an atmosphere of wonder and miracles."**

Nor was the love of *Shabbes* limited to the *shtetl.* Harry Golden, reminiscing about life on New York's Lower East Side, recaptures the feeling: "The Irish and Italian boys had Christmas once a year; we had exaltation every Friday. In the most populous neighborhood of the world, rent by the shouts of peddlers, the screams of children, and the myriad noises of the city, there was every Friday evening a wondrous stillness, an eloquent silence. So quiet was it that two blocks from the synagogue you could hear the muffled chant of the cantor and the murmured prayers of the congregation. Once the service was over, you came home to find your mother dressed in her wedding dress with a white silk scarf around her head. And your father told you all the sufferings throughout the cen-

---

* Maurice Samuel, *The World of Sholom Aleichem*, Schocken Paperbacks, 1965, pp. 62–63.
** Isaac Bashevis Singer, *In My Father's Court*, Farrar, Straus, Giroux, 1966, p. 24.

turies were dedicated for this moment, the celebration of the Sabbath."*

Now, the Sabbath was a truly revolutionary concept and institution. I am astonished that neither the Greeks nor Romans invented it. (On the contrary, Juvenal, Seneca, Horace scorned it as superstition.) When the Falasha Jews (see Appendix) were being tortured, and were goaded to name their savior, they replied: "The savior of the Jews is the Sabbath." Of which England's Rabbi Hertz wrote: "They spoke wiser than they knew."

Shabbes begins just before sunset on Friday. The wife and mother, dressed in her very best, lights the *Shabbes* candles and offers a benediction. (Before lighting the candles, the *baleboosteh*, however poor, has set aside a sum for charity.) As she lights the *Shabbes* candles, she closes her eyes and passes her palms over the candles, always toward herself ("The soul is the Lord's candle," it is said in the *Talmud*), and whispers, "Blessed art Thou, O Lord our God, King of the Universe, Who has sanctified us by Thy commandments, and has commanded us to kindle the Sabbath light." Then, silently, she asks God to preserve her family: its health, its peace, its honor. (The lighting of the candles, one of the few *mitzvas* reserved to Jewish woman, makes her a momentary priestess.)

Two braided loaves of bread (*challas*) are placed at the head of the festive board, covered by an embroidered cloth. A goblet of wine stands next to the *challa*: this is "the *Kiddush* cup," with the wine that will sanctify the Sabbath.

Traditionally, the father returns from services to bless his children; then he recites the KIDDUSH and sips the wine. The entire family joins in welcoming the Sabbath angels who accompanied the father from the synagogue, singing, "Welcome to you, O ministering angels, may your coming be in peace, may you bless us with peace, and may you depart in peace."

Jewish husbands often sing a tribute to their wives on the eve of *Shabbes*, in the words of Proverbs 31:

> Strength and honor are her clothing . . .
> She openeth her mouth with wisdom . . .

---

* In Hutchins Hapgood, *The Spirit of the Ghetto*, Funk and Wagnalls, 1966, p. 26.

> Her children arise up, and call her blessed; her
> husband also, and he praiseth her.

(The song is called *Eshes Chayil*, "A Woman of Valor.")

The *Mishna* sets forth a sizable number of Sabbath prohibitions, starting with thirty-nine activities explicitly forbidden: baking, plowing, writing, spinning, carrying, sowing, sewing, even tying a knot! (Very devout Jews would have pinned a handkerchief to their coats before *Shabbes;* a pinned object was not "carried" but was part of the clothing.)

What did the Jews do with their time on *Shabbes?* They prayed—and they studied; they read; they discussed the *Torah* and the *Talmud*. Moses had enjoined the Jews, said Philo, "[to] assemble . . . on these seventh days . . . in a respectful and orderly manner . . . [to] hear the laws read so that none should be ignorant of them." Every Sabbath, a rabbi or elder was to read the laws "and expound them point by point, until the late afternoon, when [all] depart, having gained both expert knowledge . . . and an advance in piety."

Today, every Sabbath morning a portion of the Five Books of Moses is read in the synagogue, together with an appropriate reading from the Prophets, with the entire cycle completed each year.

At home, on the six Sabbaths between Passover and *Shevuoth*, fathers and grandfathers would traditionally engage the children in discussions of the *Wisdom of the Fathers (Pirke Abot)* or portions of the *Mishna* that discuss ethical problems. I leave it to cultural historians to appraise the magnitude of the consequence of an entire people, young and old, spending one day a week, year after year, generation after generation, century after century, in a seminar on religion, morals, ethics, responsibility.

It is a long-honored custom for Jews to invite a stranger, a traveler, a student or poor man, to the *Shabbes* meal. However poor a Jew might be, he sought to find someone to be his family's *oyrech*. It is hard to overestimate how this served to make Jews everywhere feel part of one universal fellowship.

Shabbes ends at sundown, Saturday, with a home religious service called *Habdala*, which marks the "separation" of the Sabbath from the week days. A special braided candle is lighted, wine is poured, blessings are uttered, and the aroma of spices is inhaled—in the symbolic hope that the coming week will be sweet. See HABDALA.

For more about the Sabbath, from its origins to its menu, see Appendix: Sabbath. And for a hilarious lampoon on the Sabbath guest, see the note under OYRECH.

Maurice Samuel wrote this marvelous poetic passage on the meaning of *Shabbes* to poor, humble Jews.

> You must make up your mind that Tevyeh the coolie, or Tevyeh the dairyman, simply will not work . . . from sundown on Friday to sundown on Saturday. No labour-leader in the world has ever been so insistent on the forty-eight or forty-hour week as Tevyeh on his six-day week. The Sabbath is the Lord's day; that is, it is Tevyeh's day for rest in the Lord. He will not work on that day, he will not carry money about, he will not touch fire or tear paper or do anything that savours of the slavery of the body. . . . You will neither bribe, bully, nor persuade him into such transgression. For the Sabbath and the festivals are all that are left to him; they are the last citadel of his freedom. On those days he will pray, meditate, and refresh his spirit with a little learning. He may be hungry; he will contrive to rise above it. He may not know where the next day's food will come from, either; he will contrive to forget that, too. . . .
>
> There never was such obstinacy! It must not be thought, either, that Tevyeh, crushed under the double burden of the Jewish exile and the worker's slavery, clings to these practices merely as a grim protest. Not by any means. He enjoys them, thoroughly. He loves the Sabbath and the festivals. He loves prayer. . . .
>
> The Sabbath siesta is not a long affair. Who wants to sleep away the loveliest of days? Half an hour passes, an hour at most. Then you hear, issuing from the dilapidated houses, and hanging over the crooked alleys, sweet, haunting melodies in a minor key; not formal songs, but vague chants, carrying not formal phrases, but half phrases, words and half words, repeated over and over again. Melancholy but not depressed, suppliant but not importunate, the voices

linger over the townlet with the tenderness of bells.
"Ah, Father—Father—bim—bom Father in heaven—
ai—ai—look upon us—bim—bom—Thy people—Father—ai—ai—King—" The words and half words, the
melodies, the grace-notes, say nothing and say everything. They are mnemonics, mysterious and meaningless to the outsider, intimate, lucid, and vivid to the
insider, evoking dimly a long history of homelessness,
of faithfulness and hope. As the sadness of great
stretches of space informs the songs of the Russian
peasant, so the sadness of great stretches of time
haunts the truncated words, the elisions and repetitions
of these minor Jewish chants. . . . "Life is hard, God
is good, a time will come, bim-bom, remember Thy
people, hard, good, people, Father—ai, Father, little
Father. . . ." And meanwhile the Sabbath is slipping
away, the Queen is preparing her departure, the harsh
world, the daily struggle, the bitterness of life, stand at
the gates of the evening. Get everything you can out
of this heavenly interlude, an hour or two of prayer,
an hour or two of study, in the synagogue or at home.
Till the moment of the Separation comes, and with
incense box uplifted, his family gathered about him,
the Kasrielevkite takes regretful leave of the Sabbath,
and his wife sings, in homely Yiddish, the valedictory
of Reb Isaac of Berditchev, Reb Levi Isaac the Compassionate. . . .

What kind of Sabbath is it, I ask you, which leaves
the world around you utterly unchanged from the
week-days? The shops are open, the market-place is
filled, the horses neigh, buyers and sellers chaffer, the
[streetcar] thunders past the synagogue, and the Sabbath siesta is a day-mare in a din of blaring radios and
yelling children playing baseball in the street. And . . .
traditionalists and modernists alike remember now and
again with a nostalgic pang the far-off magic of those
sacred hours, those transfigured interludes of the Sabbaths and festivals for which even progress and freedom have found no substitute.*

* Maurice Samuel, *The World of Sholom Aleichem*, Schocken Paperbacks, 1965, pp. 16, 59, 60, 61.

Rabbi Korshak, the young, modern rabbi in a suburban temple, greatly loved to play golf. He played as often as he could, usually with members of his congregation; but he took his pastoral duties so seriously that he could not find time to play more than four or five times a year.

One sunny Saturday morning, after services, Rabbi Korshak saw that his calendar was clear, and felt so powerful a craving to play golf, even if only for a few holes, that he begged God to forgive him for breaking the Sabbath, tossed his golf bag into the back of his car, and sped off to a golf course a good thirty miles away, where he was certain no one would recognize him.

With an apology to his Maker on his lips, and a song of sixpence in his heart, the Rabbi teed off. . . .

Up in heaven, Moses, looking down to earth, observing the ways and follies of Man, suddenly bolted upright. "Lord! My Lord!" he cried, "I beseech Thee: Gaze down. Do my eyes deceive me? There, Holy One—beyond those clouds—do you *see?*"

"Y-yes," said the Lord.

"That's Rabbi Korshak!" said Moses. "Playing *golf!* On Your Holy Sabbath!!"

"Dear Me," sighed the Lord.

"Such a transgression!" said Moses. "From a rabbi yet. How will You punish him?"

"I," sighed the Lord, "will teach him a lesson."

And with that God cupped His hands over His mouth and —just as Rabbi Korshak teed off for the second hole—the Almighty One, King of the Universe, let out His breath in a long, mighty, cosmic *"Whooooosh!"* that caught the rabbi's golf ball in midair, lifted it 300 yards, flipped it around a tree, over a stream and against a rock, where it ricocheted in a miraculous parabola to make—a hole in one!

Moses stared at God in bewilderment. *"That* you call a punishment, Lord?"

"Mmh," smiled the Lord. "Whom can he *tell?"*

Shabbes goy

Pronounced SHAH-*bes goy*, to rhyme with "Bob is boy." *Shabbes:* Sabbath; *goy:* Gentile.

1. The Gentile who is asked on the Sabbath by Orthodox Jews to light the fire, put out candles, perform a chore—all of which are forbidden the devout on the holy Shabbes.

Since any physical exertion, any workaday routine or activity, was held to desecrate the Sabbath, Orthodox Jews in eastern Europe would ask a Gentile to fetch wood or water, light the fire in stove or oven, put out the candles, etc. A small tip, or a piece of *challa* or cake, was customary.

In America, the Orthodox would ask a non-Jewish neighbor, or the janitor, to press an electric-light switch (just as the Amish sect in Pennsylvania, forbidden by their church to own automobiles, will ride in a car hired from, and driven by, a non-Amish).

The rabbis, following the Fourth Commandment, frowned upon the custom of using a *Shabbes goy;* they said that it "breaks the Sabbath" even to ask someone else to do so.

2. (As used, on occasion, by Orthodox Jews) A Jew who is not Orthodox or "observing." "His father and mother —long may they live—are good Jews, but he, I hate to tell you, is a *Shabbes goy.*"

Shabtsitvainik

Pronounced scornfully: *shob-tzee-TVY-nik*, to rhyme with "popsy rye wick." Yiddishism: adds *-nik* to the popular pronunciation of *Sabbati Zvi*, the so-called "Messiah of Izmir."

1. A fake religious seer, prophet or self-proclaimed Messiah.
2. One who believes in, or follows the precepts of, a religious charlatan.

See Appendices: Sabbati Zvi and False Messiahs.

shachris

Pronounced SHAKH-*ris*, to rhyme with "Bach kiss." Hebrew: "morning."

The morning prayer.

One of the three daily prayers. See MINCHA, MAIREV.

shadchen

Pronounced SHOD-*khen*, to rhyme with "bodkin"—if you pronounce the *k* as a hearty *kh*. Plural: *shadchonim: shod-*KHUN-*im*. From the Hebrew: *shidukh:* "marital match."

1. A professional matchmaker.
2. Anyone who brings together, introduces, or maneuvers a man and woman into a meeting that results in a wedding.

Jewish marriages were customarily arranged by the heads of two families. Rabbis were sometimes *shadconim*, for the task of arranging marriages was considered a sacred matter: The union of two souls, and the agreement to have children and raise them as Jews, was part of Israel's obligation in its special compact with God. (Commentaries on the Talmudic tractate of *Baba Kama* deal with the role of the matchmaker in perpetuating Israel's existence; rabbinical decisions set proper fees for arranged marriages.)

The professional *shadchen* performed an important social function, gathering information about eligible mates, weighing family background, individual qualities, and personality factors in a matching undertaking that is today beginning to be assigned to computers. (See YICHES.)

As the Jewish communities in eastern Europe grew larger, more deeply rooted, the *shadchonim* became seedy Cupids, more commercial in their concern, more vigorous in their salesmanship, less exact in their representations. Soon the rabbis began to criticize the vulgarity and venality of *shad-*

chonim. The *shadchen* did become a grubby fellow, useful but distrusted, a magpie, too shrewd, fluttering around with his grubby notebooks and inevitable umbrella. (A touching story about a modern rabbi's ambivalent encounter with a *shadchen* is in Bernard Malamud's *The Magic Barrel.*)

God is considered the supreme *shadchen;* indeed, the sages of yore maintained that God pays as much attention to, and expends as much effort in, pairing off compatible couples as He devoted to the parting of the waters of the Red Sea. So every *shadchen* considers himself charged with a quasi-divine mission, and almost every Jew, and surely every *yideneh,* is an amateur but permanent *shadchen.*

Our aversion to the idea of arranged marriages is, of course, a post-eighteenth-century attitude: it did not occur to earlier Jews, nor to their contemporaries, that "love and marriage" go together. Romantic love is relatively new in human history.

The *shadchen*'s functions have been taken over today by a dozen institutional devices: Temples with social programs for young men and women, "friendship clubs," computer operations.

A wisecrack defines a *shadchen* as "a marriage broker who knows the perfect girl for you—and married the wrong girl himself."

Sholom Aleichem defined a *shadchen* as "a dealer in livestock."

A *shadchen,* having sung the praises of a female client, brought his excited male prospect to see her. The young man took one look at the damsel to whom the *shadchen* elaborately introduced him, and recoiled.

"What's the matter?" asked the *shadchen.*

"You said she was young," whispered the young man, "and she's forty if she's a day! You said she was beautiful, and she looks like a duck! You said she was shapely, and she's fat enough for two! You said——"

"You don't have to whisper," said the *shadchen.* "She's also hard of hearing."

A *shadchen* told his prospective client of a glorious girl named Rebecca.

"Rebecca? The redhead?" asked the young man.

"The same."

"You must be crazy! She's almost blind."

"*That* you call a failing?" cried the *shadchen*. "That's a blessing—because she won't see, half the time, what you're doing."

"She also stutters!"

"Lucky you," sighed the *shadchen*. "A woman who stutters doesn't dare talk too much, so she'll let you live in peace."

"But she's deaf!"

"*I* should have such luck! To a deaf wife you can shout, you can bawl her out——"

"She's also at least twenty years older than I am!"

"Ah," sighed the *shadchen*, "I thought you were a man of vision. I bring you a marvel of a woman you can spend a lifetime with, and you pick on one little fault!"

A young man, having patiently and skeptically endured the *shadchen*'s hyperbole, said, "But you left out one thing, didn't you?"

"Never! What?"

"She—limps."

"Only when she walks!" cried the *shadchen*.

The prospective groom scowled. "You lied to me."

"*I?*" said the *shadchen*. "How? Isn't she pretty? Isn't she rich? Isn't she intelligent?"

"Yes, yes, but you told me she comes from an illustrious family. You said her father is dead—and I just learned *he's been in jail for the past six years!*"

"So?" cried the *shadchen*. "That you call living?"

The *shadchen* was impressing the young man with the boundless virtues of a female, and ended: "And to look at, she's a regular picture!"

The young man could not wait for his blind date.

But when he accosted the *shadchen* the next day, his voice was frosty: "Her eyes are crossed, her nose is crooked, and when she smiles one side of her mouth goes down——"

"Just a minute," interrupted the *shadchen*. "Is it my fault you don't like Picasso?"

shah!

Pronounced SHAH, to rhyme with "Pa," "Ma," "ha."
Onomatopoetic.

An order to be quiet; a command to "shut up." *"Shah!
Shah!"*

To a group, a request or instruction to quiet down or be silent
is given as *"Zoll zein shah!"* "Let there be quiet!"

shalom

See SHOLEM.

---

shammes
shamus
shammus

Pronounced SHAH-*mes*, to rhyme with "promise." Hebrew: *shamash:* "servant."

1. The sexton or caretaker of the synagogue; the "servant" of a congregation of worshipers.

In the old country, and in the early decades of this century in
America, a *shammes* had many duties beyond the janitorial.
He was expected to keep the synagogue clean and warm; to
repair minor damage; to see that prayer books and ceremonial
objects were safely preserved. In the *shtetl*, he would go
around waking up congregation members, calling them to
prayer, announcing sunset and Sabbath times (often by trumpet). He also was used to carry messages, and acted as a
bailiff to the religious court. He collected synagogue dues,
made funeral arrangements, and rounded up a *minyan*. He
would even fill in for a cantor with a sore throat. (Jews did
not stand on ceremony.)

2. (In American slang): A detective, policeman, guard.

Shammes, in this usage, enjoys wide popularity in detective fiction and among the Irish, who spell it *shamus*, which sounds more like Gaelic than Yiddish.

Eric Partridge* and others claim that *shamus* derives from the Irish name Seamus, and say that since so many Irish immigrants became policemen, the name Seamus grew to be associated with police personnel.

3. A "private eye."
4. A functionary on a low level; an unimportant menial. "A *shammes* in a pickle factory" is a Yiddish phrase for a low man on anyone's totem pole.
5. Sycophant; a hanger-on-around someone. "Every movie producer has to have a *shammes*."
6. A "stool pigeon"; an informer.
7. The ninth candle of the *Chanukah menorah*, used to light the others.

———————————

It grieves me to tell you that neither *shammes, shames, shammas, shamas,* nor *shamus* appear in my 13-volume *Oxford English Dictionary*. Nor did it appear in the Webster's *New International Dictionary*, second edition.** Nor (to my dismay) is it indexed in Mencken's *The American Language*.*** But there are many colorful citations in Berrey and Van den Bark's invaluable *American Thesaurus of Slang*.****

———————————

On the high Holy Days, seats in the synagogue are often sold in advance, to provide revenue for synagogue upkeep. In a small *shul* in Coney Island, a Jew without a ticket came running up to the door: "Let me in, let me in! I must see Abe Baum!"

The *shammes* barred his way. "No one gets in without a ticket!"

"It's an emergency! I'll come right out! It'll only take five seconds!"

———————————

* Eric Partridge, *A Dictionary of Slang and Unconventional English*, Macmillan, 1961.
** G. & C. Merriam, 1961.
*** Knopf, 1962.
**** Crowell, 1943.

"O.K.," said the *shammes*. "But don't let me catch you praying!"

The visiting rabbi stopped in the middle of his sermon and signaled to the *shammes*. "In the second row," he whispered, "is a man sound asleep. Wake him up."

"That's not fair," said the *shammes*.

"What do you mean, 'not fair'?"

"You put him to sleep; you wake him up."

sharopnikel

Pronounced *shah-ROPP-ni-kel,* to rhyme with "bar up, pickle." Pure Ameridish.

A small object that effectuates a shutting up—hence, a baby's pacifier; a teething ring; Linus's blanket in the comic strip, *Peanuts.*

This enchanting fusion of English and Yiddish takes the English "shut up," squeezes it into "sharop" (as was the custom), adds the *-nik* to make a substantive, and tacks on the affectionate diminutive, *-el.* Amazing.

NOTE: "Pacifier" comes from "pacify," and can mean anything from a Swiss diplomat to a tranquilizing pill. *Sharopnikel,* on the other hand, sternly excludes diplomacy, international relations, or pharmaceuticals.

shaygets

Pronounced SHAY-*gits,* to rhyme with "hay kits." Hebrew origin. Plural: *shkotzim.* Feminine: *shiksa.*

1. A Gentile boy or young man. "She's going around with a *shaygets.*"

2. A clever lad; a rascal; a handsome, mischievous,

charming devil—Jewish or Gentile. "Oh, is he a *shaygets* with the girls!" "Who can say 'no' to such a *shaygets?*"

3. An arrogant cock-of-the-walk. "He strutted in as boldly as a *shaygets.*"

4. An uneducated boy; one who has no intellectual ambitions. "You won't study? Do you want to grow up into a *shaygets?*"

Lest you think meaning 3 condescending, let me remark that to the Jews, for untold centuries, the conduct of *shkotzim* hardly inspired affection. As to 4: For the same centuries, when the overwhelming majority of Europeans were illiterate, it would have been hard to find a Jewish male over the age of five who could not read. Virtually every Jewish boy *had* to learn Hebrew.

See CHEDER, CHACHEM and TALMID CHACHEM.

The two traveling salesmen, competitors in selling notions, spied each other on the platform. "Hello, Liebowitz."

"Hello, Posner."

Silence.

"So—where are you going?" asked Liebowitz.

"To Minsk," said Posner.

Silence.

"Listen, Posner," sighed Liebowitz, who was a very bright *shaygets*, "when you say you're going to Minsk, you want me to think you're going to Pinsk. But I happen to know that you *are* going to Minsk—so why are you lying?!!"

shayner Yid

Pronounced SHAY-*ner* YEED, to rhyme with "trainer deed." German: *shayn:* "pretty."

Literally, *shayner Yid* means "beautiful Jew," but the phrase is used not as a comment on physical attractiveness but to praise personal character, rectitude, and *Yiddishkeit* ("Jewishness").

A *shayner Yid* is a Jew of whom other Jews are proud, a man or woman of honor, kindness, circumspection, sensitivity to others. A *shayner Yid* can be poor as a church mouse (church mice do not discriminate; they visit synagogues, too). The butcher on our block was hailed by one and all as a *shayner Yid* because of his singular quietness, his air of gravity and refinement, his exemplary modesty.

Melnikoff and Spiegel were talking. The name of one Shmerl came up.

"Who's he?" asked Melnikoff.

"Shmerl. Shmerl Kaminsky," said Spiegel.

"I can't place him. What does he look like?"

"He's ugly, poor man, very short, has a huge nose, is pockmarked."

"N-no . . ."

"Shmerl's left hand is deformed, he holds it like this, and one ear is lopsided."

"I still don't place him . . ."

"Shmerl talks through his nose," cried Spiegel, "has a bad stutter, and he's hunchbacked!"

"Ah!" cried Melnikoff. "*That* Shmerl. Sure. A *shayner Yid!*"

Shechinah
Shekhinah

Pronounced sh'KHEE-*neh,* to rhyme with "Salina." Use the Scottish *kh.* Hebrew: "Divine Presence." Literally: "dwelling."

1. The term used to symbolize God's spirit and omnipresence, and another way of referring to God without using His Name. (See ADONAI, ADOSHEM.)

2. The actual dazzling, radiant, shining Presence of the Lord Himself.

The *Shechinah* was said to have appeared to Moses in the burning bush. It also descended in the pillar of smoke that guided the Israelites through the desert. It rested on Mount

Sinai when the Ten Commandments were given to the children of Israel.

The *Talmud* teaches that the *Shechinah* is everywhere. Observing Jews say that the *Shechinah* descends each Friday at sunset to transform each Jewish home during the Sabbath.

> 3. When someone is converted to the Jewish faith, he is said to have come "under the wings of the *Shechinah*."

Emperor Hadrian once approached Rabbi Joshua ben Hananiah and said, "I desire to see your God."

Rabbi Joshua asked the emperor to stand facing the sun and gaze upon it.

The Emperor did so for a moment, then said, "I cannot! It is too bright. It blinds my eyes!"

Said Rabbi Joshua, "If you are not able to look upon the sun, which is only a servant of God, how much less can you gaze upon the *Shechinah*."

shaytl
sheitel

> Pronounced SHAY-*tl* or SHY-*tl*, to rhyme with "fatal" or "title." Plural: *shaytlin* or *shaytlech*, pronounced SHAYT-*lin*, SHAYT-*lekh*. German: "crown of the head."

> The wig traditionally worn by Orthodox Ashkenazic Jewish women, in eastern Europe, after they were married.

The *shaytl* was made either of the user's own hair, of someone else's hair, or of false—i.e., manufactured—hair.

Sephardic and Oriental Jewish women never adopted the *shaytl*, but instead wore a shawl, turban, or veil over their own hair after marriage. Very, very few women wear a *shaytl* today.

The custom of using a *shaytl* spread slowly among the Jews of central and eastern Europe, and against opposition from the rabbis, who preferred a simple scarf. At first, a *shaytl* was only worn over the hair on the Sabbath and holidays, the head being covered by a veil or scarf at other times. Some rabbis even protested that there was nothing in either the laws or traditions of Israel that called for a wig.

The rabbis decreed that once married, a woman's hair, her well-known crowning beauty, should not be visible lest it distract men from prayer or study. (Jews also worried that attractive Jewish women might draw the attention of lecherous anti-Semites, so unmarried women braided their hair.) The *Mishna* warns a married woman never to appear outside her home with her hair visible: that was ruled grounds for divorce.

Legend has it that God prettified Eve's uncombed locks before Adam saw her—and legend will have to remain uncontested, as far as I'm concerned, because I know of no evidence to dispute it.

See also PAYESS, and Appendix: Hair.

A photograph of each of my grandmothers shows them in *shaytlin;* and if there was any doubt in my mind about how unbecoming a wig can be on a lady, that doubt was dispelled by the pictures.

I should think the *shaytl* must have discouraged adultery in the *shtetl.*

sheeny

(Vulgarism); pronounced SHEE-*nee,* to rhyme with "gleamy."

1. A thoroughly offensive name, combining contempt and disparagement, for a Jew.

C. T. Onions' *Oxford Dictionary of English Etymology** says that *sheeny* is slang and appeared in the nineteenth century, origin unknown. The *Oxford English Dictionary* calls *sheeny* slang of obscure origin, possibly from the Russian, Polish, and Czech words for Jews, emerging in the early nineteenth century. (Portuguese sailors called a Jew a *sheeny.*)

* Oxford, 1966.

The word is branded opprobrious in *The Shorter Oxford English Dictionary*, but "inoffensive" in J. C. Hotten's *The Slang Dictionary*.* The word may not have offended J. C. Hotten, but it would offend any Jew.

Ernest Weekley (*Etymological Dictionary of Modern English*, Dover, 1957, 2 vols.) suggests that *sheeny* is derived from the way Jews pronounced the German word *schön* ("pretty," "beautiful") in describing the merchandise they offered for sale.

Eric Partridge** suggests *sheeny* may come from "the sheeny, i.e., glossy or brightly shiny, hair of the average 'English' Jew." Why Mr. Partridge put quotation marks around 'English' I do not understand. As for the "average" Jew: his hair would be of "average" brilliance. Nor would older or religious Jews pomade their hair. And since it must have been early nineteenth-century Jews of whom the epithet was coined, the alleged shininess of their hair becomes all the more suspect, and the derivation of *sheeny* from *schön* the more likely. Maurice Samuel tells me he thinks *sheeny* comes from *a miesse meshina* ("An ugly fate or death"), a phrase widely used by and among Jews, the *sheeny* being a Gentile remembrance and identification of the final syllable and sound.

English slang for
2. A pawnbroker.
3. A tramp.
4. (In the military) A frugal, economy-minded man.
5. Fraudulent.
6. Base.

In such company, it is small wonder that the word raises the hackles of Jews.

Shehecheyanu

Pronounced *sheh-heh-kheh-*YAW-*noo*, to rhyme with "fella macaw Lou." Hebrew: "that He let us live."

* 1874 edition.
** Eric Partridge, *Dictionary of Slang and Unconventional English*, Macmillan, 1961, p. 753.

The main word in the benediction used for joyous events that do not occur every day.

The benediction is: "Blessed art Thou, O Lord our God, King of the Universe, who has kept us alive to this time."

A Jew "makes *Shehecheyanu*" on the three major festivals of the year: *Pesach, Succoth,* and *Shevuoth.* In addition, when an Orthodox Jew moves into a new home, or puts on a new suit, or eats the first fruit of the season, etc., he "makes *Shehecheyanu.*"

shekel

> Pronounced SHEH-*kl,* to rhyme with "heckle." Hebrew: "coin," "weight." Plural: *shkolim.*
>
> 1. A coin.
> 2. Money.

A *shekel* was the most important silver coin in Biblical times. It is mentioned in Genesis (33 : 12–16) as the money used by Abraham when he purchased the Cave of Machpela as a burying ground. And half a *shekel* was the tax Moses imposed upon the Israelites for the Tabernacle (Exodus 30 : 13).

When the first Zionist Congress was convened in Basel in 1897, the nominal sum set up for membership dues was called a *shekel.*

Shakespeare uses the word in *Measure for Measure* (II, 2). "Not with fond shekels of tested gold . . ."

Shekel or *shekels* is widely used, in American slang, to mean "coins," or "money." "Come on, lay out some *shekels.*" "He has more *shekels* than you have hairs."

H. L. Mencken's *The American Language** does not mention *shekel* anywhere. Tsk, tsk.

Which is more important: money or wisdom?

"Wisdom," says the philosopher.

"Ha!" scoffs the cynic. "If wisdom is more important than

* Fourth revised edition, Knopf, 1962.

money, why is it that the wise wait on the rich, and not the rich on the wise?"

"Because," says the scholar, "the wise, being wise, understand the value of money; but the rich, being only rich, do not know the value of wisdom."

Shema
Shma

Rhymes with "aha." Hebrew: "hearken," "hear."

The first word of the prayer that proclaims the Jews' faith: "Hear, O Israel, the Lord our God, the Lord is One. . . ."

See SHEMA YISRAEL.

Shema Yisrael
Shma Yisrael

Pronounced *sheh*-MA *yis-roe*-AIL. From Hebrew: *shema:* "hear"; *Yisrael:* "Israel."

The most common of Hebrew prayers, recited three—or four—times a day by an Orthodox Jew; it is the last prayer he utters on his deathbed.

This lyrical declaration of faith reads:

Hear, O Israel: The Lord our God, the Lord is One!—
And thou shalt love the Lord thy God with all thy
heart, and with all thy soul, and with all thy might.
And these words, which I command thee this day, shall
be upon thy heart, and thou shalt teach them diligently
unto thy children, and thou shalt talk of them when
thou sittest in thy house, and when thou walkest by
the way, and when thou liest down, and when thou
risest up. And thou shalt bind them for a sign upon

thy hand, and they shall be for frontlets between thine
eyes. And thou shalt write them upon the door-posts
of thy house and upon thy gates.

The words are found in Deuteronomy, 6 : 4–7.

Jews who were being tortured, flogged, flayed, hanged, torn
apart, burned at the stake, boiled in oil, or otherwise introduced to earnest and pious efforts to convert them, would
try to die with the prayer on their lips. Unlearned observers
of these peculiar evangelical attempts came to think that
Shema Yisrael meant "Long live the Jews!"—but they were
wrong.

See also MEZUZAH and TEFILLIN.

Shemona Esray

See DAVEN.

shemozzl
shlemozzl

Pronounced *sheh*-MOZ-*zl* or *shle*-MOZ-*zl*, to rhyme with
"den nozzle." NOTE: These words are not Yiddish, and
not Yinglish, but slang used by our cousins in England
and Ireland. I include them because they are often
spelled and pronounced like the Yiddish *shlimazl*, to
which they bear not the slightest resemblance.

A *shemozzl* or *shlemozzl* is:

1. An uproar, a fight, a confusion, a "rhubarb." "The
umpire's decision set off a terrific *shemozzl*." "He'll stir
up a big *shemozzl*."

  This usage comes from the racetrack touts and book-
makers of London.

2. To decamp, to abscond, to make off with something.
This usage is given in Eric Partridge's *A Dictionary of
Slang and Unconventional English.**

_____
* Macmillan, 1961.

Shevuoth
Shabuot

Pronounced *sheh-vu-ess*, to rhyme with "the Lewis." Hebrew: "weeks."

The Festival of Weeks, or Pentecost. (It was called Pentecost by Greek Jews, meaning "the fiftieth," for *Shevuoth* occurred fifty days after the second day of Passover.)

This two-day holiday (one day in Israel, and among Reform Jews) falls seven weeks after the second day of Passover. It is the anniversary of the covenant between God and Israel on Mount Sinai, and is called "the season of the giving to us of our Holy *Torah*."

It is also "the holiday of the first fruits," for it is one of the three happy pilgrimages to Jerusalem, when the Jews in Palestine went up to the great Temple bringing offerings of the first fruits of their harvest. To commemorate this aspect of the holiday, synagogues are decorated with greens on *Shevuoth*.

Many congregations hold a confirmation ceremony for teen-age boys and girls at this time. This links the youth's con-scious declaration of participation in Jewry with the giving of the *Torah* on Mount Sinai, and extends a tradition that began in the Middle Ages, when parents enrolled their young sons in the *cheder* on *Shevuoth*.

The section of Exodus dealing with Sinai and the Ten Commandments is read on *Shevuoth*, as is the Book of Ruth, which tells the story of the lovely Moabite who became con-verted to Judaism and accepted its laws: "Thy people shall be my people . . . and thy God my God."

It is customary to eat dairy dishes on this holiday, espe-cially delicacies made of cheese—cheese *blintzes*, cheese *latkes*, cheese cakes. It is also a time to forget diets.

shiddach

Pronounced SHID-*dakh*, to rhyme with "Bid, *ach!*" From Hebrew: *shidukh:* "marital match."

An arranged marriage; a "match." "She made a *shiddach* between Florence and Al."

See SHADCHEN.

In a certain town, there was a grievous shortage of marriageable young men. One of them, ugly but conceited, came to the *shadchen* and said. "I am considering getting married. But I warn you—I'll accept nothing but a remarkable *shiddach!*"

The *shadchen* studied the young man sourly, then said, "I have just the girl for you. Her father is rich and she is beautiful, well-educated, charming——"

"Wait a minute," said the young man suspiciously. "Why isn't such a girl married?"

The *shadchen* raised his hand. "You want to know why such a girl would accept someone who is not—excuse me—the most attractive young man in the world? I will be perfectly frank. This beautiful, educated, charming girl has an affliction: once a year she goes crazy."

"She goes *crazy?*"

"But that need not disturb you. She does not cause any trouble. She just goes a little *meshugge*—for only one day. Then she's as charming and normal as ever for another year!"

"That's not so bad," said the young man, "if she's as rich and beautiful as you say. Let's go see her."

"Not now," said the *shadchen*. "Your *shiddach* must wait."

"Until when?"

"Until the day she goes out of her mind."

shikker

Pronounced SHICK-*er*, to rhyme with "stick her." Hebrew: *shikor:* "drunk."

1. A drunk. "He's a *shikker*."
2. (Adjective) Drunk. "She got a wee bit *shikker*."

Jewish drunkards are exceedingly rare; the souse is almost

unknown in Jewish folklore or literature; yet drinking is not
foreign to Jewish culture. A Jewish child may be introduced
to a sip of wine at an early age: The blessing over wine
sanctifies each *Shabbes* and festival (see KIDDUSH).

The goodness of wine is often mentioned in the Bible: The
Psalms compare Israel to a vine which has taken deep root
and prospered (80 : 9–11); and in time of peace, every man
shall sit "under his vine and under his fig tree" (1 Kings
5 : 5). Many Biblical metaphors use wine as an allusion to
prosperity and good times.

The rabbis also believed that wine possessed splendid cura-
tive properties: "Wine is the greatest of all medicines."
"Where wine is lacking, drugs are necessary," Rabbi Huna
said. "Wine helps to open the heart to reasoning." But the
sages always stressed moderation, in drinking as in all else—
except study.

Jews have a certain contempt for anyone who loses control
of his faculties, or acts in an uncouth, "bestial," irresponsible
manner.

> ". . . drunkards were rarely seen among Jews. When
> night came and a man wanted to pass away time, he
> did not hasten to a tavern to take a drink, but went to
> pore over a book or joined a group which—either with
> or without a teacher—revered books. . . . Physically
> worn out by their day's toil, they sat over open vol-
> umes, playing the austere music of the Talmud . . . or
> the sweet melodies of . . . piety of the ancient sages."*

Drinking, if not drunkenness, has clearly increased among
American Jews; I do *not* attribute this to the injunction (one
of my favorites) in the *Talmud:* "When a man faces his
Maker, he will have to account for those pleasures of life he
failed to experience."

"A tavern can't corrupt a good man, and a synagogue can't
reform a bad one." ———PROVERB

Shikkered, to mean "drunk," is commonly used in Australia,

---

* A. J. Heschel, *The Earth Is the Lord's*, Abelard-Schuman, 1964,
p. 45.

say H. Wentworth and S. B. Flexner, in *The Dictionary of American Slang* (Crowell, 1960, p. 466). How the word got all the way down to the Antipodes I do not know.

"By three things a man gives himself away: by his tumbler, his tipping, and his temper."

—TALMUD

"When one man tells you you're *shikker*, hesitate; when two tell you, slow up; when three men tell you—lie down!"

—MY VERSION OF AN OLD SAW

In the lounge of a Catskill resort, an hour before the dinner hour, Mrs. Meckler asked Mrs. Smelkin, "How about a cocktail before dinner?"

"No, thanks. I never drink."

"No? Why not?"

"Well, in front of my children, I don't believe in taking a drink. And when I'm away from my children, who *needs* it?"

shiksa
shikseh

Pronounced SHIK-*seh*, to rhyme with "pick the." The feminine of *shaygets*. From Hebrew: *sheques*: "blemish."

1. A non-Jewish woman, especially a young one.
2. (As used, on occasion, by Orthodox Jews) A Jewish woman who is not Orthodox, pious, observing, does not keep a *kosher* household, etc.

As the Polish servant girl carried bucket after bucket of water from the well to the house, the rabbi sat down to eat with his disciples. But he sprinkled a very few drops of water on his hands, before making the traditional *broche*.

A disciple asked why he was so stingy about water.

The rabbi replied: "It is surely pious to wash before each meal; but one must not be pious at even a servant's—a *shiksa*'s—expense."

shivah

Pronounced SHI-*vah*, to rhyme with a Southerner's pronunciation of "river." From the Hebrew: "seven."

The seven solemn days of mourning for the dead, beginning immediately after the funeral, when Jews "sit *shivah*" in the home of the deceased.

The traditional practice requires members of the immediate family to remove their shoes, don cloth slippers, and sit on stools or low benches, customs derived from ancient mourning rituals. Mirrors are covered. ("Vanity of vanities, all is vanity.") The mourners wear garments with a rip in the lapel. This is the age-old symbol of grief—the rending of the garments. (The tear is made just before the funeral, and the mourner has uttered the words "Blessed be the righteous Judge," signifying his acceptance of the inevitability of his loss.)

During the *shivah* period, mourners remain in the house and do not work, or even study the *Torah* (save for certain permitted portions). A *minyan* of ten men comes to the house, morning and evening, to hold services and enable the mourners to recite the KADDISH, or mourner's prayer. Friends pay visits out of respect to the deceased and to honor the mourners. The conversation is limited to praises of the dead. The traditional expression of sympathy is, "May the Almighty comfort you among the mourners for Zion and Jerusalem." The mourners do not offer or acknowledge greetings, for they must be preoccupied with their grief and the memory of the dead.

The first meal served to the mourners upon returning from the funeral is prepared by neighbors, and customarily includes hard-boiled eggs, which are said to be symbolic of the need for life to go on—among the mourners.

The sages of the *Talmud* astutely instruct Jews not to mourn too deeply or self-accusingly. They even prescribe the protocol and phasing of grief: three days of weeping, followed by four days of eulogy. The seven-day *shivah* period is followed by a thirty-day period (*sheloshim*) of lesser mourning, and an eleven-month period during which the mourner recites the *Kaddish* twice daily. Thereafter, the deceased is remembered each year on the anniversary of his death. See YORZEIT.

The closeness and intensity of life within the Jewish community developed institutions for virtually every occasion—including a Society to Comfort Mourners, who called upon anyone struck by a death in the family, and brought food to the mourners.

———

At the funeral of a very wealthy man, a stranger joined the funeral procession, and began weeping and wailing louder than all the others.

"Are you a relative?" someone asked.

"No."

"Then why are you crying?"

"That's why."

shlemiel
schlemiel
shlemiehl
shlemihl

Pronounced *shleh*-MEAL, to rhyme with "reveal." (NOTE: *Shlemiel* is often spelled *schlemiel*, or even *schlemiehl*, but I sternly oppose such complications. In Hebrew and Yiddish, the single letter, *shin*, represents the *sh* sound. And in English, to begin a word with *sch* is to call for the *sk* sound, as in "school," "scheme," "schizophrenic." Anyway, I think a *shlemiel* is plagued by enough burdens without our adding orthographic *tsuris* to them.)

1. A foolish person; a simpleton. "He has the brains of a *shlemiel*."

2. A consistently unlucky or unfortunate person; a "fall guy"; a hard-luck type; a born loser; a submissive and uncomplaining victim. "That poor *shlemiel* always gets the short end of the stick." A Yiddish proverb goes: "The *shlemiel* falls on his back and breaks his nose."

3. A clumsy, butterfingered, all-thumbs, gauche type. "Why does a *shlemiel* like that ever try to fix anything?"

4. A social misfit, congenitally maladjusted. "Don't invite that *shlemiel* to the party."

5. A pipsqueak, a Caspar Milquetoast. "He throws as much weight as a *shlemiel*." "No one pays attention to that *shlemiel*."

6. A naive, trusting, gullible customer. This usage is common among furniture dealers, especially those who sell the gaudy, gimcrack stuff called "borax."

7. Anyone who makes a foolish bargain, or wagers a foolish bet. This usage is wide in Europe; it probably comes from Chamisso's tale, *Peter Schlemihl's Wunderbare Geschichte*, a fable in which the protagonist sold his shadow and, like Faust, sold his soul to Satan.

It is important to observe that *shlemiel*, like *nebech*, carries a distinctive note of pity. In fact, a *shlemiel* is often the *nebech*'s twin brother. The classic definition goes: "A *shlemiel* is always knocking things off a table; the *nebech* always picks them up."

Shlemiel is said to come from the name Shlumiel, the son of a leader of the tribe of Simeon (Numbers, 2). Whereas the other generals in Zion often triumphed on the field of war, poor Shlumiel was always losing.

Another theory about the origin of *shlemiel* runs that it is a variation of *shlimazl* or *shlemozzl*. (See SHLIMAZL.) I can't quite see how *shlimazl* gave birth to *shlemiel;* the words are as different as "hard luck" is from "that jerk."

The classic attempt to discriminate between the two types runs: "A *shlemiel* is a man who is always spilling hot soup—down the neck of a *shlimazl*." Or, to make a triple distinction: "The *shlemiel* trips, and knocks down the *shlimazl;* and the *nebech* repairs the *shlimazl's* glasses."

I suppose that *shlemiels* often are *shlimazls*—but that need not be. A *shlemiel* can make a fortune through sheer luck; a *shlimazl* can't: He loses a fortune, through bad luck.

Nor is every *shlimazl* a *shlemiel:* e.g., a gifted, able, talented man is no *shlemiel*, but he may run into such bad luck that he is a *shlimazl:* thus, Gregor Mendel and Thomas Alva Edison, both of whom encountered strings of perverse fortune in their experiments; one might have called them *shlimazls*, but surely never *shlemiels*.

Can a brilliant or learned man be a *shlemiel?* Of course he can; many a savant is: the absentminded professor, the im-

practical genius, are paradigms of *shlemielkeit* (*shlemiel*-ness).
N.B.: Neither *shlemiel, schlemiehl*, nor *schlemiel* appears in the
Oxford English Dictionary. Nor were they in the *Webster
New International*, second edition.* Nor are they indexed in
H. L. Mencken's *The American Language*.** I am as sur-
prised as you.

See also NEBECH, SHLUMP, SHLEPPER, SHLIMAZL, SHMO,
YOLD.

"A *shlemiel* takes a bath, and forgets to wash his face."

A *shlemiel* came to his rabbi, distraught. "Rabbi, you've got
to advise me. Every year my wife brings forth a baby. I have
nine children already, and barely enough money to feed them
—Rabbi, what can I do?"

The sage thought not a moment. "Do nothing."

A man came home from the steam baths—minus his shirt.

"*Shlemiel!*" cried his wife. "Where's your shirt?"

"My shirt? That's right. Where can it be? Aha! Someone at
the baths must have taken my shirt by mistake, instead of his."

"So where is *his* shirt?"

The *shlemiel* scratched his head. "The fellow who took my
shirt—he forgot to leave his."

Two *shlemiels* were drinking tea. In time, one looked up and
announced portentously: "Life! What is it? Life—is like a
fountain!"

The other pondered for a few minutes, then asked, "Why?"

The first thought and thought, then sighed, "So O.K.: life
isn't like a fountain."

---

shlep
shlepper

Pronounced SHLEP, to rhyme with "hep," and SHLEP-*per*,
to rhyme with "pepper." From the German: *schleppen:*
"to drag."

---

* G. & C. Merriam, 1961.
** Knopf, 1962.

shlep

1. To drag, or pull, or lag behind. "Don't *shlep* all those packages; let the store deliver them." "Pick up your feet; don't *shlep*." "They *shlepped* me all the way out to see their house." "He is a *shlep* if ever I saw one." (See also *shlepper*.)

2. To stall, drag one's heels, delay; to move or perform slowly, lazily, inefficiently. "At the rate you're *shlepping* along, we'll never finish." "He'll *shlep* that work out so that it takes twice as long as it should."

shlepper

1. A "drag," a drip, a jerk, a maladroit performer. "Who wants to act with a *shlepper* (or *shlep*) like that?" "Ever since then, she acts like a *shlepper* (or *shlep*)."

2. Someone unkempt, untidy, run-down-at-the-heels. "Why doesn't she do her hair and stop looking like a *shlepper?*" "Hike up your slip; straighten your seams; you look like a *shlepper*."

3. A beggar or petty thief. "How does he earn a living? He's a *shlepper*."

Shlepper has become a familiar word in movie and theater argot, just as have *shtik*, *cockamamy*, *bubeleh*.

See NUCHSHLEPPER, TSUTCHEPPENISH.

Mrs. Hoffenstein, visiting London, went shopping at the famous confectioners, Fortnum and Mason. She bought jars of marmalade, biscuits, tins of cookies and candies, to take back to her hotel.

"And where," asked the striped-trousered salesman, "shall we deliver these, Madam?"

"Don't bother. I'll carry them."

"But madam, we'll be *happy* to deliver this order——"

"I know, but I don't mind, I'm from the Bronx."

"I understand, madam," said the clerk, "but still—why *shlep?*"

"Queen Elizabeth will *shlep* along 95 pieces of baggage on her trip here."

—P. SANN, New York *Post*, Sept. 29, 1957

shlimazl
schlimazel (not shemozzl, not shlemozzl)

Pronounced shli-MOZ-zl, to rhyme with "thin nozzle."
From the German: schlimm: "bad" and the Hebrew:
mazel: "luck." (It is not unusual for a Yiddish word to
combine Hebrew with German, Hebrew with English,
Hebrew with Russian or Polish or Hungarian.)

A chronically unlucky person; someone for whom nothing seems to go right or turn out well; a born "loser."
Let me illustrate by combining four folk sayings: "When
a shlimazl winds a clock, it stops; when he kills a chicken,
it walks; when he sells umbrellas, the sun comes out;
when he manufactures shrouds, people stop dying."

A shlimazl wryly sighed: "From mazel to shlimazl is but a
tiny step; but from shlimazl to mazel—oy, is that far!"

A world-weary Jew once said: "They say that the poor have
no mazel, which is undeniably true, for if the poor had mazel
would they be poor?"

"Only shlimazls believe in mazel."

—PROVERB

The twelfth-century poet Abraham ibn Ezra, whom you
encountered in high school as Browning's Rabbi ben Ezra
(may his tribe increase), limpidly described the shlimazl's lot
when he wrote:

> If I sold lamps,
> The sun,
> In spite,
> Would shine at night.

Mintz came to his rabbi and said, "Whatever I do goes sour.
My wife and children soon won't have anything to eat. What
can I do?"
"Become a baker," said the rabbi.

"A baker? Why?"

"Because if you're a baker, even if business is bad, you and your loved ones will have bread!"

Mintz pondered. "And what if the day comes when I don't have enough money to buy flour?"

"Then you won't be a baker," said the rabbi, "but a *shlimazl.*"

"Hello, Yussel! *Vie gehts?*" ("How are things?")

"Good. Everything is good!"

"Really? I hear you've had a terrible year. How can you say everything's good?"

"It is," said Yussel. "Every morning, I'm good and depressed. Every evening, I'm good and tired. In the summer, I'm good and hot, and in the winter, I'm good and cold. My roof has so many leaks that I get good and wet, and my floors are so rickety that to take five steps makes me good and angry. My children are so lazy I'm good and disgusted with them, and my wife is such a *yenta* that i'm good and sick of her. In fact, everything about my life is so good, I'm good and tired of living!"

shlock
schlack
schlock

Rhymes with "clock." *Shlock* is both an adjective and a noun. From German: *Schlag:* a "blow": perhaps the Yiddish means merchandise that has been "knocked around."

1. A shoddy, cheaply made article. "It's a piece of *shlock.*" "Where did you buy that? In a *shlock-house?*"
2. A defective or fake article; an object one was cheated over. "That watch will never keep time. It's *shlock* merchandise."
3. A disagreeable, peevish person.
4. A shrew, a whining wife, a *yenta*—and a slob, to boot. "His beloved? There's a *shlock* of a girl."

shlock-house

A store that sells cheap, distressed, defective, "fire sale" articles. A gyp joint.

In the furniture business, *shlock-house* merchandise is called "borax."

The customer asked the tobacconist to recommend a good cigar.

"Here's the best cigar in the place. Fifty cents."

The customer paid, lighted up and began to cough and choke. "I asked for a good cigar and you give me *this?*" he cried.

The owner sighed, "What a lucky man you are."

"*Lucky,*" cried the customer. "Are you mad?"

"You own only one of those *shlock-house* cigars; I must have twenty dozen!"

shlub

See ZHLOB.

shlump
shloomp

Pronounce the *u* as in "put." German: *Schlumpe:* a "slovenly female," a "slattern."

As a noun:
A drip, a "drag," a wet blanket. "That *shlump* can depress anyone." "He's half-*shlump*, half-*shlemiel*."

I like to visualize a *shlump* as a *shlep* with droopy shoulders, or a *shmo* who drags his feet.

As a verb:
1. To drag about, to shuffle.

2. To perform in a *pro forma* way; to "kiss off" with nominal effort or enthusiasm. "She *shlumps* through a role." (*Time*, April 19, 1965, p. 99.)

I once heard *shlump* from two Radcliffe girls, neither of whom knew a word of Yiddish; they also tossed off *shtuss* and *nudzh* as if chatting in classical Harvardese.

Shlump seems popular on Broadway, off-Broadway, in college theatricals, and among young people.

See also SHMO, SHLEP, SHMUCK, SHLEMIEL.

On a very cold day, the faithful huddled around the stove in the synagogue. One *shlump* said, "When it's bitterly cold like this—I know exactly what to do."

"What?"

"Shiver."

shmaltz
schmaltz

Pronounced SHMOLTS, to rhyme with "doll" plus *tz.* German: *Schmalz:* "fat," "drippings."

As a noun:

1. Cooking fat; melted or rendered fat—usually, chicken fat.

A great treat, around our house, was a slice of bread spread with *shmaltz*. This happened only occasionally, because my mother, whose ideas about biochemistry I thought foolish folklore (but now turn out to be sound), was convinced that all greasy things were messengers of indigestion.

If you like chopped liver, be sure to have a little *shmaltz* over, or mixed into, it.

2. "Corn," pathos; maudlin and mawkish substance; excessive sentimentality; overly emotional mush; sugary banality.

This usage is wide in theatrical circles, which are a haven for *aficionados* of the self-dramatizing. "As an actor, he goes in for too much *shmaltz*." "Tone it down; it's as *shmaltzy* as organ music." "The way he delivered that speech, you could cut the *shmaltz* with a fork."

3. Luxury, wealth, good luck. "He fell into a tub of *shmaltz*, that's how lucky he is."

As an adjective:
Shmaltzy: corny, mawkish, hackneyed emotionalism. " 'Hearts and Flowers' is about as *shmaltzy* a song as I ever heard."

As a verb:
To *shmaltz* ("to *shmaltz* it up"): to add "corn," pathos, mawkishness.

shmatte
shmotte

Pronounced SHMOT-*ta*, to rhyme with "pot a." From Polish: *szmata:* a "rag," "piece of cloth."

1. A rag. "That you call a dress? It's a *shmatte*."
2. Cheap, shoddy, junk. "I wouldn't drive in a *shmatte* like that." "The movie? A *shmatte!*"
3. A person unworthy of respect; someone "you can wipe your feet on." "She changes her opinion to suit everyone, that *shmatte*." "They treated him like a *shmatte*." "What am I: *tata* (father) or *shmatte* (rag)?" "Stand up for your rights; don't be a *shmatte!*"
4. A woman of weak character, weak will, or wicked ways; a slattern. "She has as much self-respect as the *shmatte* she is." "As a girl, she was decent; now she's a *shmatte*."
5. A fawner; a sycophant; a toady. "Praise drips from that *shmatte* for everyone."

See the story of the shopper in Paris, under CHUTZPA.

shmeck tabac

Pronounced *shmeck* TAH-*bic*, to rhyme with "check rob lick." German: "A taste of tobacco." In Yiddish, *shmeck* means "smell."

1. A pinch of snuff.
2. Anything that is of scant value, that is worth "no more than a pinch of snuff."

A charming story is told about the three "pillars" of Judaism: *Torah* (Learning), *Avodah* (Worship), and *Gemilus chasadim* (Deeds of Kindness), who came before God and cried that, with the dispersion of the Jewish people, they would be forgotten.

"Not so," answered God. "I shall have the Jews build synagogues and they will attend services every *Shabbes*. The rabbi will teach them *Torah*, and the cantor will lead them in worship."

"But how will I be remembered?" asked Deeds of Kindness.

"Ah," said the Lord, "during the service, each Jew will turn toward his neighbor, and offer his snuffbox, saying, 'Have a *shmeck tabac!*'"

shmeer

Pronounced as it is written; rhymes with "shear." From German: *Schmiere:* "grease," or "bribe."

1. To paint.
2. To smear.
3. To spread. *"Shmeer* it on the bread."
4. A spread or paste. "With drinks, a caviar *shmeer* on crackers goes well." "Smoked fish, cream cheese, sour cream, and chives make a wonderful cocktail *shmeer."*
5. To bribe; a bribe. This is the most interesting usage, and has long been part of American slang. It is related to "greasing the palm." "Do the officials expect to be *shmeered* there?" "Do they take a *shmeer?"* There's a saying: *"Az men shmeert nit, fort men nit."* ("If you

don't bribe, you don't ride"—or, less literally, "Without bribery, you'll get nowhere.")

6. To strike or beat. "He landed a *shmeer* between the eyes."

7. "The whole package," "the entire deal."

shmegegge

Pronounced, always with disdain, *shmeh-GEH-geh* or *shmeh-GEH-gee*, to rhyme with "the mega" or "the Peggy." Ameridish slang. Origin: unknown; probably, a dazzling onomatopoetic child of the Lower East Side, or the Ukraine, some Jews say.

1. An unadmirable, petty person.
2. A maladroit, untalented type.
3. A sycophant, a *shlepper*, a whiner, a drip.

Also used to describe:

4. A lot of "hot air," "baloney," a *cockamamy* story. "Don't give me that *shmegegge!*" (This will be contested, but usage is usage: for the product of thinking of a *shmegegge*.)

I think of a *shmegegge* as a cross between a *shlimazl* and a *shlemiel*—or even between a *nudnik* and a *nebech*.

The word is popular in theatrical circles, conjuring up, by its very sound, vividly unlikable characteristics.

Miss Sophia Loren used the word with considerable *brio* in an interview with a *New York Times* reporter. The combination of great beauty, an Italian accent, an eloquent shrug, a tone of derisive dismissal, and a Yinglish word marked a high point in the life of this colorful epithet.

shmendrick

Pronounced SHMEN-*drick*, to rhyme with "Hendrick." From the name of a character in an operetta by Abraham Goldfaden.

1. A Caspar Milquetoast; a kind of *shlemiel*—but weak and thin. (That, at least, is how I visualize it.) A *shlemiel* can be physically impressive, but not a *shmendrick*. A *shmendrick* is small, short, weak, thin, a young *nebech*, perhaps an apprentice *shlemiel*.

2. A pipsqueak; a no-account; the opposite of a *mensh*. "That *shmendrick*, maybe he'll grow up to be a *mensh*."

3. Someone who can't succeed but thinks he can, and persists in acting as though he might. "He has all the unrealistic hopes of a *shmendrick*."

4. A boy, or young man; someone "wet behind the ears." "That *shmendrick* can't be trusted with such responsibility."

5. A child (affectionately). "How's my little *shmendrick*?"

6. Penis (colloquial; rarely used by men. When used by a female, the intention is to deride by diminutizing.).

A woman began to beat her *shmendrick* of a husband, who crawled under the bed.

"Come out!" she cried.

"No!" he said. "I'll show you who's boss in this house!"

shmo

Rhymes with "stow." A euphemistic neologism for *shmuck*. This is not a Yiddish word, but a Yinglish invention.

1. A boob; a *shlemiel*; a hapless, clumsy, unlucky jerk.

2. A "butt"; a fall guy; the goat of a joke.

Mr. Al Capp, the fertile intelligence who has taken L'il Abner down several exuberant decades of hillbilly hi-jinks, adopted *shmo* for the name of an egg-shaped creature that loves to be kicked and gives milk; but *shmo* was in use long before that, as a drawing-room abbreviation for the lusty, but offbounds, *shmuck*. Fred Allen, on a radio program in 1947, protested: "I've been standing here like a *shmo* for twenty minutes."

See SHMUCK.

Stolinsky came out of the richest mansion in town and confided to his wife: "I tell you, Hinda, things aren't going too well with them in there!"

"*What?* I can't believe it! What makes you say a crazy thing like that?"

"I saw both of his daughters playing on one piano!"

He was a bit of a *shmo*.

shmooz
shmoos
shmooze
shmues

Rhymes with "loose"; some pronounce it to rhyme with "ooze." Hebrew: *shmuos:* (originally) "things heard"; (in time) "rumors," "idle talk."

Both verb and noun, *shmooz* means a friendly, gossipy, prolonged, heart-to-heart talk—or, to have such a talk. "They had a little *shmooz* and settled everything." "She *shmoozed* with her father until dinner." "How about a walk and a *shmooz?*" "There's nothing better, to get something off your chest, than a *shmooz* with a friend."

I have never encountered a word that conveys "heart-to-heart chit-chat" as warmly as does *shmooz*.

Gelett Burgess, who invented the word "blurb" and was the creator of the limerick about "the purple cow," once tried to smuggle "huzzlecoo," a word he coined, into English. "Huzzlecoo" never caught on; but it was a dead ringer for *shmooz*.

shmuck

Rhymes with "stuck." From German, in some way or other, where *Schmuck* is "an ornament," "jewelry"; *shmuck* is "neat," "smart," and *schmücken* means "to decorate." In Yiddish, *shmock* means an "ornament."

1. (Obscene) Penis.

Never utter *shmuck* lightly, or in the presence of women and children. Indeed, it was uneasiness about *shmuck* that led to the truncated euphemism *shmo*—and any *shmo* knows what *shmo* comes from.

Jews tend to be puritanical about public references to the pubic.

I never heard any elders, certainly not my father or mother, use *shmuck*, which was regarded as so vulgar as to be taboo. But vulgarity has its *raison d'être*.

2. (Obscene) A dope, a jerk, a boob; a clumsy, bumbling fellow.

In this sense, *shmuck*, like its English equivalent, is widely used by males, and with gusto; few impolite words express comparable contempt. "What a *shmuck* I was to believe him!" "That *shmuck* fell for the stupidest trick you ever saw."

3. (Obscene) A detestable fellow; a son of a bitch.

I suppose that in every language the word for the male organ has been enlisted in the service of the contumelious.

NOTE: There is a Slovene word, *šmok*, that also means a fool, an innocent, a gullible dolt—but I have it on the authority of Dr. Shlomo Noble of the YIVO Institute that *šmok* came from *shmuck*, and not the other way around.

Mr. Lefkowitz—sixty-five, a widower—was having a very lonely time in Miami Beach, and he observed a man of his age who was never without a companion; people forever streamed around him, extending invitations, swapping jokes. So Lefkowitz screwed up his courage, leaned over and said to the popular paragon, "Mister, excuse me. What should I do to make friends?"

"Get—a camel," sneered the other. "Ride up and down Collins Avenue every day and before you know it, everyone in Miami will be asking 'Who *is* that man?' and you'll have to hire a social secretary to handle all the invitations! Don't bother me again with such a foolish question."

So Mr. Lefkowitz bought a paper and looked through the

ads, and by good fortune read of a circus, stranded in Miami, that needed capital. Mr. Lefkowitz telephoned the circus owner, and within half an hour had rented a camel.

The next morning, Mr. Lefkowitz, wearing khaki shorts and a pith helmet, mounted his camel and set forth on Collins Avenue. Everywhere people stopped, buzzed, gawked, pointed.

Every day for a week, Lefkowitz rode his trusty steed. One morning, just as he was about to get dressed, the telephone rang. "Mr. Lefkowitz! This is the parking lot! Your camel—it's gone! Stolen!"

At once, Mr. Lefkowitz phoned the police. A Sergeant O'Neill answered: *"What? . . .* It sounded as though you said someone had stolen your camel."

"That's right!"

"Er—I'll fill out a form. . . . How tall was the animal?"

"From the sidewalk to his back, where I sat, a good six feet."

"What color was it?"

"What color?" echoed Lefkowitz. "Camel color: a regular, camel-colored camel!"

"Male or a female?"

"Hanh?"

"Was the animal male or female?"

"How am I supposed to know about the sex of a camel?" exclaimed Mr. Lefkowitz. "Wait! Aha! It was a male!"

"Are you sure?"

"Absolutely!"

"But, Mr. Lefkowitz, a moment ago you——"

"I'm *positive,* officer, because I just remembered: Every time and every place I was riding on that camel, I could hear people yelling: 'Hey! Look at the *shmuck* on that camel!' "

shnaps
schnaps

Rhymes with "tops." German: *Schnaps:* "intoxicating spirits."

1. Brandy.
2. Any intoxicating spirits.

Any holiday or happy event was the occasion for a little toast with *shnaps*. When I say little, I mean little. None of your long drinks. *Shnaps* was poured out in a jigger-sized glass. No ice, no water, no club soda. A little drink, downed in a minute. Of course the little glass could be refilled. . . .

The phrase used to introduce the toasting is *Lomir machn a shnaps* (LAW-*mir* MAKH-*en a* SHNOPS): "Let us 'make' a *shnaps*."

Shnippishok

Pronounced SHNIP-*pi-shawk.*

A "mythical" city, used as a name in jokes—rather like Chelm or Hotzeplotz. (Shnippishok was a Jewish part of Vilna.)

See HOTZEPLOTZ.

Lupowitz returned to Warsaw, considerably miffed, and explained to the circle of listeners who crowded around him, eager to hear of his adventures: "——and the most terrible thing of all happened in one town when a man came up to me and without a word or a reason hit me a terrific *klop* on the head!"

"What?"

"No!"

"Imagine!"

"*Where* did that happen?"

"In *Shnippishok*," said Lupowitz.

"*Mn-yeh!*" scoffed a bystander. "*That* you call a town?"

shnook
shnuk

Pronounced to rhyme with "crook." Ameridish. Possibly from the German *Schnuck*, "a kind of small sheep," or *Schnucki*, the German colloquialism for "pet," a pet dog, one's "darling," or wife; but I doubt it (see below).

1. A timid *shlemiel;* a meek patsy; a passive, unassertive, ineffectual type.

2. A "Sad Sack," more to be pitied than despised. A *shnook* is pathetic but likable; if not likable, he would probably be called a *shmuck.*

Shnook is almost certainly an American-Yiddish coinage. None of my informants had ever heard it in any eastern Europe tongue, nor in German, nor in European Yiddish; and every person I questioned said he had first heard it in America.

The word was disseminated via radio and vaudeville. Thus: Jack Benny on radio, October 9, 1951: "Don't be such an apologetic *shnook.*"* In the movie *The Apartment,* the protagonist, played by Jack Lemmon, is characterized as "that *shnook.*"

Shnuckl means a customer overcharged by a dishonest salesman, according to Berrey and Van den Bark.**

---

shnorrer
schnorrer
shnorer
shnorren (verb)

Pronounced SHNOR-*rer,* to rhyme with "snorer." German: *schnorren:* "to beg." Perhaps related to *schnarchen:* "to snore"; some energetic philologists relate the whining of beggars to snoring; but Jewish beggars do not whine— as you may read below.

As a noun:

1. A beggar, a panhandler, a moocher.
2. A cheapskate, a chiseler.
3. A bum, a drifter.
4. A compulsive bargain hunter and bargainer.
5. An impudent indigent.

---

* Quoted by H. Wentworth and S. B. Flexner, *Dictionary of American Slang.* Crowell, 1966, p. 447.

** *The American Thesaurus of Slang.* Crowell, 1943, p. 521.

As a verb:
Shnorren means to beg, to panhandle, to borrow.

————————————————

Every Jewish community once had at least one *shnorrer,* and
often a platoon. The *shnorrer* was not a run-of-the-mill men-
dicant. He was no more an ordinary moocher than a *nudnik*
is an ordinary bore, or a *momzer* an ordinary child. The
Jewish *shnorrer* was not apologetic; he did not fawn or whine.
He regarded himself as a craftsman, a professional. He did not
so much ask for alms as claim them. He expected recognition
of his skill, if not encomiums for his character.

Shnorrers considered themselves respectable members of an
occupational group. They were brash, cynical, quick to take
offense, expert in needling prospective benefactors, and quick
in repartee. Their *chutzpa* was of a rare and umbrageous
order. They often baited their benefactors, haggled over the
sum proffered, denounced those who underpaid or refused to
cough up.

Many *shnorrers* considered they had a license from the
Lord, and were doing His bidding: after all, they were helping
Jews discharge solemn obligations to help the poor and the
unfortunate, through which noble acts a good Jew could
actually accumulate *mitzvas!* Any man who served as agent
for the acquisition of *mitzvas* was part of God's marvelous
scheme for improving the human race.

Shnorrers seemed to know that they were both exploiting
and assuaging one of the most powerful and pervasive psychological forces in the psyche of Jews everywhere: guilt.
They were also expediting a symbolic and magical propitiation of fate: "I, thank God, am not a pauper. How small a
coin may avert displeasure from the Compassionate One."

On the part of the Jewish community, *shnorrers* were
somehow regarded as performing a social function. Exactly
what this function was, I could never fathom, as a child; but
everyone seemed to take it for granted—and took it for
granted that no explanation was necessary. (Maybe *shnorrers*
served this purpose: often excellent *raconteurs,* they circulated stories, jokes, gossip.)

The *shnorrer* "recoiled from demeaning himself . . . from
sheer arrogance and vanity. Since he was obliged to live by
his wits," writes Nathan Ausubel, "he developed all the facile
improvisations of an adventurer. . . . He would terrorize his

prey by the sheer daring of his importunities, leaving him both speechless and wilted." *

The *shnorrer* was no fool, please note, no simpleton. He often had read a good deal, could quote from the *Talmud*, and was quick on the verbal draw. *Shnorrers* were "regulars" in the synagogue and, between prayers, took part in long discussions of theology with their benefactors. The status points involved here are too delicate for Newtonian physics, or Parsonian sociology, to handle. (Certain Hindu and Oriental groups recognize the beggar in the same way.)

Israel Zangwill's *The King of Schnorrers*, published in 1893, contains these memorable observations on London's breed: ". . . none exposed sores like the lazars of Italy or contortions like the cripples of Constantinople. Such crude methods are eschewed in the fine art of *schnorring*. A green shade might denote weakness of sight, but the stone-blind man bore no braggart placard—his infirmity was an old established concern, well-known to the public, and conferring upon the proprietor a definite status in the community. He was no anonymous atom, such as drifts blindly through Christendom, vagrant and apologetic. Rarest of all sights, in this pageantry of Jewish pauperdom, was the hollow trouser-leg or the empty sleeve, or the wooden limb fulfilling either and pushing out a proclamatory peg."

There are enough stories about the *hauteur* of *shnorrers* to fill a book ten times the size of this one. I cull but the skimpiest sample.

A *shnorrer* came to the back door on his biweekly rounds.

"I haven't a penny in the house," apologized the *baleboosteh*. "Come back tomorrow."

"Tomorrow?" frowned the *shnorrer*. "Lady, don't let it happen again. I've lost a fortune, extending credit."

The blind man stood at the corner jiggling his tin cup.

A woman stopped and dropped a quarter into the cup.

The blind man said, "God bless you. I knew you had a kind heart the minute I laid eyes on you."

---

* Nathan Ausubel, *A Treasury of Jewish Folklore*, Crown, 1948, pp. 267–268.

The pedestrian said to the *shnorrer:* "Give *you* a nickel? Why? Why don't you go to work? You've got the arms and legs of a horse!"

"Ha!" cried the *shnorrer*. "For one lousy nickel, am I supposed to cut off my limbs?"

"Better strip a carcass of its hide than beg."

TALMUD: *Pesachim*, 113.

Two *shnorrers* came before a wealthy man, and the first *shnorrer* pointed to the second and announced, "Behold a man who is the son of scholars, the grandson of saints, a scholar and a saint himself—and he is starving!"

The rich man handed the saintly *shnorrer* some money.

"And what about me?" asked the first *shnorrer*.

"You? Why should I give you anything?"

"Didn't *I* bring you this saintly scholar?!"

A *shnorrer* knocked on the door of the rich man's house at 6:30 in the morning.

The rich man cried, "How dare you wake me up so early?"

"Listen," said the *shnorrer*, "I don't tell you how to run your business, so don't tell me how to run mine."

A *shnorrer* said to a rich man, "Don't think I came here to beg. I came to make a bet with you."

"You want to bet me? What about?"

"I'll bet you ten rubles I can get something that you cannot!"

The rich man, amused, put up the ten rubles. The *shnorrer* put them in his pocket. "I," said he, "can get a certificate showing I am a pauper."

The *shnorrer* stopped the *alrightnik* and asked for "maybe a quarter."

"I," said the *alrightnik*, "don't hand out money on the street!"

"So what should I do," asked the *shnorrer*, "open an office?"

shnoz
shnozzle

Pronounced SHNOZ, to rhyme with "Pa's," and SHNOZ-ʐ'l, to rhyme with "sozzle." From German: *Schnauze*, "snout."

1. (Slang) Nose.
2. A long, very large, or unattractive nose.

shnozzola

Pronounced *shnoz-ZOB-la*, to rhyme with "Roz Ola."

The demotic embellishment of *shnozzle*, mainly used by show-business people to refer to the entertainer Jimmy Durante.

In the Brown Derby Restaurant in Hollywood, where the walls are crammed with amusing caricatures of that golden breed known as "stars of stage and screen," the representation of Mr. Durante occupies two separate frames—the second of which contains only the crowning end of the proboscis the first is presumably too small to encompass.

shnuk

See SHNOOK.

shnur
shnir

Pronounced SHNOOR. to rhyme with "spoor," or SHNEE-*er,* to rhyme with "key-er." From early High German.

Daughter-in-law.

"A good daughter makes a good daughter-in-law." ("*A gute tokhter is a gute shnur.*") "One can talk to a daughter, but mean the daughter-in-law." ("*Tsu der tokhter ret men, und di shnur meynt men.*")

Also: "Angry with the *shnur*, one yells at the daughter"—or vice-versa.

————————

Mrs. Botnick and Mrs. Krasnitz had not met in years. "Tell me," asked Mrs. Botnick, "what happened to your son?"

"My son—*oy*, what a misfortune!" wailed Mrs. Krasnitz. "He married a girl who doesn't lift a finger around the house. She can't cook, she can't sew a button on a shirt, all she does is sleep late. My poor boy brings her breakfast in bed, and all day long she stays there, loafing, reading, eating candy!"

"How terrible," said Mrs. Botnick. "And what about your daughter?"

"Ah, my daughter—such *mazel!*" beamed Mrs. Krasnitz. "She married a man, an angel! He won't let her set foot in the kitchen. He gives her a full-time maid, and a cook, and a laundress. And every morning he brings her breakfast in bed! And he makes her stay in bed all day, relaxing, reading, eating chocolate. . . ."

Et cetera.

shochet

Pronounced SHOW-*khet* or SHOY-*khet* (Yiddish); render the *kh* as a MacTavish would. Rhymes respectively with "show bet," and "joy net." Hebrew: "slaughterer."

The authorized slaughterer of animals, according to *kosher* requirements.

The *shochet* was authorized by rabbis, and his work was supervised by them. A *shochet* had to be (a) thoroughly conversant with the many rules governing *kosher* food in the *Shulchan Aruch*, the code adopted in the 16th century; (b) physically healthy; (c) mentally able to undertake and execute his responsibilities; (d) of blameless character and repute.

A *shochet* served an apprenticeship before he could use his own initials in the branding iron used to signify approval of slaughtered animals.

For more details about the *shochet* and *kosher* foods, see Appendix: Kosher.

shofar

Pronounced SHOW-*fer*, or SHOY-*fur*, to rhyme with "goiter," or SHAY-*fer*, like the name of the beer or the fountain pen. Hebrew for "trumpet," "horn," and specifically a "ram's horn."

A ram's horn, 10 to 12 inches long, that is blown in the synagogue during the high holidays of *Rosh Hashanah* and *Yom Kippur.*

The bend in the *shofar* is supposed to represent how a human heart, in true repentance, bends before the Lord. (A conch shell was also used centuries ago.) The ram's horn serves to remind the pious how Abraham, offering his son Isaac in sacrifice, was reprieved, when God decided that Abraham could sacrifice a ram instead.

The man who blows the *shofar* is required to be of blameless character and conspicuous devotion; he must blow blasts of different timbre, some deep, some high, some quavering. The ritual is elaborate—and adds up to about one hundred *tekiot* (ritualized arrangements of *shofar* sounds) for *Yom Kippur.*

See ROSH HASHANAH.

sholem
sholom
shalom

Shalom is Hebrew, pronounced *sha*-LOHM; *sholem* is Yiddish, pronounced SHO-*lem* or SHAW-*lem*. From the Hebrew root word meaning "whole," "entire": "peace."

1. Peace.
2. Hello.
3. So long, *au revoir*, good-bye.

Why is *sholem* used for both "hello" and "good-bye"?

Israelis say: "Because we have so many problems that half the time we don't know whether we're coming or going."

The Israeli Cabinet was discussing the endless and seemingly insoluble problems Israel confronted—even in a condition of *sholem*. Whereupon one member of the Cabinet said, "I have an idea. Let's declare war on the United States!"

His colleagues looked at him incredulously. "Declare war on the United States? Israel? Are you *crazy*? A war like that would last half an hour!"

"Exactly," said the minister. "And the United States, having won, would do what she always does: rebuild the vanquished country, build roads, harbors, hospitals; lend money, give free aid, send food, remodel everything! What better fate for us than to be beaten by the United States?"

"But," said a cynic, "suppose we *win?*"

sholem aleichem
sholom aleichem
aleichem sholem

Pronounced SHO-*lem* (or SHAW-*lem*) *a*-LAY-*khem;* deliver the *kh* as if clearing a bread-crumb from the roof of your mouth. Hebrew: *Shalom alekhem:* "peace unto you."

1. The traditional greeting or salutation of Jews; it is used for "Hello," "How do you do?" etc. The response to this greeting reverses the words; thus:

2. *"Aleichem sholem"* ("And unto you, peace") is the traditional response to *"sholem aleichem";* the exchange is uttered by Jews when parting, as well as when meeting.

3. (Ironically) "Finally we get to the heart of the matter!" "At long last!" "Hallelujah!" Thus:

"O.K., I owe you ten dollars."

"Sholem aleichem!"

4. The pen name of Sholom (Solomon) Rabinowitz (1859–1916), the immortal Jewish writer and humorist, often dubbed "the Jewish Mark Twain."

It is said that when Mark Twain met Rabinowitz in New York, he said, "I am the American *Sholom Aleichem.*"

Muslims use the same salutation and virtually the same phrasing, except that Muslims begin with an *s* instead of an *sh,* and use a *k* instead of a *kh;* thus: *salaam aleikum.* (This is acceptable Arabic, at no extra charge.)

"Hello, Skolnick! I haven't seen you in years. How are you, how's the wife, the children?"

"Everyone's fine. My wife is flourishing, my children are doing well, and I couldn't be happier. Well—*sholem aleichem.*"

"Wait a minute, Skolnick! Are you going away just like that? Don't you even ask *me* one question? Can't you even ask an old friend how he's doing in his business?"

"Oh, I'm terribly sorry. Tell me: How's business?"

"Don't ask. *Aleichem sholem.*"

shtchav

Pronounced *sh*-TCHOV to rhyme with *"sh*-RAHV," with the sibilant consonants, as in "fresh cheese." "Sorrel."

1. Sorrel soup.
2. Sour-grass or cabbage soup made with chopped beets.

shteiger

Pronounced SHTY-*ger,* to rhyme with "tiger." German: *Steiger:* "a climber."

Slant or style of life; ambience; mode of thought. "He

may not go to a synagogue or a temple, but his whole *shteiger* is Jewish."

shtetl

Pronounced SHTEH-*t'l*, to rhyme with "kettle," or SHTAY-*t'l*, to rhyme with "fatal." From German: *Stadt:* "a little town." Plural: *shtetlach.*

Little city, small town, village—in particular, the Jewish communities of eastern Europe, where the culture of the *Ashkenazim* flourished (before World War II).

The *shtetl*, a term of special importance in the history of the Jews, evokes special meaning and memories. In many a *shtetl*, most of the inhabitants were Jews: in others, all were Jews. And it was in the *shtetlach*—in Galicia, Poland, Lithuania, the Ukraine, Rumania, Hungary, Bessarabia, Bohemia—that certain Jewish traditions and values were preserved and embellished until they achieved a character distinctly their own.

The *shtetl* was the incubator and fortress of Ashkenazic culture—different, in many and profound ways, from that of Sephardic Jews. (See *Sephardi.*)

The Jews of the *shtetl* were poor folk, fundamentalist in faith, earthy, superstitious, stubbornly resisting secularism or change. They wrote in Hebrew or Yiddish, shunning foreign tongues among themselves. They were dairymen, draymen, cobblers, tailors, butchers, fishmongers, shopkeepers, peddlers. They considered their exile temporary and dreamed of the Messianic miracle that would—any day—return them, and their brethren around the world, to the shining glory of a restored Israel in the Holy Land.

We must remember that the Tsars had confined Jews to the "Pale of Settlement," twenty-five provinces of the Russian empire. To live outside, a Jew needed special permission from the authorities—and some skilled workers, professional men and businessmen did receive (or purchase, via bribery) such permission. But the vast majority of the Jews in the tsarist empire lived within a restricted area. They could not move without approval from the police. Entire local populations could be abruptly "resettled," forced out of their homes, with no more legality than the arbitrary impulse of an often besotted governor.

Jews were forbidden to own land. They were barred (with exceptions) from colleges and universities. They were barred from the humblest government jobs. They were not allowed to practice certain crafts, skills, and trades.

Inside the *shtetl*, life was so bound in, so shut off from the rest of Europe, so insulated from the magical world "beyond the Pale," that even the simplest amenities of city life seemed, in the words of Ruth Gay, "as legendary as Babylon or Nineveh."* Living in the *shtetl* was very hard. (In Galicia, some years, thousands literally starved to death.) Jews were spat upon, beaten, killed, their synagogues and cemeteries desecrated—either in "minor incidents" shrugged off by the authorities, or in full-scale pogroms instigated by successive regimes. The hooliganism of drunken thugs, and the ghastly bloodbaths by pious Cossacks, were alike tolerated by government officials, witnessed by unprotesting Eastern Orthodox priests, openly abetted by the notoriously anti-Semitic police.

In the *shtetlach*, the Jews produced their own people's culture, an independent style of life and thought, an original gallery of human types, fresh and rueful modes of humor, irony, lyricism, paradox—all unlike anything, I think, in history. There *Yiddishkeit* entered a golden age.

> They apologized to no one, neither to philosophers nor theologians, nor did they ask the commendation of either prince or penman. They felt no need to compare themselves with anyone else, and they wasted no energy in refuting hostile opinions. There, in Eastern Europe, the Jewish people came into its own. . . . [They] lived without reservation and without disguise, outside their homes no less than within them. They drew their style from the homespun prose of Talmudic sayings rather than from the lofty rhetoric of the Prophets.**

The world of the Jews in Germany, France, England, Holland, Italy, Austria, was vastly different from the world of

---

* *The Jews in America*, Basic Books, 1965, p. 78.
** A. J. Heschel, *The Earth Is the Lord's*. Abelard-Schuman, 1964, pp. 26, 28.

shtetl Jews in eastern Europe. The world of the first was contemporary; the world of the second only contemporaneous. City Jews in eastern, as in western, Europe were caught up in political and libertarian movements; they were both workers and bourgeoisie; they became trade unionists, social democrats, socialists, revolutionaries. But the *shtetl* was another world. . . .

The "Pale," established by Catherine II in 1791, ended, under severe economic and political pressures, during the First World War. The *shtetl* exists no more. Thousands of Jews left it for the factories of Odessa, Kiev, Warsaw, Lodz, Moscow, Petrograd—and from there went on, out of unholy Russia, anywhere: to Germany, England, South America, the United States.

History will surely record the *shtetl* as a phenomenon worthy of remembrance. It was a world isolated from time, medieval in texture, living on the daily edge of fear. And it was a triumph of human endurance, a crucible from which flamed a brilliant and unexpected efflorescence of scholarship and literature.

The attitude of American Jews to the *shtetl* is torn by ambivalence.

On the one hand [the *shtetl*] is remembered sentimentally . . . it sends up a nostalgic glow for its survivors and for those who have received the tradition from parents and grandparents. It is pictured as one of the rare and happy breathing-spells of the Exile, the nearest thing to a home from home that the Jews have ever known. On the other hand, it is recalled with a grimace of distaste. The *Shtetlach!* Those forlorn little settlements in a vast and hostile wilderness, isolated alike from Jewish and non-Jewish centers of civilization, their tenure precarious, their structure ramshackle, their spirit squalid. Who would want to live in one of them? . . . [The *shtetl* offers] a pattern of the exalted and the ignominious.[*]

An engrossing account of *shtetl* life may be found in *Life Is with People*, by Mark Zborowski and Ruth Herzog (Schocken

[*] Maurice Samuel, *Little Did I Know*, Knopf, 1963, pp. 137–138.

paperback, 1962). For a marvelously evocative reconstruction, read Maurice Samuel's superb *The World of Sholom Aleichem* (Schocken, 1965). Valuable insights and documentation are in *The Golden Tradition*, edited by Lucy C. Dawidowicz (Holt, Rinehart, 1967).

The rabbi of a *shtetl* was seen talking to a pretty woman—in the public market! The elders summoned the rabbi and dressed him down for such a breach of decorum. When they finished, the rabbi sighed, "Well, my friends, I think it better to talk with a pretty woman, thinking of the Almighty's blessings, than to pray to the Almighty—while thinking of a pretty woman."

shtik
shtikl (diminutive)
shtikeleh (more diminutive)
shtiklech (plural)

Pronounced SHTIK, to rhyme with "quick"; SHTIK'*l*, to rhyme with "pickle"; SHTI-*k'l-leh*, to rhyme with "piccolo" (with an "eh," not "o," at the end); and SHTIK-*lekh*, which rhymes with "wick loch" or "wick ech!" Just be sure to pronounce that final *kh* as a Scotsman would. German: *Stück*: "piece."

1. A piece. "Give him a *shtik* cake." (Never say a *shtik* "of" anything.)
2. A part, part of, bit of. "He is a *shtik narr* (fool)" means "He is a real fool."
3. A prank, a piece of clowning. "He made us laugh with his *shtik*." "You never saw a man with so many *shtik* (or *shtiklech*)."
4. A piece of misconduct. "In company, one should not perpetrate a *shtik* like that."
5. A devious trick; a bit of cheating. "How did you ever fall for a *shtik* like that?"
6. A studied, contrived or characteristic piece of "business" employed by an actor or actress; overly used gestures, grimaces, or devices to steal attention. "Watch

him use the same *shtik*." "The characterization would be better without all those *shtiklech*." "Play it straight: no *shtiklech*."

The last usage is spreading far beyond Broadway and Hollywood circles, where I first heard it.

SHTIKL, the diminutive of *shtik*, means:
1. A small piece. "She is a *shtikl* crazy." ("She is slightly 'off.' ")
2. A bit of. "Oh, is he a *shtikl narr*." ("He is a bit of a fool.")

SHTIKELEH, a further diminutive for *shtikl:*
A really *small* little piece.

SHTIKLECH
Plural of all the meanings cited above.
"*Shtiklech und breklech*" ("Pieces and tiny pieces") means "odds and ends."

A woman in a delicatessen saw some small pickles on the counter, under a sign *"Nosh."*

"How much costs today a pickle?" she asked.

"A pickle," said the man behind the counter, "is a nickel."

"A *nickel?* . . . So tell me: How much is this *shtikl?*"

"That *shtikl*—is a nickel."

"My God! . . . And this *pickeleh?*"

"That *pickeleh*," said the owner, "is a *nickeleh!*"

shtreimel

Pronounced SHTRY-*m'l*, to rhyme with "primal." Derivation: unknown.

A black, broad-brimmed hat, trimmed with velvet or edged in fur, worn by religious Jewish men, especially in Galicia and Poland.

A bearded man with long *payess*, in a long, black caftan-robe, wearing a high, wide-brimmed *shtreimel*, was often seen in Jewish neighborhoods in America in the earlier years of the century; now a *shtreimel* is worn only by the very orthodox, and by *Chasidim*.

shtunk

Pronounced with the short *u* of "put." From German: *Stunk*: "stink," "scandal."

(Vulgarism)
1. A stinker, a nasty person.
2. A fool, a dope, a jerk, an unpleasant *shlemiel*.
3. An ungrateful, mean person. "What a *shtunk* he turned out to be!"
4. A scandalous mess. "He made a terrible *shtunk*." "It is such a *shtunk* I don't know how to get out of it."

shtup
shtoop

Pronounced with the *u* of "put," not the *u* of "cup." Thus, *shtup* is pronounced like the first syllable of "Stuttgart," changing the *tt* to *p*, or like *putsch* pronounced backwards. From the German: *stupsen:* "to push."

1. To push, press. "Don't *shtup*," means "Don't push"— both literally and figuratively; i.e., don't be aggressive.
   "*Shtup zikh nit vu men darf nit*," means "Don't push yourself into places where you shouldn't be."
   A man who *shtups* himself in "*di hoykhe fenster*" (the high windows) is a man who is a social climber.

CAUTION: *shtup*, in vulgar vernacular, also means:
2. To fornicate. This usage is heard in American slang. "Did he *shtup* her?" "Does she or doesn't she *shtup?*" has nothing to do with hair tinting.
3. The act of copulation. "He gave her a *shtup*."
4. A female who fornicates. "That one is a real *shtup* (or *shtupper*)."

shtuss

Rhymes with "puss." Hebrew: "stupidity."

1. Nonsense. "What he says is just a lot of *shtuss*."
2. A commotion. "Pipe down; don't make such a *shtuss*."
3. A *contretemps*, a disturbance, a "rhubarb" caused by a complaint or protest. "She made such a *shtuss* that they had to go to court."

I heard this usage from a Radcliffe girl.

See also TSIMMES.

shul

Rhymes with "full." From the Greek *schola*, via the German *Schule*. The Hebrew word for a house of prayer is *bet-haknesset*, a house of assembly. Similarly, the Greek word *synagogue* means "assembly," "congregation."

Synagogue.

The *shul* was the center, the "courthouse square," the forum of Jewish communal life. Day and night men sat, read, prayed, studied, discoursed, debated in the synagogues—many of which never closed their doors. Some Jews spent more time in *shul* than at work.

Most of the study, be it noted, was in groups. "Learning is really achieved only in company" (Berakot 63). Men would drift from group to group in the *shul*, between prayers, listening with one ear to catch a word from those reading aloud, reciting or arguing. "They sang their studies; they sang them fervently and felt transported to a higher world. There was a certain enchantment to studying a page of the Talmud."[*]

The synagogue seems to date from 586 B.C., when Nebuchadnezzar drove the Jews into exile. In Babylonia they sought to replace the Great Temple of Jerusalem, which had

---

[*] Abraham Menes, "Patterns of Jewish Scholarship in Eastern Europe," in *The Jews: Their History, Culture and Religion*, Vol. I, third edition, Louis Finkelstein, editor. Harper, 1960, p. 385.

been destroyed. (A legend has it that some Jews preserved some stones from the Temple, carried them into captivity, and used them in building a synagogue in the small town of Nehardea.)

The synagogue is never mentioned in the *Torah;* it is often referred to in the New Testament. The early Catholics called a Jewish place of worship *schola Judaeorum.*

God Himself proceeds from synagogue to synagogue, says the *Talmud,* "and from *Bet Midrash* (House of Study) to *Bet Midrash* . . . [to] give His blessings to Israel."

Before the Temple was destroyed, Jews worshiped *through* priests and with animal sacrifices. In the synagogue, worshipers addressed God directly—and individually.

In time it became a solemn obligation for Jews to build a *shul* as soon as a community contained ten males (a *minyan*). Synagogues were established, in time, all through Palestine, Babylonia, Arabia, Egypt, Persia, around the Crimea, Syria— in the cities of Greece, in Rome, and eventually in every country where Jews were taken, as slaves, or allowed to reside.

Philo, who was a rabbi and a Platonist, said it was the *schola* that made all Jews philosophers.

See Appendix: *Shul, Study and Prayer.*

A visitor to a *shul* in a tiny village, whose inhabitants believed their *tzaddik* possessed miraculous powers, asked, "What miracle did your rabbi perform recently?"

"Well, there are miracles and miracles. Would you think it a miracle if God did exactly what our rabbi asked?"

"I certainly would!"

"Well, here we think it a miracle that our rabbi does what God asks *him.*"

shvartz (adjective)
shvartzer (masculine noun and adjective)
shvartzeh (feminine noun and adjective)

Pronounced to rhyme respectively with "darts," "Hartzer," "parts a." From German: *schwarz:* "black."

1. Black.
2. Unfortunate, unhappy, ill-starred. A common Yiddish curse goes: *"A shvartz yor oif ihm!"* ("A black year may he have!")
3. Ominous, gloomy, boding no good. "It looks pretty *shvartz* to me."
4. Unskilled. "He's doing *shvartz* work."
5. Contraband, "black market" goods: *"Shvartzeh s'khoyre* (merchandise) was his downfall."

shvartzer

1. (As adjective, masculine) Black.
2. (As noun) A Negro.

shvartzeh (romantic)

1. (As adjective, feminine) Black.
2. (As noun) Negress.

Shvartzer and *shvartzeh*, to mean Negro man and woman, became "inside" words among Jews—cryptonyms for Negro servants or employees. Since the growth of the civil rights movement, these uses have declined. Many Jews would not, for instance, approve of the retelling now of the following true, well-known, and (to me, at least) disarming story:

A Jewish matron dialed a number and asked, "Hello. Mrs. Weiss?"

"No, ma'am," came a melodious voice. "This is the *shvartzeh.*"

shviger

Pronounced SHVI-*ger*, to rhyme with "trigger." From German: *Schwiegermutter:* "mother-in-law."

Mother-in-law.

The folk humor of Jews is as extensive and variegated as you will find in any culture on earth; but there are fewer stories about mothers-in-law, surprisingly, than one would expect. I have no idea why this is so; perhaps a Jewish husband is careful about poking fun at his *shviger* in front of his wife.

"A daughter-in-law is always a bit of a mother-in-law."

—FOLK SAYING

Sholom Aleichem called Adam the luckiest man who ever lived—because he had no *shviger*.

Bessie Shatz had delivered triplets. Her *shviger* came to the hospital and said how unusual it is for a woman to have triplets. "No one on our side of the family *ever* had triplets!"

The new mother said, "My doctor told me it happens only once in a million times."

"My God, Bessie!" cried her *shviger*. "When did you have time to do the housework?"

shvitzbud
shvitzbad

> Pronounced SHVITZ-*bud*, to rhyme with "flits could," or SHVITZ-*bod*, to rhyme with "Fritz cod." From German: *Schwitzbad:* "sweat bath."

> Sweat bath, i.e., Turkish bath.

Men's bathhouses were a widespread and popular institution among the Jews in the old country; the Sabbath requires spotlessness of body and raiment, and few Jews could afford a bathing place of their own. (In some parts of Europe, Jews were not allowed to bathe in a stream, river, or lake—on the stern ground that the immersion of a Jew in such waters would pollute them for Christians.)

When the Jews came to America, one of the first communal institutions they required was a *shvitzbud*.

"Turkish baths" were enormously popular on New York's Lower East Side.

See also MIKVA.

Mr. Toplinski was walking down Houston Street when he saw Mr. Sverdloff. *"Sholem aleichem,* Sverdloff," he smiled.

To which Sverdloff replied: *"Gay in drerd!"* (Drop dead.)

Toplinski recoiled. "Sverdloff! I give you a polite hello and you answer, *'Gay in drerd!'* Why?"

Said Sverdloff, "I'll tell you why. Suppose I answer you politely, *'Aleichem sholem'*—so you ask me where I'm going. So I tell you to the Houston Street *shvitzbud.* So you say the Avenue A *shvitzbud* is better. So I tell you I don't like the Avenue A *shvitzbud.* So you tell me that a man who prefers the Houston Street *shvitzbud* to the Avenue A *shvitzbud* must have a hole in his head! So I holler that a man who chooses the Avenue A over the Houston Street is *meshugge!* So you call me a *shmuck!* So I holler, 'What? A *shmuck?! Gay in drerd!'* Right? . . . Well, instead of going through that whole long *hoo-ha* I answer right away, 'Drop dead,' and that ends it. *Aleichem sholem!"*

shvitzer

Pronounced SHVITZ-*er,* to rhyme with "fits her." From German: *Schwitzer,* "one who perspires."

1. Literally: one who has overactive sweat glands.
2. A braggart, a person who blows his own horn, who shows off.

See PLOSHER.

Siddur

Pronounced SID-*der,* to rhyme with "kidder." Hebrew: "arrangement," "order."

The daily and Sabbath prayer book.

The *Siddur* contains the three daily services, the Sabbath prayers, and (in some editions) the festival prayers, *Ethics of the Fathers,* and special readings.

The *Siddur* as we now know it is based on a compilation of prayers made during the ninth century in an academy in Babylonia. Additions and emendations have since been inserted, and various communities have developed slightly different liturgies.

The first printed *Siddur* appeared in 1486—just thirty years after the Gutenberg Bible. Its colophon reads: "Here is completed the sacred work for the special *minhag* [ritual] of the Holy Congregation of Rome, according to the order arranged by an expert." The Hebrew date given (2 Iyar 5246) corresponds to April 7, 1486.

simcha
simche

Pronounced SIM-*kha*, with a true Scottish *kh*. Hebrew: *simha*: "rejoicing."

1. A happy occasion; a celebration. "Come over; we're celebrating a *simcha*—our son's graduation."
2. A great pleasure.
3. That which provides great pleasure. "May you have many more such *simchas*."

A rich brother told his poor brother, "Look, you have been living off me for three years now. Enough! Good-bye! Don't come back—except for a *simcha!*"

Off went the poor brother, and back he came in the morning, saying, "When you saw me leave, you must have felt a great *simcha*, no? I have come to share it."

The poor brother would have made a splendid *shnorrer*.

'Tis said that Hitler, disturbed by nightmares, called in a soothsayer.

The seer consulted a crystal ball and said, "Ah, mighty *Führer*, it is foretold that you will die on a Jewish holiday."

"Which one?" scowled Hitler.

"Any day you die will be a Jewish holiday."

Simchath Torah
Simhat Torah

Pronounced SIM-*khess* TOE-*rah*, or TOY-*rah*, with a Mac-Gregorish *kh*. Hebrew: "the day of rejoicing in the law."

A festival, observed on the ninth and final day of SUC-COTH, that honors the *Torah*, the Five Books of Moses (i.e., the first five books in the Old Testament).

Simchath Torah is a gay occasion, with feasting and dancing, to celebrate the yearly end-and-new-beginning of the consecutive weekly readings of the *Torah* in the synagogue. On this day, the last chapters of Deuteronomy are read—and immediately after, the first chapter of Genesis is begun, to signal the continuing cycle of worship, and show that the *Torah* has neither beginning nor end.

A learned member of the congregation is usually given the honor of reading the final verses of the *Torah*. He is called *chatan Torah*, "the bridegroom of the *Torah*." And the man called to start the *Torah*-reading cycle anew is called *chatan Bereshit*, "the bridegroom of Genesis." (Reform temples may honor a woman by letting her read from the Prophets; she is called, naturally, "the bride of the Scriptures.")

The holy scrolls—adorned with silver breastplates and crowns—are removed from the synagogue's Ark on the eve of *Simchath Torah*, and each male in the congregation takes a turn in conveying them around. By tradition, at least seven "turns" are made around the entire congregation. (Seven often partakes of the magical: God rested on the seventh day of making the world; the Patriarchs of Israel were seven—if you include David.) During this ceremony, the congregation sings and the men honored by carrying the *Torah* scrolls "dance" with them. Chasidic congregations rise to a somewhat feverish exaltation during the celebration.

During *Simchath Torah*, children carry banners, join in the procession of the scrolls, and are rewarded with goodies. Children not yet of *Bar Mitzva* age gather around the *bema*, the platform or pulpit, and a prayer shawl is spread over their heads like a canopy; a passage from the *Torah* is read, and the rabbi blesses them as Jacob blessed Ephraim and Menasseh (Genesis 48 : 20).

singlemon

Pronounced SING'l-*mon*, to rhyme with "single Khan." Yinglish, from the Lower East Side.

A man who is single . . . i.e., not married.

A *singlemon* was highly prized, much propagandized, and widely courted, because of the intense feeling among Jews that everyone should marry. "He who is without a wife," says the *Talmud*, "dwells without blessing, life, joy, help, good, and peace."

See CHASSEN, SHADCHEN.

It is said that when a *singlemon's* virtues are being extolled to a maiden, by a parent or a *shadchen*, her responses vary according to her age, thusly:

At twenty: "What does he look like?"

At twenty-five: "Is he well-off?"

At thirty: "Where is he?"

succah

See SUCCOTH.

Succoth

Pronounced SUK-*kess*, to rhyme with "took us." Hebrew: "booths."

The Festival of Tabernacles, or the Feast of Booths.

This holiday starts the fifth day after *Yom Kippur*, the Day of Atonement, and is celebrated for eight days by the Orthodox, seven in Israel and among Reform Jews. Throughout the week, a pious family eats its meals in a *succah* or booth that is set up out of doors (the children love to help), roofed with branches (the stars must be visible from the inside), and decorated inside with flowers and fruit. The booth is intended to look temporary, for it represents the hastily set-up dwellings Jews used in their forty years of wandering in the wilderness. In Leviticus (23 : 43) God says: ". . . your generations may know that I made the children of Israel to dwell in booths, when I brought them out of the land of Egypt."

Succoth is a thanksgiving holiday, held at the time of the full moon, when the crops had been harvested in ancient Palestine. God told Moses: "And thou shalt observe . . . the feast of ingathering at the year's end" (Exodus 34 : 22).

On the first two and final two days of *Succoth*, special religious services are offered in the synagogue or temple. The men carry a *lulav* and *ethrog* (ES-*rogue*), a combination of palm branch, willow and myrtle twigs, and a fragrant citron, each symbolizing a particular virtue and characteristic of man.

Hoshanah Rabbah, "the great Hosanna," is observed on the seventh day of *Succoth* by a lengthy procession around the synagogue; the men carry their palm and willow branches, and the entire congregation chants special verses in praise of God. The men beat their willow branches against the pulpit or platform, some say as a symbol of penitence. (By tradition, the fate of a Jew is sealed on *Hoshanah Rabbah* in, I suppose, a celestial Bureau of Records.)

Philo considered the *succah* a democratic institution because all Jews, rich or poor, were asked to dwell in a primitive shelter. Equality of this sort, he reckoned, moved the concept out of theory into practice.

T

tachlis

Pronounced TOKH-*liss*, to rhyme with "Bach Liss." From the Hebrew for "purpose," "end."

1. Achievement; amounting to something; establishing one's self. "If only that man would arrive at a little *tachlis*." "What *tachlis* will that produce?"
2. The point, heart, nub, or substance of the matter. "Let's talk *tachlis*" means "Let's get down to brass tacks." "What's the *tachlis?*" means "What are the real effects, the practical aspects?"

It is said that when they told Levi Yitzchok, a famous rabbi, that one of his congregants, a man of seventy-four, had decided to become a Christian, the rabbi raised his eyes to heaven and cried, "How loyal are Your people, O Lord! Imagine! For seventy-four years that man held fast!"

I would call Levi Yitzchok a wizard in the discernment of *tachlis*.

tallis
talith
tallit

Pronounced TAHLL-*iss*, to rhyme with "Hollis" or "solace." Hebrew: "prayer shawl." But the plural, *talaysim* (*ta*-LAY-*sim*), is Yiddish.

Prayer shawl, used by males at prayer at religious services.

An Orthodox bride gives her groom a *tallis*, just as his father gave him one on the occasion of his *Bar Mitzva*. Sometimes a *tallis* serves as a canopy during a marriage ceremony.

The Good Book tells Jewish males to wear a four-fringed garment (fringed, that is, at the corners). It serves to remind him of his bond and duty to God. At one time, the *tallis* was a gown or cloak; but because of public humiliations the rabbis decreed it be used in the synagogue—or at home, during prayer services.

Chasidim and Orthodox Jews wear long *talaysim*; Reform Jews wear shorter, less full ones.

Black or blue bands cross the prayer shawl—to memorialize the destruction of the Temple and mourn it forever.

A traditional Jew is buried in a shroud and with his *tallis*. See also TZITZIT.

An old rabbi, passing a door, heard a faint, faint crying from within—perhaps the muffled cry of a child. He knocked on the door. There was no answer—only that soft, sad wail. He knocked again; no one answered, so he tried the door. It was open. The rabbi entered. No one was in the front room, nor in the second room, nor in the kitchen—but the muffled weeping continued; and the rabbi, deeply alarmed, traced the cries to—a drawer in a bureau. He pulled it open as fast as he could.

In the drawer was nothing but a *tallis*, and to the rabbi's astonishment he heard the *tallis* sobbing.

"Little *tallis*, little *tallis*," said the rabbi, "why are you crying?"

"Because my master," wept the *tallis*, "went off on a trip, and he took his wife and all of his children, and he left me here to cry alone."

"Ah, little *tallis*," sighed the rabbi, "do not cry. One day soon your master will take you on a trip, only you, and leave all of them behind."

talmid chachem

Pronounced TOL-*mid* KHAW-*khem* (both *kh*'s in the Scottish burr), to rhyme with "Sol would 'Hoch!' 'em." Hebrew: *talmid khakham:* "student of a wise man." NOTE: *talmid* should not be confused with *Talmud*. The plural of *chachem* is *chachamim*.

The wisest of the wise, a learned scholar, an expert on *Talmud*.

The most honored figure in the life and culture of traditional Jewry was the *talmid chachem*. He was the scholar of scholars, a sage, *and* a saint, one of the rare, entirely spiritual souls fit to be called "a disciple of the wise." He was one of those who might contribute to the vast, accumulated teachings and ruminations of savants that were known as "the sea of the *Talmud*."

The scholar was erudite, of course, but in addition he had to be: immaculate in his clothes and person; indifferent to physical comforts and material rewards; gentle in manner; sensitive to others; quiet and humble (eyes ever downcast) in bearing; impeccable in conduct. He had to combine scholarship with compassion—and conspicuous rectitude.

Indeed, these virtues were assumed to go hand in hand, in the conviction that those who study are virtuous, and that those who really know cannot do evil. A venal, vain, or salacious *talmid chachem* was unthinkable—a contradiction in terms.

No formal agency, incidentally, could make a man a *talmid chachem*. The title came via a slow accretion of recognition from his peers and colleagues. As a young scholar demonstrated greater and greater sagacity in his discussions—deeper insight, nobler humility—he began to be called a *chachem*. By that time, of course, he would no longer be young.

The *talmid chachem* remained a student throughout his life, be it noted; that is, he could not "finally" discover truth. The *chachem* is forever a seeker, a student, an inquirer. He never reaches his goal: Learning is endless.

The Jews exempted many a *talmid chachem* from paying taxes (i.e., Jewish communal taxes), not only because the *chachamim* were notoriously poor, but because Jews wanted them to spend every moment in *Talmud* study. Who could foresee what benefits might accrue from their learning? The Talmud says, "*Talmidei chachamim* strengthen peace in the world."

The *chachem* studied *for* the community, as it were, and for its welfare. In return, the *Talmud* scholar was supported by the community—and by his wife, whom the community respected, because her labors enabled her husband to study without interruption.

An impudent—an *unbelievably* impudent—young Pole put both hands behind his back and challenged a rabbi in this way: "Your attention! I hold a little bird behind my back, in one of my hands. Guess which one! If you guess right, the bird will go free; but if you guess wrong, I'll smother it and its death will be on your head! . . . What does your precious *Talmud* tell Jews about a dilemma such as this?"

The *talmid chachem* studied the young man dolorously, then sighed, "Our *Talmud* tells us that the awful choice between life and death—is in your hands."

"A table is not blessed if it has fed no scholars." —PROVERB

A famous rabbi was so wise, so great a logician, that he could answer any question his students put to him—even on the most difficult and involved points in the *Talmud*. His powers of reason seemed so great that one of his disciples cried: "Our rabbi can think his way through *any* dilemma!"

"Yes," said another, "it is true that our beloved rabbi has a mind of unparalleled powers—but I wonder what would happen if he were tired, drowsy, even a wee bit tipsy. Would his reason still prevail with all its splendor?"

And so the loving but curious acolytes decided to test the

genius of their revered *talmid chachem*. At the feast of *Succoth* they gave him enough wine to make him tipsy, then, while he slept, carried him (reverently, to be sure) to the cemetery, where they laid him on the grass—and hid behind the tombstones, waiting to see what the rabbi would say when he opened his eyes and saw where he was. . . .

What he said is a triumph of Talmudic reasoning: "If I am living, then what am I doing here? . . . And if I am dead, why do I want to go to the bathroom?"

"Understanding is a well-spring of life unto him that hath it: but the instruction of fools is folly." —PROVERBS 16 : 22

The great scholar, a true *talmid chachem*, returned from lunch and repaired to his study—but could not find his glasses. He searched for them high and low, but they were nowhere to be found.

"What to do, what to do-o?" he asked himself in a singsong pattern. "This is a prob-lem, and to solve a prob-lem, one must employ reason. Very well. Hypothesis: 'May-be someone came in and stole my glasses while I was out?' N-no. Why not? Because *if* it was someone who needed glasses to read by, he would own his own; and if he *didn't* need glasses to read by, why would he steal mine? . . . Second hypothesis: 'Maybe a *thief* stole my glasses, not to use—but to sell!' Aha! But to whom can you sell a pair of reading glasses? If the thief offers them to someone who needs glasses, *that* man surely owns a pair already; and if the thief offers them to someone who *doesn't* use glasses, why should such a man buy them? No! . . . So, where does this take us? Clearly: 'The glasses must have been taken by somebody who needs glasses and has glasses, but cannot find them!' *Why* can't he find them? Perhaps he was so absorbed in his studies that, absent-mindedly, he pushed his glasses up from his nose to his forehead, then, forgetting he had done so—took mine!"

The scholar hesitated. "I will even push the reasoning further!" he exclaimed. "Perhaps *I* am that man—the man who needs glasses, owns glasses, and moved his glasses up from his nose to his forehead and forgot that he had done so! If my reasoning is correct, that's where my spectacles ought to be right now!" He raised his hand to his forehead. His glasses were there, and he went back to his studies.

Talmud

Pronounced TOL-*mud*, to rhyme with "doll could." From Hebrew: *lamod:* "to study," or *lamade:* "to teach."

The *Talmud*. It is not the Bible. It is not the Old Testament. It is not "a" book. It is not meant to be read, but to be studied.

The *Talmud* is a massive and monumental compendium of sixty-three books: the learned debates, dialogues, conclusions, commentaries, commentaries upon commentaries, commentaries upon commentaries *upon* commentaries, of the scholars who for over a thousand *years* interpreted the *Torah* (the first five books in the Bible, also known as the Five Books of Moses) and applied its teachings to problems of law, ethics, ceremony, traditions.

The first division of the *Talmud* is the *Mishna* (from the Hebrew *shano,* "to study, to teach"), a collection of interpretations of the Biblical laws as they were applied to social conditions in Palestine between the fifth century before, and the second century of, the Christian era. These laws, which included court decisions, opinions, regulations, ethical teachings, etc., were transmitted orally; the *Mishna* is therefore known as the "Oral Law," as distinct from the "Written Law" of the *Torah*.

The wise men were afraid that written judgments might delimit and diminish the authority of the sacred *Torah*. But being sensible men no less than scholars, they knew that the Oral Laws would surely be changed and misinterpreted unless *some* written document served as authority; so they secretly made abbreviated notations! (These notes also helped them in the onerous task of memorizing the *Mishna* word by word.) Little by little, the task of codifying the *Mishna* was undertaken, and it was completed in about 200 A.D. by Judah ha-Nasi (the Prince), the head of the *Sanhedrin* (a great council of rabbis-sages-and-scribes; a Supreme Court, so to speak; see Appendix). The six sections containing sixty-three tractates are written in Hebrew.

The second division of the *Talmud* is known as the *Gemara* (from the Aramaic "to learn"), the vast compendium of commentaries upon the *Mishna*. The language of the *Gemara* is Aramaic, but contains a great deal of Hebrew.

The continuing colloquium which resulted in the *Gemara* took place in the great academies of Palestine and Babylonia from the second to the fifth centuries, when the *Talmud* was edited and assembled.

The Palestinian and the Babylonian academies produced separate *Talmuds:* the *Talmud Yerushalmi*, which was redacted around the fifth century, and the *Talmud Babli*, about a century later.

NOTE: When we speak of the *Talmud* today, we generally refer to the Babylonian *Talmud*, because it had a much greater influence on Jewish law and life. (Besides, the Jerusalem text was not preserved *in toto*.)

The legal parts of the *Talmud* are called the *Halakah*. The elements that are ethical, poetic, allegorical, anecdotal, are known as *Haggadah*.

The *Talmud* embraces everything from theology to contracts, cosmology to cosmetics, jurisprudence to etiquette, criminal law to diet, delusions, and drinking. It is a reservoir of rabbinical thought on every then-known subject under the sun—and moon. It roams from exegesis to esthetics. It is crammed with anecdotes, aphorisms, thumbnail biographies, philosophical treatises, and tiresome hair-splittings. It touches upon medicine, agriculture, geography, history, astronomy.

It is majestic—and pedantic; brilliant—and dreary; insightful—and trivial; awesome—and maddeningly obscure, superstitious, and casuistic. Sophistry runs rife, abracadabras abound, and profundity often ends in mythology, astrology, numerology, and quaint nonsense: wrestlings with the Devil and his Demons, revelations from shining angels and celestial messengers, mystical miasmas beyond measuring. Like Catholic scholastics, the Talmudists spent a good deal of time and intellect in dialectical taffy-pulls.

The *Talmud* is not dogma. Judaism has few (the *Mishna* has a few dogmas). The *Talmud* is not a catechism. It is a long, involved explication of a text, the *Torah*, and the commentaries on that text. It illustrates the *ways* in which Biblical passages can be interpreted, argued over, and reinterpreted. For over the sprawling terrain of the *Talmud* disagreements rage, views clash, arguments are marshaled, advanced, withdrawn. (The effect on the young Jews who studied *Talmud* was to encourage questioning, arguing, refinements of distinction and analysis.)

Rabbinical law, by the way, is very far from being unitary or consistent; opposing views and heated—even rancorous—disagreement are set forth in the *Talmud*'s pages. The rabbis taught that "both these [words] and these [words] are the words of the living God."

For over two centuries rival schools in Jerusalem, one loyal to Hillel, the other to Shammai, wrangled and debated on religious and juridical matters, on ethics, morality, custom, observance. No fewer than 316 of these debates are preserved in the *Talmud*. Hillel's disciples nearly always win the argument—because the Hillelites were always forbearing and humble, presenting even the argument of their opponents with exemplary deference.

It was the *Talmud*—commonly read, commonly studied, a monumental body of thought and faith—that held together a people spread and dispersed throughout Europe, North Africa, the Middle East. The *Talmud* made them one intellectual commonwealth, with a common language, a common code of laws, morals, ethics, and obligations.

Traditional Jews live not by Biblical law, but by the rabbinical teachings and decisions based thereon. Indeed, the Karaites (who, in the eighth century, rejected the tradition of Talmudic law and based their religious life solely on the Bible) were "separated" from the Jewish community and were not considered Jews by the rabbis.

The *Talmud* is not recognized by sects such as the Falashas. (See Appendix: Falashas.)

See Appendix: Talmud for historical notes and comments.

You would be surprised by the number of aphorisms now widespread that are to be found, in one form or another, in the *Talmud*.

"Give every man the benefit of the doubt."

"The ignorant cannot be pious."

"Look at the contents, not at the bottle."

"One good deed leads to another."

"Don't threaten the child: Either punish or forgive him."

"Begin a lesson with a humorous illustration."

"Bad neighbors count a man's income, but not his expenses."

"Judge a man not by the words of his mother, but from the comments of his neighbors."

"When in a city—follow its customs."

"All is well that ends well." And it certainly is.

Goebbels, the Nazi Minister of Propaganda, came to an elderly rabbi and said, "Jew! I have heard that you Jews employ a special form of reasoning, called Talmudic, which explains your cleverness. I want you to teach it to me."

"Ah, Herr Goebbels," the old rabbi sighed. "I fear you are a little too old for that."

"Nonsense! Why?"

"Well, when a Jewish boy wishes to study *Talmud* we first give him an examination. It consists of three questions. Those lads who answer the questions correctly are admitted to the study of the *Talmud;* those who can't, are not."

"Excellent," said Goebbels. "Give me the exam!"

The old rabbi shrugged. "Very well. The first question: Two men fall down a chimney. One emerges filthy, covered with soot; the other emerges clean. Which one of them washes?"

Goebbels scoffed, "The dirty one, of course!"

"Wrong. The clean one."

"The *clean* one washes?" asked Goebbels in astonishment. "Why?"

"Because as soon as the two men emerge from the chimney, they look at each other, no? The dirty one, looking at the clean one, says to himself, 'Remarkable—to fall down a chimney and come out clean!' But the clean one, looking at the dirty one, says to himself, 'We certainly got *filthy* coming down that chimney and I'll wash up at once.' So it is the clean one who washes, not the dirty one."

"Ah," nodded Goebbels. "Very clever! Let's have the second question."

"The second question," sighed the rabbi, "is this: Two men fall down a chimney. One emerges filthy, covered with soot; the other emerges clean. Which—"

"That's the same question!" exclaimed Goebbels.

"No, no, Herr Goebbels, excuse me. This is a different question."

"Very well. You won't fool me, Jew. The one who's *clean* washes!"

"Wrong," sighed the elder.

"But you just told me——"

"That was an entirely different problem, Herr Goebbels. In this one, the *dirty* man washes—because, as before, the two men look at each other. The one who is clean looks at the dirty one and says, 'My! How dirty *I* must be!' But he looks at his hands and he sees that he is *not* dirty. The dirty man, on the other hand, looks at the clean one and says, 'Can it be? To fall down a chimney and emerge so clean? Am *I* clean?' So he looks at his hands and sees that *he* is filthy; so he, the dirty one, washes, naturally."

Goebbels nodded. "Clever, Jew; very clever. Now, the third question?"

"Ah, the third question," sighed the rabbi, "is the most difficult of all. Two men fall down a chimney. One emerges clean, the other——"

"But that's the same question!"

"No, Herr Goebbels. The *words* may be the same, but the problem is an entirely new one."

"The dirty one washes!" exclaimed Goebbels.

"Wrong."

"The clean one!"

"Wrong."

"Then what *is* the answer?" Goebbels shouted.

"The answer," said the rabbi, "is that this is a silly examination. *How* can two men fall down the same chimney and one emerge dirty and the other clean? Anyone who can't see that will never be able to understand *Talmud*."

———

In the *Talmud* (Tractate of Sanhedrin, Chapter 4) the question is raised: "Why did God create only one Adam? Why did he not create an entire race?"

The discussion reaches several conclusions:

(1) God created only one Adam because He wanted to show men that any one man is an entire world. Therefore, whoever kills one man is as guilty as if he had killed all men. And whoever saves one man's life is as noble as if he had saved all men's lives.

(2) God created only one Adam to prevent men from feeling superior to one another, or boasting of their ancestry. For if God had created many Adams, you may be sure some

men would say, "My Adam was more distinguished than yours."

(3) God thought that if He created more than one Adam, pagans would think there was more than one God. So God created only one man to prove His unity.

(4) And God wanted to show men the beauty of diversity, for even though all men come from one Adam, no two men are ever exactly alike. Therefore, every man must respect his uniqueness and his integrity; and every man must, in effect, say: "The Lord created the world in me and for me; let me not impair my immortality for some trifling reason or foolish passion."

Talmud Torah

Pronounced TOL-*m'd* TOY-*reh*, or TOE-*reh*, to rhyme with "doll mid Moira" or "doll mid Nora," or "doll mid Roma."

A Hebrew school (in America).

The *Talmud Torah* in the United States offered a two-hour Hebrew session after the public schools closed each day, and classes all Sunday morning. Many Jewish children thus spent ten to fifteen hours a week in schooling in addition to their public-school attendance.

Talmud Torah schools have declined in number, partly because many of their activities were absorbed into the educational departments of synagogue and temple.*

———————————

A little boy came home from the *Talmud Torah.* "What did you learn today?" asked his father.

"Oh, the teacher told us the story about General Moses, how General Moses was leading all the Jews out of Egypt, with General Pharaoh's Egyptians hot on their trail. And there was the Red Sea in front of Moses, so he dropped an atomic bomb! Bang! So the waters parted, the Jews got across, and the Egyptians were all drowned."

———————————

* See Simon Greenberg, "Jewish Educational Institutions," in *The Jews: Their History, Culture and Religion,* Vol. II, third edition, Louis Finkelstein, editor, Harper, 1960, pp. 1266 ff.

"Is *that* what he told you?" gasped the father.

The boy shrugged. "Nope, but if I told it to you the way he did, Pop, you'd never believe it."

tarrarom
terrarom

Pronounced *teh-reh*-ROM, like "betta" bomb," or *tuh-ruh*-ROM, like "but-a-bomb." Roll the *rr*.

An onomatopoetic word, meaning a "to-do," a "hullabaloo," "a big fuss," "a big stink."

To "make a *tarrarom*" is to create a ruckus.

tata
tateleh (diminutive)

Pronounced TAH-*teh*, to rhyme with "not a," or TOT-*teh-leh* to rhyme with "not a la." From a widespread root, found in Semitic as well as Indo-European languages.

Dad; papa.

Tata is the affectionate, informal way of addressing one's father. Jews say *tata* much more often that *futter* (father). One's parents are often called *tata-mama*, not *elteren* (parents).

The phrase *"Oy, Tata!"* is often used as an evocative exclamation, as, in English, "Man, oh man!"

Interestingly enough, when one inquires of another in Yiddish: "How is your father (or mother)?" one says, "How is *the* father (or mother)?" So *der tata* or *die mama* can mean "the (your) father" and "the (your) mother."

Tateleh is the diminutive—often used to address a little boy (as *bubeleh* or *mameleh* is, for a little girl).

This is a carry-over, no doubt, from the time when stratagems to evade the Evil Eye involved magical words—in this case, loudly attributing more years to a child, to ward off child-hating demons.

"When a father helps a son, both smile; when a son must help a father, both cry."

"One father can support ten children, but ten children don't seem to be enough to support one father."

—FOLK SAYINGS

tcheppeh
cheppeh

Pronounced TCHEP-*eh*, to rhyme with "Beppa," with a *ch* as in "church." From Slavic: *tchupat*: "to pinch," "to nip."

1. To annoy, to nag. "Stop *tchepping* me."
2. To bait; to try deliberately to provoke.

I heard *tcheppeh* used to describe the kind of malicious, sadistic baiting an *agent provocateur* would use on a Jew in order to provoke an excuse for reprisal. "An anti-Semite *tcheppehs* you—to give him an excuse to beat you up."

Tcheppeh always contains the element of unpleasantness. There is a saying: "*Alle tsoris tcheppen zich tsu mir*"—"All troubles seem to latch onto me."

tchotchke

See TSATSKE.

tefillin
t'fillin

Pronounced *te*-FILL-*in*, to rhyme with "a'willin'." Hebrew: *tefilla*: "prayer."

Phylacteries.

Tefillin are two long, thin leather straps—with a 2- or 3-inch square black leather box on each. The boxes contain tiny parchments on which are inscribed, in Hebrew, four passages from Exodus and Deuteronomy. *Tefillin* are worn during morning prayers by Orthodox males past the age of *Bar Mitzva.*

The custom of donning *tefillin* is derived from the injunction in Exodus 13 : 9: "And it shall be for a sign unto thee upon thine hand, and for a memorial between thine eyes, that the Lord's law may be in thy mouth," and a similar commandment in Deuteronomy 6 : 8.

The process of putting on *tefillin* is elaborate, and carefully prescribed. They are worn while standing, as a mark of reverence. One box is placed on the inner side of the left arm, just above the elbow (this places it next to the heart when the worshiper is praying); the strap is coiled around the left forearm exactly seven times. The other box is placed in the middle of the forehead, high up, above the hairline generally, and the strap is looped around the head and knotted. The two ends of the strap are joined over the shoulder and brought forward. Then the arm-band strap is wound around the middle finger three times. This signifies *shin,* the Hebrew letter with which one of the cabalistic names for God (*Shaddai*) begins.

The entire ritual has the effect of removing mundane preoccupations from the prayer's mind and focusing his attention entirely on his devotions. Maimonides (twelfth century) thought the sanctity of *tefillin* "very great" and argued that while they were worn, a man would devote his entire mind "to truth and righteousness."

Phylacteries are not permitted to be worn on the Sabbath. Surprised? Well, on the Sabbath, the distractions of the workday week are not supposed to exist; besides, the Sabbath is a day of holiness, and does not need the added sanctification of phylacteries.

There is a charming old saying: "God himself wears *tefillin.*"

The rules regulating the way in which *tefillin* may be made, and the ritual by which they are put on, taken off, worn, under which conditions, varying according to which emergencies—all this is much too voluminous to be covered here.

(A sixteenth-century code, the *Shulchan Aruch*, lists 160 laws governing *tefillin*.)

The Jews thought that when a Jew wears the *tefillin*, "God's radiance" falls upon him and wards off all possible harm: hence, it was forbidden to cover all of the *tefillin* with the prayer shawl. Wearing *tefillin* in the street was once the custom, but since this called the attention of anti-Semites to Jews, the custom faded away.

Josephus, the great Jewish historian, wrote that the rite of *tefillin* was an ancient one—and Josephus was writing in the first century.

The word *phylacteries*, by the way, comes from the Greek word for "protection" or "fortress" (*phylakterion*) and is found in the Greek gospel, Matthew 23 : 5.

See DAVEN.

Teitsh-Chumash
Teitch-Chumesh

Pronounced TYTCH KHU-*mish*. Hebrew: *chumash:* "the first five books of the Bible" (the Pentateuch); *teitsh* or *teutsh* is a Yiddishization of the German *deutsch:* "German." Literally, *Teitsh-Chumash* means "the German Pentateuch"; but *teitsh* is used loosely to mean "translation."

The popular name for the translation into Yiddish of the Five Books of Moses (in condensed form), plus selections from the writings of the Prophets, weekly prayers, the books of Ecclesiastes, Esther, Ruth, Lamentations, and the Song of Songs.

At the beginning of the sixteenth century, translations of the Pentateuch were made to help the teachers of elementary Hebrew (the *melamdim*); these, in turn, paved the way for translations into Yiddish meant for women(!): Jewish girls were not usually taught Hebrew.

The first popular morality book of which we know is the *Sefer Midos* ("Book on Behavior"), published in 1542. The *Brantshpigl* ("Burning Mirror"), published in Basel in 1602, was aimed directly at female readers. *Lev Tov* ("The Good Heart"), 1620, was deeply religious and appealed to both men and women.

One Isaac Yanover in the sixteenth century wrote the unpretentious "home book" that became immensely popular in eastern and central Europe: The *Teitsh-Chumash*, a charming, informal array of material from Bible and *Talmud*, of course, and from the colorful reservoir of Jewish history, folklore, humor, allegories, superstitions, legends.* In its pages, the women of Israel found their devotional and instructional guide, their ethical counselor, their household reference work on every conceivable problem—from dress and dancing to prayer and proper behavior.

The *Teitsh-Chumash* was even translated into Latin, in the mid-sixteenth century: I cannot guess why.

See Appendix: Tseno-Ureno.

teivel
teuvel
teufel

> Pronounced TY-*v'l*, to rhyme with "rival." From German: *Teufel*: "devil."

1. Devil.
2. The Devil.

A common Jewish curse is *"A teivel zoll im choppen"*; "May a devil catch him!"

timtum

> Pronounced TIM-*tum*, using a short *u*, to rhyme with *"rim rum."* From Hebrew (as pronounced by Polish Jews): *tum*, "a simple or stupid child."

---

* For a brief but authoritative survey, see Yudel Mark's "Yiddish Literature," in *The Jews: Their History, Culture and Religion*, Vol. II, third edition, Louis Finkelstein, editor, Harper, 1960, pp. 1191–1233.

1. An androgynous person—that is, one who has bisexual or ambiguous characteristics; one who is hard to identify as either male or female.
2. An effeminate man.
3. A beardless youth with a high-pitched voice.

In the *Mishna*, a *timtum* is a person whose sex is not determinable—because clothes conceal the genital areas.

The original meaning fanned out, and Jews would call a young man who was beardless, delicate, high-pitched of voice, "a *timtum*."

One authority informs me that in some circles *timtum* came to mean "a total loss," an unproductive, uncreative misfit. Thus: "He may read a lot, but he's a *timtum*," or "He can't help; he's a *timtum*."

Tisha Bov
Tisha B'av
Tisha B'ab

Pronounced TISH-*a bawve*, or to rhyme with "Misha dove." Hebrew: "the ninth day of the month Ab" or "Av."

The day of fasting and mourning that commemorates both the First (586 B.C.) and the Second (A.D. 70) destruction of the Temple in Jerusalem. (The Babylonians razed the first Temple, the Romans the second.) Reform Jews do not observe this day of communal lamentation.

Down the gloomy centuries, *Tisha Bov*, known as "the blackest day in the Jewish calendar," has added disasters, catastrophes, and horrors to the destructions of the Temple: the doomed Bar Kochba revolt in 135; the slaughter of Bar Kochba's followers in 138; Hadrian's leveling of Jerusalem; the death of the brilliant Rabbi Akiba and nine other martyrs; the Holy Crusades and their unholy massacres, rapes, and depredations; England's expulsion of Jews in 1290; the Spanish expulsion of the Jews in 1492. . . .

Tisha Bov (which usually falls during August) climaxes nine days of mourning during which meat is not eaten and marriages are not performed. Many of the practices of the funeral *shivah* are adopted on this day: eating, drinking, bathing are forbidden; so are smiles, laughter, conversation. Those who enter the synagogue do not even greet one another. They sit on the floor or on low benches, as a sign of mourning. A black curtain is draped over the Ark, and only one flickering light, the Eternal Light which burns day and night at the Ark, illuminates the synagogue.

The Book of Lamentations is recited by the cantor, in a low and depressing chant. (In Sephardic communities, the Book of Job is also read.) Poems of suffering and dirges of immense sadness (some date from the Middle Ages) are intoned.

But the day ends on a note of hope, with the reading of Judah ha-Levi's (1085–1145) *Zionide:*

> Zion, wilt thou not ask if the wing of peace
> Shadows the captives that ensue thy peace,
> Left lonely from thine ancient shepherding?
> Lo! West and east and north and south
> All those from far and near, without surcease,
> Salute thee: Peace and Peace from every side.

Among some Jews, *Tisha Bov* used to include an appeal to Moses and Aaron, begging them to ask God, at long last, to help Israel—so long dispersed, despised, afflicted, tormented.

Recently Yiddish was permitted in the *Tisha Bov* prayers of some Conservative synagogues—to recount the Hitler catastrophe.

T.L.

Pronounce the letters as English: "tea el." Abbreviation for *toches* (or *tuches*) *lecker*. From Hebrew: *tokheth,* "backside," and German: *lecken,* "to lick." Yinglish.

(Vulgarism)

1. (Literally) *T.L.* stands for "ass licker" or, in the more palatable camouflage of euphemism, "apple polisher."
2. A sycophant, a fawner; one who shamelessly curries

favor with superiors. "How do you think he got where he is? He's the worst *T.L.* you ever saw!" "He's a shameless *toches lecker*."

NOTE: The Yinglish *T.L.* should in no way be confused with the American adolescent slang expression, "T.L." The latter means "trade last"; once popular among school children and suburban matrons, it is a cue phrase meaning, "I'll repeat a compliment I heard about you—if you'll first tell me something nice someone said about me."

You will find "trade-last" used by F. Scott Fitzgerald in *This Side of Paradise*. The Yinglish *T.L.* is about as far from Fitzgerald and cotillions as you can get.

tochis
tuchis
T.O.T. (abbreviation)

Pronounced TUKH-*is*, to rhyme with "duck hiss," or TAWKH-*is*, to rhyme with "caucus." Remember that guttural *kh*. Hebrew: "under," "beneath."

1. (Vulgarly) The behind, rear end, posterior, buttocks. "Get off your *tochis*" means "Get off your tail," or "Get moving." "*A potch in tochis*" is a spanking, a swat on the behind. This was a commonly heard warning to children—but never did I hear my Puritanical mother use it! Such words made her shudder.

2. "*Tochis afn tish*" does not mean "buttocks on the table," which is its literal translation, but—"Put up or shut up"; "Let's get down to brass tacks"; "Lay all your cards on the table."

3. *T.O.T.* The phrase above is lusty and picturesque, but unquestionably improper, and because it is *infra dig*, the initials *T.O.T.* are often used as genteel shorthand: "Let's stop evading the issue: *T.O.T.*, please."

I. I. Mendelson's "Ali Baba Toy Emporium" was having its problems. The tots just loved to try out the tricycles and the hobbyhorses, the swings and the teeter-totters; but whenever a parent or a salesman tried to coax the little ones *off* one of these toys, they screamed and raged and dug in their little heels and threw violent temper tantrums and the whole store sounded like a madhouse. I. I. Mendelson was sorely troubled. What to do, what to do?

One day there appeared before him a genial, cherubic, white-haired gentleman, who said: "Freibush is the name. Professor Oscar Freibush, Doctor of Child Psychology and Consultant on Infant Behavior. I have heard of your difficulties, which I believe I can solve for a fee of fifty dollars."

"Fifty dollars?" echoed I. I. Mendelson.

Mr. Freibush smiled. "No obligation. Satisfaction guaranteed or you don't pay a penny."

"Come with me," said Mr. Mendelson. He led Professor Freibush into the Toy Department. "Look. Listen. Did you ever hear such a *tarrarom?*"

On the hobbyhorse from which his frantic mother was trying to lift him, a little boy was screaming like a banshee. On a tricycle, a little girl was kicking and screeching at her father, who was trying to wrestle her off. On the teeter-totter, two children were caterwauling like demons at two salesmen.

Professor Freibush studied the howling scene but a moment, went over to the hobbyhorse, patted the screaming lad on the head, leaned over and, smiling, whispered a few words into the boy's ear. At once, the lad ceased screeching, slid off the little hobbyhorse, and let his mother lead him away.

Professor Freibush went to the little girl on the tricycle, stroked her locks fondly, leaned over, whispered something into her ear—and the hellion stopped screaming at once, descended from the tricycle, and meekly placed her little hand in her father's.

With the squawling pair on the teeter-totter, Professor Freibush plied his same swift, incredible magic. A fond pat, a kind smile, those mesmeric whispered words—and decorum promptly replaced hysteria.

"It's unbelievable!" cried I. I. Mendelson. "What do you say to them?"

"My fee . . ."

"Here! . . . Now, what do you say?"

"I pat their hair," smiled the great psychologist, folding

the $50 into his wallet, "then I put my mouth close to their little ears and whisper, 'Listen, darling, get off that toy or I'll give you such a *potch* on the *tochis* you won't be able to sit down for a week.' "

Torah

Pronounced TOY-*ra*, to rhyme with "Moira," or TOE-*rah*, to rhyme with "Bowra," or TAW-*ra*, to rhyme with "Nora." Hebrew: *Torah:* "doctrine," "teaching."

1. The Pentateuch, or Five Books of Moses: Genesis, Exodus, Leviticus, Numbers, and Deuteronomy.
2. The scroll containing the Five Books of Moses, hand-written by a scribe on parchment, and read in the synagogue on *Shabbes*, on festivals, on Mondays and Thursdays.
3. All of Jewish law and religious studies. *Torah she-be-al peh* refers to the oral teachings of the rabbis, as contrasted to *Torah sheh-bik-sav*, the written teachings of the Pentateuch, Prophets, and Hagiographa (Sacred Writings).

The very essence of Judaism—as a religion, a philosophy, a commitment, a set of values—is said to lie in the historic triad: "God, *Torah*, Israel."

The *Torah* has always held a cardinal and sacrosanct place in Jewish history, which bursts with tales of the martyrdom and sacrifices Jews endured in order to preserve and transmit "Our holy *Torah*" from one generation to the next.

The text of the Pentateuch has been carefully preserved, and scribes were specially trained to copy the ancient scrolls (*Sefer Torah*, "book of the *Torah*") with fidelity. A *Torah* scroll is considered priceless.

The highest ideal held before every Jew was the study of *Torah*. The *Talmud* is full of admonitions such as this: "A single day devoted to the *Torah* outweighs a thousand sacrifices."

"God weeps over one who might have occupied himself with *Torah* but neglected to do so."

"Not only should a person not neglect study because of the pursuit of pleasures; he should not neglect it even for his occupation."

"How long is one required to study *Torah*? Till the day of his death. . . . Some of the greatest of the wise men of Israel were wood-choppers, others drawers of water, some even blind—who, nevertheless, studied *Torah* day and night." (Maimonides.)

In order to enable even the least educated masses to learn *Torah*, a section *(parshah)* of the Pentateuch was read in the synagogue each Monday and Thursday morning (originally, these were market days in agricultural Palestine), and each Sabbath and holiday. By the end of the year, the cycle of *Torah* readings was completed—and immediately begun once more!

See SIMCHATH TORAH.

The word *Torah* is found in many epigrams and proverbs:

"Tova toireh mikol sechoireh": Learning is the best merchandise.

"Im ein toireh eim derech eretz": Without the study of the law, there are no good manners.

"May you live to introduce [him] to study [*Torah*], marriage, and good deeds." This is the expression of good wishes extended to parents at a son's *brith*.

"Prayer and the study of the Law," wrote Hutchins Hapgood after his singularly sensitive observation of the Lower East Side, "constitute practically the whole life of the religious Jew." *

Hillel, the great and saintly teacher, noblest of the Pharisees, the paradigm of modesty and grace in learning, was once baited by a heathen to condense the *Torah* into its briefest possible form. Hillel replied: "What is hateful to thee, never do to thy fellow man. That is the entire *Torah;* all else is commentary." (Another version of Hillel's historic rejoinder is: "Do unto others as you would have them do unto you." I have followed Dr. Judah Goldin's text, in *The Jews: Their History, Culture and Religion,* Vol. I, pp. 157 ff.)

* Hutchins Hapgood, *The Spirit of the Ghetto,* Funk and Wagnalls, 1965, reprint.

"... toyten bankes"

> Pronounced TOY-*ten* BONK-*kiss*, to rhyme with "Boyton konk hiss." *Toyten*, from German: *tod:* "dead"; *bankes*, from Slavic: *bankes:* the "cups" used for bleeding the sick.

> The phrase *"Es vet helfen vi a toyten bankes"* means: "It will help about as much as 'cupping' can help a corpse."

It used to be customary to bleed a sick person, in an attempt to reduce his fever, by drawing blood to the surface of his skin under a small heated cup, which formed a partial vacuum. The phrase "it will help as much as cupping will help a corpse" is about as graphic as you can get.

Mrs. Kitzman, weight 170, has brought home a new dress, size 12— plus a new "miracle girdle" which, she claims, will enable her to get into the new dress.

Will it?

"It will help *vi a toyten bankes.*"

trayf

> Pronounced TRAYF, to rhyme with "safe." From the Hebrew: *teref:* "torn to pieces."

> An animal not slain according to the ritual laws and by an authorized *shochet;* any food which is not *kosher.* "Pork is *trayf.*" "Ham is *trayf.*" "Oysters and shrimps may taste delicious, but they are *trayf.*"

To form a noun, *trayf* becomes a *trayfeneh* (woman) or *trayfnyak* (man)—someone untrustworthy, malicious, tricky, of whom you should beware.

trombenik
trombenyik

Pronounced TROM-*beh-nik*, to rhyme with "Brahma kick," or TRAUM-*beh-nik*, to rhyme with "brawn the pick." From the Polish, and/or Yiddish: *tromba:* "a trumpet," "a brass horn."

1. A blowhard, a braggart, a blower of his own horn. "That *trombenik* can drive you crazy."
2. A glutton.
3. A lazy man or woman; a ne'er-do-well.
4. A parasite.
5. A fake, a phony, a four-flusher.

Any way you look at it, *trombenik* is not a word of praise. A *trombenik* is part of the raucous gallery of *nudniks, shleppers,* and *paskudnyaks.*

"I," boasted the *trombenik*, "have been to Europe three times in the past two years."

"So? I *come* from there."

tsatske
tsatskeleh
tchotchke
tchotchkeleh

Pronounced TSAHTS-*keh*, to rhyme with "Tosca"; TSAHTS-*keh-leh*, to rhyme with "Oscela"; TCHOCH-*keh*, to rhyme with "botch a"; TCHOCH-*keh-leh*, to rhyme with "notch a la." From Slavic: *shalet:* "to play pranks."

Tsatske and *tchotchke* are used interchangeably. *Tsatskeleh* and *tchotchkeleh* are affectionate diminutives of *tsatske* and *tchotchke.*

A *tsatske* is:

1. A toy, a little plaything. "I brought the child a *tsatske*."

2. An inexpensive, unimportant thing; a gewgaw; a trinket. "He gave her some *tsatske* or other for her trouble."

3. A bruise, contusion, wound. "He had a *tsatske* under each eye."

4. A nobody; no bargain. "Don't listen to that one; he's some *tsatske*."

5. A misfit, an unadjusted child, a problem and burden to one and all. "What can we do about him? Since he joined the club he's been a *tsatske*."

6. A loose or kept woman.

7. An ineffectual person, a fifth wheel, a disappointment.

But the usages I most relish are:

8. A cute female; a pretty little number; a chick; a babe; a playgirl.

9. A sexy but brainless broad.

At one time, so I am told, West End Avenue in New York had an inordinately high proportion of *tchotchkies* (plural).

Old Mr. Gluck had finally moved to the suburbs. On a trip into New York, he met a friend who bombarded him with questions. "How do you like it? Living in the country, so far from everyone!"

"At first I had problems," said Gluck, "I thought I'd never be able to stand it! Then I listened to my neighbors, and got a paramour. From then on, everything has been fine!"

"A paramour! You? Gluck, how can you *do* such a terrible thing? What does your wife think?"

"My wife?" frowned Gluck. "Why should she care how I cut the grass?"

tsedoodelt (adjective)
tsedoodelter (masculine)
tsedoodelteh (feminine)

Pronounced *tseh-*DOO*-delt*, to rhyme with "the zoo belt."

Confused, mixed-up, pixilated, kooky, wacky.

See also TSEDRAYT.

A *tsedoodelter* said that if he found a million dollars in the street he would keep it—unless, of course, he discovered that it belonged to some poor man, in which case he would return it at once.

tsedrayt (adjective)
tsedrayter (masculine)
tsedrayteh (feminine)
tsedraydelt (adjective)

Pronounced *tse*-DRAYT, to rhyme with "de-freight." From German: *zerdreht:* "twisted," "confused."

1. *Tsedrayt* (adjective) or *tsedraydelt* means mixed-up, confused, wacky, demented. "I can't make head or tail out of it; it's *tsedrayt*."
2. A *tsedrayter* (noun) is a man or boy who is all mixed up, a kook, a crank, a crackpot. "Poor man, he's a hopeless *tsedrayter*."
3. A *tsedrayteh* (noun) is a woman or girl nut, a crank, a kook, a lunatic. "Who can believe her? She's a *tsedrayteh*."

Someone with a *"tsedrayter kop"* (deranged head) is pleasantly pixilated—or not so pleasantly demented.

See also KOPDRAYENISH and TSEDOODELT.

"If you want to live forever," a *tsedrayter* told a rich man, "come and live in our dreary little town."

"Why? Is it that healthy?"

"Listen, *never* has a rich man died there."

tsetummelt (adjective)
tsetummelteh (noun: feminine)
tsetummelter (noun: masculine)

Pronounced *tse-TU-m'lt*, to rhyme with " 'ts tumult." See TUMMEL.

Confused, bewildered. "I've never been so *tsetummelt* in my life."

tsetummelter (masculine)

A confused, discombobulated man.

tsetummelteh (feminine)

A bewildered, dotty, scatterbrained female. "Oy, is she a *tsetummelteh*."

tsimmes

Pronounced TSIM-*mess*, to rhyme with "Kim less." From two German words: *zum:* "to the"; *essen:* "eating."

1. A side dish of mixed cooked vegetables and fruits, slightly sweetened. The ingredients may be carrots and peas, prunes and potatoes. sweet potatoes, etc.
2. A dessert of stewed fruits.

Since making *tsimmes* took time and various mixings, the word came to mean:
3. A prolonged procedure; an involved business; a mix-up. "Don't make a whole *tsimmes* out of it." (Don't blow it up out of proportion: Why make a federal case of it?) "It's no *tsimmes* to me." (It doesn't bother me very much.) "Trouble? It was a regular *tsimmes*." (It was a mess, a mix-up, a real stew.)
4. Troubles, difficulties, *contretemps*. A recent newspa-

per advertisement announced: "Skip the fuss. Leave the *tsimmes* to us."

See also SHTUSS.

tsitser

Pronounced TSI-*tzer*, to rhyme with "hits 'er." An ono-matopoetic coinage.

1. One who is always going "Ts! Ts!" or "Tsk! Tsk!" or even "Tchk! Tchk!"
2. An habitual sympathizer and bystander, not a participant.
3. A *kibitzer* given to expressing his feelings with sibilant "tchk"-ings.

See also DOPPESS.

tsuris
tsouris
tsoriss
tsuriss

Pronounced TSOO-*riss*, or TSAW-*riss*, to rhyme with "jur-is" or "Boris." The plural of *tsorah* or *tsureh*. From Hebrew: *tsarah:* "trouble."

Troubles, woes, worries, suffering.

The singular is *tsorah* or *tsureh*, but trouble is rarely singular.

Tsuris has gained considerable vogue in theatrical and literary circles. "Oh, have I got *tsuris!*" "Her life these years has been one *tsorah* after another." "All he adds up to is—*tsuris*."

The phrase "He's *auf tsuris*" means "He has real troubles," "He's sick," "He's depressed."

And when *tsuris* pass beyond the cozy realm of the ordinary, they are called *gehoketh* (chopped-up) *tsuris*. Why troubles are worsened when chopped up, like chicken liver, I do not know, but the phrase certainly *sounds* authoritative.

"Troubles are partial to wetness—to tears, and whiskey."

"Don't worry about tomorrow; who knows what will befall you today?"

"From luck to *tsuris* is but a step; but from *tsuris* to *mazel* is a mile long."

"Bygone *tsuris* are good to relate."   —FOLK SAYINGS

"And how many children do *you* have?"

"None."

"No children?! So what do you do for aggravation?"

tsutcheppenish

Pronounced TSOO-*chep-peh-nish;* rhymes with "Too hep a dish." Blend of Slavic: *tchupat:* "pinch"; and German: *zu:* "to."

1. Something irritating, undesirable, that "attaches itself"; an obsession. "He has a *tsutcheppenish* that is driving everyone else crazy."

2. Someone who becomes a persistent, unshakable nuisance. "She turned into a *tsutcheppenish* I never expected."

See also NUCHSHLEPPER.

tummel

Pronounced TUM-*m'l,* to rhyme with "full pull." From German: *Tummel,* "tumult."

Noise, commotion, noisy disorder. "He can drive a person crazy; everywhere he goes he creates *tummel.*"

See TUMMLER.

tummler

Pronounced TOOM-*ler*, with the *oo* pronounced as in *took*.

1. One who creates a lot of noise (*tummel*) but accomplishes little.
2. A funmaker, a "live wire," a clown, a prankster, the "life of the party."
3. The paid social director and entertainer in those Catskill resorts that constitute "the Borscht Belt."

It is the *tummler*'s job to guarantee, to the blasé (but insatiable) patrons of a summer resort, that most dubious of vacation boons: "Never a dull moment!" The tummler performs, i.e., entertains in a formal sense, every night: as a comic, singer, actor, master of ceremonies. He acts, writes, directs, produces shows. He extemporizes, monologizes, and plagiarizes. He puts on vaudeville skits, minstrel shows, amateur nights, ordeals-by-dance.

But the rest of the eighteen-hour day the *tummler* is a noisemaker, a fun-generator, a hilarity-organizer and overall buffoon. He initiates endless tomfooleries—individual and *en masse*. He tells stories, cracks jokes, plays pranks. He wears outlandish costumes, imitates peculiar people, trips over chairs, falls off diving boards. He leads songs like "Old MacDonald Had a Farm," and games like "Simon Says." He perpetrates broad hoaxes and risqué treasure hunts. He pretends to be a waiter, a doctor, a dishwasher, a cretin. He launches public and putative romances for the favor of the fattest, shortest, tallest, or least pulchritudinous females. He forever traverses the grounds, the dining room, the recreation hall, in an uninterrupted exhibition of joking, jollying, baiting, burlesquing, heckling, clowning. He makes, in short, whatever complete fool of himself is necessary "to keep the guests in stitches"—which can be as painful as it sounds. His mission is to force every paying customer to "have a ball." His guiding principle is the maxim: "Have FUN!!!!" And his shattering resourcefulness is put to the final, awful test on those most gruesome and challenging days: rainy. For only the *tummler* stands between the guests' incipient depression and departure.

The ideal *tummler* (if "ideal" is quite the right word) would be a cross between Milton Berle and Jerry Lewis. Both have, as a matter of fact, won signal honors in the fun-loving Catskills.

The peculiar tribulations of the *tummler* have been deftly sketched by Moss Hart in *Act One*, and coyly explored by Joey Adams and Henry Tobias in *The Borscht Belt*.

To give recognition where such is deserved, "The Borscht Belt" *did* send to the glittering world of vaudeville, stage, movies, and television an astounding number of talents—comedians, playwrights, directors, singers, producers: Danny Kaye, Moss Hart, Clifford Odets, Dore Schary, Arthur Kober, Garson Kanin, Don Hartman, John Garfield, Shelley Winters, Sid Caesar, Joey Bishop, Buddy Hackett, Phil Silvers, Jackie Mason, Jan Peerce, Robert Merrill, Red Buttons, Tony Curtis, and heaven only knows how many others.

The *tummlers* of our time may not know of the historic tradition in which they function: A professional *badchen*, a jokester–M.C., used to be engaged to make merry at Jewish weddings.

See BADCHEN and Appendix: Weddings.

tzaddik

Pronounced TZOD-*dick*, rhymes with "sod Dick." Hebrew: "a righteous man." The plural is *tzaddikim*, pronounced *tsah*-DIK-*im*.

1. A most righteous man.
2. A holy man; a man of surpassing virtue and (possibly) supernatural powers.
3. (Used ironically) An unholy, wicked, cynical man.

Originally, *tzaddikim* were regarded as upright, honorable men who, by their example, brought others closer to righteousness. The medieval cabalists and, later, the *Chasidim*, attributed mirific powers to the *tzaddik*.

The famous legend of the Thirty-Six Saints (*Lamed-vav Tzaddikim*) says that on earth there live thirty-six saints—who do not know it; the world continues to exist, by God's favor, only because of these nameless thirty-six and their un-selfish ways and work. No one can tell who they are: one may be a pauper, one a drayman, a janitor, a shoemaker. . . .

The legend holds that the *Lamed-vav* disclose their identity only on rare occasions—especially emergencies, when Jews are in danger. Then a *tzaddik* will do God's bidding in a sudden, magical rescue mission—and vanish, for he must never have his identity revealed. (That, apparently, would deplete his supernatural powers.)

The idea of doing good secretly, without reward, fleeing from any recognition or gratitude, held great fascination for the men of the *Talmud*. The less publicly a good deed is done, the more for its own quintessential goodness, the more admirable it is. Heaven will know . . . God will remember. . . .

A famous old *tzaddik* was being extolled before a congregation, by a rabbi who waxed more eloquent by the second: ". . . our beloved *tzaddik* is a man of such wisdom that even the most learned sit at his feet; of such kindness that young and old alike flock to him for advice; of such honesty that men and women are uplifted by his example; with such keen understanding of human problems that even saints bare their innermost secrets to him; a man of such . . . "

At this point, the *tzaddik* tugged at the eulogist's sleeve and whispered, "Don't forget my humility."

Moishe the shoemaker was astounded to receive a letter, from the leading *tzaddik* in his town, that read:

> O Light of Israel, Eagle of Understanding, Ocean of Learning:
>
> Please come and fetch my shoes, which need mending.
>
> REB SHMUEL

Moishe dropped everything and hastened to the wise man's home. "O Reb Shmuel, I have come as fast as my feet could carry me. I am only a shoemaker, not versed in such matters— but please tell me, why did you address me in such a lofty manner?"

"Eh? What 'lofty' manner?"

"As 'O Light of Israel, Eagle of Understanding, Ocean of Learning' . . ."

The *tzaddik* looked puzzled and, stroking his beard, said, "But that's exactly the way people always write me. . . ."

"Our *tzaddik* prayed that the rich should give more to the poor—and already God answered *half* the prayer: the poor have agreed to accept."

A rabbi visited a village reputed to have a miracle-working *tzaddik*, and asked: "What miracles has your *tzaddik* actually performed?"

"Our *tzaddik* has fasted every day for three whole years now!"

"Three *years?!* But that's impossible. He'd be dead by now!"

"Certainly he would! But our *tzaddik* knows that if he fasted *every* day that demonstration of saintliness would put everyone else to shame; so he eats only to spare everyone's feelings—and conceals the fact that *privately* he's fasting."

tzedaka
tsadaka

> Pronounced *tse-DOCK-a*, to rhyme with "The Rocca."
> Hebrew: from *tzedek:* "righteousness."

> The obligation to establish justice by being righteous, upright, compassionate—and, above all, helping one's fellow man. (There is no separate word for "charity" in Hebrew, or Yiddish.)

Jews never separated charity from a *duty*, a moral and religious obligation to act justly and generously. Deuteronomy 15 : 11 says, "For the poor shall never cease out of the land; therefore I command thee, saying, thou shalt open thine hand wide unto thy brother. . . ." And Proverbs 19 : 17 tells us: "He that hath pity upon the poor lendeth unto the Lord."

The poor and needy must, moreover, be spared embarrassment. Every Jewish community placed great stress on helping the poor, the sick, the handicapped—and refugees, who have always been a saddening part of the history of the Jews. Every community had a special fund for the needy; every holiday included philanthropic activities; and every home contained little boxes into which coins, for variously designated charities, were dropped. (See PUSHKE.) Every Jewish child was told and taught very early in life to feel a duty to help those who needed it; children were often given coins to give to mendicants who came to the door. And life in any Jewish community in America is studded with "benefits," "memorials," "affairs," "parlor meetings" and other fund-raising ingenuities.

The singular independence, not to say impertinence, of Jewish *shnorrers,* those remarkable types, was rooted in a certain sense of the obligation owed them by tradition and Talmudic precept.

Maimonides set down variously rated forms of *tzedaka.* The highest form of charity, he said, is to help someone to help himself; after that, to help anonymously and secretly—so that the benefactor does not know whom he helps, and the benefactee does not know who helped him.

Jews are flatly forbidden to ignore or turn away anyone who asks for help.

"Withhold not good from him to whom it is due."
—PROVERBS 2 : 27
"He who refuses a suppliant the aid which he has the power to give, is accountable to justice."
—JOSEPHUS, *Against Apion,* ii, 27
"Wealth is fleeting, honor winged, but charity abides."
JOSHUA STEINBERG (1839–1908)

The shabby, half-starved tramp stood before the rich man, in the rich man's parlor, and asked for help, and the rich man called in his butler and said, "*Look* at this poor unfortunate! His toes are sticking out of his shoes. His trousers are patched in a dozen places. He looks as if he hasn't been able to bathe or shave for a week. He hasn't had a decent meal in God knows how long. It breaks my heart to look at this poor, miserable creature—so throw him out!"

That man clearly lacked an understanding of *tzedaka.*

"The longest road in the world is the one that leads to the pocket."

—FOLK SAYING

A teacher, meeting her class on the first day, asked each child to stand and give his or her name and hobby.

The first child rose and said, "My name is Sally Farnsworth, I'm ten years old, and I like to roller-skate."

The second student rose: "My name is James Burns, I'm nine years old, and I collect stamps."

The third student rose: "My name is Morris Wexler, I'm ten years old, and I pledge five dollars."

tzitzit

Pronounced TSI-*tsiss*, to rhyme with "kisses." Hebrew: "fringes." The plural is *tzitziot*.

The fringes at the corners of the prayer shawl (*tallis*) and the *tallis katan*—the short, jacket-like garment worn by Orthodox males under coat or vest.

Tzitzit are meant as reminders of one's duty to the laws of Judaism; more exactly, to the 613 specific instructions in the *Torah*. The authority for wearing *tzitzit* comes from God—according to Numbers 15 : 37–39, at least: God told Moses to tell the children of Israel to make fringes "throughout their generations" in the borders of their garments and "put upon the fringe of the borders a riband of blue." (Blue died out as blue dye became scarce.)

The cabalists performed all sorts of abracadabra with the number of knots, double knots, sections, and windings ("seven times around and made fast by a double knot") that are required in the *tzitzit*. The mystical gymnasts counted thirty-nine windings in each fringe, and derived an identical "value," in a numerical sense, out of the triumphant *Adonai Echod* ("the Lord is One") that ends the great *Shema* prayer.

It is said that the four *tzitziot* stand for the "four corners" of the earth. The discovery that the earth is round has not altered the metaphor.

See TALLIS.

U

ungepotchket

See ONGEPOTCHKET.

utz

Pronounced to rhyme with "foots." German: *uzen:* "to
tease," "to fool."

Verb
To goad, to nag, to needle, to torment verbally. "He
likes to *utz* you until you could scream." "Stop *utzing*
me!"

Noun
A piece of goading, verbal needling. "He's a master of
the *utz*." "Did he give her an *utz!*"

vitz

Pronounced as written; rhymes with "sits." German: *Witz:* "joke."

A pointed piece of humor; a witticism; a wisecrack.

My father, who had the readiest, most generous, loveliest sense of humor of anyone I ever knew, loved to ask me, "Well, have you heard a good *vitz* lately?"

My mother once taught me this piece of folk wisdom: "He is a hero who represses a *vitz*."

A very neat *vitz:*

When Groucho Marx, who wanted to join a certain beach club in Santa Monica, was told by a friend to forget it because the club was known to be anti-Semitic, Mr. Marx said, "My wife isn't Jewish, so will they let my son go into the water up to his knees?"

yachne
yachna

Pronounced YOKH-*neh*, to rhyme with a *kh*-guttural "Bach-na," and *not* with "botch-na." The feminine form of the Hebrew name Johanan. (There are over fifty different Johanans in the *Talmud;* the name "John" also comes from Johanan.)

A gossip; a yakkety-yak; a busybody; a coarse, shallow woman; a malicious, rumormongering, troublemaking female. "She has the manners of a *yachne.*"

Yachne is blood sister to a *yenta.*

Yachne is never used in a favorable or approving sense.

Yachne was a respectable girl's name at one time; no one knows which bearer of this appellation propelled it into immortality via the energy of her tongue and the indelicacy of her manners.

See also YENTA and YIDENEH.

"Tell me, Goldie: What do you think of Red China?"

"Please, Shirl, not with your pink tablecloth!"

Mrs. Kotchin and Mrs. Mishkin sat rocking on the porch of the Villa Lipshitz, a Catskill resort, when a young man approached.

"*Gottenyu!*" exclaimed Mrs. Kotchin. "*Look* at that boy! Did you ever see such a big nose? Such shifty eyes? Such a crooked mouth?"

In a freezing voice, Mrs. Mishkin replied, "It so happens, you are talking about my son!"

"Well," said Mrs. Kotchin, "on *him*, it's becoming!"

yahrtzeit

See YORTZEIT.

Yahveh

See ADONAI, JEHOVAH.

yarmulkah
yarmulke

Pronounced YAHR-*m'l-keh*, to rhyme with "bar culpa."
From a Tartar word, via the Polish for "skullcap."

The skullcap worn by observing Jewish males.

No religious edict I can uncover directs Jews to cover their heads—though Exodus prescribes head-covering for the Temple priests. During the early Middle Ages, the rabbis instructed Jewish men not to go about bareheaded. Why? Because man should cover his head as a sign of respect before God, whose glory and radiance are, as Maimonides said, "around and above [us]." Covering the head as a sign of respect and reverence is a custom not restricted to Jews, of course; it is common among the peoples of the East, from Arabia to India.

Reform Jews, however, hold that in the Western world it is more appropriate to bare one's head as a sign of respect, and therefore men should remain hatless when praying to God. Conservative Jews counter that baring the head is an imitation of a non-Jewish custom, and prefer to maintain the traditional head-covering during prayer.

The current custom is:

(a) Traditional Orthodox males wear a *yarmulkah* at home and at work, no less than in the synagogue, to remind them of whom they stand before at every moment.

(b) Other religious males wear a *yarmulkah* in the synagogue, while studying sacred texts, and while engaged in a religious ritual at home.

(c) Reform Jews, in western Europe and in America, do not wear a *yarmulkah* at all, although their opposition to this practice has somewhat abated.

(d) Nonreligious Jews may don a *yarmulkah* for a *brith*, Bar Mitzva, wedding, funeral—for a combination of reasons: as pure sentiment; as a concession to tradition; to please their elders; to add a note of ceremonial solemnity.

Since the *yarmulkah* has become the outwardly recognizable symbol of the Jew, the rabbis who participate in civil rights marches (including Reform rabbis) often wear *yarmulkahs* to serve as an identification of their faith.

See Appendix: Hair.

Old Hirshbein, in a *yarmulkah*, appeared at Nazi police headquarters carrying a newspaper, in which he had circled an advertisement.

Exclaimed the sergeant: *"You* came about this ad?"

"That's right."

"But it reads: 'Wanted: young man, well-built, over 6 feet tall!' You're at least seventy, thin as a match, and not over 5 feet 2. The ad says: 'Must have excellent eyesight.' Your glasses are so thick you can barely see! The ad says, 'Must be Aryan,' and you are obviously a Jew! Why did you come here?"

"I just want to tell you," said Hirshbein, "that on *me*, you shouldn't depend."

A cartoon in an Israeli newspaper showed the Pope, during his historic visit to Palestine in 1964, with the President of Israel. The caption read: "The Pope is the one with the *yarmulkah*."

Yekke

Pronounced YEK-*keh*, to rhyme with "Mecca." Origin: unknown. A German.

Yekke is the colloquial name Ashkenazic Jews used for a German. In Israel, Jews from Germany or Austria are called *Yekkes*, even by Israelis who don't approve of Yiddish. The name suggests "Teutonic," "pedantic," "rigid,"—in any case, not popular. (Some Israelis think *yekke* an acronym for three Hebrew words, meaning "A Jew of scant intelligence," but my experts call this folklore, not philology.)

yekl

Pronounced YEK-*k'l*, to rhyme with "heckle." From German: *jäck*, "batty."

1. A stupid person; a sucker.
2. A "greenhorn," a newcomer to the United States who is taken advantage of; a yokel.

Abraham Cahan, author, journalist, founder and editor of the Jewish Daily *Vorwärts* (Forward), and perhaps the single most important person in the story of the spread of Yiddish in the United States, wrote a novel called *Yekl* that described the adventures of an innocent and often-wronged immigrant in New York.

yenta
yente

Pronounced YEN-*ta*, to rhyme with "bent a." *Yenta*, I am told, was a perfectly acceptable name for a lady, derived from the Italian *gentile*—until some ungracious *yenta* gave it a bad name. (So, too, the Spanish *esperanza* became the basis for the Jewish name "Shprintza," *señor* the original for "Shnaiur," and "Phoebus" the origin of "Feivish.") It is also suggested that *yenta* is an ironic corruption of the French feminine for well-bred, *gentille*, but I doubt it.

1. A woman of low origins or vulgar manners; a shrew; a shallow, coarse termagant. "She is the biggest *yenta* on the block." "She has the tact of a *yenta*."
2. A gossipy woman; a scandal-spreader; a rumormonger; one unable to keep a secret or respect a confidence. In this sense, men are sometimes described as *yentas*, just as one might call a male blabbermouth "an old woman."

Yenta Telebende was a famous character in a Yiddish newspaper published in New York; she was invented by the humorous writer "B. Kovner," the pen name of Jacob Adler.

The rapid-fire comedian Jack E. Leonard once called the garrulous moderator of a television discussion program "a *yenta* with facts."

Two *yentas* met in Miami.

"So tell me, Molly, have you been through the menopause?"

"The menopause? I haven't even been through the *Fontainebleau* yet."

For the first time in her life, Mrs. Samuelson went to a gynecologist.

After taking her medical history, he said, "Now, please go into the next room and take off your clothes."

"My *clothes?*" gasped Mrs. Samuelson.

"Yes."

"Listen, Doctor, does your mother know how you make a living?"

One of the more amusing buttons worn by the button-happy hippie young reads:

> MARCEL PROUST
> IS A
> YENTA

yentz

Rhymes with "rents." From German: *jenes* (see below).

1. To copulate.
2. To cheat, to swindle, to defraud. In this usage, *yentz* is akin to the English slang use of "screw." Thus: "Don't trust him; he'll *yentz* you."

Yentz is a most coarse word, an obscenity never used in the presence of women, children, or elders who are likely to blush.

The Yiddish equivalent of the best-known four-letter English word for sexual congress, *yentz* has become part of the vernacular of the American underworld.*

The origin of the word is interesting. *Yentz* comes from the German demonstrative pronoun *jenes*, meaning "that," "that thing," "the other," "the other thing." The German pronunciation is YAYN-*es;* the Yiddish rendition became YENTS. But how did "the other" or "that thing" become infested with carnal content? Quite simply, as a euphemism—i.e., "that unmentionable thing." In the United States, in the twenties, the word "it" was used for copulation: "They did it"; "Does she—do it?"

NOTE: Hebrew contains no words for the sex organs; the male member is called "that organ" (*ever* or *gid*); the female receptacle is called "that place" (*ossu mokum*).

With such a prudish tradition, it is not surprising that Jews seized upon *jenes*, which, incidentally, is how genteel ladies'

---

* See Berrey and Van der Bark's *Dictionary of American Slang*, Crowell, 1943; and Mencken's *The American Language*, Knopf, 1962.

maids and governesses in Germany referred to you-know-whats.

yentzer

Rhymes with "rents 'er." Yiddish vernacular.

(Obscenity)

1. One who copulates—male or female.
2. One who is promiscuous. "She left him because he is a *yentzer*."
3. One who copulates rather more than most, or who claims inordinate sexual powers. *Yentzer* might have served Dr. Kinsey as a synonym for "sexual athlete."
4. A crook; a swindler; someone who takes advantage of others by guile, cunning, misrepresentation or outright dishonesty. "He is a born *yentzer*."

yeshiva
yeshiba

Pronounced *yeh*-SHEE-*va*, to rhyme with "believe a." From Hebrew: *yeshov:* "to sit." (Students sat while studying, and the places where they so sat became known as *yeshivot*.) Plural in Hebrew: *yeshivot*; in English usage, *yeshivas*. (The Hindu Upanishads are named for the Sanskrit words "to sit near"; students sat near teachers for oral instruction.)

1. A rabbinical college or seminary.
2. (In the United States) A secondary Hebrew school; an elementary school in which both religious and secular subjects are studied.

The *yeshiva* was an outgrowth of the *Bet Midrash*, the "House of Study," the place in every Jewish community where men met to study and discuss the *Torah* and the *Talmud*. The great *Mishnah*, compiled by Judah the Prince in the latter part of the second century, drew upon the vast accumulated body of knowledge, interpretations, and debates of the innumerable and unending seminars in the innumerable "houses of study" where Jews carried on their unending discussions on God, faith, good, evil, responsibility.

One of the earliest *yeshivot* was established in Palestine, at Yavneh, by Rabbi Johanan ben Zakkai. This rabbi, who was looked upon with favor by the Roman Emperor Vespasian (he had predicted Vespasian would become emperor), asked Vespasian as a special favor to spare Yavneh and its scholars from the destruction Rome visited upon Jerusalem and other centers of Jewish religion and nationalism. After the destruction of Jerusalem and the great Temple, the *Sanhedrin* (council of rabbis and sages) moved to Yavneh, and the academy there attracted many scholars and became the seat of Jewish scholarship. Permitting the *yeshiva* at Yavneh to exist enabled the Jews to continue their studies, to write the *Mishnah* and the *Gemara*, to maintain their tradition of learning, to perpetuate themselves as a people—albeit without a land or political structure.

During the Talmudic period, *yeshivas* were established elsewhere in Palestine and Babylonia, and they were the creative source and critical laboratory of all Jewish theology, law, ethics and moral guidance. From the tenth century on, *yeshivas* spread wherever Jews lived or migrated—to North Africa, Spain, France, Italy, Germany, England, Holland, and especially in eastern Europe.

Relatively few of the students at a *yeshiva* in eastern Europe received or wanted a rabbinical degree. The purpose of the *yeshiva* was *not* primarily to produce rabbis, but to produce Jews who were well versed in the *Talmud*, learned men, erudite men, men disciplined in their thinking and ascetic in their habits, men who would dedicate themselves to live according to the *Torah*, men who would spend several hours a day for the rest of their lives studying the ever-discussable tractates of the *Talmud*.

> The cities and towns of Eastern Europe were . . . full of learned householders, who studied not only . . . to fulfill the commandment to study, but because they actually felt an urge to study. They sang their studies;

they sang them fervently, and felt transported to a higher world.*

In most *yeshivot* it was unheard of to read anything but the Bible and the *Talmud*. All secular works—philosophy, science, fiction, poetry—were strictly excluded. Religious Jews greatly feared that secularization and a falling away from piety would follow if worldly and non-Jewish influences were permitted to attract the Jewish young. In the late nineteenth century, however, the *Yeshiva* of Volozhin (Poland) advocated the acquisition of secular knowledge.

The traditional *Talmud*-studying-only, no-secular-courses *yeshiva* is rare in America. The first American *yeshiva*, Etz Chayim Talmudical Academy, was organized in New York City in 1886. It later merged with the Rabbi Isaac Elchanan Yeshiva and eventually grew into Yeshiva University, which in addition to a rabbinical seminary includes institutions ranging from high schools to its own medical school. The first rabbinical college for Reform Jews was established in Cincinnati in 1875: Hebrew Union College. The Jewish Theological Seminary was founded in New York in 1886, was reorganized in 1902, and is today the leading Conservative rabbinical training center.

For more about *yeshivas*, see Appendix: Yeshivas and Shul, Study, and Prayer.

A great scholar, a luminary of his *yeshiva*, was taking a journey on a ship. The other passengers were tradesmen, bringing their merchandise to foreign markets.

"What kind of merchandise are you carrying?" they asked the poorly dressed scholar.

"What I carry is the most valuable merchandise in the world," said he.

"And what is that?"

He smiled and would not answer.

The merchants searched the scholar's cabin and interrogated the crew and learned that the scholar was, in fact, escorting no merchandise whatsoever. So they laughed and made fun of him and called him a fool.

* A. Menes, "Patterns of Jewish Scholarship in Eastern Europe," *The Jews: Their History, Culture and Religion*, Harper, Vol. I, p. 385.

Several days later, pirates attacked the ship and robbed all of the passengers, stripping them down to their clothes. And when the ship reached port, the merchants scarcely knew what to do. They had no money. They had nothing to sell. But the scholar went to the "House of Study" and sat down and began to discuss the law. And when the local Jews saw how learned he was, they gave him food and fine clothing and lodged him in the finest house in town.

And the merchants, begging in the street, saw him pass and said, "Yes, his merchandise *is* the most valuable in all the world: It is Learning."

A young scholar at a *yeshiva* was so learned that men came from all over Poland to marvel over his erudition.

One day, a visitor asked the head of the seminary, "Rabbi, what do *you* think of this young man? One wonders how he knows so much."

The rabbi said, "I wonder about something else; this young man reads so much that I wonder when he will find the time to *know*."

yeshiva bucher

Pronounced ye-SHEE-va BOO-*kher* or BAW-*kher*, with a Scottish *kh*. Hebrew: *yeshov:* "to sit"; *bachur:* literally, "chosen"; also "young man" or "bachelor." The plural of *bucher* is *bachurim*, but in English usage may be (and often is) given as *buchers*.

1. A young man who is a student at a *yeshiva* (college for Talmudic study).
2. A scholarly, shy, unworldly type. "He is as gentle as a *yeshiva bucher.*"
3. (Used ironically) A naive, gullible type; an inexperienced and unrealistic sort. "He has about as much knowledge of girls as a *yeshiva bucher.*" "Don't ask him for an opinion; he's a *yeshiva bucher.*"

The archetypical *yeshiva bucher* was an eastern European, seventeen or eighteen years old, who studied the *Talmud* at an academy of higher studies. Study at a *yeshiva* was extremely demanding, beginning with early prayers and continuing all day, in rigorous cerebral discipline, until late at night. It took about seven years of *yeshiva* study to become a rabbi. The *Mishnah* tells the young scholar to "eat a morsel of bread with salt, drink of water a measure, sleep upon the ground—and lead a life of deprivation while you toil in *Torah*."

Poor students were supported by the community. Those who came from far distances to a *yeshiva* were boarded and lodged with local families. It was considered an act of piety to feed and lodge a *yeshiva bucher*, many of whom went from home to home, eating and sleeping in a different place each night. (The custom of the *essen tug*, or eating day, was widespread.) Some slept on the benches in the *yeshiva* where students studied all day. The *yeshiva bucher* often lived on the edge of malnutrition, and not without humiliation.

With his wide black hat, his long black caftan, his uncut sidelocks (*payess*), pallid skin, soft hands, modest ways (it was the style of scholars to walk with downcast eyes, absorbed in some Talmudic problem—never letting their eyes fall on a woman!), the *yeshiva bucher* was a familiar figure in eastern Europe. His innocence, his asceticism, his gentleness became legendary. (Rabbi Jonah, in the *Talmud*, told Jews never to behave "frivolously" in the presence of a scholar.)

A *yeshiva bucher* was a matrimonial prize. The *Talmud* (*Pesahim*) says: "If you must, sell everything and . . . marry your daughter to a scholar."

The father of the bride would settle an amount on the scholarly groom as dowry; or would provide him with support; or would guarantee to pay his bills for a year. Honor attached to any family that included a *yeshiva bucher*.

A student who dedicated himself to perpetual study—daily, lifelong study—was called a *matmid* (plural: *matmidim*).

The story is told of a *yeshiva* in Russia where all the *yeshiva buchers* were once drafted into the Tsar's infantry. To everyone's surprise, the would-be rabbis turned out to be superlative marksmen.

Came war.

The Talmudic regiment went into the front lines. The enemy advanced.

"Fire!" shouted the Russian C.O.

No shot was heard. The enemy came closer.

"Fire!" cried the officer again.

His rifles were silent, the enemy at pistol range.

"What's the *matter* with you?" cried the C.O. *"Why don't you shoot?"*

One of the *yeshiva* soldiers blurted, "But those are *men* coming toward us, sir. If we fire, someone will get hurt!"

I am told that a student at a *yeshiva*, who had become interested in Freud, was asked by one of his classmates: "Tell me, Abe, what's the difference between a psychotic and a neurotic?"

Abe scratched his chin but a moment before replying: "A psychotic thinks that 2 plus 2 makes 5. A neurotic knows that 2 plus 2 makes 4—but he just can't *stand* it!"

YHVH

See ADONAI.

yiches
yichus
yihus

> Pronounced YIKH-*ess*, with a strong uvular *kh* sound, in the Scottish or German manner. Hebrew: "pedigree," "genealogy."

> Family status or prestige.

Yiches refers to more than pedigree or family "name," for *yiches* must be deserved, earned as well as inherited.

The crucial ingredients of *yiches* are: learning, virtue, philanthropy, service to the community. One who does not live up to his family's past record swiftly "loses" his *yiches*.

The highest *yiches* attaches to the man of learning. *Yiches* is the hallmark of the "aristocrat"—in the sense that the highest deference among Jews was accorded those learned in the *Talmud*.

Yiches does not attach itself merely to the successful or the wealthy; wealth or success never warrants or receives the respect accorded knowledge.

A *shadchen* would enter in his record of a marriageable male or female a careful listing of the scholars, teachers, rabbis in the family background. The more the learning, the higher the *yiches*.

Newly rich Jews would try to marry their daughter to a young man of illustrious background, however poor—i.e., a boy with true *yiches*. And for their sons, they sought a rabbi's daughter.

A universe of *yiches*-aspiration lies in the heartfelt cry of a Jewish woman at the seashore:

"Help! Help! My son the doctor is drowning!"

Yid

Pronounced YEED, to rhyme with "deed." (If you pronounce it YID, to rhyme with "did," you will be guilty of a *faux pas*: "YID" is offensive—and the way anti-Semites pronounce it.) From the German: *Jude:* "Jew." And *Jude* is a truncated form of *Yehuda*, which was the name given to the Jewish Commonwealth in the period of the Second Temple. That name, in turn, was derived from the name of one of Jacob's sons, *Yehuda* (Judah, in English), whose descendants constituted one of the tribes of Israel and who settled in that portion of Canaan from Jerusalem south to Kadesh-Barnea (50 miles south of Beersheba) and from Jericho westwards to the Mediterranean.

A Jew (male or female).

Yid is a neutral term (if pronounced YEED, not YID)—but *yideneh* never is. See YIDENEH.

So sensitive are Jews about racial aspersions, that when a Vassar girl told her father they were experimenting in the psychology lab with guinea pigs, he drew back in horror: "At college haven't they told you never to say 'guinea' for Italian?"

The Klan, deciding to harass Mr. Levine, who ran a tailor shop in a hamlet in Mississippi, told the school children to stand in front of the shop every afternoon and shout, *"Yid, Yid!"*

The children set to their work with enthusiasm. Out came Mr. Levine. "Thank you, thank you," he said. "If you'll come back and do that tomorrow, I'll give each of you a dime."

The next day the children came back—with reinforcements; and after the hooting began, Mr. Levine distributed dimes to each *kleine* Klanner.

The following day—more children, more catcalls. But this time Mr. Levine only distributed nickels.

On the morrow the children returned, but got not a penny. "What's the idea?" they wanted to know.

"I'm sorry, kids, but I can't afford any more advertising," sighed Mr. Levine.

The children never came back.

In the days of the Tsar, Koplinski fell off a bridge and proceeded to drown—threshing around and shouting for help at the top of his lungs.

Two tsarist policemen heard his cries and ran to the rail, but when they saw it was a Jew in the water, they simply laughed.

"Help! Help!" cried Koplinski. "I'm drowning!"

"So drown, *Zhid (Yid)!*"

And just as Koplinski started under for the proverbial third time, he had an inspiration: "Down with the Tsar!" he shouted.

At once, the policemen jumped into the water, pulled Koplinski out, and arrested him for sedition.

Yiddish

Pronounced YID-*dish*, to rhyme with "mid fish." From German: *jüdisch*, "Jewish."

The language of East European, or Ashkenazic, Jews. (The vernacular of Sephardic Jews is Ladino.)

Jews do not speak "Jewish" any more than Methodists speak "Methodist" or Canadians speak "Canadish." "Jewish" is an adjective, not a noun. (But because "Yiddish" means "Jewish" *in* Yiddish itself, many Jews use the two words interchangeably, and refer to "a Jewish newspaper," for instance. The distinction between the adjective "Jewish" and the noun/ adjective "Yiddish" is, accordingly, widely ignored.) *Yiddish,* the name of a language, need not be pronounced with embarrassment—even by German Jews, who long despised it as a vulgar jargon; or by Hebraicists, who loathed it as the shabby vernacular of the masses; or by ardent Israelis, who consider it a demeaning tongue of hated German and ghetto ancestry.

Yiddish is not Hebrew, which remains (with Aramaic) the Jews' language of prayer and religious ceremonies. Hebrew is the official language of Israel.

Yiddish uses the *letters* of the Hebrew alphabet; it is written from right to left; its spelling, which has been standardized, is emphatically phonetic. (But see Appendix: Spelling of Yiddish Words in English.)

Perhaps fifteen to twenty percent of the vocabulary of *Yiddish* consists of Hebrew words and phrases—but *Yiddish* and Hebrew are as different as, say, English and Hungarian. In addition to its quotient of Hebrew words, the vocabulary of *Yiddish* is adapted from German (seventy to seventy-five percent), and from Polish, Russian, Rumanian, Ukrainian, various Slovene dialects, and, within the last century, English.

Yiddish is not a "new" or even a "young" language, believe it or not. It is older than modern German, which may be said to have begun with Martin Luther's translation of the Bible, and it is older than modern English, which dates from 1475, according to the *Random House Dictionary.*

Yiddish is descended from the form of German heard by Jewish settlers from northern France, about a thousand years ago. As Jews settled in towns along the Rhineland, they adopted and adapted the local vernacular. They wrote German with their Hebrew alphabet, phonetically—just as Jews used Hebrew letters to write many other languages. They shunned Latin and its alphabet, for Latin was associated with things Christian, including pogroms.

The Germanic tongue, heavily studded with Hebrew words and phrases (names, holidays, all religious or ritualistic matters), added words from other languages as the Jews traveled. The new linguistic mélange took root and expanded in the ghettos—and flourished in Eastern Europe; it became the beloved native tongue of the Ashkenazim—and was never used by, or known to, the Sephardim.

Since Jewish women were not taught Hebrew, the "sacred tongue," they spoke *Yiddish* to the children—who, in turn, spoke it to their parents and, later, to their own children. So *Yiddish* became known as *Mame-loshen*, "mother's language," to distinguish it from *loshen-ha-kodesh*, "the sacred language."

As the *Haskala* or Enlightenment among Europe's Jews spread, in the eighteenth century, its proponents, who were intensely conscious of their Jewishness, championed Hebrew and wanted to revive it as a modern tongue. (They were themselves resented by the Hebraicist-purists who opposed making Hebrew secular.) The champions and publicists of *Haskala*, called *Maskilim*, attacked *Yiddish* as vulgar, as slang, as an illegitimate, déclassé, low-grade jargon. Enters a paradox: The *Maskilim* had to use *Yiddish* in order to reach the very people they were trying to wrench away from it! So it was that their earnest campaigns served to strengthen the attachment of the Jewish masses to that vernacular they already called "the people's tongue" or "the language of the masses." (It was not the first time that Jews became entangled in paradox.)

Yiddish is only one of many vernaculars fashioned by Jews throughout the ages (see Appendix: Dialects) but it is the one that spread most widely, adapted itself most vigorously, and has flourished most successfully. It has been estimated that at one time (in the 1920's) about two-thirds of all the Jews in the world could *understand Yiddish*. Hitler's gory harvest changed that forever.

Today, familiarity with *Yiddish* appears to be correlated directly with age: the older the Jew, the more can he be expected to understand *Yiddish*. I think it is safe to generalize that more Jews understand *Yiddish* than speak it; more can speak it than read it; more can manage to read it than write it.

I was long ago struck by the fact that any Jew who gives an affirmative answer to the question, "Do you understand *Yiddish?*" does so with a sudden grin. Whatever else may be said of this gamin of a language, it inspires enormous affection.

In the technical world of linguistics, *Yiddish* is classified as "Judeo-German." But it also contains what philologists call "Loez"—which is Jewish correlates of Old French and Old Italian. *The Standard Jewish Encyclopedia* (Doubleday, 1966) offers this chronology: Initial Yiddish: 1000–1250 A.D.; Old Yiddish: 1250–1500; Medieval Yiddish: 1500–1750; Modern Yiddish: 1750 to date.

Philologists identify three main types of *Yiddish:* Lithuanian, Polish, South Russian (Ukrainian). (Rumanian *Yiddish* is close to Polish *Yiddish;* Austrian and Hungarian versions are close to Ukrainian.) In the newspapers and journals published in the United States, Lithuanian *Yiddish* predominates.

In the United States, Jewish immigrants, who were as noteworthy for their resourcefulness as for their rectitude, cheerfully borrowed English words, altered them to suit their own resilient requirements of case, mood, and inflection, arranged them in startling variations of traditional syntax ("A raise I should ask him for yet?", "Him you call a philosopher?"), negated negatives with breezy assurance ("I didn't agree and I didn't not agree"), and garnished Anglo-Saxon words with the heady spices of enthusiastic mispronunciation: *donton* (downtown), *izebox* (ice-box), *svit-hot* (sweetheart), Abraham Lincohen, Judge Vashington. Even as a child, I was enchanted by such blithe spirit.

Yiddish possesses an incomparable vocabulary of words to express shades of feeling; a juicy catalogue of praises, expletives, and curses; and a richer array of characterization-names than can be found, I think, in any other language on this globe: consider *nudnik, nebech, shlepper, shlump, shmendrik, shlemiel, tummler, kibitzer, gonif, shnook, momzer, bren, A.K., kochleffel, platke-macher, yenta, shtunk, yachne, alrightnik, bulbenik, plosher, boytchik, chachem, tsedoodelter*—each of which holds an honored place in these pages.

It has been said that *Yiddish* is the only tongue in the world in which you may speak three languages with three words: "Good *Shabbes*, madame." I make it five languages in five words: *"Guten erev Shabbes*, Madame Chairman." (In order: German, Hebrew, *Yiddish*, French, English.)

The purists who sniff at *Yiddish* for its exuberant adoption of words from other languages should pause to reflect on the fact that of all the languages in the world, English has, from its very origins, been the most energetic borrower and lifter. "No language can show a more varied assortment of foreign 'loan-words' and foreign-inspired locutions." So say the distinguished Sir William A. Craigie and H. Kurath.*

Yiddish possesses a rich and immensely attractive literature —stories, novels, poems, essays; but much of it has not been translated and that which has is deflavored in the process.

Before Hitler, 11,000,000 people are said to have understood *Yiddish*, whose newspapers, journals and books flourished in the United States, Latin and South America, Australia. An energetic and fecund *Yiddish* theater existed all over Europe, Russia and America, performing the classics of Russian, German, English—in translation—and plays in *Yiddish* and Hebrew.

The reader will, I trust, forgive me for quoting myself:

> One thing is certain: It was in *Yiddish* that was created the unique and radiant culture, a triumph over excruciating adversity, of the *shtetl*. And it is in *Yiddish* that that civilization—so poor, so rich, so realistic, so romantic, so frightened, so brave, so raucous, so sensitive, so anxious, so gallant, so pathetic, so proud, so cynical, so sentimental, so irreverent, so pious, so resigned, so passionate and honorable and majestic— is preserved.

For further data, see Appendices: Yiddish; Yiddish and Hebrew; Yiddish and German; Spelling of Yiddish Words in English.

"*Yiddish* incorporates the essence of a life which is distinctive and unlike any other." —ISRAEL ZANGWILL

"With this cosmopolitan jargon, made of the rags of every language, he [Morris Rosenfeld, poet] created a music like that of a lamenting harp." —LÉON BLOY

* In *Chambers' Encyclopedia*, Vol. V, p. 278. Appleton-Century-Crofts, 1954.

"To call *Yiddish* an offshoot of Middle High German with an admixture of Hebrew and Slavic [is entirely misleading] . . . the tone and spirit of [*Yiddish*] are as remote from German as the poetry of Burns is from the prose of Milton."

—MAURICE SAMUEL

I am sure this never happened, but how I wish it had: Yusseleh Shpeisel, reporter for the *Jewish Daily Forward*, dashed into a phone booth on Delancey Street, dropped his coins, dialed, barked "Managing Editor!" and cried, "Chief? Shpeisel. I've got a story that'll rip this town wide open! Hold the back page!"

Leonard and Manny, both lovers of *Yiddish*, were comparing its charms to those of other languages, and Lenny observed, "Do you know something remarkable? There's no word in *Yiddish* for 'disappointed'!"

"Really? I can't believe it. You *must* be wrong. Wait, I'll call my mother."

And to his mother, who barely spoke English, Manny said in fluent *Yiddish*, "*Mameleh*, listen. Suppose I told you I was coming to dinner on Friday. And suppose you worked all day Friday to make me the finest meal ever—from *challa* and chopped liver and *gefilte fish* and *knaydlach* soup down through the chicken and *kugel* and *tsimmes* and applesauce and two kinds *strudel* for dessert. And on Friday, two minutes before I'm supposed to arrive, I telephone and say that something so important has come up that I just can't come to *Shabbes* dinner! What would you say?"

"What I would *say?*" wailed his mother. "I'd say, '*Oy, bin ich* (am I) disappointed.' "

yideneh

Pronounced YID-*eh-neh*, to rhyme with "lid in a."

1. (Derogatory) An elderly Jewish woman. *Yideneh*, the feminine of *Yid* (pronounced YEED), is always used in a scornful sense—to mean gossipy, interfering, stupid. *Yideneh* is a synonym for *yachne* and *yenta*, and it is

almost impossible to draw exact distinctions between them.

2. Any gossipy, uncultivated, shallow person, whether male or female, Jew or gentile. In this usage *yideneh* is like "silly old woman," which in English is used for male fuddy-duddies.

See YENTA and YACHNE.

Two *yidenehs* were talking about their children. "My son?" said the first. "Who could ask for a better boy? Every Friday, rain or shine, he eats dinner at my house. Every summer, he makes me spend a month with him in Bayshore. Every winter he sends me to California!"

The second woman said, "I have a son, an angel, too. He's going to the most expensive psychiatrist in New York—every day, month in, month out, he goes there, and he talks, talks, talks each day for an hour. And do you know what he talks about, paying twenty-five dollars an hour? Me!"

The ladies were having tea. As the hostess passed the cookies around, she said, "So take a cookie."

"I already had five," sighed Mrs. Bogen.

"You had, excuse me, six, but take another: Who's counting?"

"My wife is so well-read," said Nudelman, "and goes to so many lectures, and is so up-to-the-minute on current events, that she can talk all night on any subject!"

"*My* wife," said Kugelman, "doesn't require a subject."

Yisroel
Yisrael

Pronounced *yis*-RO-*el* or *yis*-ROY-*el*, to rhyme with "this goal," or "miss royal." Hebrew: Israel. (In Hebrew the pronunciation is *yis-ra*-EL.)

1. The land of Israel. See ERETZ YISROEL.

2. The people of Israel, the Jews. In Jewish literature

Yisroel is used interchangeably with "Jew" and "Hebrew."

3. The name assumed by Jacob after he fought with the Angel of the Lord and subdued him (Genesis 32 : 29).

4. The collective name given the twelve tribes who left Egypt and settled in Canaan.

5. The name of the northern kingdom of Israel (933–722 B.C.) that was formed when the ten tribes seceded after the death of King Solomon.

6. The name of the state of Israel (*Medinat Yisroel*).

In Tel Aviv, one dark and ominous night, 06 Dash 4 looked up and down the street, darted into the apartment building, slipped the Colt into his outer pocket, knocked on the door of 2-D twice, paused, knocked once, paused, knocked twice again.

From inside, a voice inquired, "Who is it?"

"Horowitz?" whispered 06 Dash 4.

The door opened; a bald-headed little man in pajamas said, *"Sholem aleichem."*

"The oranges," murmured 06 Dash 4, "are ripe in Valencia."

"Ha-anh?" asked Horowitz.

"The oranges," repeated 06 Dash 4, more slowly, "are ripe . . . in Valencia!"

A light entered the eyes of the bald-headed little man. "Ahhh! I'm Horowitz the violin teacher. You want Horowitz the spy. Upstairs, 3-E."

Yizkor

Pronounced YISS-*kor*, to rhyme with "disk oar." Hebrew: "May (God) remember."

Memorial service for the dead, held in a synagogue.

Yizkor is the shortened, popular name for the memorial service, *Hazkarat Neshamot* (Remembrance of the Souls), which is recited on the eighth day of *Pesach*, second day of *Shevuoth*, eighth day of *Succoth*, and on *Yom Kippur*.

The service opens with a reading which emphasizes the

living more than the dead, asking that those in the congregation be permitted to "complete in peace the number of our years . . . [and] bear ourselves faithfully and blamelessly during the years of our pilgrimage." The deceased kinsfolk and parents, "the crown of our head and glory," are recalled: "Their desire was to train us in the good and righteous way, to teach us Thy statutes and commandments, and to instruct us to do justice and to love mercy. We beseech Thee, O Lord, grant us strength to be faithful to their charge while the breath of life is within us."

Private prayers are then recited in memory of close relatives, in which God is asked to "bind [his, her] soul in the bond of eternal life, in the company . . . of all the righteous. . . ." Those reciting *Yizkor* also pledge to perform "acts of charity and goodness" in honor of the deceased's memory.

The service continues with a congregational prayer *El Maleh Rachamim*, which petitions God to grant peace and eternal life to the departed souls. This concept is interpreted as the continuing communion of the generations, the idea that children and grandchildren are a man's life after death— for their memory keeps the beloved dead "alive."

Part of the *Yizkor* service is a memorial to the martyrs, of all generations, who died for the sanctification of God's name (See KIDDUSH HASHEM). Many synagogues recite a special memorial prayer for the six million victims of the Nazis. In Israel a *Yizkor* prayer is said for the men and women who fell while defending Israel in its War of Independence.

yold

Pronounced YULD, to rhyme with "culled." From Hebrew: *yeled:* "child," "boy."

A simpleton; a fool; a boob; a yokel; a harmless dolt; one whose gullibility and naiveté get him into trouble. "Oh, is he a *yold!*" "He fooled me completely; I acted like a real *yold.*"

See SHLEMIEL.

A *yold* is a man who walks into a friend's antique shop and calls out, "Hello! What's new?"

———————————

A *melamed*, discovering that he had left his comfortable slippers back in the house, sent a student after them with a note for his wife.

The note read: "Send me your slippers with this boy."

When the student asked why he had written "your" slippers, the *melamed* answered, "*Yold!* If I wrote 'my' slippers, she would read 'my' slippers and would send me her slippers. What could I do with her slippers? So I wrote 'your' slippers; she'll read 'your' slippers and send me mine."

Yom Kippur

> Pronounced *yum-*KIP*-per*, to rhyme with "hum dipper." Hebrew: "Day of Atonement." (Some scholars trace *kippur* to the Babylonian for "purge," "clean," "wipe off.")

> The last of the annual Ten Days of Penitence; one of the two high Holy Days of the Jewish calendar. *Yom Kippur* is, perhaps, the day which has the strongest hold on the Jewish conscience.

Rosh Hashanah marks the first day of the Ten Days of Penitence (*Yamin Noraim*). On that day, say the Orthodox, all men stand before God for judgment; but the Lord's decision is made on the *last* of the Ten Days—and that day is *Yom Kippur*.

The *Mishnah* instructs pious Jews not to eat or drink, wash or wear shoes on *Yom Kippur*. Maimonides gravely advises: "Every man should confess his sins, and turn away from them on *Yom Kippur*."

Because Jews hold that offenses against other men can only be forgiven by other men (and not by God!), on *Yom Kippur* eve, before *Kol Nidre*, Jews would hurry around to those they had offended or been unfriendly to during the year—and beg their pardon. Pious families would gather and ask forgiveness of each other for any slights, insensitivities, or injustices they might have committed against each other in the preceding year. Husband and wife would ask each other's forgiveness; children would ask forgiveness of each parent and of each other; each parent would ask each child for forgiveness! The custom is still observed in part or in whole, according to the degree of religious commitment. The idea is that each mortal should enter upon *Yom Kippur* with a clear conscience.

The synagogue service begins just before nightfall the evening before *Yom Kippur*. In the synagogue, the cantor stands before the Ark; on each side of him stands an honored worshiper from the congregation. Each carries a large scroll of the *Torah*. The cantor and two worshipers act as spokesmen for the congregation, standing before an invisible Judge and Tribunal; they recite:

> "By the authority of the Court on high, and by the authority of the Court below, by the permission of the Lord, blessed be He, and by the permission of this sacred congregation, we declare it lawful to pray with those who have transgressed."

This is thrice repeated; then the cantor begins to intone *Kol Nidre*.

Prayers on *Yom Kippur* continue, virtually without interruption, from morning until after sunset. Since purity of conscience is the *leitmotif* of the day, white predominates. The curtain of the Ark and the *Torah* coverings are white (they may be of varied colors during the year). The rabbi and cantor wear white robes; many men in the congregation wear white skullcaps (*yarmulkahs*), instead of the traditional black.

The primary feature of *Yom Kippur* is the Confession, repeated several times during the day. It involves a cataloguing of no fewer than fifty-six categories of sin. Tradition-observing Jews repeat the formula: "For the sin we have committed before Thee by [stating one of the fifty-six varieties], O God of forgiveness, forgive us, pardon us, grant us remission," and beat their breasts.

It is interesting to note that the confession of guilt is recited as a collective "we," not as an individual "I." On *Yom Kippur*, Jews "share" each other's transgressions—plus general responsibility for the misdeeds and shortcomings of mankind. The ecumenical spirit is not new to Jews.

The morning reading from the Prophets teaches the kind of repentance God seeks of man (Isaiah 57 : 14–58 : 14):

> . . . Is not this the fast that I have chosen?
> To loose the bands of wickedness,
> To undo the heavy burdens,
> And to let the oppressed go free,
> And that ye break every yoke?
> Is it not to deal thy bread to the hungry
> And that thou bring the poor that are cast out
> to thy house?
> When thou seest the naked, that thou cover
> him;
> And that thou hide not thyself from thine
> own flesh?

During the afternoon, the reading is the Book of Jonah, whose theme is God's clemency toward those who truly repent.

The liturgical readings, which describe the atonement ritual as it was practiced in the ancient Temple, hold a prominent place in the *Yom Kippur* service. When the cantor describes how the High Priest would pronounce, on this one occasion during the entire year, The Ineffable Name of God, he follows the ancient practice, bowing and prostrating himself, and many of the pious join him.

As the long day of fasting, prayer, inner searchings and new resolve draws to a close, the *Ne'ilah* service is held. This service begins the moment the setting sun is level with the treetops; and it is timed to end with the appearance of the first stars. The congregation makes one last profession of repentance, and one last request for forgiveness.

> Lord, though every power be Thine
> And every deed tremendous,
> Now, when heaven's gates are closing,
> Let Thy grace defend us.

Yom Kippur ends with the cantor proclaiming in a loud voice: "Hear, O Israel, the Lord is our God, the Lord is One," followed by a thrice repeated "Blessed be the Name of Him whose glorious kingdom endures forever." (These are the words with which the worshipers responded when the High Priest pronounced God's Name in the Temple.) Then he repeats seven times, "The Lord, He is God." These are the statements a pious Jew is expected to utter at the moment of his death; they have indeed been the last words of many martyrs.

Yom Kippur ends with the call of the *shofar*.

For further information, see Appendix: Yom Kippur.

Yom Kippur is sometimes called "Instant Lent."

Belinsky could scarcely believe his eyes: There, on the Day of Atonement, at a table right in the window of the Sea King Restaurant, sat his old friend, Herman Hochshuler—eating oysters!

Into the Sea King dashed Belinsky. "Herman! *Gottenyu!* Eating?! Today?! And *oysters?!!*"

"So?" shrugged blasé Hochshuler. "Isn't there an 'r' in *'Yom Kippur?'* "

yontif
yontiff
yom tov
yontifdik (adjective)
yontifdig

Pronounced YUN-*tiff* in Yiddish, to rhyme with "bun miff." From Hebrew: *yom:* "day"; *tov:* "good."

1. Holiday. "The post office is closed; it's *yontif.*" (Third-generation Jews would say: "a *yontif.*") "A good *yontif* to you!" "Happy *yontif!*"
2. A celebration, a festivity. "I felt all *yontifdik* that day."

Several odd facts about *yontif:*

The two Hebrew words *yom tov* were joined to make a

Yiddish word, even though there already was a Hebrew word for holiday: *chag*.

To say "Good *yontif!*" would seem redundant, like "a good good-day," except that *yontif* has been given its own meaning: "holiday."

In Israel, people use the Hebrew phraseology: *chag same-yach:* "Happy holiday."

———————

A denizen of Flatbush, having seen the Pope in one of the large, public, papal audiences, felt obliged to send His Holiness a Christmas greeting. It ran: "Good *yontif,* Pontiff."

Yortzeit
Yahrzeit

> Pronounced either YAWR-*tzite*, to rhyme with "court site," or YAR-*tzite*, to rhyme with "dart site." The first pronunciation is Yiddish, the second German. *Yahrzeit* is, of course, German: "year's time," or "anniversary."

> The anniversary of someone's death.

Many observances are incumbent on religious Jews to commemorate the death of someone in the family. (See KADDISH and YIZKOR.)

On the annual anniversary, a memorial candle or lamp is lighted in the home, and another in the synagogue, where it burns from sunset to sunset. A burning light is connected with the idea of immortality—perhaps as suggested in Proverbs 20 : 27: "The spirit of man is the candle of the Lord . . ."

Orthodox Jews fast all day at *Yortzeit*.

The *Yortzeit* ceremony, by the way, is the one religious ritual of Jews that has no Hebrew name (although *Yom hashana* means "day of the year.")

The idea of an annual prayer for the dead probably was adopted when the Jews were in Persia. The custom of lighting a candle for the dead may come from that proverb in Proverbs that compares the soul of man to a candle; it may also have come about after the Christians spread the ceremony so widely.

zaddik

See TZADDIK.

zaftig

Pronounced ZOFF-*tig*, to rhyme with "boff wig." From German: "juicy."

1. Juicy. "What a *zaftig* plum."
2. Provocative, seminal, germinal. "The book is full of *zaftig* ideas."
3. Plump, buxom, well-rounded (of a female). This is the most frequent American usage.

Zaftig describes in one word what it takes two hands, outlining an hourglass figure, to do.

Two *zaftig* matrons talking:
  "I think women like us should take a greater interest in

politics. . . . Tell me, what do you think of the Common Market?"

"I still prefer the A & P."

zayde
zeyde

Pronounced ZAY-*deh,* to rhyme with "fade a." Probably of Slavic origin.

1. Grandfather. "My *bubbeh* and *zayde* came to visit yesterday."
2. An old man. You may say to any old Jew, "How are you, *zayde?*" just as a Frenchman or Chinese will affectionately greet an old man who is not his grandfather.

In Israel, an American visitor saw an elderly Jew praying, tears simply pouring down his face.

The American, who could not bear the old man's wailing, asked, "*Zayde* . . . please . . . why are you weeping so bitterly?"

"Because—I want to be with my people!" sobbed the old man.

"But you *are,* in Israel, the Promised Land."

"I mean with my people in Miami!" said the *zayde.*

zchuss

Pronounced z-KHUSS. From Hebrew: "the legal right in possession."

1. *Originally:* A legal right by virtue of possession. An heir may claim a *zchuss* in an estate.
2. A man's right to, or claim upon, reward for special deeds or *mitzvas.* "His *zchuss* justifies such luck."
3. The special consideration a man may acquire because of his ancestry. "He may not be worthy, but he has the *zchuss* of his ancestors." "Judge every man on the side of *zchuss,*" says the *Talmud;* which means "give a man

the likelihood that he is right before condemning him"—
that is, when judging give the benefit of doubt, with a
kindly *zchuss*.

An excellent example of *zchuss*:

As the rabbi walked home from the synagogue on *Tisha
Bov*, lost in sorrowful thoughts, he encountered a member of
his congregation happily chewing away on a chicken.

The rabbi, shocked, exclaimed, "Have you forgotten that
today is *Tisha Bov?*"

"Not at all."

"Then you must be sick. I suppose the doctor forbade you
to fast?"

"Oh, no, rabbi. I'm not sick. I feel fine."

The rabbi promptly raised his eyes to Heaven: "Oh Lord,
see how pious are Israel's children. This man would rather
admit his sins than tell a falsehood!"

zetz

Pronounced as spelled; rhymes with "gets." From German: [*zurück*] *setzung*, literally, "a setting back."

A strong blow or punch.

Note that *zetz* is purely descriptive, and has no emotional
overtones, as has *chmallyeh*.

"He gave me a *zetz* I'll never forget!"

zhlub
zhlob

Pronounced ZHLUB or ZHLAWB, to rhyme with "rub" or
"daub." From Slavic: *zhlob*, "coarse fellow."

1. An insensitive, ill-mannered person. "He acts like a
zhlub, that *zhlub*."
2. A clumsy, gauche, graceless person. "Vassar-Shmas-
sar, the girl's still a *zhlub*."

3. An oaf, a yokel, a bumpkin. "What can you expect from such a *zhlub?*"

A Jew came running into a railway station, the perspiration pouring down his face, panting and crying, "Stop, train, stop!"

A *zhlub* said, "What's the matter?"

"I missed my train!" the man exclaimed. "By twenty measly seconds!"

"The way you're carrying on," said the *zhlub*, "one would think you had missed it by an hour!"

See also KLUTZ, BULVON, GRAUB.

Zion
Tziyon

Pronounced TZEE-*yone*, to rhyme with "see bone." Hebrew: *Zion*.

The land of Israel; Jerusalem.

Since the first exile of the Jews to Babylonia, *Zion* has been synonymous with the idea of a reunited Jewish people in their own, original homeland. "By the rivers of Babylon, there we sat down, yea, we wept when we remembered *Zion*." (Psalm 137.)

Wherever they have lived, traditional Jews have turned in the direction of *Zion* when they prayed. The great Hebrew poet of the Middle Ages, Judah ha-Levi, who was also a physician and a philosopher, wrote:

My heart is in the East
But I am in the farthest West,
How then can I taste what I eat,
And how can food to me be sweet?

Pious Jews would seek to be buried in *Zion*, and it became customary to bring a small sack of earth from the Holy Land to be placed in one's coffin, to provide a symbolic burial, at least, in the soil of *Zion*.

Chaim Weizmann, who later became the first President of Israel, was an ardent Zionist. As an illustrious scientist, he had access to many important European personages. One day he visited Paul Ehrlich, the discoverer of "606," a drug used in the treatment of syphilis. Weizmann sought to convince Ehrlich of the importance of the Zionist cause, and to enlist his support. He spoke earnestly and at great length, until Ehrlich broke in, "You know, Dr. Weizmann, hundreds of people come to see me each week. I never give them more than five minutes each. You have already taken up forty-five minutes of my time!"

"The difference, Dr. Ehrlich," replied Weizmann, "is that they come to get an injection—and I, to give you one."

Zohar

> Pronounced zoH-*harr*, to rhyme with "go far." From *Sefer ha Zohar*, or "Book of Splendor." The most important book of the cabalistic movement, probably written in the thirteenth century.

The most influential book in the literature of the cabala is the volume called the *Zohar*, believed to have been written/assembled by the Spanish rabbi Moses or Moshe de Leon—who deliberately attributed the work to a second-century rabbi, Simeon ben Yohai.

The *Zohar* is an utterly fantastic compendium of superstitions, mysticism, folklore, and abracadabra used to reveal supposedly hidden meanings in the Bible. It is a hodgepodge of abstruse codes, dreams, symbols; a cryptic excursion into demonology (and angelology); it explains ways of exorcising devils; it delves into the transmigration of human souls; it is steeped in supernaturalism and astrology. The *Zohar* is especially beholden to a "science of numbers" that endows numbers with special meanings and powers in a method called *gematria* (see Appendix); e.g., a numerical value is assigned to each Hebrew letter, then a text from the Bible is analyzed, the text arranged in every conceivable pattern—vertically, backwards, diagonally, upside down, in a triangle shape, as a hexagon, a palindrome, an acronym, an acrostic, etc., etc.

One name—of a prophet, say—may be arranged in all the possible permutations of its separate letters.

The *Zohar* also contains some wonderful stories, ethical pronouncements, and moving prayers. The book exerted a significant influence on the religious thought of large groups of Jews, particularly the *Chasidim*. The rabbis often warned the laity not to court mental danger by too-deep immersion in the *Zohar*'s cosmological mumbo-jumbo—and I can only agree with them.*

---

* For an interesting exploration of the influence of cabalism, the *Zohar*, and *gematria* on Christian mysticism, see Richard Cavendish, *The Black Arts*, Putnam, 1967.

One name—of a prophet, say—may be arranged in all the possible permutations of its separate letters.

The Zohar also contains some wonderful stories, ethical pronouncements, and moving prayers. The book exerted a significant influence on the religious thought of large groups of Jews, particularly the Chasidim. The rabbis often warned the laity not to court mental danger by too-deep immersion in the Zohar's cosmological mumbo-jumbo—and I can only agree with them.*

*For an interesting exploration of the influence of cabalism, the Zohar, and gematria on Christian mysticism, see Richard Cavendish, The Black Arts, Putnam, 1967.

Appendices

Contents

Anointing

Long before the Jews appear on the scene of history, anointing (which means applying ointment to) was endowed with mirific powers; "sacred" stones were anointed with "holy" perfumed oils; so were the furnishings in pagan tabernacles. Priests were anointed; and a king, having been anointed, thereby partook of the charismatic.

Anointing, as a sacerdotal rite, was widely used in Canaan, where it was adopted by the ancient Israelites.

The title, *Mashiach YHVH*, "the anointed of Yahweh," itself indicates the supernatural properties allegedly conferred in the ceremony of anointment.

The Jews made a distinction between ordinary cosmetic anointment of the body (*sukh*) and the pouring of sacred oil, as a consecration rite (*mashah*), on the head of a priest or king.

A guest was often honored by anointing his head—or feet.

The first anointed king mentioned in the Bible is Saul.

Except for one phrase in the Book of Esther, where "oil of

461

myrrh" is mentioned, all (over 200) scriptural references to anointing seem to mean olive oil.*

Ashkenazim and Sephardim in the United States

Until the fourth decade of the eighteenth century, the *Sephardim* (from England, Holland, the West Indies) were the dominant Jewish group in the United States. The *Ashkenazim* began to arrive, from central and eastern Europe, after 1740 or so.

There was no significant conflict in the New World between Sephardic and Ashkenazic Jews, as there clearly was, a century later, between German and Polish/Russian Jews. The *Ashkenazim* adopted some Sephardic rituals with no difficulty, and marriages between Ashkenazic and Sephardic Jews were not uncommon.

All this was markedly different from the hostility that came to characterize the feelings among German Jews in the United States to East European Jewry. To the prosperous, Americanized, bourgeois German Jews, the new immigrants—poor, gaunt, bearded, ear-locked, black-hatted, dressed in long black caftans—looked like "medieval apparitions." To the *Deutsche Yehudim* (German Jews), the new *Ashkenazim* were religious fanatics or—doubly puzzling—"agitators," union organizers, socialists, radicals. And the German Jews loathed Yiddish, which they thought a vulgar corruption of their own language.

Stephen Birmingham's lively *Our Crowd* (Harper and Row, 1967) contains many revealing anecdotes and pungent comments, by descendants of the Teutonic patricians, about the German Jews' strong sense of responsibility—and ambivalence—toward their poorer, less worldly coreligionists.

For more scholarly explorations of Ashkenazic-Sephardic tensions, see Jacob Rader Marcus' *Early American Jewry*, Vol. II, Philadelphia, 1951, 1953, pp. 390 ff.; Nathan Glazer's perceptive "Some Characteristics of American Jews," in *The Jews: Their History, Culture and Religion*, Vol. II, edited by

---

* See "Anointing" in *The Jewish Encyclopedia*, Funk and Wagnalls, 1901–1906, Vol. I, and the *Dictionary of the Bible*, edited by James Hastings, Scribners, 1963, p. 710.

Louis Finkelstein, Harper, 1960, pp. 1694–1735, and Glazer's invaluable *American Judaism*, University of Chicago, 1965.

Bar Kochba and Akiba

Surprisingly little is known of the life of the great Bar Kochba ("son of the star"), Simon ben Cozeba, also known as Barcocheba, Bar-Cochab and Bar Kokba, the last being the name you will find in Christian accounts. (Roman histories apparently never mentioned him.) Bar Kochba was the military leader of the revolt against the Romans in 132 A.D. (Trajan had crushed a rebellion in 113 A.D., in a three-year war.) Bar Kochba—a self-willed and irascible leader—was hailed as a messiah. Letters from Bar Kochba were recently discovered near the Dead Sea.

The revered scholar-saint, Rabbi Akiba (also spelled Akiva), supported Bar Kochba—whom most rabbis and the Sanhedrin regarded with some distaste. Rabbinical sources called him Bar Coziba, which means "son of deceit"! (Bar Kochba was so irreverent as once to have cried, "O Lord, don't help us—and don't spoil it for us!") And the great Akiba, head teacher of a rabbinical academy where he is said to have had some 24,000 pupils, supported Bar Kochba's claim to being the Messiah, descended from King David. Both Akiba and Bar Kochba called the Jews to arms against Rome. Akiba acted as Bar Kochba's sword-bearer.

It took the Emperor Hadrian and his ablest general, Julius Severus, three long, brutal, bloody years to defeat the greatly outnumbered Jews—580,000 of whom were casualties! The rest were sold into slavery.

Bar Kochba was slain at Bethar in the year 135. Akiba was captured, flayed alive with a cruelty exceptional even for those dreadful times, and died with singular composure:

> Akiba was found guilty and condemned to death. Still attended by his faithful Joshua, he retained his courage and his strength of mind until the very end. The popular story tells that the Romans killed him by tearing his flesh from his living body. As he lay in unspeakable agony, he suddenly noticed the first streaks of dawn breaking over the eastern hills. It was the

hour when the Law requires each Jew to pronounce the *Shema*. Oblivious to his surroundings, Akiba intoned in a loud, steady voice the forbidden words of his faith, "Hear, O Israel, the Lord is our God, the Lord is One. And thou shalt love the Lord thy God with all thine heart, and with all thy soul, and with all thy might."

Rufus, the Roman general, who superintended the horrible execution, cried out: "Are you a wizard or are you utterly insensible to pain?"

"I am neither," replied the martyr, "but all my life I have been waiting for the moment when I might truly fulfill this commandment. I have always loved the Lord with all my might, and with all my heart; now I know that I love him with all my life." And, repeating the verse again, he died as he reached the words, "The Lord is One."

The scene, indelibly impressed on the eyes of Joshua ha-Garsi, became part of Jewish tradition. The association of the *Shema* with the great martyr's death made its recitation a death-bed affirmation of the faith, instead of a repetition of select verses: and to this day the pious Jew hopes that when his time comes he may be sufficiently conscious to declare the Unity of his God, echoing with his last breath the words which found their supreme illustration in Akiba's martyrdom.*

Also see Appendix entry, False Messiahs.

Bible: Notes

The oldest part of the Bible (that is, the part written down first) may be the Book of Amos, which is dated by scholars around 750 B.C. The Pentateuch was probably completed in the fifth century B.C. Oral transmission clearly preceded the dates given above. "The earliest writings probably consisted of ballads, such as the Song of Deborah (c. 1200 B.C.), law

* Louis Finkelstein, *Akiba*, The Jewish Publication Society, Philadelphia; World Publishing Co., 1962, pp. 276–277.

codes . . . and epic narratives such as the Joseph saga in Genesis."*

Most of the Old Testament was written in Hebrew, without vowel points or marks. Some parts were written in Aramaic—which became the everyday language of the Jews after their Exile. (Hebrew was reserved for the language of the Law.)

Many of the incidents recounted in Genesis, and in the writings of the Prophets, can be traced back to much earlier customs and traditions.

The story of the Flood, for instance, appears to be a later version of the account in a Babylonian epic, the *Gilgamesh*—a tale, dating back to around 2000 B.C., that was probably based on the annual floods in the Euphrates valley. It impresses me that in the Sumerian–Babylonian version, too, an Ark is constructed, the righteous are spared, birds are dispatched from the vessel to the shore, etc. (The *Gilgamesh*, said to be the earliest written epic yet discovered, is a reconstruction of cuneiforms on twelve clay tablets found in Mesopotamia.)

The Tower of Babel legend is found, in an earlier version, in the story of the *ziggurat*, a "stepped" temple, of Babylon.

God's destruction of Leviathan (Psalm 74) seems to have its roots in an earlier myth of the Canaanites—myth reconstructed from newly discovered clay tablets excavated in North Syria.

Isaiah's description of the Leviathan (27 : 1) as "the piercing serpent . . . the crooked serpent" repeats the exact words of an earlier text.

See Professor T. H. Gaster, *Customs and Folkways of Jewish Life* (William Sloane, 1955), for other striking, not to say startling, parallelisms. Gaster is considered "extreme" by traditionalists.

For an informative history of the Bible itself, see William Albright's excellent *The Biblical Period from Abraham to Ezra* (Harper, paperback, 1963); John Bright's *A History of Israel* (Westminster, 1959); the entry "Bible" in *Dictionary of the Bible*, edited by James Hastings (Scribners, 1963), pp.

---

* *Dictionary of the Bible*, edited by James Hastings, Scribners, 1963, pp. 102–105.

102–105; Otto Eissfeldt, *The Old Testament* (Harper & Row, 1965), and *The Old Testament and Modern Study*, edited by H. H. Rowley (Oxford, 1951).

Cabala

God was known to the cabalists as *En Sof* (Infinite One); His existence was made known through ten *sefirot* or "divine radiations": Crown, Wisdom, Intelligence, Mercy, Judgment or Strength, Beauty, Victory, Glory, Foundation, and Kingdom.

Some cabalists followed the example of Christian flagellants and mortified the flesh; others set themselves prodigious tasks of fasting, penitence, prayer, and fearsome ordeals of suffering—all to atone for evil, purge the soul of sin, redeem the spirit or break the dread Devil's awful hold.

The world's leading authority on cabala and Jewish mysticism is Professor Gershom G. Scholem; see his renowned *Major Trends in Jewish Mysticism* (Schocken, 1961) and *On the Kabbalah and Its Symbolism* (Schocken, 1965). An earlier (1929) and quainter work is Arthur E. Waite, *The Holy Kabbalah: A Study of the Secret Tradition in Israel* (University Books, reprint, 1960). Christian D. Ginsburg, who surely bore an odd combination of names, has written a learned analysis and history in *The Kaballah: Its Doctrines, Development and Literature* (Routledge and Kegan Paul, London, 1920).

Calendar

To find the Hebrew year, add 3,761 to the present date—but remember, the Hebrew calendar year began, and begins, in September or early October.

Back around the year 360 of the Christian era, Hillel the Second established the Hebrew calendar, according to which the year is divided into 13 months, alternately 30 and 29 days in length. To make the Hebrew calendar jibe with the solar system, a month is added every 3 years—7 months in 19 years.

The year starts on the first day of the month called *Tishri*—the day the new moon appears, nearest to the autumnal equinox. This date, which is the first day of *Rosh Hashanah*, shifts, from time to time, according to ancient regulations: e.g., New Year's Day must not fall on a Friday or a Sunday, because that makes two consecutive days on which certain tasks may not be performed, which would create problems; for example, no Jew may be left unburied for two days and the toil of burying may not be done on *Shabbes;* it may not fall on a Wednesday, either, because that might cause *Yom Kippur* to fall on a Friday.

The months, with their Gregorian Calendar equivalents, are:

Tishri	September–October
Heshvan	October–November
Kislev	November–December
Tebet	December–January
Shebat	January–February
Adar	February–March
Veadar	Intercalary month
Nisan	March–April
Iyar	April–May
Sivan	May–June
Tammuz	June–July
Ab	July–August
Elul	August–September

Orthodox Jews date the year 1 as the time when God, according to the Bible, created the world—3,760 years before the beginning of the Christian era. This naive chronology had no benefit of science, I think it safe to say. But the faithful explain that the numbers used are not to be taken literally: "A day in the mind of God is like a millennium in the reckoning of man," one rabbi told me. "The first seven 'days' of Genesis," said another Orthodox scholar, "were not days as we use the word or measure time: they were millennia. That is why I find no contradiction between *Torah* and modern scientific findings."

Symbols and metaphor certainly permit of variant interpretations, and certain kinds of scholarship, far from heightening clarity, may only add complexity to ambiguity.

Cantors

Jews thought vocal music a divine art that could express true religious rapture, touch the soul, effect a special *rapport* between man and the holy.

The use of instruments in synagogues was discontinued after the destruction of the Temple (where harp, cymbal and horn *had* been used to accompany the worshipers).

Among Jews, prayers were directed by a precentor, or "master of prayer," who stood before the Holy Ark, draped in his prayer shawl, intoning the liturgy as the "advocate of the congregation" *(shaliach tzibbur)*.

As Catholic and Protestant religious services grew more and more melodious, to say nothing of opulent, Jewish worshipers, too, sought musical enrichment, and toward the end of the Renaissance, in a quite radical departure from tradition, congregations began to employ professional cantors, men with singing talent. (Few congregations could afford to pay them very much, so cantors also taught Hebrew to the young; some even served as sextons.)

In Italy, where Jewish musicians headed important music schools, the traditional singsong of the Middle East was embroidered with the lush melodic interplay of baroque Italian music.

One famous *chazzan*, Salomone Rossi of Mantua, advocated the introduction of a choir and soloists and an organ into synagogue services. This simply scandalized the Orthodox. (Rossi wrote many lovely hymns for religious services.)

By the middle of the eighteenth century you could hear music (a choir, an organ) in the synagogues of well-to-do congregations across Europe—in England, France, Germany, Italy, but *not* in eastern Europe, where the idea was anathema to the pietists.

In time, a special *bravura* style of rendering the prayers, with remarkable falsetto effects, won over even the fundamentalists of Poland.

The cantors, of course, loved long, solo recitatives, and were important in altering the monotonous singsong of services that were part-praying, part-mumbling, part-keening and much wailing, rather than singing.

Nathan Ausubel notes, in his article in *The Book of Jewish Knowledge* (Crown, 1964), that after Franz Liszt went to hear a famous cantor sing in Vienna he wrote: "Seldom were we so deeply stirred by emotion as on that evening, so shaken that our soul entirely surrendered to . . . participation in the service." (p. 94)

The cantors also served to spearhead a remarkable rebirth of music among East European Jews. Music offered one nearly magical way to "break out of the ghetto"——to have a career, to win fame and fortune, to travel, to become renowned and honored in an otherwise inhospitable Gentile world. Soon Russia, Poland, Germany, Hungary, Austria, Lithuania, Galicia, Rumania, produced an amazingly large and remarkably gifted stream of Jewish violinists, pianists, cellists, composers, conductors. In this century, of course, Jewish musicians have scored spectacular successes around the world. And in America, rare was the Jewish boy who was not hounded to play the fiddle, or the girl not *mutched* to play the piano.

Chanukah

The four sides of the *draydl* or *trendl*, the spin-toy used during Chanukah, were originally initialed *N, G, H, S*—for the German-Yiddish words *Nichts* (nothing), *Ganz* (all), *Halb* (half), and *Stell* (put). In time, the *N, G, H, S* were reinterpreted to be the first letters of the Hebrew "*Nes Gadol Hayah Sham*," meaning "a great miracle occurred there." The miracle referred both to the Maccabean victory and to a one-day supply of oil that somehow burned for eight days when the Temple was rededicated.

The pre-Biblical roots of some Jewish holidays and celebrations are interesting. Hermes, the Greek god, became the angel Hermesiel, leader of a heavenly choir; and he in turn may have become identified with David, "the sweet singer of Israel," who played his harp before the throne of God.

And where pagans used the symbol of the vine of Bacchus, Jews used the "vine of Israel." Traditionalists strongly object to such interpretations, regarding the Jewish symbols as quite different in content and meaning from all that preceded them.

For a study that is unpopular with some of the Orthodox and Conservative rabbis I consulted, but is nevertheless a careful and scholarly undertaking, see Theodor H. Gaster, *Customs and Folkways of Jewish Life* (William Sloane, 1955).

Circumcision

Among Jews, the baby boy to be circumcised is carried into the room where the circumcision is to be performed. One of the waiting men (the *sandek*, or godfather) receives the boy, and the males, standing, recite a Hebrew greeting: "Blessed be he that cometh."

The *sandek* seats himself on a chair known as the "Chair of Elijah." The baby is placed on the knees of the *sandek*, and a service begins. Prayers—before, during and after the circumcision—are pronounced.

After the circumcision, the *mohel* or a rabbi utters this prayer: "May the lad grow in vigor—of mind and of body— to a love of *Torah*, to the marriage canopy, and to a life of good works." A name is given to the baby. Then a blessing is offered over wine, a drop of which is placed on the baby's lips.

A celebration follows, favoring wine and sponge cake, which I think well named.

Circumcision is described as "the seal of God"—a seal in the flesh, as it were. (In the early days of Christianity, baptism was called "sealing.")

In Genesis 17 : 10, you may remember, the Lord says: "This is my covenant . . . every man child among you shall be circumcised." And Abraham, who was a very great man, circumcised himself.

The circumcision is held to signalize an obligation—to observe the Covenant between God and Israel, to live and exemplify the life of virtue, to obey, teach, and transmit God's law.

In a wider sense, circumcision imprints into a man's body a lifelong sign that Israel will be perpetuated through him—

that his seed, passing through the circumcised portal, will create children who will in turn be pledged to the Jews.

Down the ages, circumcision met with vicious repression: Antiochus Epiphanes made it punishable by death; Hadrian forbade circumcision (an edict contributing to the rebellion led by Bar Kochba); and a Visigoth monarch named Sisebut, which is a peculiar name for a king, ordered Jews to baptize, instead of circumcise, their sons. But circumcision remained one of the most unalterable practices among Jews everywhere.

Jewish Hellenists, eager to Grecianize themselves (and to pass muster in a gymnasium), used to undergo an operation to remove all signs of circumcision. The rabbis countered this ploy by emphasizing that the glans be laid bare through a firm pushing back of the skin during circumcision.

The Jews did not invent circumcision. Herodotus mentions the custom among ancient Egyptians, whose hieroglyphic sign for a phallus is a circumcised specimen.

The Syrians, Phoenicians, Ethiopians, practiced circumcision—as did (and do) many tribes around the world, in India, Africa, Oceania, Indonesia, the Philippines, Australia.

Among Muhammadans, of course, circumcision is universal: it is called "purification." (In Lahore, India, the ceremony is known as "wedding.")

Most Eskimos and American Indians circumcise the young male.

In some cultures, the women refuse sexual congress with an uncircumcised man.

But few peoples circumcise as *early* (the eighth day) as Jews do. In Africa, the rite usually occurs at puberty, or just before marriage. With other peoples, circumcision may be performed at the fourth, fifth, or even sixth or seventh year.

Among primitive peoples, circumcision is usually performed *en masse*, as part of an annual ritual or seasonal festival.

Genesis (17 : 25) tells us that Ishmael was circumcised at the age of thirteen. This led some (who apparently had not read Genesis 17 : 12) to conclude erroneously that to be Hebrews circumcision was a puberty rite, just as it is, say, among the Masai of Africa—who circumcise (if that's the

right word) the girls as well as the boys at this develop-
mental stage.

The medical and hygienic advantages of circumcision are
so widely known today that I need not expatiate upon them.
And circumcision has become so widespread in the United
States that it is no longer possible to distinguish Jews from
non-Jews in a locker room.

Even nonobserving Jewish families have their male young
circumcised, on or before the eighth day. I know of Jews who
never go to a temple or synagogue, who know no Hebrew,
understand no Yiddish, were not *Bar Mitzva*—but were
circumcised. I have done only casual research in this area.

Cochin (India) Jews

Most of the 1500 Jews of Cochin, on the Malabar coast of
South India, have emigrated to Israel, leaving a population of
only two hundred. The old community was established in
1523. It became divided into strict castes, after a historical
process of symbiosis with the Hindu world: "White" Jews,
descended from Syrian and Turkish immigrants, occupied the
peak of the pyramid of status; the other castes ranged in color
from light brown to mahogany to very dark brown, almost
black. Some native slaves were converted to Judaism. The
darkest-hued Jews seemed the most numerous and had seven
separate synagogues.

The Cochin Jews live devoutly, use the Sephardic liturgy,
and follow the Orthodox code, the *Shulchan Aruch*, with its
more than six hundred detailed prescriptions. All Cochin Jewish children learn to read Hebrew (girls included). Their
native language is Malayalam.

The men wear a *yarmulkah*—plus appended *payess*, and
nothing much else except the standard male garment of the
area: a loincloth. This strikes European and American Jews
as an odd way for a Jew to dress.

The *kosher* laws are observed in India—to the extent that
meat-rice-and-curry is not mixed with dairy forms of curry.

Dr. David Mandelbaum, on whose report of customs and
rituals I have relied above, observes that an Orthodox Jew

from the Bronx would find the Cochin synagogues exotic—at first, but "the devotion of the Cochin Jews to Jewish law and learning would soon make him feel at home."*

Crucifixion: Notes

The Jews never crucified anyone, nor ever demanded it of the political authorities; in all of the Old Testament, there is no case of a living person being crucified. The *Mishnah's* four forms of sanctioned execution do not include crucifixion.

The practice of crucifixion has been traced back to the Phoenicians, and was quite commonly used by the Romans to punish slaves, criminals, foreigners—but not Roman citizens. (That is why Paul was beheaded, not crucified, by the Romans.)

The Jews in ancient Palestine were most severely treated by the Romans; in Josephus (*History of the Jewish War*, Vol. II) you may read the sanguinary account of the crucifixion of 2,000 Jews by Varus (died 9 A.D.).

For an interesting and scholarly inquiry, see Solomon Zeitlin, *Who Crucified Jesus?* (Bloch Publishing Co., 1964). For a provocative and illuminating discussion, see Joel Carmichael, *The Death of Jesus* (Macmillan, 1962).

Dialects of the Jews

Yiddish is only one of many dialects created by Jews or adapted from other languages.

Judeo-Greek was spoken in Byzantium, under Christian rule. Some Greek Jews still write Greek using the Hebrew alphabet, in a Judeo-Greek that contains relatively few Hebrew words or phrases, and virtually no Yiddish.

Persian Jews speak Judeo-Persian—which takes different forms in Central Asia.

Jews in the Caucasian mountains, who date back to the

* See David G. Mandelbaum, "The Jewish Way of Life in Cochin," in *Jewish Social Studies*, Vol. 1, 1939, p. 424, quoted in *The Jews: Their History, Culture and Religion*, edited by Louis Finkelstein Harper, 1960, p. 1495.

time of the Second Temple, use a form of Farsi-Tat and have their own literature, rich in Hebraic, Aramaic and Biblical phrases.

The Jews of Spain wrote Spanish with the letters of the Hebrew alphabet; after they were driven out, in 1492, they brought this form to the Muhammadan countries where they found temporary asylum: Bulgaria, Greece, Turkey, North Africa. (See LADINO.)

In Italy, a Judeo-Latin vernacular arose that used Hebrew letters to write Italian (in prayer books and a translation of the Bible) because many Jews in Italy could not, or would not, decipher Latin letters, which were considered "monkish."

Many beautiful and priceless manuscripts and books, in various languages and dialects, may be seen in the great library of the Jewish Theological Seminary in New York, in the Bodleian collection at Oxford, etc.

Elijah

The prophet Elijah plays a leading and greatly beloved role in Jewish lore; it is Elijah who shall come just before the Messiah, and will blow his ram's horn to signal the Redemption and prepare the way for the Messiah.

According to the Bible, you may remember, Elijah never died: He was transported directly to heaven—in a chariot of fire, within a whirlwind.

Elijah became the most popular of seraphim among Jews: He was thought to be a special protector of the sick, the poor, the harassed, and was credited with all sorts of miracle-working powers and wondrous disguises.

Jews are still given to reserving a special, if symbolic, place in their ceremonials (the Passover *seder*, circumcision) for Elijah—and his ever-hoped-for and "imminent" appearance on earth.

See Louis Ginzberg's monumental *Legends of the Jews,* 7 volumes (Jewish Publication Society of America, Philadelphia, 1954).

For a dossier on Elijah and other angels, including the fallen, see Gustav Davidson's charming *A Dictionary of Angels* (Free Press, New York, 1967).

Essenes

The Essenes were a small Palestinian religious sect, numbering some 4,000 in Philo's time, active during the period of the Second Temple (built 538–515 B.C. and destroyed by the Romans in 70 A.D.).

The remarkable resemblances between the Judaism of the Essene sect and Christianity itself have been analyzed and elaborated by many scholars. Consider:

The Essenes believed in a divine Messiah, whom they referred to as "Teacher of Righteousness." He would preach humility, poverty, penitence. They called themselves "the elect of God." They initiated members via baptism. They called their community the "New Covenant." They observed a ritual identical with Communion, and seating arrangements identical with the Last Supper. And John the Baptist taught the Essene doctrine of baptism, i.e., a symbolic cleaning of the soul through immersion in water. They believed in the soul's immortality, but not in physical resurrection.

Essenism became a monastic sect—perhaps the first organized in the world of Mediterranean cultures. Many Essenes were celibate. The sect vanished after the Romans destroyed the Second Temple in Jerusalem.

For the similarities between the Essenes and Christianity, see Martin Larson's *Religions of the Occident* (Philosophical Library, 1959), Duncan Howlett's *The Essenes and Christianity* (Harper, 1957), and Volume II of Emil Schürer's *History of the Jewish People in the Time of Jesus Christ* (Edinburgh, 1890), pp. 188–218. A lively, if overly emotional, survey of historical data on the roots of Christian creed and history will be found in Nathan Ausubel's entry, "Jewish Origins of Christianity," pp. 100–111, *Book of Jewish Knowledge* (Crown, 1964). See also Gershom Scholem, *The Essenes/The Kaballah* (Routledge and Kegan Paul, London, 1956).

Evil Eye

Envy and the Evil Eye are closely linked in popular mythology, and as aspects of the lore of hoodoo, voodoo, "the hex."

The malignant forces of darkness are believed especially to

covet any beautiful, bright, talented child; hence, elaborate magical methods were enlisted by mothers in the effort to protect their beloved young. From this came the swift and automatic formula *"Kayn aynhoreh!"* ("[May] no Evil Eye [harm him!]") uttered by a Jewish mother immediately after anyone chanced to comment on her child's graces or virtues.

The Chinese, incidentally, seek to outwit the demons by loudly announcing that a pretty girl is ugly, or a bright lad stupid. And a well-educated Greek friend of mine periodically stuffs garlic into his pockets to ward off the *kalikantzaroi*, certain cloven-footed demons who are said to inhabit certain islands, on one of which he was born.

For more recondite forays into evil eye-ism, see Joshua Trachtenberg's *Jewish Magic and Superstition* (Jewish Publication Society, Philadelphia, 1961), Frederick T. Elworthy's *The Evil Eye* (London, 1895), and the crisp entry by Ludwig Blau in Volume V, p. 280, of the *Jewish Encyclopedia* (Funk and Wagnalls, 1901–1906). Evil eye-ism in stolid England is summarized by Edwin and Mona Radford in their *Encyclopedia of Superstitions* (Philosophical Library, 1949).

Falashas

The Falashas (the Ethiopic or Geez word for "emigrants") are some ten to fifteen thousand dark-skinned Jews in Ethiopia north of Lake Tana. Probably descended from converts to Judaism, they claim to be direct descendants of the Ten Tribes ejected from Palestine; romantic commentators think them descended from Solomon's son—by the Queen of Sheba.

The Falashas know no Hebrew. They know only the Old Testament (in Geez), and nothing of *Talmud*. They regard Moses' story as explicitly meant for them. Very strict in morals and literal in observance, they fast every Monday and Thursday, at every new moon, and on Passover. They worship in synagogues and observe the *Te-e-sa-sa Sanbat*, or laws of the Sabbath. They also practice rites that would make a European or American Jew's hair stand on end (an unchaste female, for instance, must leap into a roaring fire to purify herself; how long she remains there, I do not know). The

Falashas have Jewish monks, and believe in the evil shadow, rain doctors, assorted soothsayers and raisers of the dead.

For more about the Falashas' exotic ways and rites see Jacques Faitlovitch's *The Falashas*, Joseph Halevy's *Travels in Abyssinia*, H. A. Stern's *Wanderings Among the Falashas*, M. Flad's *The Falashas of Abyssinia*.

False Messiahs

I know of no single volume on this tantalizing subject, yet history is studded with stories of self-designated Messiahs— holy men, mystagogues, paranoidal visionaries genuinely convinced that they had received God's personal message, and outright charlatans. Pseudo-Messiahs clearly range from the sincere to the mad, the naive to the brazen.

I suppose that one difficulty the writer of a volume on fake Messiahs would encounter is criteria of definition—and choice: a seer revered by Tweedledum is ludicrous to Tweedledee. Men have tortured, enslaved, and slaughtered one another, performed the most monstrous outrages, perpetrated the most odious obscenities, all in the name of aberrations parading as revelations.

Messianic hopes, like hallucinatory visions, may be directly correlated to adversity, hunger, suffering, despair, and the obsessional-paranoidal quotient of any population at any time. Maimonides set down rules for the judging of allegations, prophecies, and "miracles" purporting to be messianic.

The fall of an empire—the Persian, the Byzantine, the Roman—always and understandably raised the Jews' desperate messianic hopes. I know of no better passage on this tragic theme than the résumé of Professor Hugh Trevor-Roper, who writes:

> . . . when Popes and Kings allied themselves with the blind prejudices of the Church and the mob, such patronage availed the Jews no more than the Moriscos of Spain or the Huguenots of France. Whither then were the persecuted remnant to turn for relief? Whither indeed but to that stock refuge of the oppressed: mysticism, the Messiah, the Millennium. As the de-

feated humanists of Spain sank into private ecstasies, as the *marabout* on his African dunghill promises a Mahdi to the dejected beduin, as the Anabaptists of the seventeenth century manipulated their Scriptural logarithms to hasten the Apocalypse, so also the Jews of the Dispersion deviated into mystical heresies, counted the days to the Millennium, or discovered the Messiah. He appeared to the persecuted Jews of the Yemen in the twelfth century; a Portuguese Jew announced him in Italy in the sixteenth century; and in the middle of the seventeenth, in those propitious days when the English millenarians had already pin-pointed the Second Coming and Manasseh ben Israel was reviving the hopes of his people, there arose in Turkey the most spectacular of all such Messiahs, Sabbatai Zevi of Izmir.*

Josephus, in his *Antiquities of the Jews,* cites the case of a Jew called "Judas of Galilee" who, in the year 6 A.D., led a rebellion against the Romans, claiming to be a Messiah come to deliver the Jews.

In 44 A.D. a gaudy character yclept Theudas led his bedazzled followers to the Jordan, where he promised to part the waters, as had his predecessor Moses at the Red Sea. There is no record that the ambitious Theudas parted a single liquid yard of that river, which is considerably narrower than the Red Sea. The iconoclastic Roman authorities terminated the post-Mosaic mission of Theudas, first by crucifying, then by beheading, him.

Around 58 or 59 A.D. one "Benjamin the Egyptian" managed to assemble twenty-five thousand or more followers, with whom he marched up to the Mount of Olives. Benjamin announced that he would now make the walls of Jerusalem tumble down, à la Joshua before Jericho, but an unimaginative Roman procurator broke up the historic meeting. Of Benjamin, "the Lord's anointed" (so he said), no more was ever heard.

Around 66 or 67 A.D., the inventive grandson of the "Judas of Galilee" cited above, one Menachem, announced that *he* was the *Mashiach* and, with men armed from and by a raid

* *Historical Essays,* Macmillan, London, 1963, pp. 148–149.

on the fortress of Masada, marched upon holy Jerusalem—
before reaching which, he was stopped by superior Roman
forces and disappeared from history's pages, at least those
possible to believe.

The immortal Simon Bar Kochba (or Kokba, or Cochba),
who led the great revolution of the Jews against Hadrian
from 132 to 135 A.D., was called the *Mashiach* by no less
than the most celebrated rabbinical figure of his time, Akiba.
Bar Kochba seems to have claimed to be *a* (if not "the")
Messiah. He is sometimes referred to as Simon, the Prince
of Israel. The rebellion he led was long, bloody, characterized
by phenomenal courage and perseverance. It took the Romans
three years to suppress it; the Jews lost 580,000 (!) men in
the fighting, to say nothing of thousands more—men, women,
children—who starved or died of one or another disease
brought on by the revolution. (In 1953 and 1960, letters
written by Bar Kochba were discovered by archaeologists in
Israel.)

In 431 A.D. there appeared on the island of Crete a new
Messiah, called Moses, who told his followers that he would
lead them to the Holy Land—right across the water from
Crete. Moses seems to have disappeared (not under or over
the waters) after many of his gullible disciples were drowned,
in both their faith and the Mediterranean.

In the eighth century, pseudo-Messiahs sprouted in many
places; examples are the brazen Abu Issa al-Isfahani, in
Persia; one Severus, or Serene, which I do not doubt, in
Syria; and an obscure Yudghan in Hamadan, a city in western
Persia.

In the ninth century, an enthusiastic Eldad Ha-Dani an-
nounced that the lost 10 tribes of Israel had been discovered:
The glorious Messianic Age would now commence. Exit
Eldad Ha-Dani.

The Crusades, which spelled repeated horrors to thousands
of powerless and innocent Jews, saw a predictable uprise in
the market for Messiahs: the singular David Alroy of
Mesopotamia (about 1160 A.D.) and *Mashiachs* of a lesser
luminosity who flourished in Persia, Morocco, Spain, and
France.

Alroy, whose real name was Menahim ben Solomon, was a
leader of considerable intellectual stature. He was killed by

assassins sometime between 1135 and 1160. *The Standard Jewish Encyclopedia,* edited by Cecil Roth (Doubleday, 1966), states that Benjamin Disraeli's romantic novel, *The Wondrous Tale of David Alroy,* is "unhistorical."

In 1295, a *Mashiach* appeared in Ávila, Spain. Born Nissim ben Abraham, he announced he would inaugurate the Redemption on the last day of the month of Tammuz. Mass fastings promptly began, worldly possessions were given away, prayers and ecstasies accompanied the impatient wait for the commencement of the kingdom of God. Alas, poor Jews. . . .

A Spanish Jew named Avrum (Abraham) Abulafia (1240–91), who had steeped himself in cabalistic writings and assorted abracadabra, went on a trip to the Holy Land, where he had a vision: A voice told him to hasten home and announce himself to be a prophet. Later, the voice told him to convert no less than Pope Nicholas III! This, believe it or not, he set about attempting. Abulafia actually obtained an audience with the Pope who, discovering what the astounding Spanish Jew was up to, promptly condemned him to be burned at the stake. Abulafia escaped this incendiary fate because Nicholas III died a few days after issuing his awesome order. So Abulafia went on to Sicily, where the Voice now told him he was the Messiah long promised to the Jews. So he said, so he said. . . . Farewell, Abulafia.

A most remarkable, brave (or presumptuous) genius of a charlatan was one David Reuveni, or Reubeni, a dwarf, who in the year 1524 announced in Venice that he was the brother of the King of one of the Lost Tribes, the Tribe of Reuben. Dwarf David Reuveni sought to win the Pope's support for a joint crusade against the Turks, who were marching into Europe. The dwarf disclosed that his "brother" commanded thousands of splendid Jewish soldiers *behind* the Turkish lines, a most happy place to be. Pope Clement VII did grant little Reuveni an audience; and the papal astrologers not only approved the dwarf's credentials, whatever they could be, but even certified his prophecies of a fraternal military victory.

The Pope then communicated with the King of Portugal—and David Reuveni sailed for Portugal, under a Jewish flag! . . . The *Marranos* in Portugal hailed Reuveni as the Messiah —and one Diego Pires (1500–1532) became so entranced by Reuveni that he underwent circumcision and changed his name to Solomon Molko or Molcho, under which sobriquet you may encounter him in encyclopedias. Molko joined Reuveni in Italy, then fled to the Holy Land to escape the Italian Inquisition, and in time returned to announce the happy tidings that *he* was the Messiah. The Pope exempted him from the mounting umbrage of the Holy Inquisition.

Reuveni and Molko together went to Charles V, Emperor of the Holy Roman Empire, to ask for support for the apocryphal Jewish legions in Arabia. Charles turned both of them over to the Inquisition.

Molko refused a chance to recant and, apparently thinking his sacrifice would redeem mankind, was burned at the stake in Mantua. The year was 1532. Reuveni was shipped off to Spain and ended in an *auto da fé*. (His travel diary is in the Bodleian Library, Oxford.)

At the beginning of the sixteenth century, one Asher Lammlein (or Lemmlin) proclaimed himself Elijah, herald of the *Mashiach*. . . . Some Jews thought that Lemmlin was actually the Messiah himself, and not merely Elijah, but was too noble to admit it. Many Jews were "baptized" in purification ceremonies to hasten the Messiah's arrival. Exit Lammlein or Lemmlin.

The most spectacular of fake Messiahs, of course, was Sabbatai or Shabbatai Zvi (1626–1676), who deservedly enjoys an appendix entry all to himself later in this volume. He came from Smyrna.

The flamboyant, thoroughly detestable Jacob Frank (1726–1791) attacked rabbis and Talmudists, and deplored the Jews' devotion to holy books and book learning; Jews should become warriors, he cried, and Israel a military nation. "The Resurrection will be by the sword," said Frank. So far, so good. But the odious Frank, a traveling salesman by trade, was a sensualist by inclination. He became a member of a Sabbatean sect, then issued a novel ukase: Redemption was to be achieved through *im*purity. The road to heaven ran through the boudoir. It is said that his religious sessions were small saturnalia and featured quite orgiastic rites.

In Poland, Frank claimed to be Sabbatai Zvi—reincarnated. Indeed, he altered the personnel of the Trinity to include himself. The audacious Frank lived in great splendor off the donations of his gullible followers, and soon ennobled himself —or at least called himself "Baron."

The rabbis anathematized Frank for licentious behavior, to say nothing of blasphemy and heresy; and the Church in time jailed Frank (who had been converted, along with many of his followers) because of his startling and sacrilegious alteration of the doctrine of the Trinity. After thirteen years in prison, Frank was freed (by the Russians).

He now journeyed to Vienna, where he became a great society favorite. He was known as "The Man with the Gospel," and favorably regarded by the Empress herself, Maria Theresa. Frank's followers again showered funds on him, and they paraded around in Uhlan uniforms, on splendid steeds, and carried lances and pennants adorned with various mystic symbols.

After Jacob Frank's unmessianic death in 1791, his energetic daughter Eve carried on Daddy's fakery. She was known as "the Holy Lady." Apparently as lustful as her father had been, little Eve, like the Byzantine Empress Theodosia, joined venery with hocus-pocus—a combination certain to appeal to many mortals.

The eighteenth century also records false Messiahs such as Löbele Prossnitz, Judah Hasid, and Mordecai Mokhliah, about whom I know nothing.

Also see Appendix entry Bar Kochba and Akiba.

The literature on the flamboyant characters identified above is lamentably sparse. For an introduction, see H. G. Friedmann's "Pseudo-Messiahs," in Vol. X, pp. 251–255, of *The Jewish Encyclopedia* (Funk and Wagnalls, 1901–1906), and Albert Hyamson's essay "Messiahs (Pseudo)," in Vol. VIII, pp. 581–588, of *The Encyclopedia of Religion and Ethics*, ed. by James Hastings, *et al.* (Scribner's, 1913–1922).

A scholarly survey of the theoretical underpinnings will be found in Abba Hillel Silver's brisk *History of Messianic Speculation in Israel, from the first through the seventeenth centuries* (Beacon, 1959). I have found bizarre facts and useful clues under various entries in Nathan Ausubel's *The Book of Jewish Knowledge* (Crown, 1964); see especially pp. 286–290.

Family Members, Relatives (Mishpoche)

father	*tateh* or *tata* (TAH-teh)
mother	*mameh* or *mama* (MAH-meh)
husband	*mann* (MON)
wife	*veib, froy* (VIBE, FROY or FRO)
son	*zun* (ZUHN)
daughter	*tochter* (TAWKH-ter)
brother	*bruder* (BROO-der or BREE-der)
sister	*shvester* (SHVES-ter)
uncle	*fetter* (FEH-ter)
	onkel (AWN-kel)
aunt	*tante* (TAHN-*teh*)
	mummeh (MOO-meh or ME-meh)
nephew	*plemenik* (pleh-MEN-ik)
niece	*plemenitza* (pleh-MEN-it-zeh)
cousin	*kuzin* (m.) (KOO-ZIN)
	kuzineh (f.) (KOO-ZEE-neh)
	shvesterkind (SHVES-*ter-kind*) *
grandchild	*aynekel* (ANE-ek-el)
grandchildren	*ayneklach* (ANE-*ek-lekh*)
grandfather	*zayde* (ZAY-deh)
grandmother	*bubbe* (BAW-beh or BUB-beh)
great-grandfather	*elter zayde* (EHL-ter ZAY-deh)
great-grandmother	*elter bubbe* (EHL-ter BAW-beh)
great-grandchild	*ur-aynekel* (oor-ANE-ek-el)
great-grandchildren	*ur-ayneklach* (oor-ANE-ek-lekh)

The Family-by-Marriage (Mechutanim)

father-in-law	*shver* (SHVAYR)
mother-in-law	*shviger* (SHVI-ger)
brother-in-law	*shvoger* (SHVAW-ger)
sister-in-law	*shvegerin* (SHVEH-geh-rin)
son-in-law	*aidem* (AID'm)
daughter-in-law	*shnur* (SHNOOR or SHNEE-air)

* The aphetic form of the German, *Geschwisterkind,* "sibling child."

Gematria

The letters of the Hebrew alphabet represented the following numerical values: *aleph* 1; *bet* 2, etc., through *yud* which is 10; *kaf* is 20, *lamed* 30, etc., through *tzadi* which is 90; *koof* is 100, *resh* 200, *shin* 300, and *taf* 400. Thousands are indicated by a letter with an apostrophe after it.

Here are four examples of gematria:

(1) Genesis 14 : 14 says: "And when Abraham heard that his brother was taken captive, he armed his trained servants, born in his own house, 318, and pursued them into Dan." Why is the number 318 mentioned—a specific number, not a "round number" like 300, or 350? Ah: this number *"really"* refers to "Eliezer," which also has the value of 318, and he was the only servant of Abraham's known to us by name!

(2) Simon the Just used to say: "Upon three things the world is based: upon the *Torah*, upon worship, and upon the practice of loving kindness." (*Sayings of the Fathers*, 1 : 2) So:

> *Torah*, numerical value of 611;
> *Avodah* (worship), value of 87;
> *Gemilut chasadim* (deeds of loving kindness), value of 611.

From this we are supposed to learn the co-equality of *Torah* and practicing loving kindness! Moreover, if Israel observes the obligations it assumed when it accepted the Lord "to be your God" (value, 611), then "His Kingdom will come" (611)!

(3) The place of *avodah* (worship), between *Torah* and the practice of loving kindness, is held to be highly significant: Worship is central to the other qualities, because it inspires us to fulfill them. Why do we worship? Because we accept God: "I am the Lord," which adds up to 87. Moreover, 87 emphasizes the Jew's responsibility for his brethren: "Where is Abel thy brother?" (87). Et cetera.

(4) Hillel's Golden Rule has the numerical value of 1021; here we must realize, said the rabbis, that we and our neighbors are different kinds of people, with variant characters, just as are the branches and fruits we use at the Feast of *Succoth* (which are said to represent the diverse types that make up the Jews). Now, "The boughs of goodly trees,

branches of palm trees, and willows of the brook" (Leviticus 23 : 40) have the numerical equivalent of 3063, which is 1021—three times!*

God's Names

Adonai literally means "My Lord" in Hebrew; but, as Rabbi I. Rackovsky told me, when God, speaking, uses *Adonai* in the Bible, the word obviously cannot mean "*My* Lord." *Adonai* has come to assume an identity independent of its strict literal meaning.

Adonai is but one of the words used to indicate the divine attributes of God. These attribute-referents are enumerated by Maimonides as seven in number: 1. *YHVH* 2. *El* 3. *Eloha* 4. *Elohim* 5. *Elohai* 6. *Shaddai* 7. *YHVH Tsevaot*.

YHVH (which I read somewhere appears 6,823 times in the Old Testament) means "the essence of His being" and is never really uttered or used, for it deals with a most abstract conception: the approximation of God through those characteristics by which He manifests Himself to men. *YHVH* (see ADONAI) is called, by theologians, "the essence of God's Being," and is considered far too rarefied for ordinary men to comprehend. The concept was handed down not in writings but orally, only to the highest, wisest *cognoscenti*.

Shaddai, according to *Midrash*, indicates God's contentment with the size of the world after He had created it and it had grown and grown. God said "*Dai!*" (Hebrew: "Enough!") and the universe stopped growing. . . . So *Shaddai*, for "The One Who Said 'Enough!'" rep....nts the divine attribute of Plenty. (Modern cosmologists, torn between the steady-growth and "big bang" hypotheses, will find the regal "Dai!" a delightful explanation of extremely complex matters.)

Note: Hindus have no less than 108(!) names for the holy river, *Ganga Ma* ("Mother Ganges"), and the pious cry "Ganga!" to atone for their sins. (See E. Newby, *Slowly Down the Ganges*, Scribners, 1967, pp. 19–22.) And the Chinese, during the T'ang dynasty, believed that whoever truly pronounced the name of Amithabha, one of the many Bud-

---

* For the material on 611, 87, and 1021, we are indebted to Harold Roland Shapiro, who published these and other interpretations in "The Light," February, 1963, and February–May, 1964.

dhas worshiped, would be reborn in a lapis lazuli paradise with jeweled trees. (See E. H. Shafer, *Ancient China*, Time–Life Books, 1967, pp. 70, 72, 74.)

Other names for God among Jews are *Bore Olam* (the Creator of the World), *Kedosh Yisrael* (Holy One of Israel), *Ha-Makom* (the Omnipresent Place), *El Elion* (Most High One), *En Sof* (Infinite One).

Why monotheists should go in for such elaborate nomenclature has intrigued as many scholars as it has baffled. I suspect that the answer lies in the psychological need to extend, prolong, and embellish veneration—by citing holy attributes with fervor and attenuating the time used therein: The All-Forgiving One, the Omniscient One, the Father of All Things, Lord of the Universe, the Compassionate One, et cetera.

See "Names of God," *Encyclopedia of the Jewish Religion*, edited by R. J. Werblowsky and G. Wigoder, Holt, Rinehart, Winston, 1965, pp. 160–161.
See also Appendix: Names and Magic.
On any aspect of Jewish mysticism, one should refer to the works of Professor Gershom Scholem. See his *Major Trends in Jewish Mysticism* (Schocken, 1941).

Hair, Hair Magic,
Hair Covering,
Shaving and Tonsures

The awesome symbolic powers men attribute to human hair are too numerous (and too childish) to be explored properly here. Consider the story of Samson; or the potent erotic influence a woman's locks are presumed to exercise over helpless males.

Under Mishnaic law, incidentally, if a married woman went out of the house bareheaded, that was grounds for divorce. (*Ketubot*, 7.6)

Jews wore high hats, fur hats, hats of Persian lamb, silk turbans, fezlike coverings. The *Chasidim* favored fine, round velvet hats, trimmed with fox, called *shtreimel*. Orthodox male Jews always wear a *yarmulka*, praying or not—for the name of God may come up in conversation.

Married Orthodox Jewish women in eastern Europe cropped their hair and donned a *shaytl*, wig, for life.

The *Midrash* (on Genesis) states that after God created Eve, He decided to give her a pleasing coiffure before presenting her to Adam.

The *Talmud* reports that in the olden days brides appeared for their nuptials with disheveled (or, at least, unbraided) hair.

The custom of unbraiding the hair (for instance, when in labor) is affiliated with the old superstition that evil spirits cast "binding spells" which can be avoided by loosening. (So, too, the clothes of the dead are arranged so as not to contain "binding" loops or knots.)

Did Jews in Biblical times cover their heads while praying? Hieroglyphs, written texts, monuments do not tell us. Prof. Samuel Krauss believes Jews in Palestine prayed bareheaded, and that Paul followed the custom in II Corinthians 3:15, 16. See *Hebrew Union College Annual*, Vol. 19, 1945–46.

Catholic and Greek Orthodox monks wear skullcaps over their tonsure—i.e., a shaved circle on the back-top portion of the skull.

A Catholic novitiate's hair was, originally, entirely cut; now the tonsure is reduced to a small circle, principally as a sign of the renunciation of sexuality. Tonsuring was performed immediately upon the uttering of the vow of chastity. Today, the bishop in ordination ceremonies cuts only three locks (symbolizing the Trinity?) and a barber does the rest.

In many Eastern countries, religious novitiates cut their hair as a sign of virginity—and dedication to it.

Life and strength are believed to reside in the hair, by many people and in many cultures: hence the ancient fear of cutting a baby's hair during the first year of its life; or the widely held notion that warriors gain strength from letting their hair grow long. The *Iliad*, you may recall, speaks of "long-haired Achaeans."

A bride's locks, in ancient Greece, were shorn just before she took the wedding vows, and the tresses were dedicated to a goddess.

In some societies that border the Black and Caspian seas, the bride's hair was cut off on her wedding eve, and she wore a headshawl or turban, thereafter.

For Jewish tradition and practice *vis-à-vis* the hirsute, see appropriate entries in *The Jewish Encyclopedia* (Funk and Wagnalls, 1901–1906) and Joshua Trachtenberg's *Jewish Magic and Superstition* (Jewish Publication Society, Philadelphia, 1961).

Holidays and Feasts *

Rosh Hashanah (New Year, Tishri 1)
Tsom Gedaliah (Fast of Gedaliah, Tishri 3)
Yom Kippur (Day of Atonement, Tishri 10)
Succoth (Tabernacles, Tishri 15–22)
Simchath Torah (Rejoicing over the Law, Tishri 23)
Chanukah (Feast of Dedication, Kislev 25)
Asereth B'tebet, Fast of (Tebet 10)
Purim (Feast of Lots, Adar 14)
Pesach (Passover, Nisan 15–21)
Shevuoth (Feast of Weeks, Sivan 6)
Tisha Bov (Fast of Ab, Ab 9)

Jewish holidays always fall on the same date if you use a Jewish calendar, which is governed by the 354–355 day lunar year, not the 365–366 day solar year of Gregorian reckoning. To synchronize the dates with the heavens, a month is added seven times every nineteen years. (It's too complicated for me, too.)

---

* See Appendix: Calendar for the Hebrew months used here.

Immigration of Jews: The United States

Up to 1825, there were only about 6,000 Jews in the United States—and only 500 in New York City. Then, as the waves of immigration from Germany began, New York's Jewish population grew.

It was heavy German immigration which, by 1848, made New York's Jewish population the largest in the United States (12–13,000); after that, the Jewish population of New York grew pretty much in proportion to the growth of the Jewish population in the United States. By 1880, 60,000 Jews were living in New York City—about 25 percent of the number in the United States. See Hyman Grinstein, *The Rise of the Jewish Community of New York, 1654–1860* (Jewish Publication Society, 1945).

The first census of American Jews, conducted by the Union of American Hebrew Congregations in 1877–1879, disclosed some surprising data:

There were Jews in every state in the Union, and in every new territory except Oklahoma. And the Jews in the West represented a higher percentage of the population than those in and around New York: 1.6 percent in the West, and only 0.6 percent in the Northeast. Of course, the population was exceedingly sparse in the Far West, as compared to the Northeast. See *Statistics of the Jews of the United States*, Union of American Hebrew Congregations, 1880, and H. S. Linfield, in the *American Jewish Yearbook for 1928–1929*, Vol. XXX, p. 159.

In some thirty years after 1880, about one-third (!) of the entire Jewish population of eastern Europe emigrated—over 90 percent of them came to the United States.

Here is a vivid and memorable account:

> These immigrants packed their few household belongings, pots and pans, samovar, pillows, and bedding, much of which would be lost or pilfered on the way, and forsook their native towns and villages to embark on the greatest journey of their lives. They parted with loved ones, seemingly forever, and made their way by foot, coach, and train, to the bewildering port cities of

Western Europe. There they sailed direct from Hamburg or Bremen at a cost of thirty-four dollars, some for a saving of nine dollars traveling by way of Liverpool. Crammed into steerage for as long as three weeks, Jewish immigrants were confined to herring, black bread, and tea by their loyalty to dietary laws, until the water journey's end. It was "a kind of hell that cleanses a man of his sins before coming to Columbus' land," insisted a popular immigrant guidebook that attempted to minimize the torments of the ocean voyage. Whatever the spiritually therapeutic values of that epic crossing, few immigrants would ever forget its terrors.*

Jews, Drinking, Crime

"Jews did not drink; Jewish students were docile, accepting—as lower class children rarely do—today's restraints for tomorrow's rewards; Jewish workers stayed out of jail," says Nathan Glazer. "When we look at the working class Jewish neighborhoods of the great American cities of the 1920's and 1930's, it is clear we are not dealing with ordinary workers. It was not dangerous to walk through the New York slums at night when they were inhabited by Jews. The Jewish workers . . . were in many important ways indistinguishable from the non-Jewish as well as the Jewish middle class." That is, poor and proletarian Jews did not conform to the general pattern of behavior found among the working classes. See Glazer's excellent survey in *The Jews: Their History, Culture and Religion,* edited by Louis Finkelstein (Harper, 1960), Vol. II, pp. 1694–1735.

Judaism: A Note

Judaism in eastern Europe, as in Germany, tended to ignore everything that might be considered theology. Only the practices of Judaism were taught. One was brought up to observe the commandments, and, for

---

* Moses Rischin, *The Promised City: New York's Jews: 1870–1914.* Corinth Books, 1964, p. 33.

this reason, as soon as one came in touch with a kind of thought which questioned fundamentals, one was at a loss. In other words, it may be said Jews lost their faith so easily because they had no faith to lose: that is, they had no doctrine, no collection of dogmas to which they could cling and with which they could resist argument. All they had, surrounding them like an armor, was a complete set of practices, each presumably as holy as the next. Once this armor was pierced by the simple question, Why?, it fell away, and all that was left was a collection of habits. Not that these habits could be dismissed completely. In some cases these were enough to supply the individual with a repertory of religious observances of a variety and complexity that would put the piety of any Christian to shame. A non-believing Jew might still, from habit, observe the dietary laws, go to synagogue now and then (and when he went, so thorough was the East European training, he often knew most of the prayers by heart), say Kaddish (a memorial prayer) for his father.*

Karaites

The Sadducees, Jewish priestly rulers under the Roman hegemony, opposed the *Talmud*—or any authority other than the sacrosanct *Torah*.

In 760 A.D., an anti-rabbinical movement known as Karaism, created by Anan, held that only the *Torah* and the words of the Prophets were valid for Israel. The Karaites attacked the Oral Law and the *Talmud* as a mare's nest of absurdities and pipe dreams. The most important Karaite leader was Benjamin ben Moses Nahavendi, who wrote the first systematic exposition of the Karaite position.

The supporters of the *Talmud* waged polemical battle against Karaism, under the leading Talmudist of his time, Saadia Gaon (892–942).

See the discussion by Judah Goldin, "The Period of the Tal-

* Nathan Glazer, *American Judaism*, The University of Chicago Press, 1965, pp. 69–70.

mud," pp. 115–216, in *The Jews: Their History, Culture and Religion,* edited by Louis Finkelstein (Harper, 1960), Vol. I, and the excellent entry "Karaites" in *The Standard Jewish Encyclopedia* (Doubleday, 1966), pp. 1106–1107.

Kol Nidre

Kol Nidre was originally regarded with disdain by the learned.

Rab Natronai, the rector of one of the rabbinical academies in Babylonia, wrote: "Of what use is an annulment to a man who makes the condition after he has taken a vow that that vow is to be void? . . . It is not the custom in [our] two academies . . . to annul vows. Neither on *Rosh Hashanah* nor on *Yom Kippur* is the *Kol Nidre* recited . . . we never saw, or heard the like, from our fathers." (Cited in Ibn Giat, *Shaare Simcha.*)

It was Rabbi Yehudai the Gaon, an eighth-century sage of Babylonia, who introduced the *Kol Nidre* into the synagogue, according to Professor Eric Werner of Hebrew Union College.*

Kosher

Genesis 9 : 4 forbade animal blood to all the seed of Noah. Moses himself, in Leviticus and Deuteronomy, forbade Jews to consume animal blood, internal fat or suet, carrion or the carcass of an animal that has died, instead of having been slain in the ritual manner.

In the *Talmud* it is written that forbidden foods "pollute the body and the soul."

The *Midrash* says that God is just as compassionate to beasts and birds as He is to men; hence Jews are told to be "kind and compassionate to all the creatures [God] created in this world. Never beat or inflict pain on any animal, beast, bird, or insect." (From the medieval *Book of the Pious.*)

---

* *The Jews: Their History, Culture and Religion,* edited by L. Finkelstein, Harper, 1960, Vol. II, pp. 1288–1321.

Eating and drinking, said the rabbis, are *religious* acts, for during them man partakes of God's bounty. Even in eating, the mind should dwell on God: any meal, therefore, should begin with a benediction of thanks, and end with grace.

This praying of the Jews before and after eating was carried into Christian practice.

Paul also asked Christians to avoid the blood of meat and the meat of strangled animals (Apostles 21 : 25).

For over 2,000 years rabbis developed and refined an elaborate code of regulations concerning food. The ritualistic details became so minute that a major part of the rabbis' *expertise* lay in their mastery of the elaborate rules: What is proscribed and what permitted; the occasions when one food or another is allowed; the order in which one food or another may be consumed; how food must be prepared, how it must be cooked, etc.

The Orthodox Jews' horror of eating pork was (and is) indescribable. When Antiochus, the Seleucid king, conquered Judea, he ordered Jews to sacrifice pigs on their holy altars; the Jews simply rose in fury (the Maccabean revolt, 168 B.C.).

The persecution of Jews down the centuries often involved one or another mob's forcing a God-fearing Israelite to pollute his soul by eating pork.

Whatever it was that originally prompted the Jews to taboo pork, it was a fortunate decision for them. As is now well known, pork is the commonest carrier of the parasites of the dangerous disease trichinosis. Similarly, hepatitis has in some cases been traced to contaminated clams, which are also taboo for observing Jews.

Some Jewish religious leaders in America hold that strict observance of the laws of *kashrut* (*kosher*-ness) served ghetto functions that are inappropriate to modern times. Others hold that observing *kashrut* at each meal helps remind the Jew of his identity and keeps the Jewish people intact.

For a brief, authoritative summary of these and other aspects of *kashrut*, see Samuel H. Dresner, *The Jewish Dietary Laws*, and Seymour Siegel, *A Guide to Observance*, both in paperback, Burning Bush Press, N.Y., 1959. This pamphlet may be obtained from the United Synagogue of America. Also see Simon Glustrom, *The Language of Judaism* (Jonathan David, pub., 1966), pp. 128–129, and the excellent summary in *Dictionary of the Bible,* ed. by James Hastings (Scribner's, revised edition, 1963), pp. 300–303.

Any textbook in anthropology can testify to the ancient origin of, and universal human preoccupation with, food taboos: totemism, animal sacrifices, magical rites of propitiation, symbolic accretions of strength *via* ingestion, etc.

The Babylonian laws of Mani forbade the eating of birds of prey.

In Egypt, priests were forbidden to eat birds that eat fish. Egyptians would not, of course, eat "deities": cats, cows, bulls.

Romans would not offer the gods scaleless or finless fish in their sacrifices. (Iranians still will not eat them.)

Many South Sea Islanders will not eat eel.

Natives of Borneo, Guiana Indians, Laplanders, Navaho Indians, and the Yakuts of Turkey eschew (no pun) pork.

Muhammad forbade his followers to eat of the pig.

See articles on "Tabu," "Totemism," "Diet," and "Malnutrition" in the respective volumes of the *Encyclopaedia Britannica.*

Ladino

Ladino, or Judesmo, as it is also called, can be written in either Hebrew or Roman characters. It is generally printed in what is called Rabbinical Hebrew letters, or in Latin characters. In writing Ladino, the cursive Hebrew letters are used —just as in writing Yiddish.

The first book to be printed in Ladino appeared in 1510, in Constantinople, but some Ladino texts date back to the Middle Ages.

Ladino is spoken along the southeastern littoral of the Mediterranean—notably in Turkey, North Africa and, of course, Israel—and in Brazil and other parts of South America.

As in Old Spanish, Ladino uses an *f* or *g* instead of the *h (fablar* instead of *hablar);* often omits the *h* at the beginning of a word *(ermano* instead of *hermano);* replaces *n* with *m (muestros* for *nuestros);* uses *s* instead of *z* and *c;* and never uses a double *r*. And it changes the *ll* of Spanish to a *y (caballero* becomes *cabayero)*. See George F. Ostermann, *Manual of Foreign Languages* (Central Book Company, Inc.), p. 151.

Messiah

The Gospels, and contemporary historical sources, draw a vivid picture of the intense expectations held among the Jews in the time of Jesus that the beloved Elijah, the herald of the Messiah, would soon appear (Elijah being, like Moses, a prophet) to end their travail.

John the Baptist explicitly said he was neither Elijah nor the Prophet nor the Messiah.

Note that Luke (24) said ". . . we trusted that it had been which should have redeemed Israel," and that the Angel tells Mary, "And, behold, thou shalt conceive in thy womb, and bring forth a son, and shalt call his name Jesus . . . and the Lord God shall give unto him the throne of his father David; and he shall reign over the house of Jacob for ever." (Luke 1 : 31–32.)

See the scholarly and detailed entry "Messiah," in *Dictionary of the Bible, op. cit.,* pp. 646-655, and the present Appendix: False Messiahs.

Money Changers

It was the custom for men to hawk their wares outside the Temple in Jerusalem (especially sacrificial pigeons and doves) to pilgrim Jews who came to offer sacrifices. Since different currencies were involved, it was customary for money to be "changed." What Jesus did was drive *these* money changers from the stairs outside the Temple—and so had rabbis before him.

Note that Jews never take up a collection inside a traditional synagogue or temple; they do not "pass the plate"; they pay annual dues, or pay for seats during the High Holidays, or pledge sums for synagogue or temple needs.

See Appendix: Talmud, Economics.

Names and Magic

Words are believed to exercise magical power in many societies. Much folklore revolves around the spells that are cast, or removed, by the mere utterance of a name. (See also Appendix: Naming and Names among Jews.)

Isis, the goddess of the ancient Egyptians, won ascendancy over the sun-god, Ra, by turning his saliva into a snake that bit him. To escape virulent death, Ra was then forced to divulge to Isis his most secret name (he had many). The name provided Isis with final power over Ra.*

Many American Indian tribes considered their names an integral part of themselves, and were convinced that if anyone pronounced a name balefully or malevolently their very bodies would suffer.

In some Australian tribes, every man has two names, the secret one being known only to the ceremonially initiated.

In one Congo tribe, no one dares pronounce a man's name if he is out fishing: that would ruin his chances of catching a fish. Another African tribe makes taboo the naming of a warrior who is off warring.

Rumpelstiltskin, if I remember correctly, killed himself when the miller's daughter discovered his name.

The Kirghiz in Asia forbid a woman to utter her husband's name or any word like it.

In Hungary, centuries ago, men tried to outwit ghoulish spirits, who were all around searching for human prey, by using horrid, magically protective names for their children. The idea seemed to be that an incubus would give a wide berth to a child who is loudly called, say, "Death." The Chinese had a similar custom.

A useful introduction to magic is Kurt Seligmann's *The History of Magic* (Pantheon, 1948).

---

* See *The Spell of Words*, by John and Joan Levitt, Philosophical Library, 1963.

Naming
and Names among Jews

Sephardic Jews often name a child after a living relative, but the *Ashkenazim* have a distinct and abiding dread of doing so. A certain trepidation is felt by old-fashioned parents even when a young man or woman selects a mate who bears the same given name as a living parent. (In some cases of this sort, the bride- or groom-to-be will adopt a second name or nickname.) Anxiety about names and naming is, of course, not limited to Jews. See "Names" in Edwin and Mona Radford, *Encyclopedia of Superstitions* (Philosophical Library, 1949).

Ashkenazic Jews generally named a child after a deceased relative. This was, however, only a custom and in an increasing number of cases is being ignored. Even where the custom is still honored, the "naming after," in recent decades, may be as nominal as it is farfetched: *Mervyn* for *Moshe; Barton* for *Benjamin; Natalie* ("Christmas child!") for *Nechama.*

Every Jewish child was once given a Hebrew name at birth. (Some parents gave the child a Yiddish name, unaware of the difference between the languages.) Some parents sought a name which "sounded like" Hebrew.

First-generation Jews in America took *Yitzchak* (Hebrew for Isaac) or *Itzik* (Yiddish) and Anglicized it to Isadore, Irwin, Irving; similarly, *Avraham* (Hebrew) or *Avrum* (Yiddish) became Alan, Allen, Allan, Albert, Alvin, Arnold; *Chaim* became Hyman, Herman, Herbert, even Charles.

Jews adjusted Biblical names to the orthography of the language in their country of residence: *Yosef* (Joseph) appears as Yussuf, Giuseppe, Beppo, Peppo, José, Pepe, Pepito, Josko, Joska, Joey.

Yaakov (Jacob) has the following variations: Jacques, Giacomo, Giacobbi, Jacobus, Jakob, Jaime, James, Jake, Jack.

Despite the feeling among religious Jews that Mary and John are "Christian" names, they are both Hebrew, of Biblical origin: Miriam and Jochanan.

Many common Yiddish names are of Biblical or Talmudic origin:

Avrum (Abraham)	*Dovid* (David)
Yankel (Jacob)	*Dvora* (Deborah)
Yisroel (Israel)	*Mayer* (Meir)
Itzik (Isaac)	*Leib* (Levi)
Yussel (Joseph)	*Yudel* (Judah)
Rivke (Rebecca)	*Shmuel* (Samuel)
Ruchel (Rachel)	*Michel* (Michael)
Moishe (Moses)	*Chana* (Hannah)

Names like Sarah, Leah, etc., are identical in both Bible usage and Yiddish.

Other Jewish names have their origin in other languages, mainly German:

Freda, Freida, Freyde (Joy)	*Raizel* (Rose)
Fruma (Grace—pious)	*Sheine* (Grace—pretty)
Feigel (Birdie)	

In Biblical times, children seem never to have been named after relatives—not even in the royal family. Scholars hold that not one of the twenty-one kings of Judah was named after a predecessor.

After the Exile, Jews began to use foreign, rather than Hebrew, names—such as Abba (Aramaic), Alexander and Philo (Greek). During the Hellenistic period, Jews began to name a boy after his grandfather.

The use of surnames first became common among Arabic-speaking Jews; Arabs form family names by adding *Abu* (Abudarham), *Ibn* (Ibn Ezra) and *Al* (Alharizi).

During the Middle Ages, the Jews often took names from the languages of the countries in which they lived, although they kept Hebrew names for "sacred" purposes (*brith, Bar Mitzva,* marriage, blessings attendant to reading from the *Torah,* etc.).

Surnames were not unknown among Jews (they were common among *Sephardim*) but came into general usage among the *Ashkenazim* only in the eighteenth century.

The Austrian Empire compelled the Jews to adopt surnames in 1787; Napoleon followed suit in 1808. Part of the reason, at least, was the difficulty presented to the authorities in collecting taxes in communities where individuals were known as Shmuel the Red-Haired, Harry the Cobbler, Isadore the Lame, etc.

The names *Alte* (fem.) and *Alter* (masc.) have a double origin, from the Latin ("other") and from German ("old"). These names, often given a child born after someone in the family had died, were designed to confuse the Angel of Death—should that malevolent worthy come looking for the newly born baby; for he would find "another" or "an old one"! A boy who was precocious was sometimes called *alter*.

For a discussion and list of English and Hebrew names, and their equivalents, see *The Name Dictionary* by Alfred J. Kolatch (Jonathan David Publishers, 1967). For superstitions about names not limited to Jews or Jewish tradition, see Edwin and Mona Radford's *Encyclopedia of Superstitions* (Philosophical Library, 1949).

Passover, Seder

For the family *Seder*, these foods (in addition to those listed in the word list) are required: a shank bone of roast lamb, to remind everyone of the paschal lamb that once was sacrificed; a hard-boiled egg (a *beitzah*), which varying allegories explain as standing for life or immortality, even for Israel itself (the egg becomes harder the more you boil it); a piece of radish or horseradish *(maror)*, to symbolize how bitter life was during the bondage in Egypt; salt water, to dip the parsley in, to recall the tears shed by mothers in Egypt whose babies were snatched from them—and the miracle of the Red Sea; a sprig of parsley *(karpas)*, to remind Jews that this is a spring festival; a little mound of crushed apples-raisins-almonds-nuts-cinnamon-wine, to represent the brick and mortar with which Jewish slaves built the palaces and monuments of their oppressors.

The opening of the door during the *Seder* has several interpretations: It invites Elijah to enter; the Prophet Elijah, being the Messiah's herald and messenger, may speed up God's appearance on earth. But some hold that it was the terrible

"Blood Accusation" against Jews, used both to terrorize and murder them (the charge that Jews drank Christian blood at Passover), that led the Jews to open their doors during the holiday feast—to allay any suspicion on the part of Gentile neighbors that secret or dastardly practices were being followed inside.

The repeated, fanatical slaughter of Jews during Passover finally led some rabbis to ban the use of red wine at the *Seder:* until a hundred years or so ago, white wine, raisin wine, was used sacramentally on Sabbaths and holidays alike.

The Festivals of *Aviv* ("spring," "greening") and of *Matzot* preceded Passover. *Aviv* was a festival to propitate God in order to obtain a good crop. (The Greeks, Canaanites, Assyrians, Sumerians, Babylonians had similar rites.)

Exodus 12 : 15 is very severe about those who eat bread during *Pesach:* "that soul shall be cut off from Israel."

Prayer among Jews

Orthodox Jews were, and are, prodigious pray-ers. They spend a great deal of time praising the Lord, the Holy Name of the Lord, the will and acts and mysterious goals of the Most High. In Jewish religious life, God is thanked, petitioned, invoked, or acknowledged many times a day.

An observing Jew will recite the *Shema* four times daily. The *Shema* is today what it was over 2,500 years ago: "Hear, O Israel: The Lord, Our God, the Lord is One." Then comes the passage from the Bible: "Thou shalt love the Lord thy God with all thy heart, with all thy soul, and with all thy might" (see SHEMA).

The Silent Devotion, an extraordinary prayer of eighteen (really nineteen) benedictions, is also offered four times daily by Orthodox (and many Conservative) Jews. Recited or chanted while standing, it involves three thoughts: wisdom, learning, immortality. It extols God's glory; it offers a hope for the welfare of the pray-er, his family, and the community at large; and it thanks God for His blessings.

Reciting the Ten Commandments is no longer customary among Jews, as it was long ago. One school of thought holds that the practice ended when rabbis astutely observed that the incessant recitation of the Commandments tended to over-glorify them as against God, and tended to fortify the impression that the Commandments are "all there is" to Judaism.

A large part of Jewish praying entails reciting the Psalms.

For centuries, Jews have had the sense of being part of one flowing, continuous, uninterrupted prayer to (and dialogue with) God.

Consider the psychological importance of that moment when the weekly readings from the *Torah* have reached the final paragraph of each of Moses' Five Books, and on the holy day, *Simchath Torah:* Instantly the entire congregation declaims with excitement, "*Chazak, chazak, venit chazak!*" "Be strong, be strong, and let us gather new strength!"

And at once, all over again, the cycle of reading-praying begins, from the first words in Genesis.

See DAVEN.

Prayer Shawls and Phylacteries

Orthodox and Conservative Jews wear a prayer shawl *(tallit or tallith)* and phylacteries *(tefillin)* when praying—the former every morning, the latter only on weekdays. Reform Jews do not wear phylacteries.

Ancient Palestinian Jews used a *tallith* with four tassels or fringes at the corners—to carry out the Biblical command to Jews that they remember their obligation to observe the 613 commandments of the *Torah*. (The fringes represent 600, the strings 8, the knots 5; total, 613.) The fringes were white and blue, traditionally; these are now the colors of the state of Israel.

The *tallith* is striped at the ends, across its width—usually in black. This may signify the mourning of Jews over the ancient destruction of the Temple.

In America, most Jews fold the *tallith*, which is made of silk, and wear it rather like a long scarf.

The Orthodox use a voluminous, robelike *tallith* and cover their shoulders and back with it when praying, the better to "take refuge in the shadow of God's wings." During the most solemn portions of prayer, Orthodox Jews place part of the shawl over their heads—to shut out anything that might diminish the intensity of their concentration on the All-Holy.

At the *Bar Mitzva*, the boy is usually given a *tallith* of his own.

See TALLIS, TEFILLIN.

Purim

Scholars have long questioned the authenticity of the colorful and dramatic Esther-Mordecai-Haman story.

One theory holds that the Purim festival is a carry-over from an old pagan carnival that used to take place on the Babylonian New Year—a festival that Persians and Jews alike loved because of its masks, dances and Mardi Gras shenanigans; the Jews could not be persuaded by their rabbis to reject such unseemly disportment, so (it seems) the wise men finally decided to use the Esther-Haman drama as the purported reason for carnival celebrations they could neither ignore nor condone.

There are close resemblances between Purim and non-Jewish holidays such as Shrovetide, and ordinary carnivals descended from pagan festivities. The burning of Haman in effigy, the choosing of a special "Purim Rabbi," the masks and dances and mummeries—all these are related to celebrations that burn "the spirit of the preceding year," or burn evil and malevolent demons, or appoint a "Bishop of Fools" just for the holiday, or stage masques and miracle plays.

See Theodor H. Gaster, *Customs and Folkways of Jewish Life* (William Sloane, 1955). Also see "Purim," in *The Book of Jewish Knowledge*, Nathan Ausubel (Crown, 1964).

Rabbis: Notes

The first rabbis were not professional clergymen at all, but men superior in character, probity, learning, whom the community respected. They exercised moral leadership, acted as judges, counselors, exemplars of conduct.

Beginning with Ezra, Jewish scholars established the precept that no man should use the *Torah* as a "spade" with which to dig for wealth. The great names of the *Talmud* are the names of workmen-scholars: Hillel was a woodchopper; Shammai, a surveyor; Ishmael, a tanner; Abba Hoshaiah, a launderer.

The extreme sense of humility among rabbis, which extended to their walking always with lowered eyes, is seen in the case of the famous and learned Rabbi Shalom Shakna of Lublin, to whose *yeshiva* came scholars from all Europe. The rabbi never wrote a single tract or book, though students and colleagues pleaded with him to leave a written record of his brilliant Talmudic inquiries, his juridical decisions and the reasons for them. Rabbi Shakna said it would be wrong for him to do this, because he could not bear the thought that future scholars and students and laymen might attribute too much and too great importance to his writing, or might be influenced too strongly in their own thinking and judgment!

Rabbi Shakna's renowned teacher, Rabbi Jacob Polak of Cracow, wrote no book, either.

Neither of these good and learned men, said Shakna's son, made "any copies of their responses to be sent abroad, for the same reason."

The secular and the scholarly can only mourn the disappearance of the cerebrations of such *chachamim*.

Rosh Hashanah: Notes

Johanan ben Nappaha said that on *Rosh Hashanah* three ledgers are opened in heaven: the Book of Life, in which the names of the truly righteous are inscribed; the Book of Death, in which the names of the unredeemably wicked are entered; and a sort of in-between ledger, where the rest of mankind is found. The fate of the in-betweeners is held in abeyance for ten days, until *Yom Kippur*.

Between *Rosh Hashanah* and *Yom Kippur*, those who gain merit, by penitence and deeds, are written into the Book of Life; the rest are marked for Death.

"On *Rosh Hashanah* and *Yom Kippur*," says a passage in the Yerushalmi *Talmud*, "Jews should not appear depressed and in somber clothes, as suppliants before a human judge, but joyous, dressed in festive white, betokening a cheerful and confident spirit."

Rosh Hashanah used to be called *Yom ha-Zikaron*, "the Day of Remembrance," *Yom ha-Din*, "the Day of Judgment," or *Yom Teruah*, "the day of blowing of the horn."

The earliest mention of *Rosh Hashanah* appears to be in a second-century passage in the *Mishnah*.

The first month of the Hebrew calendar is *Nisan* (which comes in March–April) and commemorates the Exodus. Yet the Jewish New Year is the first day of *Tishri*, the seventh month. This suggests a close relationship to the same timing for the Babylonian "Day of Judgment," the New Year's day when, the Babylonians believed, all their gods assembled in the temple of Marduk, their chief deity, to pass judgment on man and to record each individual's fate for the next year.

Sabbatai Zvi

One of the more amazing, if minor, episodes in the history of the Jews involves the fascinating figure of one Sabbatai Zvi—or Zevi, or even Sebi, as he is called in the *Encyclopaedia Britannica* (Vol. 19, p. 787). In Yiddish, he is also known as "Shabtsai Zvi," pronounced "SHOP-*tzee-tzvy*."

Repeated and terrible pogroms in the mid-seventeenth century (Cossack bloodbaths slaughtered about half the Jews in the Ukraine, some 300,000 souls) led many pious Jews to think that the Messiah was about to appear—for an ancient tradition held that when the misery of Israel reached the point of utter unendurability, God would end it by sending a Messiah down to earth.

In Salonika, in the year 1648, a twenty-one-year-old Turkish Jew announced that he was the Messiah. His name was Sabbatai Zvi.

Sabbatai Zvi was born in 1626, in Smyrna (Izmir). He was of Spanish descent, apparently. His father was the local agent for an English firm. Sabbatai, who sang psalms very sweetly and was much loved by children, was engrossed in the mystical teachings of Rabbi Isaac Luria, a famous cabalist known as Ari (the Lion).

Zvi seems to have been able to induce prolonged ecstatic states in himself, and he came to believe that he was destined to fulfill the prediction of certain Christians in England who had set 1666 as the year in which the Millennium would begin. (Jewish cabalists, by elaborate numerical mumbo-jumbo, had concluded that 1648 was the year of salvation.)

Sabbatai Zvi went to Jerusalem in 1662, after Safed had been sacked by the Turks and Tiberias had been laid waste by the Druses. There he prayed fervently at the tombs of the patriarchs of old; he fasted, and mortified his flesh—and won followers by the score.

Sent to Egypt by his zealous believers, Zvi was received with great honors. In Cairo, he married a prostitute named Sarah, a rather remarkable lady who had been raised in a Polish convent (her parents had been slain in a pogrom). She had traveled to Amsterdam, where she experienced a vision, she later claimed, that told her of the miracle-worker, Sabbatai Zvi, who would become her husband. One legend indeed held that the Messiah would take an unchaste woman for his bride. (Remember that Hosea received a divine command to marry a harlot—to symbolize the way Jews had prostituted themselves to false gods. Hosea took as wife one Gomer: Some scholars hold Gomer to have been a heathen "temple prostitute," a hierodule, or temple slave, used in pagan rites; other scholars stoutly call her a woman who, after her marriage, became indubitably unfaithful.)

Sabbatai returned to the Holy Land, his visionary pronouncements greatly aided by one Nathan of Gaza, who took it upon himself to act as "Elijah," the prophet and pathbreaker for "Our Messiah, Sabbatai Zvi."

The rabbis of Jerusalem, furious, threatened to anathematize Sabbatai Zvi, who went back to Smyrna where he was received with fantastic enthusiasm. And the Sabbatean movement began to spread through the Jewish centers of Asia Minor.

Sabbatai Zvi attracted great crowds, many of whom called him "The Anointed One," or met him with waving myrtle and palm branches and acclamations of "Our Messiah!" And Zvi promised to lead the faithful up to Mount Zion in a mighty procession, there to set up the Kingdom of God. And thousands believed him, and prepared for the holy moment.

The ecstasy and hysteria produced by Sabbatai Zvi's mystical evangelism is difficult to describe. A messianic fever spread from Turkey to Venice, on to Hamburg, to Amsterdam, and even to London. Sabbatai became "the King of the Jews" to many, on whom the earlier parallel of Jesus was not lost.

Thousands of Jews actually prepared for the end of the world, sold all their possessions, settled their affairs, prayed for the Day of Judgment, left their homes, covered themselves with ashes and sackcloth, started prolonged fasting and praying.

I quote with wonder the following passage from Hugh Trevor-Roper:

> What lunacy overcame the whole Jewish world in the days of Sabbatai's antics! A Polish prostitute, having boasted her reservation for the Messiah, was fetched unseen from Leghorn to be his bride; a high-powered secretariat proclaimed his mission throughout Europe and the East; and prosperous jewellers and grain merchants in Hamburg and Amsterdam giddily declared that Sabbatai Zevi would "take the royal crown from the Sultan's head and place it on his own." "Like a Canaanitish slave," they repeated, "shall the King of the Turks walk behind him, for to Sabbatai is the power and the glory."*

In 1666, Zvi went (or was ordered) to Constantinople, where he was arrested by the Turkish authorities. Accounts of his miraculous doings continued to spread, nevertheless, and many a Turk now began to believe in the Jewish "Messiah."

Zvi was brought before the Sultan and given the choice of having his head chopped off or embracing the faith of Islam: Zvi kept his head on his shoulders. . . . He and his wife became, respectively, Mehemet Effendi and Fatima Radini.

---

* *Historical Essays,* Macmillan, London, 1963, p. 149.

Many ardent, if embarrassed, followers found a way to explain Sabbatai Zvi's apostasy, and a small sect of Muhammadans in Turkey are still Sabbatean.

Sabbatai Zvi died a Muslim, obscurely, it is reported, in Albania, in 1676.

For a memorable literary vignette of this altogether incredible figure, see Israel Zangwill's *Dreamers of the Ghetto* (Harper, 1898), pp. 115–186. A useful biography is Joseph Kastein's *The Messiah of Ismir* (Viking, 1931). Historians draw heavily on Heinrich Graetz's *History of the Jews* (Jewish Publication Society, reprinted 1956), Vol. V, pp. 118–167. For the place of Sabbatai Zvi in Jewish mystical thought, see Gershom G. Scholem's *Major Trends in Jewish Mysticism* (Schocken, 1961), pp. 287–324.

Sabbath: Notes

The *Shabbes* feast is fairly standardized among Jews: It includes *gefilte* fish, soup with noodles or *matzo*-ball dumplings, and chicken (boiled or roasted). Horseradish invariably accompanies the *gefilte* fish, and *tsimmes* the meat. My mother always served chopped liver, celery, radishes, olives, then *gefilte* fish, then *knaydel* (dumpling) soup, then the chicken —and apple sauce for either a side dish or dessert.

On Saturday, the traditional lunch (prepared by the Orthodox the day before, of course) was *cholent* and *kugel* (noodle or bread pudding).

Genesis says: "God blessed the seventh day and sanctified it" (2 : 3); Exodus commands men to "Remember the sabbath day, to keep it holy" (20 : 8). The Fourth Commandment calls the seventh day "a sabbath of the Lord thy God."

NOTE: The Babylonians observed a festival of the full moon which they called *Shapattu* or *Shabbatu;* these words meant "to rest," as does the Hebrew *shabbat*. Work, labor, business were taboo to Babylonians during *Shapattu*.

Scripture commanded the Israelites: On the Sabbath "thou shalt not do any work," nor shall "thy son, nor thy daughter, thy manservant, nor thy maidservant, nor thy cattle, nor thy stranger that is within thy gates . . ." (Exodus, 20 : 10.)

According to Deuteronomy, God commanded the Jew to observe the Sabbath so that he would "remember that thou wast a servant in the land of Egypt, and that the Lord thy God brought thee out thence through a mighty hand and by a stretched out arm" (5 : 15).

The *Torah*'s fourth commandment ordains the Sabbath for beasts of burden no less than men. (Jews were allowed to break the Sabbath if that was necessary to save the life, or relieve the pain, of an animal.)

The radical idea of one labor-free day each week did not appeal to the Greeks and Romans: They owned slaves.

Seneca, the Stoic, abandoned his stoicism to attack the Hebrew custom that, he admitted, was spreading. ("This most outrageous people . . . lose almost a seventh part of their life in inactivity.")

Juvenal jeered at the Romans, who, influenced by the Jews, "adore nothing but clouds and the divinity of heaven . . . to whom every seventh day is idle."

Horace scorned, and Martial maligned, the *Shabbes*.

The historian Josephus records the fact that Roman military men knew that Jewish soldiers would fight on the Sabbath only in dire extremity (the rabbis permitted fighting on *Shabbes* if it was absolutely necessary—to save life, or in immediate and unmistakable peril). The Romans exploited this fact in the timing of their military actions against the Jews.

A *Talmud* sage asserts that on *Shabbes* eve a good angel and a bad angel hover over each man who returns from the synagogue to his home. "If the man finds the candles lit, the table set, and the bed made, the good angel says, 'May next Sabbath be like this one,' and the evil angel perforce responds, 'Amen.' Otherwise the evil angel answers, 'May next Sabbath be like this!' and the good angel is compelled to answer, 'Amen.' " (José ben Judah, second century. Quoted in the *Talmud*.)

"Tell nothing on the Sabbath which will draw tears," is written in *Sefer Hasidim* (13C, No. 625).

"Let melancholy and passion, born of spleen and bile, be

banished from all hearts on the Sabbath day." (Moses Hasid, a moralist who lived in Prague; 1717.)

"Who spends for Sabbath," says the *Talmud*, "is repaid by the Sabbath."

Asher Ginzberg, better known as *Achad ha-Am*, made the succinct and memorable observation: "More than the Jews have kept the Sabbath, the Sabbath has kept the Jews."

Sanhedrin

There is considerable contradiction, and irksome ambiguity, in the historical accounts of this religio-juridical institution. The *Mishnah*'s data do not coincide with the material in Josephus, and the New Testament varies from both. Modern scholarship tends, I think, to follow the conclusions reached by Adolf Büchler (see S. B. Hoenig's interesting *The Great Sanhedrin*, Bloch, 1953).

Moses said "Gather unto me seventy . . . elders of Israel" (Numbers 11 : 16). That would mean that Moses sat as the Patriarch, or presiding judge, over seventy wise men. But we do not know when the first Sanhedrin was established. The *Talmud* says after Simon the Just died, which means (*if* Simon the Just is the same Simon who was Patriarch, or High Priest) in the third century B.C.

There were probably two types of Sanhedrin, one of twenty-three members, a court concerned with political-civil matters, and the Great Sanhedrin of seventy-one elders, that ruled on religious problems.

It is difficult to know exactly what civil powers the Sanhedrin exercised, over whom and in which "jurisdiction," because of the vicissitudes of its history. Local matters in Judea, and, under the Roman Empire, such matters as the Roman procurator allocated to the Sanhedrin (or simply failed to take care of himself) fell in its domain; it was the final court of appeals on Mosaic Law, with judges of the lower courts bound to support it, on pain of death. But the Sanhedrin dealt mostly with noncriminal matters.

The Sanhedrin usually met in "The Hall of Hewn Stones" in the Temple. The members were seated in a semicircle, so that each could easily see, or be seen by, the others. Behind the clerks, who stood before the court, were three rows of disciples of the judges—who clearly were learned and distinguished men. The accused before the court was required to wear mourning.

When the Temple in Jerusalem was destroyed, in 70 A.D., the Sanhedrin vanished; the *Beth Din* (court of law) and later academies of study, in various parts of the Middle East, assumed their functions.

The Romans both permitted and encouraged the Sanhedrin to operate as the Jews' political governors and high court. In 57 B.C. the procurator of Judea, one Gabinius, abolished the Sanhedrin and set up five different councils of Jews, supported by Rome: in Jerusalem, Jericho, Hamath, Gadara, Sepphoris. These councils were stripped of religious and ethical duties. Some historians hold that these Jewish councils served to consolidate Roman rule against rebellious, anti-Roman Jews. (See Appendix: Crucifixion.)

When Napoleon was trying to formalize relations between the state and the Jews in his far-flung empire, he established a Sanhedrin of seventy-one members that included distinguished Jewish laymen as well as rabbis. It does not seem to have carved much of a niche in either French or European history.

See articles on Sanhedrin in *Dictionary of the Bible, Standard Jewish Encyclopedia, Encyclopedia of the Jewish Religion*, and other standard source books cited throughout this lexicon.

Shofar

The rabbis, sensitive to symbolic values and overtones, would not permit Jews to use an ox or bull horn as a *shofar;* after all, the Hebrews had hurt God deeply enough when they took up the worship of the Golden Calf. The ram's horn symbolizes the ram who appeared as a substitute for Isaac.

Shofars were often used in Palestine to announce holidays, to signal danger or call for defense, as a war sign, to signalize a peace, to usher in the new moon, to inaugurate a religious fast or feast, to call together convocations, or as a regular watchman's sound of reassurance.

In Israel today, the *shofar* is used on high official occasions. In Orthodox neighborhoods, the *shofar* is sounded on Friday eve to herald the Sabbath.

When Moses went up to Mount Sinai for the second time, a great *shofar* sounded—to tell Israel never again to become idolators.

The Bible enjoins the sounding of the *shofar* only for *Rosh Hashanah* (Numbers 29 : 1), and nowhere describes the nature, sequence or meaning of the blasts; the rabbis developed complex rules—e.g., that the broken notes should resemble sobbing, and that a long, unbroken note *(tekiah)* precede and follow broken notes of sobbing *(shevarim)* and wailing *(teruah)*.

Maimonides said that the *shofar*'s message is this: "Awake, ye sleepers from your sleep; and ye that are in slumber, rouse yourselves. Consider your ways, remember God, turn unto Him" *(Laws of Repentance, 3 : 4)*.

Shul, Study, and
Prayer among Jews

At bazaars, in markets, at country fairs or trade fairs, Jews were always seen studying, even while "minding the store." That was because a male might pledge himself to read a certain part of the *Mishnah* or *Midrash* or *Gemara*. Itinerant Jews—peddlers, salesmen, tradesmen—usually carried something to read while away from home, to fulfill their pledged "appointment."

Part of this singular obsession with "reading *Torah*" (or *Talmud*) rested in the notion that a man could actually earn a "portion of bliss" in the hereafter by performing certain acts—among which reading his "portion" ranked high. Some Jews were eager to read aloud from the pulpit in the synagogue, not simply as an honor, which it was, but as a means of winning extra merit in the heavenly record.

Whatever the motives, however naive the reasoning, an entire culture was·structured around reading, study, a reverence for words. And this, please note, for centuries and centuries during which the overwhelming majority of mankind was illiterate.

". . . the study of the Talmud gave the student exceptional intellectual satisfaction. Most of the students in the *yeshibot* did not aspire to be rabbis. The cities and towns of Eastern Europe were, as we have seen, full of learned householders, who studied not only for the sake of studying, i.e., to fulfill the commandment to study, but because they actually felt an urge to study. They sang their studies; they sang them fervently, and felt transported to a higher world. There was a certain enchantment to studying a page of the Talmud."—A. Menes, "The Pattern of Jewish Scholarship in Eastern Europe," in *The Jews: Their History, Culture and Religion,* Vol. I, ed. by Louis Finkelstein (Harper, 1960), p. 385.

A special role was played by the synagogue (Yiddish, *bes-medresh;* Hebrew, *bet hamidrash*). One can say, without exaggeration, that a considerable portion of the Jews spent more of their time in the synagogue than in the marketplace. It was in the synagogue that the Jew began his day, and it was there that he said his prayers, met his friends, and occupied himself with public affairs. There were synagogues whose doors were never closed: night and day men studied and prayed. They studied both alone and in groups. There was a widespread custom of "appointments" (Hebrew, *keviot*), according to which each man pledged himself to study an appointed page of the *Talmud,* a chapter of the *Mishna,* a portion of the Pentateuch, etc. each day. Merchants would frequently take along a book while on the road, to be able to keep up with the daily portion. Rabbi Abraham Danzig, the author of *Hayye Adam,* who remained a merchant until the last years of his life, wrote about himself as follows: "And the merchants will bear witness that it was always my custom to take along copies of the *Talmud,* Bible, and *Mishna* with me on the road, and that even during trade fairs I would study one and a half pages of the *Talmud,* in addition to the *Mishna,* every day." *Ibid.,* pp. 380–81.

Should a merchant have to miss his daily lesson, he would "repay" his debt on his return home. There were also some who would learn a certain section of the *Talmud* by heart and repeat it on the road, lest they violate the Commandment to study, even when they had no books with them. Collective study was also very popular. The Talmudic sentence "Learning is achieved only in company" (*Berakot,* 63) was always highly thought of, and it was not particularly difficult to find friends with whom to study in the cities and towns of Eastern Europe. Indeed, the Jewish communities were full of study societies. In a description of the small town of Kroz in 1887, nine study societies were listed. Among them the *Talmud* Society, which was "full of scholars well-versed in the Law," occupied the highest prestige position. The town of Kroz at that time had a total of 200 Jewish families. Yet this small, poor town supported by its own means as many as ten male teachers, two women (who probably taught girls), a rabbi, two slaughterers (of *kosher* cattle), three sextons, and—what is perhaps exceptionally important to note—two bookbinders.*

Soul

The *Talmud* never mentions the soul's transmigration—i.e., leaving the body after death. Many rabbis considered such stuff idolatry and superstition—and a challenge to monotheism itself. Yet mystics and ordinary folk clung to the idea.

It was in the Middle Ages that Jewish cabalists suggested the idea of souls wandering around, as punishment, to atone for sins; the concept even filtered into the explanation for the *Galut,* the dispersion of Jews in exile from the Holy

* A. Menes, "The Pattern of Jewish Scholarship in Eastern Europe," in *The Jews: Their History, Culture and Religion,* edited by Louis Finkelstein, Harper, 1960, Vol. I, pp. 380–381.

Land; prayers refer to this as God's punishment "for our sins."

See *Standard Jewish Encyclopedia, op. cit.,* p. 1743.

Spelling of Yiddish Words in English

The authoritative YIVO Institute for Jewish Research has tried energetically to create a standard Yiddish orthography, and standard rules for the transcription of Yiddish into Roman letters. These were "established" in 1937—and have been rather widely ignored ever since.* Jewish philologists and editors, too, have attempted, not successfully, to set abiding standards and rules. In 1954 a publication, *The Field of Yiddish,* was established for this purpose, and in 1958 an international conference on the study of Yiddish was held in New York.

The American Jewish Press Association appointed a Committee on Transliteration in 1950. A report of that committee, some sixteen years later, confessed: "All were in agreement on the desirability of a uniform system of transliteration . . . but unfortunately there was no agreement on a specific plan." Part of the problem lay in the fact that certain linguistic rules, necessary for scholarly and scientific publications, are intensely resisted—by the popular press, by deeply ingrained habits, by the preferences of influential Jews to whom their own version of the vernacular remains sacrosanct.

Indecision continues to plague those who seek a uniform system for the transliteration of Yiddish. Accordingly, words like *Chanukah* and *Rosh Hashanah* have been spelled in some 15 different ways. "Since there existed no authoritative guide, every writer was a law unto himself," said the American Jewish Press Association, which finally decided to sacrifice all for simplicity and uniformness, and agreed that its members would

(1) set aside formal philological rules;

---

* See *The Standard Jewish Encyclopedia,* ed. by Cecil Roth, Doubleday, 1966, p. 1943:

(2) recognize the Israeli/Sephardic *pronunciation* of Hebrew words, which would be spelled phonetically in Yiddish;

(3) write the Hebrew letter "het" (given in English as *ch* or *kh*) as "*h*";

(4) omit the "h" letter where it is silent at the end of a word (Rosh Hashana);

(5) write the Hebrew "tzadik" as "tz," not "ts."*

Certain variations of spelling in the present lexicon occurred however much I would have preferred uniformity: Quoted material contained variant ways of spelling Yiddish words in English, and my own transliterations changed—to satisfy contexts, niceties of print, or in behalf of clarity rather than consistency. Many compromises had to be made—sometimes simply to simplify pronunciational cues to readers unfamiliar with Yiddish or Hebrew. Finally, not ignorance but economics dictated the preservation of certain variations as they appeared in the galley proofs. Since many words may be spelled quite correctly in more than one way (e.g., *Mishna* or *Mishnah*) I sometimes decided to allow either version, in a given passage of texts, depending on the other material that surrounded it.

Synagogues and Temples in the U.S.: Note

Synagogues and temples sprang up everywhere (3,100 congregations in 1927; 3,700 in 1937), but these religious centers took on new forms: in addition to areas for prayer, study, classroom, they now contained such unheard-of features as "social rooms," music rooms, art or dance studios, gymnasiums.

Orthodoxy in religion, the observance of tradition in customs, were maintained even after Jews began to "move up"—i.e., away from the so-called "ghetto" areas of New York—in the 1920's.

When Jews moved to better neighborhoods, Orthodox

---

* I have drawn all this material from an undated copy of a "copyrighted, 1966" one-page résumé by Leo H. Frisch, editor of the *Jewish World*, entitled "War of Words Is Peacefully Resolved," distributed by the American Jewish Press Association.

synagogues still predominated—even though some were becoming far less East European; some even began to offer sermons in English!

Synagogues that departed from strict Orthodox ritual and procedures began to call themselves "Conservative," to distinguish themselves from the Old-World and the Orthodox. German Jews, for the most part, belonged to Conservative temples. And in the neighborhoods still later populated by Jews (upper-middle-class, well-to-do) Reform temples began to outnumber the Orthodox. Many Conservative synagogues were to be found there, too. Soon, the Orthodox Jews formed a decided minority among the well-to-do.

See Nathan Glazer's excellent survey, *American Judaism*, University of Chicago Press, 1965.

Talmud, Midrash, Mishnah, Gemara

The first time *"Talmud"* was used as a written name for the burgeoning body of knowledge that began as far back as the fifth century B.C., seems to have been 1100 years later—in the sixth century A.D.

Ezra and Nehemiah (fifth century B.C.) established the canon of the *Torah*, the Five Books of Moses. This virtually sealed the contents against change. They initiated the custom of having an interpreter present in the synagogue to explain complex passages whenever the *Torah* was read aloud. Since it became increasingly difficult to interpret ancient injunctions so that they seemed relevant to contemporary problems, the interpreters began to stray from the text, offering more pertinent or imaginative interpretations; so was born an exegesis, a "science" of analysis and interpretation called *Midrash* ("exposition") and what was to become the *Talmud*.

Out of *Midrash*, in time, came *Mishnah* ("repetition"), a more advanced commentary-interpretation. The *Mishnah* began, apparently independently, in both Palestine and Babylonia. The Pharisees held *Mishnah* to be an exalted effort to probe into and reveal God's meaning, but this was opposed by many Sadducees, who held a fundamentalist position: The sacred text of Scripture was self-revealing and unalterable;

interpretation was not needed and, indeed, verged on blasphemy.

Whatever each faction hoped for, the masses took to *Mishnah* with enthusiasm, for now any ordinary Jew could read the holy books, and discuss and question the sages' interpretations. New exegetes rose from the ranks of common people; their occupations were no bar to the once-priestly privilege and monopoly of interpreting the holy books. And since the rabbis foresaw the energy and growth that *Mishnah* would acquire, and feared that it might in time replace—or, at least, compete with—the *Torah,* they decreed that no one was allowed to *write down* any *Mishnah;* this meant that *Mishnah* had to be memorized and could be passed on only orally. Hence, *Mishnah* became known as "Oral Law."

A great first-century (A.D.) debate was waged between the sages Hillel and Shammai, and their intense followers. Shammai was a "conservative," a strict textual adherent, a legalist. Hillel was a "liberal," a philosopher-humanist. Shammai stressed a position somewhat similar to what we would call "strict Constitutionalism"; Hillel was concerned less with "property rights" than "human rights." The views of Hillel finally prevailed.

Akiba (or Akiva), who died around 135 A.D., the greatest scholar of his time, to whom thousands upon thousands of students flocked, perfected his own method of Biblical exegesis and collected the Oral Law, which he classified by subject matter. This great work was used by Judah Ha-Nasi (see below) and his co-workers as the basis for the *Mishnah.*

Judah Ha-Nasi ("the Prince," about 135–200 A.D.), a great scholar, fearing that *Misnah* would depart too far from *Torah* and might even create heretical departures from the true faith, declared *Mishnah* to be closed (as Ezra and Nehemiah had "closed" the *Torah*). "Oral Law" was to be frozen.

But such fundamentalist constraints succeeded no more in Judaism than in other religions. For in the *yeshivas* of Babylonia there soon arose (indeed from the efforts of several of Judah Ha-Nasi's disciples) a continuation of *Torah* interpretation called *Gemara* ("supplement"). This *Gemara* observed the solemn restrictions governing Oral Law, used Aramaic instead of Hebrew as its language, and appeared to be, at first, simply an extension of *Mishnah* itself. Like *Midrash,* like *Mishnah,* so *Gemara* was strictly oral for centuries, and the academies of Babylonia reigned as authority, in Judaic thought and discussion, from 200 to 600 A.D.

The historic shift to a *written* form was born of a political crisis in the sixth century A.D. Zoroastrian fanatics, rebelling against the influence of both Judaism and Christianity, came to power and launched severe repressive programs against Jews and Christians in the Persian realm. Jews fled, dispersed, were killed, and the rabbis realized that the collective "memory" of *Mishnah* and *Gemara* was in peril of extinction. A group of scholars, the *Saboraim*, who were at home in both Hebrew and Aramaic (not too hard, given the similarities of the two languages), were now set the task of writing down the precious interpretative materials. These are to be found in the Babylonian *Talmud*.

The work went on for over two hundred years (!). And the new interpreters, being only human, often resolved points of unclarity or ambiguity by becoming high courts themselves —adding, interpreting, interpolating, ingeniously revising— until a *Gemara* of their own grew up around the *Gemara* they were reducing to written form.

Talmud, Economics, Moneylending

The role the *Talmud* has played in the economic life of the West has been sparsely cited by historians. True, Werner Sombart attributes much of the beginnings of capitalism itself to Europe's Jews, and W. E. H. Lecky stresses the part Jews played in organizing and injecting life into trade between nations. Other historians remark upon the part Jews played in devising a money system, a credit system, a sense of investment and capital accumulation, the idea of legitimate interest rates as against "usury," etc.

The *Talmud* was of immense economic value to Jews. Along with its application of dialectics to *Torah*, the *Talmud* laid down abiding (and remarkably intelligent) rules about property, commerce, contracts, insurance, real estate, trade governance, equity, torts—and international law! Back in 1200 A.D., Maimonides wrote that economic life, to grow, required that money be used by being lent—and that interest far from being usurious and wicked, served a crucial and salutary function.

The activity of "moneylending," so hated by Christian theologians (though not by kings and popes, who enlisted the aid of Jews to finance the building of cathedrals), was a *sine qua non* of economic growth in medieval times. But the laws governing interest and finance were as startling as they were ill-advised. Roman law held that a debt was personal, that a note could not be transferred. In Germany, a man who owed money was obliged to pay it only to the original lender—hence, debts died when a creditor died. Even in enlightened England, up to the middle of the nineteenth century (!), some debts were not transferable. But the *Talmud* says a debt must be honored even if a creditor or debtor dies. The Talmudists understood the concept of the negotiable.

Christian Church fathers made the economically catastrophic error of considering any form of banking usurious, no matter how proper or modest the interest rate charged. (The *Talmud,* incidentally, forbids Jews to take "excessive" interest; the rabbis determined "proper" rates.) To buy tools, seed, livestock, to recover from a drought, to pay taxes, to tide a man over a disastrous season or harvest, accident or disease—for any of these, loans were imperative. And for these, the kings and barons, and the clergy, too, went to the Jews. The Church considered it a sin to lend money for a fee; but since Jews were not part of the Christian community, and were doomed to perdition anyway—let the Jews take on one more sin.

Students of economics will not be surprised to learn that, almost invariably, when Jews were forced out of banking, investment, and moneylending activities, to be replaced by Christians (who persuaded the authorities to push the Jews out), interest rates rose.

Several popes denounced Christian moneylenders for their "heartless" rates, and Dante put them into the deepest abyss of his Inferno.

Seventeenth-century English monarchs earnestly asked Jews to lend money—so as to undercut the high interest rates being charged by Christians. (William of Orange even knighted Solomon Medina, a Jewish banker.) William Pitt also enlisted the aid of Jews against English bankers whose interest rates were strangling the Treasury's efforts to raise money.

Talmud and Science

For the first nine centuries of the Christian era, there is in the literature of the Jews simply nothing even approximating science, or the scientific spirit, or the scientific cast of inquiry and analysis. The marvels of nature excited awe and veneration—but not curiosity in our meaning of the word.

Within the *Talmud* and its system of discourse, its debates and casuistries and sophistical distinctions, there just was no place for anything resembling science. Professor Charles Singer points out that even though many Greek names may be found in the *Talmud*, there is not the name of one Greek scientist. Most surprisingly, even Aristotle is not mentioned.

It was through Islam, ironically enough, that science and philosophy (as the West defines it) finally came to the Jews—who, in turn, played a significant role in spreading science throughout the Christian world.

See Charles Singer, "Science and Judaism," in *The Jews: Their History, Culture and Religion,* edited by Louis Finkelstein (Harper, 1960, third edition), Vol. II, pp. 1380–1383. The works of George Sartor on the history of science are invaluable. Also see A. Koyré, *From the Closed World to the Infinite Universe* (Johns Hopkins, 1957); and *The Legacy of Israel,* ed. by E. Bevan and C. Singer (Oxford, 1927).

Tisha Bov

The prophet Zechariah, asked whether a Jew should weep on *Tisha Bov,* inquired whether the mourning was for the sake of God or for the self-consolation of the mourner. This austere, if not superhuman, standard was raised by Zechariah, who advised Jews that, however horrible their experience, and however just the cause for weeping, they should evidence true piety by showing mercy, acting justly, and displaying "compassion by every man to his brother." Zechariah bade his people "oppress not the widow nor the fatherless, the stranger, nor the poor."

Tseno-Ureno

Literal translations of the books of the Bible, removed as they were from the sphere of everyday life, failed to gain especial favor, and it was not until several efforts, such as the translation of the Pentateuch by Reb Isaac ben Samson, had been made that the most widely read and influential work of all Yiddish literature, the *Tseno-Ureno (Go Out and See)* by the Polish Jew, Jacob ben Isaac Ashkenazi (1550–1628), appeared. Ostensibly a translation of the Pentateuch, the *Haftoros* and the Five Scrolls, it is actually a unique mosaic of commentary, legend, allegory, epigram, and ethical observation. The author drew upon the entire popular literary heritage from the canonization of the Bible to his own day, choosing those stories which related to the passages of the Pentateuch he was paraphrasing. Directed to the feminine reader, the work became a kind of woman's Bible which has been the source of Jewish knowledge for generations of mothers, who, Sabbath after Sabbath, have absorbed its Cabala-flavored philosophy of life.

The *Tseno-Ureno*, reflecting the triumph of individual interpretation over literal translation, the prominence of the woman's role in everyday Jewish life and the paramount influence of Polish ritual over the more worldly Germanic, overshadowed all previous works in Yiddish and affected the life of the general population more deeply and more lastingly than any other. . . .*

Weddings

The rabbis held the first positive commandment of the Bible to be the one that enjoins "Be fruitful, and multiply" (Genesis 1 : 28), and looked favorably upon early marriage.

* Yudel Mark, "Yiddish Literature," in *The Jews: Their History, Culture and Religion*, edited by Louis Finkelstein, Harper, 1960, Vol. II, p. 1196.

The *Talmud* sets eighteen as the proper age for marriage; some rabbis encouraged marriage as early as fourteen.

A man who remained unmarried after twenty was considered cursed by God Himself, living without joy and without blessing. (Compare this with Paul's strange views on marriage.)

Legend had it that forty days before a child is born, its *chassen* (or *kallah*) is determined in heaven.

Jewish wedding ceremonials vary greatly throughout the world. In ancient times, a Jewish bride and groom followed the Greek custom of wearing garlands and wreaths, like crowns. In Roman days, Jews used lighted torches. In some Arab countries, fireworks were set off. In the Middle Ages, the Jews in Germany married only during a full moon, the Jews in Spain only under a new moon.

The breaking of the glass, after the rabbi has pronounced his benediction over one glass, and after both bride and groom have sipped from another glass, has many interpretations. Some maintain that the breaking of the glass reminds the wedding party of the destruction of the Temple. The *Talmud* often counsels Jews to remember that happiness is transient, and that Jews must never forget the sufferings of Israel; it records the example of a fourth-century wise man who was so disturbed by the high jinks at his son's wedding that he broke "a very fine glass . . . and they became sad."

Many people other than Jews follow a similar custom. Some nationalities break a dish or a jar, or the glass from which all the guests have drunk, or old crockery. Egyptians smashed clay pots on which they had entered the names of their enemies. It may even be that breaking objects was a form of magic to frighten away evil spirits.

Orthodox Jews celebrate a wedding for seven days running, for that is the Bible's account of the festivities after Jacob married Leah; and each wedding added to Israel's estate— and children.

It was customary for teachers to adjourn their classes and join a wedding party with their students: It was a *mitzva* to participate in the happiness of a bride and groom.

Under the old laws, groom and bride fasted on their wedding day, to atone for past sins and start connubial life with a clean slate. (In the synagogue, the groom would recite the *Yom Kippur* confession before the congregation.)

Most *shtetl* weddings occurred on Fridays. This gave everyone a chance to celebrate on the Sabbath.

At one time, a procession of lighted torches and gay musicians preceded the groom, his *mishpocheh,* and the rabbi; then the procession hurried off to provide the same triumphant parade to the bride.

Guests would shower the couple with barley grains or kernels of wheat—as explicit a hope for fertility as rice, it seems. Further to enhance fertility, a hen and rooster once preceded the couple.

A fertility "fish dance" was the custom of Sephardic Jews in the Balkans, because fish were considered exceptionally fecund; a bride and groom often made their post-hymeneal dinner one of fish.

The Orthodox bride was customarily shorn of her hair and given a wig (*shaytl*) while seated before her girl friends who, holding lighted candles, bade a ceremonial farewell to her maidenhood.

The dancing at weddings was spirited (see *klezmer*) and the dances at weddings were many: the *mazel tov* dance, the dance for the parents of bride and groom, etc. A *badchen* often enlivened the proceedings with mock songs and laments, traditional jokes and free-wheeling badinage.

At some Orthodox ceremonies, the bride, her parents, her "sponsors," circled the groom seven times, each holding a lighted candle. (This may derive from a cabalistic practice of making a mystic circle to shut out the dastardly demons who resent happiness.)

Elaborate premarriage "arrangements" or "conditions" (*tena'im*) were once required. A dowry (*nadan*) was, of course, part of every Orthodox nuptial contract. Presents of value were exchanged between bride and groom-to-be. The latter usually gave his betrothed a prayer book (*siddur*), a veil, a fine comb, a sash, and a ring. The bride-to-be gave her "intended" a prayer shawl (*tallith*), a gold or silver chain, or a watch, or both.

Yeshivas

Jewish schools of learning were created in Galilee, Caesarea, Tiberias (where the "Babylonian" *Talmud* was put together), and in Babylonian centers like Sura.

At one time (twelfth century) the *yeshiva* in Baghdad had over 2,000 students, plus 500 in graduate work. There were impressive *yeshivas* in Tunisia, in Morocco, and, of course, in Europe, in virtually every large city.

In Spain, unlike eastern Europe, the *yeshivas* included courses in secular philosophy, astronomy, medicine, mathematics.

Yeshivas underwent a dynamic growth, both in number and distribution, during the Renaissance—especially in central and northern Europe.

The most distinguished *yeshiva* for a time was the one in Cracow, where the Aristotelian influence was permitted to exercise itself via the writings of Maimonides.

The *yeshivas* of Poland came to dominate Jewish theological scholarship, especially after the expulsion of the Jews from Spain: Poland suffered less from Roman and secular interference than did most European countries.

See Julius B. Maller, "The Role of Education in Jewish History," and Simon Greenberg, "Jewish Educational Institutions," both in *The Jews: Their History, Culture and Religion*, edited by Louis Finkelstein (Harper, 1960), Vol. II, pp. 1234–1288.

Yiddish: Historical Notes

Starting around 4000 B.C. the ancient Israelites spoke Hebrew, a Semitic language of the Canaanite group, until Solomon's Temple was destroyed (586 B.C.) and they were taken into captivity. A hundred or so years later, when the Jews returned from Babylonia, they found the inhabitants of the Holy Land speaking Aramaic—the vernacular of the Near and Middle East, the tongue used in daily life. Aramaic crept into the prayers of the Jews (e.g., *Kaddish, Kol Nidre*) despite strong resistance from the rabbis. But Hebrew was the language in which the *Torah* was read and studied, and Hebrew was the language used in prayers and religious ceremonies.

After the rise of Islam, Arabic displaced Aramaic (and other tongues) as the oral language of Jews in the Arab world; many scholars, physicians, poets, wrote in Arabic (Maimonides, Saadia Gaon and others), often using Hebrew letters.

How and where did Yiddish, as distinct from Hebrew, begin?

The Standard Jewish Encyclopedia (Doubleday, 1966, pp. 1945–1946) offers the following chronology for the development of Yiddish as a language:

Initial Yiddish	:	1000–1250 A.D.
Old Yiddish	:	1250–1500
Medieval Yiddish	:	1500–1750
Modern Yiddish	:	1750 on . . .

The Yiddish language consists of four basic components: German, Hebrew, Slavic tongues, and what philologists call Loez—the Jewish correlates of Old French and Old Italian.

About a thousand years ago, Jewish emigrants from the north of France began to settle in a number of towns along the Rhine. These Jews spoke Hebrew and Old French, to which they now added the Germanic dialects of the Rhine.

The Jews *wrote* the new vernacular with Hebrew characters (Jews had good reason to eschew Latin—i.e., "monkish"—letters). Jews had always used the letters of the Hebrew alphabet—to write Persian, Greek, Latin, etc. And they wrote from right to left, as Hebrew was and is written.

It was in the ghettos (begun by Lateran Councils in 1179, 1215) that the new linguistic mélange took root and flourished: a mixture of Middle High German, some Old German with Hebrew pronunciations and inflections, some relics of French, Italian, local dialects, and a considerable stock of Hebrew words and idioms.

The terrible pogroms that accompanied the First Crusade and the Black Plague drove Jews into South Germany, Austria, Bohemia, and North Italy; they brought their language along. The great eleventh-century Talmudist, Solomon ben Isaac of Troyes, who is called "Rashi," said that these Jews spoke *loshen Ashkenaz*, "the German tongue." (*Ashkenaz* was the name medieval rabbis used for Germany.)

Jews from the Rhineland were invited to Poland, to become traders and, accordingly, to rank in a social stratum between the nobility and the serfs. And in Poland these immigrants now found old settlements of Jews who spoke Slavic, did not live in ghettos (though in separate sections of cities), and were not worried or threatened about their Jewishness. These Polish Jews assimilated their Ashkenazic brethren, newly arrived, and themselves began to speak—Yiddish. "Since the golden age of Jewish life in Babylonia," writes Abraham Menes, "Jews had not felt as much at home in a country as they now did in Poland."*

Yiddish departed from German—in structure, spelling, grammar, pronunciation. And it continued freely to borrow, to adopt, to adapt, and to absorb words, phrases, locutions—from Czech, from Polish, from Russian, from any and every Slavic and Romance tongue. (But for abiding links to German, see my Appendix: Yiddish and German.)

As far back as the fifteenth century, the gifted Elijah Bochur, a Hebrew scholar, wrote and published poems in Yiddish. He wrote two stories in Yiddish that were adaptations from Italian.

In 1602 there appeared a Yiddish storybook or *Maase Bukh*, a collection of folk tales, legends, stories out of the *Talmud*, that exercised a powerful influence on Yiddish prose.

A book on morals and manners, the *Sefer Mides*, or "Book on Behavior," meant for Jewish women, appeared in 1542.

Religious and moral literature for the ladies also included a *Burning Mirror (Brantshpigl)*, published in Switzerland in 1602, and *Good Heart (Lev Tov)*, published in Prague in 1620.

The first Yiddish newspaper in the world was *Di Dinstogshe Kurantn* and *Fraytogshe Kurantn (Tuesday and Friday Courant)*, which began publication in 1686–1687 in Amsterdam. It was "a semiweekly publication which com-

---

* See "Patterns of Jewish Scholarship in Eastern Europe," in *The Jews: Their History, Culture and Religion*, edited by Louis Finkelstein, Harper, 1960, Vol. I, pp. 379–380.

pared favorably with contemporary Dutch papers," says Yudel Mark, editor of the great multi-volume Yiddish dictionary now being produced.

In 1544, one Joseph Bar Yokor produced a prayer book in Yiddish—but it was not successful.

Much poetry was published by Jews in Prague in the second half of the sixteenth century.

Josephus's *Antiquities of the Jews* was adapted into Yiddish in Zurich, in 1546.

The earnest champions of the eighteenth-century Enlightenment among Jews (the *Haskalah*), seeking to restore and renew Hebrew as the modern tongue of then-modern Jews, inveighed against Yiddish with great eloquence—and reverse, or boomerang, effect. For, as has been said in the earlier entry, *Yiddish*, the *Maskilim* had to use Yiddish in order to reach the very souls they were trying to coax into abandoning it.

J. C. Rich of the *Jewish Daily Forward* writes that modern Yiddish may be said to have begun in the year 1856, when a story by Isaac Meir Dick was published, in Yiddish, in the city of Warsaw.

No student of the history of Yiddish in the United States can fail to pay tribute to the prodigious role played by Abraham Cahan (1860–1951), founder and long-time editor in chief of the *Jewish Daily Forward*, the most influential Jewish newspaper in the United States. Cahan also wrote a novel in English, *The Rise of David Levinsky*, one of the best books ever written on the immigrant.

To an analyst who seeks to remain objective, it seems clear that Hebrew had become too emphatically "sanctified," too closely tied to the holy writings, to religious services, to theology and *Talmud;* had become the language of Jewish men and not Jewish women (who were rarely taught the exalted tongue); was too deeply steeped in the arcane preoccupations of rabbis, exegeticists, casuists; was far, far removed from the sweat and tears, the homely jokes and endearing anecdotes of daily living that Jews so cherish.

Yiddish—a lusty, pliable, eclectic tongue—was certain to exercise a profound, indeed an irresistible, attraction to Jews. How could it be otherwise when it was Yiddish, not Hebrew, that Jewish women spoke—and spoke, if you please, to the children, who spoke it to the parents and relatives, and, in time, to their own offspring?

German Jews, of course, considered (many still do) Yiddish a vulgar, even barbarous, dialect—low-class in origin, an East European "ghetto vernacular" that hampered Jewish assimilation. In America, Yiddish unpleasantly reminded proud second- and third-generation *Deutsche Jehudim* of the new, grubby, superstitious immigrants: Polish, Galician, Rumanian, and Russian Jews with their outlandish *payess,* their phylacteries, their caftans and beards, their "medieval religion" and un-American ways.

In the twentieth century, Yiddish became a political football because, among other reasons suggested in the foregoing, it was championed by the Bundists—in Poland, Lithuania, Russia. The Bundists were socialists and social democrats, deeply involved in the Russian revolutions of 1905 and 1917. They were energetic exponents of a new Enlightenment, of a bold secularism, agnosticism, even atheism. They adamantly opposed the use of Hebrew and the rising credo of Zionism.

The Zionists, on the other hand, sought to revive Hebrew and make it the Jews' everyday language. Yet Orthodox Jews clung to Yiddish, paradoxically, for Hebrew was too sacred to be used outside of religious discourse! The Zionists wanted to make Hebrew a contemporary tongue; and many Hebraicists who were not Zionists ardently supported them.

To complicate even further these snarled lines of affiliation and hostility, the first Yiddish schools in America were established in 1910 by Zionists—who were also socialists! *They* supported Yiddish because it was "the language of the masses."

It is estimated that before World War II, 11,000,000 people throughout the world spoke Yiddish. Yiddish newspapers and journals existed all over Europe, the United States, Latin America, Australia. A vital Yiddish theater flourished in Europe, the United States, South America. The Golden Age of Yiddish literature—novels, stories, plays, social criticism, journalism—began in the middle of the nineteenth century and reached its peak in the early decades of the twentieth.

The Workmen's Circle, the extremely influential labor-socialist, once anti-Zionist organization, organized schools, in various cities, in which Yiddish was taught (speaking, reading, writing, literature) to the children of working-class, and largely trade-union, immigrants. The Bundists were antireligious and antitraditional, as were most Jewish labor leaders—yet they feared that their children would "lose their Jewishness" along with their piety.

I find a moving moral in the fact that a very old book, rescued from the libraries that were burned in Europe during the depredations of the Nazis, a book now to be found in the collection of the YIVO Institute in New York, bears this *ex libris:* "The Society of Woodchoppers for the Study of *Mishnah* in Berditshev."

In Israel, where Hebrew became the national language, the state officially shunned Yiddish; many Israelis refused to speak Yiddish entirely (its Germanic ancestry would hardly endear it to refugees). It was a shattering experience for elderly Jews, arriving in Zion, to find Yiddish derided. True enough, Hebrew was the national, the revered tongue—but Yiddish was "the language of the heart," of suffering, the encapsulated record of Jewish history and suffering for a thousand years. (Fifty years ago, in Palestine, zealots rebuked anyone who spoke Yiddish.)

Nor is the attitude of more recent *sabras*—native-born Israelis—hard to understand. Hebrew is their native tongue. Yiddish? Yiddish is a language disgraced—the bastard tongue of Jews in the long Exile, and worse, the offspring of detested German, with its reminders of the Nazi nightmare.

Today, Israel has relaxed its antipathy to Yiddish. In Tel Aviv one may read Yiddish newspapers and magazines and attend Yiddish theater. But the governing attitude is still reverence and pride *vis-à-vis* Hebrew. The frank and affectionate recognition of Yiddish as the container and crucible of sixty generations of experience seems missing.

Alexander Harkavy's *English-Yiddish Dictionary,* the first of its kind, was published in 1891 (English and Hebrew Publication Company).

No authoritative English textbook of Yiddish grammar appeared until 1949 (!)—the late Uriel Weinreich's *College Yiddish* (YIVO Institute for Jewish Research).

In 1950, the Yiddish Scientific Institute (YIVO) published a scholarly *Thesaurus of the Yiddish Language,* in Yiddish.

A *Great Dictionary of Yiddish,* under the editorship of the esteemed Yudel Mark, has already published two of its many projected volumes.

YIVO, the Yiddish Scientific Institute, now headquartered in New York, was founded in 1925, in Lithuania, and has become the authoritative academy for the regulation of standards in Yiddish, and for the standardization and reform of spelling.

The B'nai Yiddish Society, 387 Grand Street, New York, publishes a bimonthly called *B'nai Yiddish*, devoted to the defense and perpetuation of the language.

For valuable insights on Yiddish and the Yiddish language see N. Buchwald, "History of Yiddish Literature in America," in *The Cambridge History of American Literature*, Vol. IV, New York, 1921; "Yiddish Literature," by Yudel Mark, in *The Jews: Their History, Culture and Religion*, edited by Louis Finkelstein, Harper, 1960, Vol. II, pp. 1191–1233; "Who Needs Yiddish? A Study in Language and Ethics," by Joseph C. Landis, in *Judaism: A Quarterly Journal*, Vol. 13, No. 4, Fall 1964, pp. 1–16; "Yiddish and American English," by Lillian Mermin Feinsilver, in *Chicago Jewish Forum*, Winter 1955–1956, Vol. 14, No. 2, pp. 71–76; "Yiddish Language and Literature," by A. A. Steinberg, *Encyclopaedia Britannica* (1957), Vol. 23, pp. 891–893; Shlomo Noble, "Modern Yiddish Literature in English Translation," in *Jewish Book Annual*, Vol. 7, Jewish Book Council, 1948.

Yiddish and German: A Note

Some differences between Yiddish and German, *as advanced by Yiddishists:*

GRAMMAR: Yiddish has developed its own characteristics—not unlike those of other German dialects: e.g., the imperfect tense in the verb has virtually disappeared; so has the genitive case in noun declension; so has the final unaccented *e*. (This is the claim of Yiddishists, but experts on German tell me that almost all High German dialects have dropped past and future tense, using compound formations—with auxiliary verbs or prepositions.)

SYNTAX: The structure of Yiddish has come to resemble English much more than German. (But German experts say that Yiddish syntax is still the same as most High German dialects.)

VOCABULARY: Americanisms and Slavic phrases abound in Yiddish to a degree unknown in German, naturally.

SPELLING: Hebrew words are written phonetically in Yiddish; words from German, Russian, Polish, Czech, have undergone distinctive (and un-Germanic) change.

For the Yiddishist views summarized above, see "Yiddish Language and Literature," by A. A. Steinberg in *Encyclopaedia Britannica*, (1957), Vol. 23, pp. 891–892.

Yiddish and Hebrew

Generally, Yiddish uses Hebrew words for all references to the Bible, the *Talmud*, religious tenets, observances, rituals; for customs and ceremonies, holidays and historical events; and for certain concepts (*emmes*, truth; *eytse*, advice). The words are spelled as they are in Hebrew.* But Hebrew words are pronounced differently in Yiddish than in Hebrew. Hebrew words accent the last syllable, Yiddish do not; the Hebrew *th* is pronounced as *s* in Yiddish, etc.

Hebrew, presumably the language God used, is one of the oldest languages on earth. Around 4000 B.C. the Jews used a Semitic language like the Akkadian tongue—spoken in Assyria and Babylon (or like the Phoenician parlance used in Sidon and Tyre). During the Babylonian Captivity, the Jews took up Aramaic, which was the language common to all the Semites and Semitic tribes who lived under Babylonian rule in the ancient Babylonian empire.

The Hebrew alphabet consists only of consonants—22 of them. In Yiddish, four of these consonants are used (like our *a, e, i, u*) to represent vowel sounds: points above and below these letters indicate the pronunciation. This is less complicated than it sounds. It is as if "fame" were spelled *fām*, "dawn" d*a*n, "light," l*i*t.

Experts differ in their estimates of the number of Hebrew

---

* Except in the U.S.S.R., where official pressure forced changes in spelling.

words that are part of Yiddish. Mr. Yudel Mark, perhaps the world's ranking authority, editor of the many-volumed Yiddish dictionary now being compiled, has said that 10 percent of all Yiddish words derive from Hebrew.* The late Uriel Weinreich, professor at Columbia University and author of a college textbook on Yiddish, said that Hebrew comprises over 15 percent of Yiddish.** Nathan Ausubel guesses that Yiddish today contains 20 percent Hebrew, 70 percent German and 10 percent other languages (chiefly Russian, Polish, Hungarian, Rumanian).*** My learned friend Maurice Samuel, who has as sensitive an *expertise* as one could hope for, guesses that Hebrew words account for 10 to 15 percent of the Yiddish vocabulary.

Yiddish has influenced Hebrew, much to the discomfiture of Hebraicists. For instance, the diminutive suffix, so widely employed in Yiddish to express affection, has been adopted in Hebrew.

Professor Joseph C. Landis has written a charming essay "Who Needs Yiddish?" (in *Judaism*, Fall 1964) that explores the endless resourcefulness of Yiddish in expressing or embroidering affection. A name such as *Leye* (Leah), for instance, is rendered as Leyele, Leyenyu, Leyinke, Leyinkele, Lyke, Leykele, Leykenyu, Leyche, Lychele, Leychenyu. *Yosef* (Joseph) becomes Yosel, Yosseleh, Yoshke, Yozifl, Yosheh, Yosenyu, Yoshenuy, Yosinkeh, Yoshkenyu, Yosinkleh, Yosinkeleh.

Hebrew, incidentally, contains no "four-letter" obscene words. Its speakers, when driven to cursing, resort to Aramaic —or Yiddish.

Yizkor

Traditional Jews observe *Yizkor* four times a year: on *Yom Kippur*, on the eighth day of Passover, on the eighth day of *Succoth*, and on the second day of *Shevuoth*.

In the United States, some Jews who observe virtually no

---

* *Invitation to Yiddish*, American Jewish Congress, 1962, p. 90.
** *College Yiddish*, YIVO, 1965, p. 66.
*** *Book of Jewish Knowledge*, Crown, 1964, p. 227.

other religious service continue to observe *Yizkor*. Some close shop, or do not report to work, for the entire day, to attend a synagogue or temple.

Yizkor began long ago in the west of Germany, to honor and remember the great number of Jews who had been slaughtered (I do not think "slaughtered" too harsh a word) during the First Crusade (1096 A.D.).

The idea of naming the dead and celebrating their martyrdom probably came from Catholic practice, where it began as long ago as the fourth century.

Yizkor services are held at different times for different communities within Jewry: Sephardic Jews observe a *Yizkor* on *Yom Kippur* eve; Reform Jews include the *Yizkor* in their *Yom Kippur* morning service.

Yom Kippur: Notes

The idea of collective confession, the use in prayers of "we" and "us" (instead of "I" or "me"), stems from an ancient belief that the gods become infuriated with a whole tribe when one of its members transgresses; hence, collective crops, livestock, and wells suffer the gods' wrath.

In Jewish tradition, the community is responsible as long as even one sinner is left on earth: e.g., the thief would not have sinned had "we" provided for him, or taught him proper morals.

Note that the *Yom Kippur* release from promises applies only to promises made to God. Vows made to another man, to the community, to a court, to the political regime—no divine or religious annulment is possible for these. (A kind man may forgive a promise made to him and broken.) The observing Jew must ask forgiveness from another three times.

Yom Kippur began, very long ago, as a ritual in which God was both petitioned and propitiated. Animals were sacrificed (goat, bull), to the accompaniment of appropriate incantations.

The Jews, horrified by the human sacrifices pagan peoples made to appease their gods, instead sacrificed a "scapegoat" to whom the community's sins were "transferred." In the Temple, the High Priest performed the sacrifice on the altar, before the whole congregation, and in behalf of all Israel.

Two goats were used: one was sacrificed on the altar, its blood then sprinkled eight times in front of the sanctuary. The second goat, to appease Azazel, "the demon of evil of the wilderness," was taken up a cliff, in a ceremony, and pushed over. And at this moment, a strip or banner or something white would be waved from one of the Temple's walls or gates—the signal for all who were watching to burst into hosannahs. (All this seems far removed from Judaism's lofty ethical precepts—but it *was* an immense improvement over the ghastly human-sacrifice practices of the time.)

Kapparah, a sacrificial rite, was introduced after the Temple was destroyed (70 A.D.). Maimonides condemned it as idolatrous. Only very Orthodox Jews practice this vicarious rite of atonement today: It involves swinging a chicken over the head thrice while reciting a formula which makes it clear that the chicken's blood atones for the year-past's sins. I have never myself witnessed any chicken-waving over the head. Money is sometimes substituted for chickens—then given to charity.

See entry KAPOREH, Yiddish for *kapparah*.